Freedom and Reform

Frank H. Knight

Freedom and Reform

Essays in Economics and Social Philosophy

FRANK H. KNIGHT

LibertyPress

Indianapolis

Liberty*Press* is a publishing imprint of Liberty Fund, Inc., a foundation established to encourage study of the ideal of a society of free and responsible individuals.

The cuneiform inscription that serves as the design motif for our endpapers is the earliest known written appearance of the word "freedom" *(ama-gi),* or liberty. It is taken from a clay document written about 2300 B.C. in the Sumerian city-state of Lagash.

Copyright © 1947 by Harper & Brothers. Published by arrangement with Harper and Row, Publishers, Inc. All rights reserved. Foreword to Liberty*Press* edition copyright © 1982 by James M. Buchanan. All inquiries should be addressed to Liberty Fund, Inc., 7440 N. Shadeland, Indianapolis, Indiana 46250. This book was manufactured in the United States of America.

First edition published 1947 by Harper & Brothers.
Liberty*Press* edition published in hardcover and paperback 1982.

Photo courtesy of Mrs. Ethel V. Knight.

Library of Congress Cataloging in Publication Data

Knight, Frank Hyneman, 1885–1972
    Freedom and reform.

    Reprint. Originally published: New York: Harper, 1947.
    Includes index.
    1. Liberty—Addresses, essays, lectures.
2. Social problems—Addresses, essays, lectures.
3. Economic policy—Addresses, essays, lectures.
I. Title.
HN18.K5   1982   303.3'72   81-83237
ISBN 0-86597-004-1   AACR2
ISBN 0-86597-005-X (pbk.)
10 9 8 7 6 5 4 3 2 1

Contents

Foreword

*T*o those who may not know Frank H. Knight or his works, I can commence by making a "contribution to your education," one of his own most familiar phrases. Frank Knight was born in 1885 on a farm in Illinois, and was variously educated in schools, colleges, and universities in Illinois and Tennessee (in chemistry, German drama, and philosophy) before settling down for a doctorate in Economics at Cornell (1916). His dissertation, *Risk, Uncertainty, and Profit*, published in 1921, quickly became and remains a classic in economy theory. His broader ranging interests were reflected early in essays written over the period 1921–1935 and published in *The Ethics of Competition* (1935), the first of his three volumes of collected papers.

Knight's active teaching career included Cornell and the University of Iowa before the University of Chicago, which he joined in 1928 and where he became the primary intellectual source for the original, or pre-Friedman, "Chicago school" of economics. At Chicago, Knight put his stamp on several generations of students who learned economics with philosophical overtones. After visiting stints at several universities in his post-retirement years, he died in Chicago in 1972 at the age of eighty-seven.

Do other students of Frank H. Knight experience reactions similar to mine when I reread one of his essays? Having struggled to develop a plausibly coherent intellectual position, and in one sense, feeling a bit of pride in my achievement, I find myself confronted time and again with Knight's much earlier and more sophisticated statement of the same thing. It is as if in rereading Knight I am retracing the sources of my own thoughts, which themselves have somehow emerged without conscious recognition that they are derived from him.

My own relationship to Frank Knight in this respect is, I think, quite different from the more straightforward teacher-disciple connection. When confronted with an intellectual-philosophical "puzzle," I do not go back to search out and see what the master may have written on the subject. For me, Knight's works are not reference materials. In response to a "puzzle," my own proclivities are those of Knight himself (which I surely got from him also), which are those of working out my own preliminary "solution," independent of *any* authority or *any* text.

This characteristic is central to everything Knight approached. The intellectual-moral courage to treat nothing as sacred shines through all his work, perhaps most notably in the philosophical essays of the sort included in *Freedom and Reform*. Honesty, sincerity, integrity—these are the qualities that mark the writings and the man. Frank Knight knew who he was and where he was. He possessed the elementary gumption to stake out his intellectual-moral position unawed by either the "wisdom of the ages" or the potential censure of his peers in the academy. He was willing to acknowledge his own vulnerability to error, and when he was confused, he was not reluctant to say so.

Frank Knight did not preach a gospel (despite the old University of Chicago saying that "there is no God, but Frank Knight is his prophet"). There was, to him, no gospel to be preached. He made no effort to present the "truth according to Frank Knight." He taught that "truth" was whatever emerged from the free discussion of reasonable men who approached the dialogue without prejudice and as good sports. The question as to the possible existence of something external to such a discussion-agreement process was not within his range of interest for the simple reason that it could never be answered.

Knight's audience was made up of the other potential participants in the discussion process. He did not address his words to the agents who might hold positions of governmental-political power over others. Even in a remote conceptual sense, Knight was not an adviser to governments, a characteristic that, in itself, separates Knight from so many of his fellow economists, in his time and now.

As he himself acknowledged, and as many others have recognized, Frank Knight was essentially a critic. His work, aside from *Risk, Uncertainty, and Profit,* can be interpreted as a series of long book reviews. His "social function" was that of exposing the fallacies, nonsense, and absurdities in what was passed off as sophisticated-scientific discourse. He emphasized repeatedly that the problems we face in modern society are not problems of science and education in the standard meaning of these terms. "The main task of society . . . is *education,* but of the will more than the intellect; it is to develop a more critical attitude."[1] I have personally heard Knight repeat many times the Josh Billings aphorism: "It

---

[1] *Intelligence and Democratic Action,* Harvard University Press, 1969. Page 14.

ain't what we don't know that hurts us. It's knowing so darned much that ain't so.''

Frank Knight was not pleased with developments in modern economics. He shared with the Austrians a highly skeptical attitude toward the value of empirical research. I recall sitting with him at the American Economic Association Presidential Address by Paul Douglas, during which Douglas paraded a panoply of charts and diagrams purporting to demonstrate relationships in aggregate production functions. At the close of the presentation, Knight muttered. ''Proving water runs down hill,'' a comment that he would surely have found applicable to much of the empirical trivia that fills the journals of the 1980s.

He would have been particularly disturbed by the image of man that the modern emphasis on empirical testability forces on the economist as practitioner. To make hypotheses operational, arguments in utility functions must be specified. Old-fashioned *homo economicus,* man as net-wealth maximizer, reemerges as the actor on center stage. To Frank Knight this reemergence could only reflect retrogression into a simplistic and wrongheaded usage of the valuable insights that economic theory can offer. *Homo economicus* exists in every man, but one of Knight's most persistent themes through all his works is that there exist all sorts of other men (the romantic fool, the sportsman who enjoys the fray, the prejudiced ignoramus, the man who wants to be a ''better'' man) alongside the rational maximizer of economic interest.

To Knight the task for economists (and for social philosophers) is not to be located at the extensive margin of ''science.'' The task is to be located squarely at the level of elementary common sense. No sophisticated analysis is required to recognize that legally-enforced wage floors cause unemployment or that inflation cannot increase production in any long-term sense. But many men are prejudiced and romantic fools.

The job is to cut through the cant of the professional and tackle the intellectual prejudice where it exists. In staking his own effort toward some ultimate attainment of common sense by ordinary citizens, Frank Knight categorically rejected the elitism too often met in the academy and at the same time reaffirmed his own faith in a society of free men. While he remained always pessimistic as to its potential realization, such a society was, for Knight, the only one worthy of serious consideration.

I am especially pleased that Liberty*Press* is republishing *Freedom and Reform*. Over and beyond the desirability of insuring that the essays here will now be available again to potential readers, there are particular reasons that make Liberty*Press* republication appropriate. Pierre Goodrich, whose works made Liberty*Press* possible, shared with Frank Knight more than membership in the same age cohort. These men shared a respect for ideas and a love of individual liberty. They were also men of mid-America, and the location of the source of the republication is itself of value. Frank Knight personified the mid-American scholar-skeptic-critic of his age. The man and his mind could never have emerged from the culture of either Europe or the American seaboard. And, sad to say, such a man could probably not emerge anywhere in the culture of the late twentieth century.

In this connection, I shall conclude by recalling a conversation with Professor Ronald H. Coase when he and I were colleagues at the University of Virginia, where Frank Knight had visited for an extended period. Coase and I were walking along Mr. Jefferson's Lawn, and we had been discussing famous economists. Ronald said something like the following to me. "I can think of almost any famous economist, like ———, ———, ———, or ———," naming the obvious world-renowned figures in our discipline as evaluated from the perspective of the early 1960s, "and I can sort of imagine myself in their position of fame with a bit of luck, persistence, and effort. But I simply cannot imagine myself to be like Frank Knight. I guess that amounts to saying that Knight is a genius.'' I have always remembered that conversation because Coase put so well what so many of us feel when we think of the professor from whom we learned so much.

James M. Buchanan

James M. Buchanan is the author of many books and articles, including The Calculus of Consent *(with Gordon Tullock),* The Limits of Liberty: Between Anarchy and Leviathan, *and* What Should Economists Do?

Preface to the First Edition

F*reedom and Reform* is in a sense a sequel to the volume, *Ethics of Competition*, published in 1935. The content is chiefly papers of a philosophical or interpretive character that have appeared in various journals and symposium volumes since that time; two earlier items and an expanded version of a lecture not hitherto printed are also included, but nothing belonging to the field of technical economic theory.

The assembly and publication of these papers is due to the initiative of certain of Professor Knight's students and junior colleagues, and the selection has been made in consultation with the author. The material has been brought together and presented in book form because of its significance in relation to serious problems that have been prominent in public discussion—both in and outside of academic circles—in recent years. It seems unlikely that these problems will lose their importance or their interest in the near future.

The papers deal with the nature of social science and its relation to social problems, the place of the methods and concepts of natural science, the interrelations of the several disciplines, and the interpretation of conspicuous features— many of them recognized as ominous—in the trend of events in the western world during our generation. It is hoped that these essays will contribute something to historical understanding and to the clarification of the values and procedures involved in social action in a free society.

We wish to thank the various publishers who have so kindly given us permission to reprint the selections included in this volume.

HUBERT BONNER
WILLIAM GRAMPP

The University of Chicago   MILTON SINGER
December, 1946   BERNARD WEINBERG

Freedom and Reform

Freedom as Fact and Criterion

S tudents of ethics or social science hardly need to be reminded that one of the leading modern schools of ethical thought has been dominated by economists. The English-speaking world in particular has been utilitarian in its theory and its folk-mind from the age of the Enlightenment. Hence some reflections by an economist on utilitarianism and ethics generally may be worth consideration.

For present purposes, it is the political rather than the properly ethical aspect of utilitarianism, and especially the separation of the two, which is of interest. It is one thing to ask what is Good, and another to inquire as to what social policy is to be carried out, and by what agencies, in order to realize the Good as far as possible. There might, indeed, be such a connection between the two questions that the answer to one would largely involve an answer to the other; but it is

Reprinted by permission from *The International Journal of Ethics*, vol. 39 (1929), pp. 129–147.

an essential feature of utilitarian theory that it makes the separation complete.

The good, according to the utilitarians, is pleasure, which is a purely individual matter. We shall not stop to criticize this conception of the good. The issue regarding it is in fact largely verbal. Utilitarians expressly define the term "pleasure" in an all-inclusive sense; it covers high pleasures and low pleasures, the pleasure of being good and that of being bad, the pleasure of peace and also that of strife, even the "pleasure" of martyrdom. If pleasure is defined as identical with motivation in general, there naturally can be no motive but pleasure—and if it is defined in any other way, there will necessarily be other motives. And that is all that appears to be worth saying on that point, with the possible exception of questioning whether it is an economical use of language to take two perfectly good words to mean the same thing when there are significantly different ideas which they might be used to distinguish with less departure from their ordinary meaning in speech and writing. The important point, however, is that for utilitarianism good is individual, and the individual is the ultimate judge of it; what is good is that the individual shall get what he wants. To Bentham especially, the particular beauty of the theory was that it definitely removed the ethical question from the domain of practical politics and set up an "objective criterion" of public policy.[1]

The actual goal of political action then became the essentially negative ideal of *freedom*, i.e., the "greatest good" will be realized through "maximum freedom."[2] Details were worked

---

[1] We need not pause to consider expressly the now familiar fact of a contradiction between two aspects of the pleasure theory, psychological and ethical hedonism. If every individual universally and necessarily seeks his own maximum pleasure, it is hard to see sense in saying that he ought to do so.

[2] Dean Pound derives the doctrine of maximum freedom in legal theory from the "metaphysical" foundations of Kant (*Law and Morals*, p. 103, etc.); but he elsewhere admits that all the modern schools of jurisprudence come out at

out by the British laissez-faire economists, beginning with Bentham's older contemporary, Adam Smith, and culminating in Herbert Spencer, a biological sociologist rather than an economist of technical competence. In practical application, the doctrine of maximum individual freedom necessitates a further assumption, namely that the individual is the final judge of the *means* to his own happiness, as well as of the result. The utilitarian-economic position on both points is, however, relativistic. It need not be assumed that the individual's knowledge is perfect, or even very good, but only that it is *better* than that of the outside agency of control, practically speaking a political bureaucracy. Smith and his followers notoriously placed their emphasis on the stupidity of governments rather than the competence of individuals, and the modern reader must keep in mind the character of the governments which formed the basis of their judgments.[3]

Sharply definite formulation of the principle of freedom waited for Herbert Spencer. In contrast with Smith, who mixed genial humanity with his hard common sense, Spencer was the cold, passionately dispassionate thinker. He explicitly defined pleasure as any mental state men strive to get or keep, and pain as the opposite. He traced conflicts of interest to

---

essentially the same practical conclusion. It seems to be the only kind of political ideal which has meaning for the modern mind, especially the Anglo-American mind.

[3] In England it was, of course, the period of the ''rotten-borough'' Parliament and the Hanoverian Kings whom Thackeray rhymed so spicily:

> "Vile George the First was reckoned;
> Viler still was George the Second;
> And what mortal ever heard
> Any good of George the Third!
> When George the Fourth to Hell descended,
> Thank the Lord the George's ended."

It is not clear just how much of a theoretical hedonist Smith was when he wrote the *Wealth of Nations*. His views seem to reflect rather ''hard common sense'' than rigorous analysis, and undoubtedly contain an element of the Puritan conviction that it is good for the soul as well as conducive to happiness for the individual to make his own decisions and take the consequences of his own acts.

biological-economic roots in the distribution of the material means of individual enjoyment and gave the freedom theory its classical, quantitative expression as the right of each to the maximum freedom compatible with equal freedom for all others. He also supported it with a deduction from an evolutionary-biological law that life is necessarily increased and improved by making each individual free to act and to reap the consequences of his acts, since pleasure-giving and life-sustaining acts are "necessarily" identical. The good in life is its balance of pleasure over pain, and Spencer was unconscious of the absurdity involved in combining ethical with psychological hedonism.

Contemporary with Spencer, the subjective-value school of economists worked out the implicit rationale of the economic utilitarian political philosophy of maximum freedom or laisser faire. The result may be summed up in a series of propositions: (1) The good is pleasure (or happiness, the substitution of terms being largely an evasive effort to soften the position). (2) Each pleasure has its specific desire or motive, which impels conduct with a force proportional to the magnitude of the pleasure. (3) The intensity of any pleasure and the force of the desire for it decrease together as more of any pleasure is enjoyed, in comparison with other pleasures sacrificed to obtain the first (law of diminishing utility). (4) Consequently, an individual if left "free to choose" must automatically proportion his activities in such a way as to secure the maximum total of pleasure from the available means. (5) Interrelations between individuals work automatically, so as to bring about a maximum of pleasure all around, if such relations are also "free," or voluntary, on both sides (free exchange), including the freedom of each individual to bargain with whichever opposing party offers the best terms (free competition). Hence the field of group control is restricted to the prevention of relations other than those of competitive free exchange, specifically the protection of property and enforcement of contract.

Passing over various mechanical implications or hidden assumptions which still trouble economic theory,[4] our purpose here is to show that the very notion of freedom as a "criterion" is illusory. The theory of maximum freedom if really followed through, ends in a question-begging justification of whatever human relations happen to exist, and the only way to escape this result and arrive at any ethical judgment is to appeal to an ethical judgment as such. If the notion of freedom has any ethical significance, it is derived from prior ethical norms.

The fatal defect in the utilitarian doctrine of maximum freedom as a goal of social policy is its confusion of freedom and power. Its advocates overlook the fact that freedom to perform an act is meaningless unless the subject is in possession of the requisite means of action, and that the practical question is one of power rather than of formal freedom.[5] As its actual test of equality of freedom, the utilitarians set up voluntary exchange. That is, no individual is to be asked to make a sacrifice or render a service at the behest of another unless he receives in return what he himself considers a full equivalent. Plausible this argument undoubtedly is, but there is a gaping

---

[4] Such as the tendency of freedom to eventuate in monopoly rather than competition, the fact that bargains between individuals usually have effects, good or bad, for persons other than the immediate parties, the further fact that many wants like culture and a beautiful environment must practically be provided for on a local group basis if at all, etc. See Pigou, *Economics of Welfare*.

[5] Another deficiency of utilitarianism on the side of ethics proper is its restriction of the notion of the Good to values realized through conduct and use of material means. It has nothing to say about purely internal problems of appreciation or attitude such as are the chief concern of religion in its esthetic and mystical aspects.

In our opinion it is unwise to attempt to vindicate freedom as an ideal by defining it to include power. Thus Graham Wallas calls freedom the capacity for continuous initiative, and others distinguish between positive and negative freedom. It is surely better to work out clearly the relation between freedom and power as distinct factors in conduct.

hole in the logic. An "equivalent" to the choosing individual himself is simply the maximum that the other party will pay, a standard of force with no flavor of fairness. An ostensible provision for "fair" equivalence comes in only through the workings of the competitive market, establishing a general scale of prices. Thus the *most* that exchange relations can do is to assure that each individual shall keep, quantitatively unimpaired, the stock of values originally possessed, as measured by free exchange among persons whose original stocks were whatever they happened to be. The principle merely settles the ethical problem by decreeing fixity for all eternity of the *existing* distribution of means of enjoyment, as measured by a process the results of which also depend on the starting point. By a twofold *petitio principii* it sanctifies the *status quo*. The result rests on an ethical judgment, and on an ethically indefensible one. Its ethic is in the first place the right to keep what one has. But it does not stop there, as will presently be pointed out more in detail; it also sets up the right to use what one has to get more, without limit!

The weakness of this theory of maximum benefit through maximum freedom defined by voluntary exchange could not go entirely unnoticed. Theorists of the subjective-value school were accused of bringing forth their doctrine as an answer to the socialistic labor theory of value. But if it might be used apologetically in that connection, its net significance was clearly against the fairness of the established value scale rather than in its favor. For the principle of diminishing utility seems to lead at once to the conclusion that total utility can always be increased through one-sided transfers from persons who have more to those who have less, and hence establishes an equalitarian ideal of society. Early in the history of the subjective-value movement, one of the leaders of the Austrian school wrote a book to deal with this difficulty. He got around it theoretically by admitting that value or price does not correspond to personal significance or utility in the actual world, and making the theory "hypothetical," to fit the ideal conditions of a communistic society.[6]

Two other ways out of the difficulty presented themselves. Economists might insist on a strict separation of their subject from ethics and set up as a "science," devoted to the description and explanation of things as they are in an actually existing social order,[7] or if persistent in the interest to justify or criticize as well as explain, they might go back of inequalities in income to conditions of production and distribution. To a considerable degree both courses have been followed, though with by no means the clarity of distinction between the procedures of explanation and criticism that would be desirable. As our interest here is in the ethical question, we shall glance at the workings of the system of "free" exchange at the source of individual incomes.

It goes without saying that men's status with regard to their supply of the means of enjoyment is not finally a matter of stocks of goods, but of a stream of total production and its division into streams flowing to the consumers individually. In modern society it is worked out through money income, which in turn is secured through the continuous offer in exchange of "productive services" (of person, or goods of indirect usefulness). How about the freedom and equality of these exchanges and their result in maximizing total benefit? It is easy to make of the pain-cost theory of value of the classical political economy a social apologetic along this line;

---

[6] *Der natürliche Wert*, by Friedrich von Wieser, 1889. Wieser seems almost evasive in his reference to the conditions under which value would actually equal utility. He seems to mean equality of money income, which is not theoretically conclusive, as differences in individual capacities for enjoyment might distort the result in various ways.

[7] This procedure saves the theory of marginal utility, since if men choose intelligently, the *relative* utilities of all dollar's worths of different commodities are equal for every consumer, whether rich or poor.

this is not fair, but we must limit ourselves to the logic of the question.

Under "perfect competition" it is theoretically true that the income share paid to the individual who furnishes any unit of productive service is equal in market value to the share of the social product causally imputable to that unit of productive service as its contribution to the total. But is there anything ethical about these equivalences? In order to give them ethical significance, two assumptions have to be made, as in the previous case. In the first place, the ethical claim of the owner of any productive service to its contribution to product can be no better than his ethical claim to the "ownership" of the service itself. The distribution of *income* is ethical if we "sanctify the status quo" in regard to the distribution of *wealth,* including personal endowments given by nature and those developed through opportunity and training. In the second place, again, the value scale by which products and contributions are measured is itself a reflection of the existing distribution of ultimate purchasing power.[8]

As a matter of fact, it is superficial to look at the productive resources in a quantitative way. Concretely, they are not amounts, but *kinds,* and only become amounts, so that it is possible to think of quantitative equivalence, through the pricing process. One income receiver furnishes "land," another "labor," and another "capital"; one wheat land and

---

[8] The working of the price mechanism in the control of production is a matter of technical economics rather than ethics, but has its ethical side also. If business men, or "entrepreneurs," act intelligently, the higher price offers for productive services can be made by those who use them to produce the goods most in demand and employ the most efficient productive methods. Consequently all productive power is theoretically directed into the channels of greatest usefulness. But again, usefulness is measured by the existing value scale, which reflects the existing distribution of ownership. If a man of wealth chooses to spend a million dollars' for a drawing room or a tomb, that becomes the most useful employment for a million dollars' worth of labor and materials, no matter how much want and distress might be relieved by using the labor, etc., to produce necessities of life.

another banana land, one pick-and-shovel work, another bookkeeping or blacksmithing and another managerial service or direction of investments, and so on almost without end. On looking into the price-fixing process by which these services become comparable, we see that it is a matter of "demand" and "supply," or rather the reciprocal of supply, namely scarcity. Hence the amount of income received by any individual depends chiefly on the two considerations of being in a position to render (*a*) services of a sort for the products of which there are consumers who can and will pay large amounts, and (*b*) services of a sort which few or no other persons are prepared to offer. To be sure, one's income also depends on the amount of any given kind of service rendered, other things being equal. But the natural quantitative differences between men are relatively insignificant, and the large incomes are actually received on the ground, either of owning a large amount of wealth or exercising some highly unique and scarce personal capacity, which again is some mixture of natural gift with the results of opportunity and training. It is mainly the scarcity that counts; it matters relatively little what the personal peculiarity is. One has to be a rare specimen indeed to make much money writing poetry or playing the cornet, while if exceptional enough one can make a very comfortable income by merely being large, or small, or deformed. Exceptional lawyers, doctors, and business managers also make large incomes, partly on the ground of scarcity but more on that of another principle. The price they command depends on their reputation, more than on concrete performance, and reputation tends to grow cumulatively. In large part their prestige depends on the pay itself, while it is for the prestige that the pay is received.

How far does the principle of freedom go in justifying the differences between incomes? It goes just as far as people really are free, that is, as far as the rendering of (*a*) a larger

11

amount of a given service, (*b*) a service more in demand or (*c*) a scarcer service, is a matter of voluntary choice. That is not far, and it calls for no argument that actual differences rest to an overwhelming extent on differences in power. The evaluation of the separate contributions of individuals to the social total is overwhelmingly a matter of force and not of right, and the inequalities tend overwhelmingly to reduce and not to increase "total satisfaction." [9]

To be sure, there is still another step in the argument. Existing capacities to render service, including ownership of wealth, are in turn the result of the working of the economic process in the past. If we pursue our ethical inquiry backward through the process, we shall find that the same principles work cumulatively, but also that two new ones come into play. The amount and kind of economic power possessed by

---

[9] The classical political economy came, in its final expression in the works of J. S. Mill and Carines, to recognize that the tendency of values to reflect pain costs is hopelessly obstructed by the lack of freedom of laborers to move from low-paid to high-paid occupations, even over a period of generations. The economists never regarded rent as a remuneration for pain, and Senior, who was the originator of the "abstinence" doctrine, explaining interest on the ground of a pain, explicitly said that after the capital has passed by inheritance or gift from the possession of the original saver the payment for its use should be regarded as a rent. A doctrine of equivalence of reward and sacrifice *at a margin* and *to each individual* was, like the corresponding doctrine of relative marginal utility, wanting in the economic theory of the classical period. It would have saved the pain-cost doctrine from absurdity in the scientific sense, and written its lack of ethical significance where he that runs might read. But a clear separation of the two points of view is still in slow process of achievement.

Regarding the precise extent to which the classical economics and the pain-cost theory of value were, or are, consciously or unconsciously, formulated and taught for the purpose of apologetic, it is clearly useless to speculate. But viewing the matter historically one can hardly help watching the sanctity of property take the place of the divine right of kings as the main principle of social order, as the latter had displaced ecclesiastical hegemony, with theorists shifting their ground as the facts change. All these while established were really principles of order, and as such so useful as to justify calling them sacred. All were also bases of exploitation of the many by the few. Whether the human race is capable of establishing order on a principle which does not expressly sanctify exploitation remains for the remote future to determine.

any person "now" depends largely on the amount and kind he possessed "last year." For economic power is used not merely to produce satisfaction-yielding goods, but also (through investment in capital or personal training) to multiply itself. The important point is the powerful tendency for inequality to increase cumulatively, compounding at an enormous rate. For the more wealth or income-producing capacity one possesses the easier it is to invest not merely the same but an increasing fraction of the yield.

The two new principles which come in when considering longer periods of time are inheritance and uncertainty. In an economic order based on the private family, the ownership of wealth by individuals is not dependent alone on the economic rôle played by them in the past, but largely on the accident or brute fact of inheritance. It is not easy to see how any ethical significance can be attached to the receipt of income from inherited wealth (or training, social position, etc.) on grounds of "equal freedom" or any sort of personal desert. The second new factor, uncertainty, is much harder to reduce to formal principles, but is just as obviously important. In fact, the results of productive operations over long periods of time are highly unpredictable. In the use of given resources in producing commodities, uncertainty is relatively unimportant; but in committing productive capacity to new forms and uses it is very great. In other words, the maintenance and increase of productive capacity is in no small degree a matter of *luck,* as well as of the character of choices made.

The conventional classification of productive factors recognizes the three classes, land, labor, and capital, or nature, man, and waiting. From an ethical point of view it would be more significant to analyze income into three sources of free choice or effort, inheritance, and luck. And the greatest of these is luck! The principle of equal freedom, as expressed through a social order based on free exchange, simply takes us nowhere in the solution of the problem of economic justice. Everything depends, not on the character of exchange, but on what individuals bring to the exchange, and this is ultimately a matter of fact and not of ethics. Historically viewed, the significance of the doctrine is to justify inequality, and the project is a failure. A consistent application of the principle of maximum satisfaction would yield a theory of distribution according to effort, if individuals are recognized only as producers, and according to some composite of effort and need if they are treated as abstract human units. And this seems to be in harmony with ordinary moral common sense if the latter breaks away from mere convention and becomes reasonably critical.

A more direct psychological examination will also show the notion of freedom to be question-begging or meaningless. Scrutiny of any typical case of unfree behavior reveals that the coercive quality rests on an ethical condemnation, rather than the ethical condemnation on a factually established unfreedom; or perhaps it is more accurate to say that they are merely different names for the same thing. Illustrations are at hand in the commonest business or legal relations. The ordinary citizen who sees a desired article in a store does not feel oppressed or constrained because he is not permitted to appropriate it without submitting to the condition of parting with the price—as long as he considers the price necessary or reasonable. And his standards of necessity and reasonableness, moreover, are entirely relative to the accepted economic organization at large. He may know that the price might be much less if some possessor of unique skill or a unique natural resource would consent to furnish the special service at a much lower yet perfectly possible remuneration. As long as everything is assumed to be in accordance with accepted standards of *fairness,* there is no feeling that freedom is interfered with. All taxes and legislative or administrative regulations take away property values, but they do not "confiscate" if sound social-moral reasons clearly underlie them. We do not feel constrained in having to take the right side of the street or sidewalk. We simply do not have the feeling of coercion except in connection with one of ethical disapprobation. There is psychological truth in the famous story of the cowboy coroner who brought in a verdict of suicide by doubting the superiority of four deuces to a full house. Freedom cannot afford an objective standard of policy, a way of escape from the subjectivity of moral judgments, when the feeling of freedom itself is derived from, or at best is another aspect of, moral approval.

Freedom is also relative to power. Our ordinary citizen, again, feels no coercion in not being able to buy an object which he does not have money enough to pay for (unless, again, the fact is due to some "unfair" manipulation). It is nonsense to say that I am not "free" to fly (without mechanical aid) or that a paralyzed man has his freedom restricted by locking his door. But it may well be that under different conditions, if society were organized or administered on different principles or certain individuals had behaved differently, the individual excluded or helpless in a given situation would have had power to act. And so he may perfectly well be the victim of a heinous wrong. But it is a clear misuse of words to describe the wrong as a deprivation of freedom. It is a deprivation of *power*. The "wrongs" on grounds of which social organization or policy is to be criticized undoubtedly have the character of inequitable distribution of power rather than unethical coercion or interference with the use of power. But for *neither* sort of wrongs is the notion of freedom a criterion by which definition or identification is possible.

From an abstractly logical standpoint, again, the difficulties of the notion of freedom go still deeper. In the world view of natural science freedom is simply a meaningless word. In

15

terms of physical causality (behaviorism) all human acts alike and equally have their physical antecedents from which they inevitably follow, and beyond the description of these antecedent conditions no intelligent statement can be made. Nor do we in any way escape from the difficulty by recognizing mental states, attitudes, or motives as causes. In that case all acts alike and equally have their adequate motives. No factual attribute or descriptive difference in either physical antecedent or motive will make one act (of a private individual or government official) right and another wrong. At most the ethical question is merely carried back a step. If we adopt the view that acts are to be fully accounted for by motives, then in order to validate any difference between right and wrong acts we must find some basis for discrimination between right and wrong motives. If we say that acts are to be fully accounted for by antecedent physical conditions it seems to be nonsensical to talk about ethical differences at all, for we can hardly call one physical configuration right and another wrong.

It will be seen that the issue regarding freedom is entirely unconnected with the old metaphysical problem of free will. If one believes in freedom, in that sense, all choices are alike and equally free, within the limits of the possible alternatives open. If one does not believe in freedom, then all acts are alike and equally *determined* (by physical or psychological conditions, or both, according to taste). Practical requirements, however, call for a working distinction between two sorts of acts, some free and some unfree, and for a valid means of assigning some acts to one class and some to the other. The thinker whose mechanistic bias is strong enough will simply deny that the distinction has any meaning; but he will hardly convince any jurist or legislator who is "up against" the practical problem that he does not have to make the classification. Our suggestion is that the fallacy comes in seeking an objective standard, or one which does not finally rest on a judgment of ethical approval and disapproval. We say that the victim of a highwayman is coerced, not because the character of his choice between the alternatives presented is different from any other choice, but because we think the robber does "wrong" in making the alternatives what they are.

In no other sense is it possible to speak of coercion. No human being can ever literally "force" another to do anything (though one may of course forcibly prevent another from acting). It is most unfortunate that the word "force" has come to have such a confusing ambiguity of meaning; for the *threat of violence* (or threat of inflicting some other injury or loss) as a means of controlling the conduct of a human being has only a figurative kinship with the action of a physical force in changing the state of rest or motion of a mass of matter. It is interesting to note that when conduct is influenced by an offer to improve one's condition, instead of a threat of worsening it, we do not call it force or duress. The intensity of "moral pressure" exerted by a bribe is felt to be less than that due to a threat, no doubt because of the tendency to assume that the person affected must have been in a tolerable situation to begin with. Perhaps it is generally true that men feel a negative change in condition more keenly than a positive change, or perhaps we should have to seek for some historical or accidental explanation of the fact that the law takes a different attitude toward bribes than toward threats. The point of this discussion is presumably clear, and need not be labored further. It is simply and briefly that freedom is itself an ethical category and cannot possibly furnish an objective criterion for moral judgments of legislative policy.

However, if the argument for this negative result is sound, it can be followed out to some broader and more positive conclusions, of significance for the character of social "science," and that of ethics. This general argument may be summarized in two main stages, both of which are perhaps "self-evident" in the only sense that expression ever rightly carries. The first of these conclusions or propositions is that the notion of economy, or efficiency, or degree or extent of desire satisfaction is not "objective" in the sense in which physical occurrences and magnitudes are objective. Yet the very notion of policy, or of a practical problem, involves at a minimum the former notion of a possible greater or lesser degree of achievement of a desired end. There can be no such subject matter as economics nor any intelligent discussion of conduct in a practical sense which does not run in terms of teleology. One might treat of the movements of the human body or its members in terms of physiology,[10] or perhaps admit the possibility of conscious accompaniments of such changes on a merely factual level.[11] But such a discussion would not hold any place for recognition that such movements present a problem to the behaving organism itself; the movements so treated would not be conduct, in the meaning which the term actually has to educated human beings. If, at a minimum, the concepts of desire and satisfaction, end (in a personal sense), and achievement of end, are not "real" or "objective" in the sense of being valid units in disclosure,

---

[10] The same logic will in fact just as conclusively eliminate the physiological point of view also, reducing physiology to physics and chemistry. Nor will it end there. The premises of modern physics eliminate all *content* in that field also; matter is resolved into energy, a pure intangible, a physical non-existent, and one is left with a sort of higher geometry of an indeterminate number of dimensions, a system of abstract relations of a purely ideal character.

[11] It is more than doubtful whether this is in fact logically allowable. No human being could have any way of knowing the existence of such purely phenomenal conscious states unless we admit the validity of processes of inference totally different from those involved in our knowledge of physical reality and hence just as subjective, metaphysical, and inadmissible as the notion of value which the scientific intellect finds so repugnant, and the effort to get rid of which raised all these questions in the first place.

then the whole content of economics, technology, and all practical discussion whatever is illusion, and the discussion itself is without meaning, mere raving. That this is not true is as certain as any assertion whatever—*at least* as certain as any assertion regarding those external physical objects which are the subject matter of the natural sciences. The conclusion in regard to the status of the notions of desire and satisfaction does not need to be put into words.

The second general conclusion is fully as repugnant as the first to the intellectual cravings of twentieth-century man, but is also unescapable. No *discussion of policy* is possible apart from a moral judgment. The argument of the body of this paper has shown that an appeal to maximum freedom as a "standard" involves a fallacy. The result is dogmatic acceptance of an existing distribution of power, which is an ethical proposition, a value judgment in disguise, and an ethically indefensible one. Moreover, it involves logical contradictions. Freedom means freedom to use power, and the only possible limitation on the use of power is intrinsically ethical. To say that one is restrained from the use of power by other than ethical considerations amounts to saying that he does not really have the power, that it is cancelled by some opposing force. Freedom and coercion are ethical categories, and the only question in regard to which *discussion* can possibly be carried on is the question of what power *ought* to be exercised, or how and under what circumstances. Why should one not be as *free* to use political power as economic power? As far as the mere notion of freedom is concerned, there is no reason why the majority in a democratic state, or the sovereign group in any state, should not dispossess and exploit the rest of society at their pleasure. And the consistent theoretical utilitarian would have to pronounce the result, whatever it might be, in perfect conformity with his ethical principles. Those principles can never carry him beyond a begging of the question in justification of the *status quo*. The only real objection that could be raised is some form of the statement that political power ought not to be used in that way.

Indeed, it appears to be self-evident, as stated above, that the only reason one person should yield to another, in pleasure or well-being or self-realization or whatever it be called (for they are all merely different words for value or the good) is either (*a*) that he must (in which case he has no choice, no problem exists), (*b*) that he wishes to do so (and hence there is a purely personal problem), or (*c*) that he feels a duty or obligation to do so, which gives rise to a new sort of problem, a moral or ethical problem. The notion of duty or obligation is an ultimate fact of experience—as much so as desire and satisfaction, or space, time, matter, motion, and force.

Or (we might add) life, or consequences, or beauty; and a more detailed examination would greatly extend the list of kinds of "reality" which the exigencies of talking sense compel us to recognize in this "pluralistic universe." But there appears to be justification for giving special recognition as above, to three levels of experience and of subject matter for intelligent discussion. There is first, the field of external fact (science in the narrow sense) in which the relations of events in space and time present no problem in any sense to the material undergoing change. Questions arise in this field only to man as an outsider, as problems of knowledge, in relation to pure curiosity (if there is such a thing) or to the *means* of action. Human behavior may be conceived and studied in either of these two ways: either as scientific data in which the only problem can be to discover "uniformities of coexistence and sequence,"—in more modern terms, stable configurations in space-time—or as a problem of "economy," the adaptation of means to ends. The ends are *data,* but not physically existent data, nor yet values; they are purely personal desires. Discussion on this second level, however, involves something over and above the description of actual events. It involves a judging of conduct, but only from the standpoint of the *intelligence* displayed. The norm is that of efficiency.

On the third level, ends and not merely means are problematic, and are to be discussed and judged. That men do pass such judgments, rating some aims or objectives of action to be higher or more worthy than others and recognizing that it is possible to be in *error* in regard to such ratings as well as in regard to choice of means for securing given ends, is perhaps more of an observed fact than a conclusion established by reasoning. It is hardly necessary to remark to people who have reflected at all about the foundations of knowledge that the common distinction between what is observed and what is inferred is naïve and untenable.

So finally, the argument as to the interpretation of freedom as an ethical standard leads even to a suggestion to the philosopher in his supreme function of ontologist. Viewing the matter in terms of the ineluctable practical exigencies, it is hard to deny "reality" to any notion which has to be recognized as a condition of a tolerable ordering of conduct or of intelligible discourse, or "truth" to any proposition the opposite of which is indisputably more wrong than the proposition itself. Accuracy is a matter of degree, even in the most exact measurements of space. From such a point of view, both private motives in behavior and ethical evaluations have to be recognized as real, and ultimately just as real as behavior itself, considered merely as a change in physical configuration or movement of matter in space.

From the point of view of "radical empiricism," indeed, the problem presented is that of explaining why the modern mind has developed the tendency to explain everything by correlating it with some change in physical configuration, to refuse to accept any other explanation or to regard anything else as truly real. The tendency itself is unquestionably "real" (and this proposition might go far in deciding the ultimate nature of reality and truth, for matter and motion are after all ideas, culture facts with a culture history and explanation). The writer of the present argument feels the bias toward physical-mechanistic thought as strongly as anyone does or can. Primitive atomism, which explains all change as a rearrangement of hard inert particles in space, is unquestionably more solid and satisfying to the mind, gives one more the feeling of really knowing what one is talking about, than any other view of phenomena. But a little study of physics, more effectively than any amount of psychology and philosophy, shows conclusively that such a description of the world leaves out most of the facts, and those rather the most interesting and important. The first thing that physical theory does to the physical world of common knowledge is to annihilate it; all its properties of visibility, tangibility, etc., by which it can be known, are shown to be purely subjective and the reality back of them to be unknowable. Neither the hard particle nor even the space in which it moves stands up under critical examination, or can be at all what it seems. The equations will not balance without putting in various intangibles, force, energy, and potential energy, which are fully as bad as creative will, if indeed they can be kept from running into the latter.

We have to face the fact that our craving for a simple, monistic, mechanical explanation of experience is intrinsically doomed to frustration. However, an explanation of why men have such a craving will go far to take the place of satisfaction for the craving itself. Our final suggestion is that there is a fairly obvious explanation for the phenomenon along pragmatic lines. Thought is to begin with, mainly, and throughout its history in considerable part, a biological function, a phase of organic adaptation, which in its developed stage is more and more adaptation of the environment rather than the organism. Now the only way in which the organism which has developed to the stage of purposiveness can change his environment in the least is by *moving* some part of it in space.

The sole point of effective contact between mind and matter is through the voluntary muscles and the sole activity of which they are capable is precisely this change of physical configuration or rearrangement in space, first of the members of the organism itself and secondarily of external objects. Is not this the source and meaning of the bias for reducing all existence to physical existence and all change to change in spatial configuration?

Social Science and the Political Trend

I

The question whether men as scientists can understand the behavior of men as statesmen and citizens is closely connected with the question how far the latter's behaviour is itself of an intelligent or understanding sort; and such issues are hard to discuss in purely descriptive terms.

Even before the current political trends, which have become increasingly noticeable since the Great War, a number of writers had been questioning how far political activity could be described as consciously intelligent behaviour. The mention of such names as Sorel and Pareto, Cooley, Wallas, and Lévy-Bruhl, is sufficient to emphasize the point, to say nothing of the interpretations of human nature derived from psychopathology. The methodological controversy in economics of the past quarter-century or so looks in the same direction. The rationalistic assumptions of the older classical economics

Reprinted by permission from the *University of Toronto Quarterly*, vol. 3 (1934), pp. 407–427.

have been under fire, and the type of analysis based upon them has been yielding ground to other "approaches."

II

On the nature of the current political trend, most of what can be said with confidence is negative. It is something different, change, revolution, a break-down of the old system and of the theory and ideology on which it rested. In particular, it is irrationalistic, romantic, away from thinking, toward action. Well before the War, this tendency was manifest in the declining faith in parliamentarism. Then came the War, with its inevitable regimentation of economic and social life, followed by a brief liberal reaction, and then by the Depression, which more and more has come to be seen as a breakdown of the old order on its economic side. *Either* economic science failed to find the cause and prescribe a cure *or* political leadership failed to discern in the babel of claims the true economic science, and to follow its behests. In any case, we have seen a discrediting and discarding of old economic and political points of view and axioms, and the rise of a new type of leadership which contrasts strangely with old norms. It does not claim to know, or make its appeal on grounds of knowledge or reason, but rather advocates action as such, the following of an emotional direction or frank experimentation.

The latest main episodes in a change going on all over the world of European liberal civilization are the "New Deals" in Germany and the United States. They use different catch-words, but are variants of the same theme. The German "Leader" is perhaps more frank in his call to his people to "think with their blood" but the American pose of experimentalism is at bottom the same thing, the appeal to follow leadership—of the appealer; the cry is "All pull together," meaning "Follow me" (and don't ask critical questions). And the public likes it. The whole West-European social mind is tired of thinking and of argument which seems to lead nowhere, and responds with enthusiasm to the confident proposal to do something about it. The meaning of action, again, is familiar enough; the keynote is to "crack down" on somebody, to make the protestant and non-conformer "feel the full weight of public disapproval." The social science on which the present adult generation was brought up much exaggerated, it would seem, the distance western society had travelled from "primitive" African political ideas with the witch-hunt as the correct procedure for dealing with any public crisis. As to experimenting with social life, it is not good form to question the wisdom of distinguishing food from poison by eating it or to ask who is to experiment and who to be experimented upon.

Of course there *is* thinking—at least there is mental process expressed in sentences which have subjects and predicates— along with the battle-cries. As reasoning, however, it is sometimes hard—for one with an old-fashioned education (or "reactionary" political sentiments!)—to follow. Thus the favourite American recipe for curing the depression is to encourage employment by forcing up wages, and revive business by increasing its costs, while guarding against a corresponding rise in prices. Again, the bulk of the unemployment being in the industries producing for investment needs, everything must be done to throttle investment and increase the demand for products for immediate consumption. The latest broadcast from the Leader in Washington argues that because "the people in this country whose incomes are less than $2,000 a year buy more than two-thirds of all goods sold here, [therefore] it is logical that if the total amount that goes in wages to this group of human beings is steadily increased, merchants, employers, and investors will in the long run get more income from the increased volume of sales.'' Thus employers are to be aided by forcibly transferring incomes from them to wage-earners; what general effects the indirect procedure followed would probably have, is another matter, too far from the workings of the political mind to be inquired into here.

It will be seen that such analysis tends to imply criticism. This is utterly foreign to our intent. The point is simply the difficulty of understanding intellectually the political process when it takes on such forms. The first business of a political leader is to keep on being a political leader, and his acts and words are to be appraised solely from the point of view of their effectiveness to that end. Rather to be criticized is the familiar habit of criticizing politicians for playing good politics. This is palpably stupid. For a politician to do what the voters do not like is neither possible nor conformable to democratic ideals. Whoever is leader will play politics; the business of the student is merely to find out what is good politics, and why.

To the critical historian, the acts of individuals seem to be more the effects, or incidental accompaniments, of funda- mental changes than determining factors. As to the underlying causes, the most we know is that our knowledge and under- standing are very limited, that we have no clear conception of the material that is changing, or of the forces, processes, or laws of change. Yet we must and will try to understand the historical changes of the past and, by this light, those we are going through. Statements as to the limited achievements to date and the difficulties of the problem must in no wise be taken as pessimistic. If intelligence is to accomplish anything, it must both face candidly its mistakes in the past and appraise critically the inherent limits of its power.

For the first two years or so after the economic crisis of 1929, I was one of the large group of students of economics who condemned the idea that this was fundamentally different

27

from other depressions. But I have become convinced that I was in error, that we are actually in the course of one of the world's great economic and political revolutions. Even if we see some business revival, it will be limited and temporary. The nineteenth-century liberal system is played out, and the world of West-European civilization, based on political "democracy" and economic "freedom," will go through a drastic revaluation of its "modern" ideas and values. This change leads backward historically, toward some combination of nationalism—though a nationalism different from that of the post-Renaissance centuries—with a quasi-religious intellectual absolutism, comparable to, yet different from that of the Middle Ages.

The significance of this for education is profound. If the civilization of the visible future is to be more like that of the thirteenth and sixteenth centuries than that of the nineteenth, the most important thing for youth to be taught today is that most of what the writings of our fathers treated as established is for the future the opposite of the truth. Natural science and scientific technology may not go backward to a serious extent—they are too important for war!—but the conditions of free initiative under which they are studied and applied will be entirely changed; and in everything connected with political life ideals will be practically inverted. Fixity will take the place of progress, security that of adventure; individuality, independence, and diversity will make way for conformity, uniformity, and unity; consequently, love of truth will give place to loyalty, and love of liberty to unquestioning obedience to authority. The basic mystery of the relation between thinking and social process could have no better illustration than the fact that those who are striving most zealously to bring this about are liberals, and though predominantly educated (as well as honourable) men—even professors of social science in universities—they think they are working to promote freedom and democracy.

III

The evidence for all this can only be suggested. The first item would be the course of events—Russia, Italy, Germany, Japan, etc., and then America, England, and France. More important is the visible decay of the ideal of liberty. Particularly noteworthy is the shift of radical reformism away from the democratic faith, the decline of Socialism in favour of Communism (which was in evidence long before the War), while even professed democratic Socialists hasten to disclaim the "fetish of legality." An argument perhaps intrinsically stronger, if less tangible on the face of it, is the *a priori* presumption that, as in the age of democracy the cure for any weakness shown by democratic institutions was always to make them more democratic, it is much more inevitable that the cure for any weakness of planning and regulation will be more regulation and a further concentration of power. The movement toward "control" once under way, we must surely expect for the visible future a process of plugging the holes in the system.

But the strongest, and in my own mind, the conclusive argument, is to be drawn from the inherent impossibility of nineteenth-century civilization itself, to certain essential features of which the social science of the age was strangely blind. From the vantage point of the present, we can see that only a remarkable accidental and inherently temporary set of conditions made it possible, for a time, for such a "free" social system—private initiative in economic life and government through representative institutions—to seem to work, or seem to have the capacity of solving the problem of combining liberty with order. Democracy, such as it was, was possible only in so far as there were no vital political problems, no serious differences of opinion or conflicts of interest. Whenever a democratic nation confronted such a problem as a foreign war, democracy folded up as a matter of course; and any really serious internal problem, such as slavery in the United States, had also to be settled by fighting to the exhaustion of the weaker party.

The conditions under which free government was possible, meaning under which there were no serious political issues, were an incident of the "frontier." The geographical discoveries and technical inventions of the seventeenth and eighteenth centuries relieved social and economic pressures in the countries of western Europe. With an essentially unlimited domain awaiting economic conquest, life ceased to be seriously competitive for individuals. A practically unbounded sphere of action and of self-aggrandizement was open for any and all with sufficient energy and ambition to count seriously in social or political affairs. Such a world could be individualistic, and would naturally tend toward individualism—while the situation continued. It did so, and experienced a brief period of "freedom," a literal "withering away of the state." But with the filling up of the world and the passing of frontier conditions, requirements would revert to older norms of stability through discipline. That is essentially what has happened though other changes, more or less predictable concomitants of the same development, have contributed to the resurgence of the state and of politics.

This reasoning may help us to grasp our present situation, but it is not encouraging as regards the capacity of intelligence to create social science. For it is essentially hindsight. None of this was seen by the leaders of the old order itself, whether political or intellectual and scientific. On the contrary, "everyman" was taught to view the state of liberty as a solid achievement which would both live and grow, and so was encouraged to live in a fool's paradise. Under the conditions of the moment, the problem of making a success in life was primarily that of exploiting nature, rather than other men, as normally in the world. The individual's requirements for getting ahead were enterprise, technical capacity, and a minimum of small-scale organizing ability. Thought habits and moral ideals were moulded accordingly, especially in the New World. Intellectually, the age became one of "scientificism," and of "management"; in philosophy it was the age of utilitarianism, which evolved, in America, around the end of the century, into pragmatism, the negation of philosophy, philistinism transformed into a cult.

IV

If the intellectual leadership of nineteenth-century society failed to grasp the underlying physical situation, it failed just as egregiously to understand the spiritual foundations of its own institutions. In liberal society, as in any other, these were mainly unconscious or emotional. Social behaviour must always be largely habit, while of that part which receives conscious attention a large fraction must be based on sentiment and loyalty rather than on critical deliberation. Moreover, sentiment and loyalty must be not merely uncritical, but definitely above criticism, protected from intellectual examination by social sanctions. The objects of loyalty must be sacred. In other words, next to unconscious tradition, *religion* is the foundation of social order.

The religious basis of liberalism was peculiar in that it was separated almost completely from current professions and practices of a formally religious sort, those which were current being a survival from an age and culture long past and thoroughly repudiated. The real spiritual foundations of the social order had been laid in the early "modern" centuries following the "Middle" or "Dark" Ages, as this past civilization was disparagingly called, the process culminating in the eighteenth century, the "Age of Reason." But rationalism is as emotional and anti-critical—as religious—as any other creed. Liberalism considered itself intellectual because it was based on a religion of irreligion, of intelligent self-seeking (verbally reconciled with deistical professions in the maxim that God helps those who help themselves). In all ideas and practices relating to the supersensible, there was in theory the utmost tolerance, showing that these things were not taken seriously in connection with the problems of social life.[1]

But the religion of liberalism had a positive social-moral content, read into the notion of intelligence (in somewhat Socratic fashion). This was the sanctity of property. Only on such a basis could the *ordre naturel* of the French *économistes* or Adam Smith's "obvious and simple system of natural liberty" exist and function.[2] This unexamined, emotional-religious absolute which, objectively viewed, is Property, was generally called by the more appealing name of Liberty. It is a purely negative idea, meaning freedom to use power, and without power, completely empty. As gradually came to be frankly stated, the liberty of liberalism is "the right to do as

---

[1] Professor Tawney tells us that a nineteenth-century prime minister met a protesting church delegation with a remonstrance to the effect that things had come to a pretty pass if religion was going to interfere in the affairs of everyday life.

[2] As has often been pointed out, the economic laws were conceived in much the same way as the principles of Newtonian mechanics, i.e., as having a similar significance for society to that which the Newtonian principles had for cosmology. The basic difference, that the operation of the Newtonian principles does not depend on their recognition or acceptance, still less their enforcement by man, was overlooked. But this is a phenomenon so common in social thinking as to be almost typical.

one wills with one's own." The economic individual has but
two attributes, will and power, or in economic terms, wants
and property. Property, in turn, includes two kinds, the
personal capacities, having salable value, of the biological
human unit himself, and rights to and over external things.
Property is a part of personality, or personal capacities are
owned, as one may choose to look at it.[3] The essential content
of property as a constitutional principle is a sacred immunity
from interference either by society itself through political
agencies, or by other individuals. The latter immunity is, like
other sanctities, enforced by political sanctions.

V

Under liberal theory, the role of government and government itself were reduced to a minimum. The positive tasks
of social organization were to be turned over to an automatic,
two-stage system of markets which was rapidly developing,
the system which economists call free enterprise. Competition
of business firms in buying productive services and selling
products should guarantee the use of productive capacity in
the manner yielding the greatest want-satisfaction on the

---

[3] It is a mere accident, and true only within limits, that incomes from property
are larger than incomes from labour, and represent a greater quantity of power.
The peculiar weakness of the position of one who owns earning power only in
the form of personal capacities is, somewhat paradoxically, a consequence of the
guarantee of personal freedom, general in modern nations, but logically not a part
of the property system; in fact, it is a limitation on the ownership of one's own
person. Because of such "inalienable rights" a man cannot "capitalize" his
earning power because a contract to deliver labour in the future will not be
enforced. Hence, one who has no other source of income can satisfy current needs
only by the current sale of services; he has no power to "wait." Also, the ethical
contrast commonly drawn by radical critics of the competitive system between the
two forms of exchange power, labour and property, or their respective incomes,
is almost entirely false. Both sources of income arise genetically from similar
unanalysable mixtures of inheritance, conscientious effort, and luck.

whole. The state would get by taxation its small share, needed to support its limited functions, chiefly the protection of property and enforcement of contract, plus certain general services to the economic system.[4]

Thus were reversed a number of the main assumptions of previous political thinking. The notion of the universal conflict of economic interests gave place to a presumption of mutual advantage. The view of the state as an entity with its own ends and of the main social problem as that of getting individuals to subordinate, to a requisite degree, their private purposes to these ends—with the corollary that economic problems were a subordinate part of political—gave place to the conception of the state as a means to individual ends, of politics as a subdivision of economics, and of the main political problem as the negative one of preventing government from interfering unduly with private affairs.

The political side of these new ideas is democracy—government by elected officials. Much the most thorough-going embodiment in an actual constitution naturally occurred in the United States of America, a new nation starting relatively free from older traditions, populated predominantly from the European country most advanced in the liberal direction (and indeed with people selected in large measure for an attitude of dissent), and also immediately dominated by frontier conditions. There the political constitution followed through on the principle of "checks and balances," assuring a government able to preserve "law and order" but prevented from undertaking positive functions which would interfere with liberty. To the founding fathers this connection between

---

[4] The classical exposition of the new doctrine in its positive aspect was Adam Smith's *Wealth of Nations,* published in 1776. Interestingly enough, the political and legal theory had been stated in a series of classics, well in advance of the formulation of the economic theory by Smith. The leading names are, of course, Locke, Montesquieu, and Blackstone.

democracy and economic *laisser-faire* was so obvious that they were hardly conscious of it.

In western Europe the political evolution was toward democracy in the American sense.

VI

The system seemed to work fairly well in the political and economic spheres while frontier conditions lasted. Certainly the world has never seen anything comparable to the nineteenth century, or to America, in the way of scientific and technical progress, particularly the diffusion of material well-being over the general population, and many sorts of humanitarian advance. If the results were not so satisfying from the standpoint of "culture" taken in a more aesthetic sense, there were grounds for generous allowances in the present and hope for the future. (And pre-liberal and Old-World civilizations were not actually all pure beauty and refinement.)

Turning points are never points, and evidences of fundamental change go back at least to the first English factory acts. But it is interesting that not far from the date usually given for the "passing of the frontier" in the New World, we begin to hear in Britain of a New Liberalism essentially antithetical to the old, repudiating the automatic economic order and substituting the positive care and activity of the state as a main reliance for securing the realization of fundamental human values. The new liberalism, however, retained the faith in democratic forms for carrying out its constructive programme, an idea which would have been unintelligible to the founders of liberalism in France, America, or Britain itself. The corresponding political development was the creation of an expert civil service, otherwise known as a bureaucracy; government was to be conducted by "experts," men with special technical and administrative competence.

The role of the people would be restricted to choosing legislative representatives who would determine general policies, and this power of choice would maintain "responsibility."

VII

But there is an ambiguity amounting to paradox in the theory of responsibility, which could be seen in the workings of the democratic machinery all through the nineteenth century, most clearly in the United States. The question was whether a political representative is supposed to do the *will* of his constituents or to act as a custodian of their *interests,* being guided in action by his own presumably superior knowledge and judgment. Whatever theory might say, the exigencies of political life forced professional politicians, as a condition of success, more and more to advocate and to inculcate in the people the theory of direct democracy, the "rubber stamp" view of the representative function. But the result was that officials became more incompetent, and in addition, more corrupt. Platforms and pledges ran to verbiage, decreasing in content as they increased in length, and were taken less and less seriously. Political life appealed more and more exclusively to two main types, outright crusaders and self-seekers— the former not generally conspicuous for sound judgment, the latter either professional place-fillers, power-lovers (overlapping with crusaders), or servants of special interests. A new word, "graft," quickly became one of the most used items in the political vocabulary.

The mystery is not that representative institutions were discredited, but that any other result could have been expected. The agency relation presents a problem for which there is no mechanical or intellectual solution, while direct democracy, on any considerable scale and with positive functions, is out of the question. To illustrate the first point, we need only look at the problem of selecting a physician.[5] A patient who would choose his doctor scientifically would, in the first place, have himself to know all medical science, or at least all that known to any and all candidates for the place, and in addition know just the amount of this knowledge possessed by each candidate. But this is only half the story, and perhaps the smaller half. Our poor patient would further be required to know the degree in which each candidate would use his knowledge in his, the patient's, interest.

If the problem of competence in an agent admits of no solution because of its magnitude and complexity, that of the moral factor admits of none, of an intellectual sort, by its very nature. One who is to act for another with special competence, superior to that of his principal, and with fidelity, must be picked for competence and trustworthiness by some intuitive process, and must then be trusted. Sanctions of the sorts found in every society no doubt help in securing trustworthiness. About all these matters we have little knowledge, and the one thing that can be said with assurance is that (peace to the shade of Jeremy Bentham!) no machinery of sanctions can conceivably function without very large aid from moral forces.

Turning from the agency relation to the process of decision by a group as such (direct democracy), we confront the vast problem of the group mind and its changes, conscious and unconscious, or in other words the problem of history. Our concern here is with the rôle of specialized intelligence with respect to understanding and influencing historical change. On this topic, only two brief observations are possible. The

---

[5] *Cf. Faust,* Part I, II. 1022–63.

first has to do with the theory underlying nineteenth-century liberalism. The suggestion in Smith's famous phrase, "the invisible hand," received more definite content nearly a century later from Darwin and Spencer in the conception of natural selection among spontaneous variations. To make it fit the social process the theory must be modified by recognizing that both in initiating variations and in selection, intelligence is assumed to be involved, but the mechanism has the same automatic beneficence. The individual is free (if he has, or can get from others by mutual agreement, the necessary resources) to "start" any change in the production and marketing of economic services, and similarly, to advocate any change in the laws or constitution. In the economic field the change survives or grows to the extent that it is selected by consumers' expenditures, in competition with other uses of income, old and new. A suggestion for political change survives only if it is selected for the group in question as a whole, by the democratic political machinery as it actually exists and functions. To insure that only intelligent changes from the group standpoint will be made, the theory relies on the selective process; if initiation is unintelligent, as shown by failure of selection, the initiator's effort is wasted, but society is not materially affected.

On the political side, the error is that the people cannot select either ideas or leaders intelligently and are disposed to prejudice and hero worship rather than thinking or judgment. That the theory must presently break down on the economic side, in the absence of considerable political management, could have been predicted by fairly simple economic analysis, if any such had been forthcoming. Discussion there was in abundance, but that which got any hearing was a mixture of crude analysis with shallow apologetic, or with criticism of a sort to distract attention from the real weaknesses of the system,[6] or even with both. The criticism typically took the form of debating advocacy of alternatives obviously worse, particularly that of substituting for the system of organization through free markets the political bureaucracy. But one of the most fundamental weaknesses of the market system is the use of persuasive influence by sellers upon buyers and a general excessive tendency to produce wants for goods rather than goods for the satisfaction of wants. Influencing men's judgment, however, is almost the essence of democratic political process, and is definitely more sinister where the advocate appeals to men in the mass, and they decide in the mass, rather than individually.[7] To substitute competitive politics for competitive business is to jump out of the frying pan into the fire. No possible "machinery" will preserve responsibility without actual crowd rule, or will give political guidance (or even finally preserve order, once the traditional-religious basis of order is broken up) in the absence of moral leadership (good or bad) accepted as such by the masses. The real breakdown of *bourgeois* society is only superficially economic: as a structural break-down it is rather political, since indisputably it is the business of the political system to make the economic system function; fundamentally, however, the breakdown is not structural at all, but moral. The intellectual mistake of liberalism was two-fold: it failed to see that the social problem

---

[6] It is impossible to go into this economic analysis here. The basic fact is that, in the absence of preventive measures, concentration of wealth (aggravated by inheritance) and still more concentration of power (through organization) would be inevitable and must before long smother the competitive process in monopoly and other impediments to readjustment.

[7] Adam Smith seems not to have thought of advertising and salesmanship, which developed long after his death. The founding fathers of democracy, notably in America, thought of campaigning, though apparently not of political party "machines"; but their careful provisions against the crowd mind were soon condemned as antidemocratic and did not count for long in a system which actually put the crowd in power.

is not at bottom intellectual, but moral, and it utterly misconceived the genuinely intellectual element involved. Individual intelligence in the instrumentalist sense, so far from being a solution of the problem, is a perfect formula for the war of each against all.

The crux of current change lies in the loss of faith in intelligence as an agency for social problem-solving; it manifests the inevitable downfall of the religion of individual intelligence. First to fall of the idols erected to this religion were faith in the automatic competitive system and the belief in the supreme political competence of the untutored plain man, the special romanticism of Rousseau. Then universal education became the panacea. Faith in the natural capacity or educability of the masses was not much longer-lived, and emphasis was shifted from mass education to the training of leaders. Then the problem was teachers for the leaders, and how to get the trained leaders to lead and others to follow— the problem of agency added to that of mass decision. Education provides no formula by which a society can lift itself culturally by its bootstraps, and the faith in education now appears as one of the most pathetic items in the entire creed of liberalism.

Loss of faith in intellectual leaders was followed by the final step, a turning away from belief in the very reality of truth. For a generation, left-wing political agitation has preached that ''sound'' and ''unsound'' doctrine in economics and politics mean the advocacy of the special interest of the proponent (though why or in what sense it should be ''class'' interest is a mystery); orthodoxy is merely the doctrine favourable to the dominant social class. And not different is the dominant academic philosophy, in the United States specifically, for this is the meaning in the social field of the pragmatic test of truth.

VIII

This leads to the final observation referred to, in connection with which a constructive suggestion may be offered. In the doctrine of liberalism the theory of natural selection by an invisible hand applies to the intellectual, aesthetic, and spiritual, and even to the religious life, as well as to the economic and political. Anyone is free to propose "variations," and advocate them, within wide limits, by any sort of arguments. It is assumed that selection by the ultimate consumer will produce agreement on the "fittest" alternative where agreement is requisite, or otherwise will select what is fittest for the particular individual or group. In the intellectual field, the issue is especially acute, since the notion of truth implies that it is the same for all. Moreover, the field of public policy is peculiar in that there *must* be agreement; it is *impossible* for each to have it his own way. But under liberalism, political truth is decided by mass judgment selecting among opinions or personalities advocated under conditions of free competition.

It is perhaps in economics that, within the field of culture, the largest element of impersonal truth is presumed and that there is the largest necessity for social policy. Trained economists have been put in the position of appealing to the crowd against each other, of making the crowd the judge of their intellectual differences. Selection has tended to staff the profession with persons who accept this democratic process as the final and right method of reaching intellectual validity. The tendency is cumulative. It places increasing pressure on the diminishing remnant of minds interested in getting the right answers to problems to enter the forum where the issues are really determined and where they see a growing majority of their professional colleagues engaged in the only activity which can either be practically significant or afford any community of intellectual life, or even, in the not-very-long run, any chance to live by one's work. It is surely unnecessary to explain here that what this process selects is not truth, but effective technique in persuading the crowd, and that it can only eventuate, as we have seen it do, in the destruction of the notion of truth in any matter connected with public policy. And of course the attitude tends to spread to other fields.

Our suggestion, then, is that a few people in the fields most directly affected, such as economics, might recognize this situation and deliberately stand out against it, striving to preserve in a small area an atmosphere of cooperative critical truth-seeking, apart from mutual destruction in public controversy. There must be no delusion that this is easy. The purely intellectual difficulties are stupendous. Even material obstacles are considerable, for intellectual intercourse must be costly where it does not result in a marketable product. But the really serious difficulty is moral. We are all children of our age, the age of liberalism, the age of publicity and of personal competition. We are all soaked in the tradition of "fighting for the truth," which implies that truth is defined by victory, and puts love of victory, which is easy, in place of love of truth, which is hard. A genuine religious conversion would be necessary for most or all of the members of any group which should really devote itself to love of truth and faith in truth. They must both renounce personal emoluments and resist the temptation to place power behind truth, which actually tends rather to prostitute truth to power.

There is no backward yearning for any golden age in this suggestion. There has never been any promotion of truth (practically speaking) which was not connected with promotion of the promoter as a human individual. Yet the problem is a new one, as the idea of social direction by popular discussion is new. It was created in the first place by the printing press and then by modern civilization, which drew the whole population, willy-nilly, into the discussion of questions previously reserved for specialists. This is not the place for details as to how to meet the difficulties. But it would seem that it ought to be possible to have a political and economic science, on some scale, which would not rest on a competition among those of special competence in ''selling'' to the public ideas and doctrines which they cannot sell to each other.

Pragmatism and Social Action

I

In his latest book,[1] Professor Dewey's three Page-Barbour lectures at the University of Virginia are published as chapters under the titles: i, "The History of Liberalism"; ii, "The Crisis in Liberalism"; iii, "Renascent Liberalism."

II

The first chapter contains many illuminating and suggestive insights. The most interesting to me is the suggestion that it

Reprinted by permission from the *International Journal of Ethics*, vol. 46 (1936), pp. 229–236.

[1] John Dewey, *Liberalism and Social Action*. New York: Putnam's, 1935. Pp. x and 93. These paragraphs represent a slight revision of some "notes for a possible review," written for local circulation, intended to provoke discussion, and not for publication in a philosophical journal. Responsibility for publication in this form, without benefit even of the private discussion which was the original aim, rests with the editors of the *International Journal of Ethics!* The writer would concede that an exhaustive study of Professor Dewey's work might lead to modification of some of the general statements about his system as a whole. His own interest is in issues and not in the exegesis of a particular corpus of philosophic writing.

is because America had no Bentham and no Benthamite movement that we tended to follow in the more negative, individualistic liberalism of Locke and Adam Smith, while English liberalism in the nineteenth century showed a strong reverse tendency toward positive political action in the interest of social well-being. Professor Dewey also emphasizes in this connection the role of Thomas Hill Green, a mediator of German ideas, but one who remained liberal, without the extreme "stateism" which characterized the idealistic movement in German philosophy.

III

Professor Dewey's conception of the "crisis of liberalism" is not easy to grasp, or certainly to state briefly. In moving toward concrete "diagnosis," and constructive suggestions, we move into the vagueness and ambiguity which is (to me) the outstanding characteristic of his thought. The "crisis" has something to do with two opposed conceptions of intelligence, on the one hand as "an individual possession and its exercise as an individual right" (p. 65), on the other as "integrated with social movements and a factor in giving them direction" (p. 44). The first quotation is from Lecture iii, and it is here that the author's main conceptions become fairly clear, especially (I think) as to the fundamental confusion underlying them.

IV

Professor Dewey is clearly right in the general abstract position that the conception of intelligence in its connection with social relations is the crucial issue confronting "liberalism," by which I mean here simply the hope and the project of maintaining a democratic social order, in contrast with autocracy or dictatorship. He is further right in recognizing (or at least in coming very near to explicitly recognizing [cf. esp. pp. 65–67]) that intelligence in this field must be something more than an individual quality or possession or right (see foregoing quotation). But I should want to go further and say, a form of individual *power*, and to add that this false conception has been largely promulgated and re-enforced by the whole pragmatic movement in philosophy. Professor Dewey's pragmatism always strikes me as fundamentally ambiguous, oscillating between a conception of knowledge as "technique," essentially a biological function, and some vague mystical conception of it in terms of "shared life" or "shared experience." Of this latter notion I can make nothing except a kind of intellectualized gregariousness; it seems to be intellectual only in the sense that the manifestations of the herd instinct take the form of verbal, grammatical, and in various senses meaningful, intercommunication, instead of rubbing noses or similar physical manifestations. What shared experience has to do with social problems in any sense in which these can be called intellectual, I am unable to make out. What it naturally suggests is rather the mob-spirit than rational deliberation. And no more can I find, in the fairly large sample of Professor Dewey's writings known to me, any successful or even real attempt to build a bridge between his two conceptions of intelligence.

Whenever we approach anything concrete, or in any sense "get down to cases," in Professor Dewey's treatment of intelligence, we usually find it to be "pragmatic" in the first and more literal sense, of crude instrumentalism, which may be summed up in the formula, "knowledge is power," really meaning physical power. In particular, this is the meaning of taking "scientific" activity as the type illustration of intelligence, which is Dewey's regular practice. But as far as problems of human relations are concerned, knowledge as technique or power means individual power, over other individuals or society as a whole, and is definitely an antisocial force. The habit of thinking of life problems in terms of means and end, power and technique, is necessary in our relations, individual or group, to the physical environment; but it must be *prevented* from carrying over into the social field itself if ethical society—which is to say any true society—is to exist. And this prevention is perhaps the main or prior practical social problem. No *social* interest of the individual (or of society in the sense in which a society can be said to have social interests) can be promoted by scientific knowledge or technique, and any attempt to do so must have the opposite effect.[2]

V

It is at this point that, as I wish to maintain, Professor Dewey's theories of liberalism and his program for its salvation go definitely and catastrophically wrong. He seems to confuse the unquestionable fact that scientific and technological knowledge is in a fundamental sense social in genesis and transmission with the view that this style of intelligence is applicable to social problems, which is the antithesis of the truth. What is the matter with liberalism in connection with the use of intelligence is especially the fact that in its view of society it has taken intelligence in the instrumentalistic-scientific sense. This is shown especially in the whole endeavor to build social

---

[2] Even the antisocial interests centering in the quest of power over others—virtually the definition of the immoral in the Kantian sense, which is the liberal sense—are not really promoted by intelligence in any form closely resembling that by which men "predict and control" in connection with inert natural objects. Power in the human field takes such forms as suggestion, persuasion, pleading, and coercion, which are alike without meaning in connection with natural objects. But this point cannot be developed here (cf. *International Journal of Ethics*, October, 1935, pp. 1–33).

sciences on natural-science models, and at the same time to view them as guides for, or in any way relevant to, social action. Natural science in the predictive sense of astronomy (social analogue: science of history, in any form) rests on postulates which exclude the possibility of action in the social field, since this means action of the subject matter on itself; natural science in the "prediction-and-control" sense of the laboratory disciplines is relevant to action only for a dictator standing in a one-sided relation of control to a society, which is the negation of liberalism—and of all that liberalism has called morality.[3]

VI

The basis of Dewey's diagnosis of the failure of intelligence to develop freer and more effective forms of social co-operation is the theory of "culture lag," especially the lag of other phases of life behind industrial changes (p. 52). Like most critics not especially trained in economics (and many who should know better), he greatly exaggerates the role of power relations in the economic life of today, practically ignoring the role of competition (in the economic sense—not that of rivalry). An enterprise economy would break down completely unless predominantly competitive, and, in so far

---

[3] In my view, only the problem of agreement upon ends and upon modes of cooperation is really social. A pragmatist critic has objected that my position would exclude a doctor using medical science in treating a human patient. I hold that the social problem ends when the doctor-patient relation is established and accepted by both parties. Professor Dewey quotes from Henry George as an ideal statement of the nature of intelligence in its social office, "the wider and fuller union of individual efforts in accomplishment of common ends" (p. 68). I agree as to the objective, but with the fundamental qualification that the social problem for intelligence is exclusively that of finding the right ends and the right organization for their pursuit. A scientific problem, in so far as it is relative to action at all, is one of control; but a social problem is one of *consensus*, especially on rules of action and forms of cooperation, both of which in political society are matters of "law."

as it becomes monopolistic, the major conflict of interests is between the different monopolists. Any opposition between "producers" and "consumers" is a logical absurdity, a "fallacy of composition." Now, in the first place, what the culture-lag theory really amounts to is the assertion that some social changes of which the theorist approves have taken place, while others of which he thinks he would approve have not, or "wrong" changes have occurred instead; the word "lag" has no proper application. In the second place, the particular phase of social changes which Professor Dewey finds to have "lagged" has to do with "patterns of thought and belief," or "of intelligent purpose and emotion" (p. 58), or "habits of desire and effort" (p. 59). Liberal society is by implication exhorted to save itself by "speeding up" changes in this regard. But as already noted, what has happened is that such changes have been taking place in "wrong" directions, rather than lagging. Moreover, these things are assumed to be under the control of "society," a matter of free election and choice, or for the application of scientific intelligence. It is impossible to argue this question here, but it should hardly be necessary; intelligence must take something as given, in the way of objectives and ideals, as well as conditions of their realization; and intelligent choice between ends is a very different thing from "science" which adapts means to ends.

VII

The nearest we get to the concrete, in the way of a program of action, in this book, is, as one might expect, the appeal to "education." As usual, nothing is said about who is to do the educating of "society." Presumably "we" are to do it— we reformers, saviors of society. This throws us squarely into communistic, or possibly fascistic, theory, the antithesis of democracy, of freedom, and of any liberalism. It is to be noted especially that there is no approach to agreement among the reformers themselves, and the first, and perhaps the main, task of "me and my gang" would be to suppress a vast congeries of competing aspirants for the same role. The conflicts among reformers are at least as violent now as those they wage with advocates of the *status quo*, and surely more acute than the latter would be if the reformers were reasonably in agreement. Organized education, democratically controlled, is, on its face, as regards fundamental ideals, an agency for promoting continuity, or even for accentuating accepted values, not a means by which "society" can lift itself by its own bootstraps into a different spiritual world.

Moreover, to repeat, the contention that our moral sentiments and emotions have "lagged," or that they are in any sense a survival from preliberal ages (pp. 75, 77), does not even have the merit of historical accuracy. The excessive individualism which is the real threat to liberalism is definitely a modern development, the product of liberalism itself—or, more accurately, each has produced the other, or the various aspects of liberalism have evolved in interaction, as is always the case with the major aspects of any cultural form. The real weakness of liberalism is that by taking certain general principles, such as individual freedom and scientific intelligence, too naïvely and carrying them to extremes, it has educated against itself, against the fundamental conditions of its own permanence. (Perhaps this is what any social system naturally does, and some kind of cycle in political forms is a "law of history," as Plato and Aristotle believed.)

VIII

The author's argument must be followed one step farther. He lists three changes, all essentially economic, in relation to which our "patterns of emotion and feeling" are supposed to have lagged. These have to do with scarcity, insecurity, and the scale of economic productive organization. His treatment of all seems to me completely superficial. (There is most "sense" in the third, from the standpoint of such a general position as his, but the point cannot be developed.) Speaking as a student of economics, I must say briefly that economic conditions have extremely little to do with the really fundamental social problems. It is not, of course, a mere accident that the individualistic quest of prominence, power, and aggrandizement has in our age taken a somewhat predominantly economic form, while the mode of insecurity of which people are most conscious naturally corresponds. But there is no reason to believe that, given individualism, in something like the current sense, as the general moral outlook on life, the social problem would be *essentially* different if life had no economic aspect whatever. If all our material wants were automatically gratified, or if we had none; if we had no "work" in any sense to do, and the social problem in, say, the United States, were simply that of organizing play activities for the relief of boredom, there is no reason to believe that social conflicts would be either less intense or essentially changed in character. (Moreover, there would probably be "classes" and "class struggles" in essentially the same meaning as now—which is no definite meaning at all, as Professor Dewey seems to recognize.) Indeed, it is a sobering reflection that the competitiveness of play is a phenomenon indefinitely older and more general than the competitive organization of economic life. There is a strong case for the view that the whole development of economic and political individualism represents essentially a release of general, if not universal, human tendencies which formerly were held in leash by institutions—a release under the peculiar conditions created by an open frontier, in which this did not mean immediate social disintegration. An outstanding phase of the development has been the carrying of the play attitude into work, which is a splendid thing in itself—though the routinizing of work under the influence of minute division of labor and mechanization tends to reverse this tendency for a large part of the population.

On the one hand, Professor Dewey, like most of the reformers of the day, grossly exaggerates the possibilities even of economic abundance, defined by any standard of living which would be satisfactory to the reformers themselves. But, on the other, the real scarcity which seriously afflicts individualistic civilization is the scarcity of such things as distinction, spectacular achievements, honor, victory, and power—which is clearly not to be cured by any application of scientific technique. (The meaning of insecurity in this connection does not call for elaboration.) The problem of control (over nature by man) has not been solved. But the social problem, for those interested in freedom, is the very different one of securing consensus *without* control. It is a problem of discovery and definition of values—a moral, not to say a religious, problem; and, Professor Dewey notwithstanding, the relation of the procedure of attack on such problems to intelligence in the scientific sense is primarily one of contrast. As already suggested, the two do have in common a moral attitude of recognition that there is a problem, which has a solution, or better and worse solutions, which must be sought and found, and not arbitrarily chosen and imposed. In other words, social problems must be solved by *discussion*, which implies a kind of objectivity in the result pursued. But it is the objectivity of "valid value" which contrasts sharply with that of either logically demonstrated or experimentally discovered and verified truth.[4]

---

[4] At various places in this book Professor Dewey expresses the view that we have too much discussion, too little scientific control. Cf. esp. pp. 71 and 73. At the latter point he links discussion with persuasion, against which I must protest.

To forestall misinterpretation, in a milieu in which science as such is a religion, and practicalism as such the accepted ethics, it may be advisable to specify two things which this position does not mean. On the one hand, the rejection of experimentation—except within narrow limits, and in a sense very different from that of natural science—as a mode of attack on social problems does not imply any leanings toward rationalism, or any kind of "a priorism." I certainly do not want to place myself on the "side" of any such philosophy, or want any "aid or comfort" from that quarter. From the standpoint of human liberty, a rationalistic philosophy will virtually begin where scientificism is bound to end, in the effort of each individual to bring up society in the way in which it should go. This is evidently a formula for a war of all against all, with dictatorship by some individual as the only possible basis for peace. It is, moreover, uncertain whether it is better or worse to have the whole procedure carried out ostensibly in the interest of society rather than openly in that of the "bringers-up."

On the other hand, the position here taken does not imply that there is no place for the use of intelligence in the solution of social problems. What I mean is that intelligence in the selection of ends is fundamentally different from intelligence in the use of means, and that intelligence in establishing agreement on common ends—and on common, cooperative, procedure in the pursuit of individual ends—is considerably different still. This is admittedly negative and unsatisfactory, but as far as I can go here. The task of indicating the nature of the differences and the positive meaning of intelligent procedure in the field of social problems is certainly difficult,

---

Persuasion is a form of control, of force, ethically on the same level as any other—or even a lower one, since it always contains a large element of deceit. The technique, as noted above, is not based on science in the proper sense, but on what might be called quasi-science.

not to say forbidding. I would suggest, however, that some progress would have been made if writers in philosophy and social science clearly recognized that the following three things, among others, are *not* discussion: (*a*) talking machines grinding out sound waves at each other; (*b*) "economic men" confronting each other with propositions beginning with, "I want"; and (*c*) "prophets" uttering divergent dicta beginning, "God says." But my point here is simply that the discussion of social problems, and of ends generally, requires and presupposes norms of validity other than those of natural science; and I maintain that we must, and can, and do discuss ends, including social problems.

IX

The really discouraging thing about the position of liberalism in the world is the character of intellectual leadership which is able to secure recognition. Whether we look at philosophy or social science, or radical politics or the labor movement, a sound and comprehensive grasp of the nature of social conflicts and problems is hardly to be found in utterances which succeed in making themselves audible or getting into print. Typically, the proposals for action which do get a hearing either do not make sense at all—one cannot imagine them enacted and carried out by free political process—or they are such as would aggravate instead of cure or alleviate the evils at which they are directed. That is, unless the communists are right, and the only hope for a humane social order is to put society absolutely in charge of a dictatorship of force (and "propaganda") to re-educate men morally to ways of tolerance and truth and gentleness, through ruthless violence applied over an indefinitely long historical epoch. Professor Dewey does at least recognize the incongruity of this particular method of "reform." But it is hardly enough to ask of reformers that each individually should be able to see the weakness and fallacy and menace of the measures proposed by others.

Ethics and Economic Reform

I. The Ethics of Liberalism

*T*he problem of ethics is the most baffling subdivision of the social problem as a whole. For on the one hand, it seems clearly impossible to "talk sense" at all, in the way either of criticism of the existing state of affairs or of any proposal for change (which two things are properly inseparable, for to call a situation hopeless is for practical purposes the same thing as calling it ideal) unless we have a defensible, and hence reasonably clear and stateable ideal to indicate at least a direction of change if not an ultimate goal. Society depends upon—we may almost say that it *is*—moral like-mindedness. But on the other hand, an essential feature of the present social problem itself is the fact that our ethical common sense, the ethical common sense of modern Western civilisation—now commonly referred to as "capitalistic"— seems to be little more than a tissue of vague generality and

Reprinted by permission from *Economica*, N.S. vol. 6 (1939), pp. 1–29, 296– 321, 398–422.

contradiction. It seems hardly possible to find ethical premises which can be used as a basis for reasoning and which are not matched by other premises equally valid or plausible in the abstract, and as generally accepted, often by the same people, yet which are opposite in sense and lead to different and conflicting conclusions.

Perhaps the basic contradiction, from the standpoint of such a discussion as this, is that which subsists between the absolutist, negativistic, personal idealism taught by Christianity, the religion generally professed in some form in Western civilization, on one hand, and on the other the positive, activistic, relativistic and practical norms of utilitarian mutualism and sportsmanship which actually prevail in workaday life, in so far as this rests on ethical ideals at all. According to the first view, all that is good is the good will; according to the second, "good intentions" are contemptible: it is "results" which count. The situation is well pictured in a sports writer's newspaper headline: "The meek may inherit the earth, but hits win ball games"; and some blasphemous wag has also observed that faith will remove mountains but engineers recommend dynamite, in spite of the expense.

Corresponding to this confusion is that which obtains in the attitude towards power. The Christian ethic repudiates power as a virtue or a value, viewing it rather as an evil temptation; but the ordinary behaviour of Christian-European man suggests as the reason for such professions a sense of shame because he "really" admires or desires little else. Another inconsistency which is almost as fundamental as that just mentioned is the opposition between personal loyalty or fidelity and loyalty to abstract principle, especially to truth. In the attitude toward truth is centred, in fact, much of the paradox of modern ethical convictions. On one hand, truth as integrity is the most essential value, the corner-stone of our ethical thought and our social life; and it is especially sacred in science, where men typically pose as despising all sanctities and values. And yet the least effort to formulate the conditions under which it is really good or proper, or conducive to the general peace and well-being, to speak the truth, rather than some variety and some degree of untruth, will surely bewilder anyone who undertakes the task. Plays have, of course, been written on this theme, but writers find difficulty in dramatizing it effectively without seeming to belabour the commonplace, a commonplace which is unpleasant without rising to the level of the tragic.

What may conceivably be done, or reasonably attempted, in the scope of an article, on the ethical phase of the social problem, is limited at best. This paper will attempt only to give an intelligible statement of the main ethical assumptions involved in free enterprise as a social-economic form, i.e., the ethical axioms which are assumed and must be assumed to be valid in accepting or defending the system—assuming always that it can be and is made to work in accord with its theoretical or mechanical ideal. We must always keep in mind the relations between ethical and mechanical aspects of the critical discussion of the economic system. In so far as undesirable results are due to obstructions or interference of a frictional character in the workings of the organization machinery, the correct social policy will be to remove these or to supplement the natural tendencies of the system itself. In so far as these natural tendencies are wrong, the effort must be to find and substitute some entirely different machinery for performing the right function in the right way. There is much confusion in the popular mind on this point: critics of enterprise economy who do not have a fair understanding of how the machinery works cannot tell whether to criticize it because it doesn't work according to the theory or because it does. And the same dilemma arises if the critic does not know what are his ethical ideals.

It may be well to say frankly in advance that the net constructive achievement of two articles will not be very large. We shall not get much beyond an elaboration of the negative theme already announced, that ethical reflection in modern civilization has hardly come to grips at all with the fundamental ethical problem of social organization. This is true whether we look at the ethical common sense of the man in the street, or at the assumptions taken for granted in our non-scientific literature, essays and *belles lettres,* or at the ethical teachings of our religion, or, finally, at the ethical writings of philosophical specialists and the teaching in our universities. We shall be concerned here with that preliminary clearing and survey of the ground which study has seemed to show is necessary before construction on sound lines can begin.

For lack of a better term, we shall refer to the general type of social order accepted as a working ideal in European civilization in the later nineteenth century, and which until recently was supposed to be in process of realization, as "liberalism." It is the "ethics of liberalism" that this article will attempt to examine. The main content of the liberal ideal was economic and ethical individualism. The tenet which received most emphasis in political and social discussion was economic *laisser-faire,* or political negativism, with specific reference to economic relations. Stated positively, the essential principle of *laisser-faire* liberalism is that each "individual" (really meaning each family—see below) shall be free to use his own resources in his own way to satisfy his own wants. The primary ethical claim on behalf of free enterprise as a mechanism of economic organization is that it leads to this result, i.e., that under this system the "individual" gets the consequences of his own activities, takes out of the social enterprise what he puts into it. In so far as this is true it is of course in a quantitative sense; the individual or family cannot get what it "produces" in the direct sense in which this is true of a primitive self-sufficient household. The assumption is that in the ideal working of such an economic system each contributor takes from the joint product the "equivalent" of his contribution in productive service. The measure of equivalence is exchange value or money price, and the question of its validity involves a correct interpretation of the valuation process of the economic system as a whole, considered both in mechanical and in ethical terms.

At first sight, it seems arguable that in such a system there is little or no place for ethics, that it is non-ethical if not unethical; for it makes little reference to moral obligation, especially in a positive sense. But this view can be shown to be an error. Every social order, in fact all organized action, all social life and all human life, is necessarily ethical, in so far as its character is a matter of deliberation and conscious acceptance on the part of its participants. Our main task in this article is to show that the social system of liberalism embodies a genuine ethical ideal and to make clear what the ideal is.

It is a political commonplace that in no society do its members obey the laws from sheer self-interest or purely because of "sanctions." They must be believed to be "right," in principle, and in the main. And personal rulers are followed or officials obeyed because their position is accepted as, first, legal, and secondly, in accord with a law which itself is fundamentally "right." Social institutions must be in harmony with what those who live under them think to be moral— whatever theory one may hold as to the causal relation in history between institutions and moral ideas. Our point here is merely that the basis of social order is opinions on matters of right which are viewed as objective, i.e., as knowledge and not merely or mainly as individual and subjective interests, desires, wishes, or even opinions. As will appear throughout, the relation between interests and opinions is one of the crucial aspects of the social problem. One of the vices of Western thought in the social sciences and of certain of the most popular schools of philosophy is that of "reducing" value judgments to statements of preference, asserting that "this is better" or "ought to be done," "really" means merely, "I like it." Popular and practical thinking, on the other hand, characteristically shows the opposite tendency to erect every personal wish or comparison into a cosmic value.[1]

The essential social-ethical principle of liberalism or liberal individualism may now be stated, for the purpose of examination. It is that *all relations between men ought ideally to rest on mutual free consent, and not on coercion, either on the part of other individuals or on the part of "society" as politically organized in the state.* The function, and the only ideally right function, of the state, according to this ethic, is to use coercion negatively, to prevent the use of coercion by individuals or groups against other individuals or groups. Some of the main aspects and implications of this ideal principle may now be considered point by point.

1. In explaining what is involved in this notion and—of at least equal importance—what is not involved in it, we must in the first place maintain a clear distinction between the political and the personal aspects of ethical doctrine. The principle as stated is a theory of the right sphere of political coercion, not of what is right and wrong in individual conduct, or in social conduct, outside the single matter of the individual's rôle in determining the answer to this one question, in his

---

[1] Much of our "philosophic" thought carries the first, or reducing, process another step, holding that all felt motives "really" are "merely" incidents in world mechanics or positive natural law somehow conceived. Idealism in the Hegelian sense is not practically different from mechanism in this regard.

own political group (or conceivably in other groups).[2] What the leading proponents of liberalism have thought about other ethical problems, such as the nature of the good life, the meaning and content of moral obligation, etc., is a separate question. As we shall see, it has a much less direct and vital bearing on the meaning of liberalism, and calls for notice chiefly for the purpose of illuminating the really central, positive issue, the sphere of politico-legal coercion.

2. Our second point is that this principle itself was never advocated in any strict or absolute interpretation. The *laisser-faire* economists of the straightest sect made exceptions of a sort which opened the way to much wider departures from the principle when and as changed conditions might seem to demand. This applies particularly to the great apostle of the movement, Adam Smith. All liberal individualists have recognized the necessity for restriction on individual freedom, and also for action by the state, for purposes of defence [*sic!*] and police, and for carrying out various public functions, including "certain public works" of obvious public utility but which it would not be profitable for any individual or private group to construct and maintain. The state was to be supported, of course, by taxation, and the liberal notions of tax policy always inclined rather to equalizing the burden than to imposts in accord with benefit received. Moreover, liberalism has always accepted without question the doctrine that every member of society has a right to live at some minimum standard, at the expense of society as a whole—i.e., out of

---

[2] In a rough way the sphere of coercion is that of law, but this needs qualification. For law may be taken to include recognised rules of social behaviour which are not "coercively" enforced, and, on the other hand, political coercion may take the form of administrative action which only indirectly if at all comes under the rubric of law enforcement. Law-making, or legislation, presumably does not ordinarily refer to promulgations not meant to be enforced by penalties intended to be adequate.

taxation levied as indicated above—if unable to provide such subsistence through his own efforts, the proceeds of sale of services, or through help from his family or voluntary private charity. Finally, Adam Smith and other liberals recognized as a legitimate function and task of the state, provision for the education of the youth, and, in varying degrees, for activities designed to promote the diffusion of knowledge and the advancement of science, art, and general culture.

3. Thirdly, the liberal ideal of mutual free consent applies in all relations of life and not merely in those called economic. The predominant emphasis on economic liberty in the nineteenth century literature no doubt reflected some bias and some misunderstanding on the part of the liberal leaders; but this is explicable in terms of the particular problems which were important at the time and the historical background out of which liberalism took its rise. In its historical setting it was primarily a movement for the removal of restrictions on economic freedom which had prevailed in Europe in the preceding epoch—that of mercantilism or nationalism. This epoch had also greatly stressed the economic side of life, but had leaned in the opposite direction, namely, political control or direct political action. We must remember, too, that as a matter of historical fact, the struggle for freedom in its earliest phases related directly to religious freedom even more than to economic, and the mutual-consent principle was always meant to apply equally to all fields of human relations. But this tended to be taken for granted, because the situation did not seem to call for important changes in this respect in fields other than the economic, after the subsidence of the wars over religion. No doubt also, liberals were inclined for historical and other reasons to assume, rightly or wrongly, that it is primarily in the sphere of economic life that opportunity arises for the coercion of individuals by individuals, and that in consequence preventive coercion by the state is called for;

and they were perhaps even more disposed to assume that the "temptation" of the state itself to exercise positive coercion is a danger chiefly in the economic sphere.

It should be emphasized that, apart from the historical circumstances under which the liberal political faith arose— as a reaction against measures of economic control which had become anachronistic—these assumptions have no high degree of validity. The truth is rather that the economic sphere of action is inseparable practically, and even theoretically, from other spheres, and the contrary position, in the form of the "economic interpretation," is one of the worst fallacies, or vices, of current thinking. But for various reasons, it was the "mode" in the nineteenth century to think of social problems of conflict and struggle, between men (or "private" groups) and between the "individual" and the state, and between states, primarily in economic terms. In general, this view cannot be maintained. Every form of human association necessarily gives rise to power relations and to conflicts of interests within the group and between groups, and to rivalry and struggle in both these areas. And these will ultimately lead to violent conflict, "human nature being what it is," in the absence of some regulatory restraint, i.e., of "law" and enforcement, in some form. In any fair appraisal, the casualty list of cultural rivalry and of purely personal clash is far longer than the list for conflicts of economic interest in any proper definition. And there is no reason to believe that if all properly economic problems were solved once for all through a fairy gift to every individual of the power to work physical miracles, the social struggle and strife would either be reduced in amount or intensity, or essentially changed in form, to say nothing of improvement—in the absence of some moral revolution which could by no means be assumed to follow in consequence of this change itself.

The idea that the social problem is essentially or primarily economic, in the sense that social action may be concentrated on the economic aspect and other aspects left to take care of themselves, is a fallacy, and to outgrow this fallacy is one of the conditions of progress toward a real solution of the social problem as a whole, including the economic aspect itself. Examination will show that while many conflicts which seem to have a non-economic character are "really" economic, it is just as true that what is called "economic" conflict is "really" rooted in other interests and other forms of rivalry, and that these would remain unabated after any conceivable change in the sphere of economics alone.

Especial emphasis on economic freedom might however be justified within very wide limits by the fact that it is basic to other forms of freedom, as historical fact and general considerations join in proving. But it is not clear, to the present writer at least, how far the leading nineteenth-century proponents of liberalism actually saw this relationship and took this ground.

4. It cannot be denied that liberal leaders propounded views on the nature of the good in individual life, and these were often vulnerable to criticism. The liberals inclined to hedonism, the doctrine that the good means pleasure. Indeed, they were much addicted[3] to the absurdity of combining or confusing ethical and psychological hedonism, holding that pleasure is at once what men do universally and necessarily pursue in conduct, and at the same time what they "ought" to pursue, the content of "duty." But whatever any individual, however great or important, may have thought, liberalism is not logically committed to any particular conception of the nature or content of the good, individual or social. The importance of this fact can hardly be too much stressed. As an economic movement, the primary immediate objective of liberalism was freedom

---

[3] Notably Jeremy Bentham.

for the individual in relationships of exchange, of goods and services, i.e., relations of *quid pro quo*. Beyond freedom of transactions was the more remote objective of increasing "efficiency." This is a synonym for economy, which is not an end, but an auxiliary or instrumental conception relative to any end whatever, in so far as its achievement is a matter of degree and the degree of achievement depends upon the mode of employing means. The relationship between economy or efficiency and various types of real end or value cannot be discussed here, though we may refer again to the "straddle" in our customary valuation axioms referred to at the outset, that nothing is good but the good will, and that nothing is good but results; obviously the notion of efficiency fits the second axiom and not the first, and it is also irrelevant to such ideals as obedience and ascetic self-discipline. But the ideal of freedom is relevant to these also.

Regarding the end of action, it is of the essence of liberalism properly conceived to have no concrete position. The end of action is whatever the individual wants and strives to do, or to get, or to be, as the case may be—as far as the main issue, namely freedom from coercion, by others or by the state, is concerned, and as long as he does not infringe on the like freedom of other individuals to pursue their own ends in their own way. The theory is that the individual is, in general (but not without exceptions—cf. use of narcotics, etc.), the "best" judge of his own ends and of the procedure to be used in promoting them. The doctrine never meant that the individual is a perfect judge, but only that he is a better judge, and especially a more impartial judge, than "the government" or any other person likely to claim the right to judge for him. Consequently, according to the liberal view, a greater total achievement of ends actually desired and pursued, and in that sense a greater realization of "good," will result from a general application of the principle of freedom, with the limitation of mutual consent, than from the application of any other general rule.

5. The principles of liberalism involve no pressure on anyone to practice efficiency in any sense, or to pursue ends in connection with which it has meaning, rather than other ends. He is free to pursue such ideals as "poverty, chastity and obedience" (assuming that he can find someone willing to be obeyed), or universal "love" or any form of ascetic practice, as long as he does not attempt to coerce others or infringe upon their similar freedom. He is also free to join with others in forming groups voluntarily devoted to the practice of any ideal of life which is not so offensive to the tastes of the larger community as to create danger of violence.

6. In particular, liberalism allows any collection of individuals to organize economic life in any way they may choose. They do not have to establish markets or make exchanges under any form, to say nothing of conducting "enterprises" for profit. They may practice any type of cooperation, and adopt any mode of apportioning burdens and benefits upon which the members themselves can agree. And under the liberal regime groups have tried widely various schemes. But on seeing that cooperative or planned or controlled economic organization does not work out as it figures out (to some figurers), instead of learning their lesson, opponents of liberalism typically pour contempt and scorn upon such experiments as "Utopian" and demand political authority over whole nations or the whole earth. The reasons for this attitude are not so very far to seek in the nature of human nature, but they cannot be explored in detail here. The fact that such propaganda wins adherents among the educated as well as the masses, and threatens to subvert liberalism itself and replace it with a most extreme dogmatic and violent illiberalism, is of course a matter for the profoundest concern. But to return to our theme (and to repeat), liberalism means only that

individuals and groups shall not coerce others, and not merely in economic relations, but in any department of life, though freedom for the conduct of enterprise economy was the main immediate objective of liberalism as a general political movement.

It should be pointed out, however, that liberal doctrine involved a tendency to oversimplification of values and motives, for which the hedonistic bias was no doubt partly to blame, or of which this bias was a consequence, as the case may be. The main argument for *laisser-faire* was instrumental, in the general meaning of the term; it was intended to increase efficiency. On one hand, this obviously involved taking the individual's actual endowment with means as a datum (either as "right" or as unalterable) along with his tastes and other characteristics. This is the main weakness of the system, from an economic standpoint, as will be emphasized presently. Freedom is freedom to use power, of which the individual may possess much or little or none at all, and be equally free.

Apart from this shortcoming, the liberal position itself can be maintained on quite different grounds, some at least as cogent as the tendency of freedom to increase efficiency, and different lines of argument are more or less confused in the literature. (In general, the writings of the utilitarians were not characterized by any great subtlety or analytic profundity.) The context, if not the explicit wording, frequently suggests more penetrating views. Freedom may be, and often was, considered an end or value in itself, and not merely as instrumental to efficiency in realizing other values. And going still farther, the writers would occasionally recognize that freedom is a "good," not merely in the sense that men actually want it, but in the deeper and more truly ethical sense that men "ought" to be free, more or less independently of whether they wish to be or not. This latter view, that it pertains to the dignity of human life to live responsibly, to make one's own decisions and take the consequences, is in keeping with the religious ethic of Puritanism, which certainly played an important rôle in the historical culture movement of which liberalism was a phase. Moreover, still another (a fourth) more "practical" line of argument for economic *laisser-faire* is important, and is occasionally met with. This is that the capacity of the state is limited, and that loading it with tasks which it cannot perform will cripple its effectiveness for functions which are possible for it as well as vital for the social life.

7. As already noted, the "end" of the enterprise economy is, in liberal theory, productive efficiency, which means the transformation of the ultimate productive capacity possessed by each individual into the maximum "income," consisting of "goods and services" reduced to a common denominator in terms of each individual's preferences. The notion of the economic individual will have to be further discussed presently. We now observe that the concept of income contains a twofold ambiguity which has been the source of much difficulty and confusion in technical economics itself. On the one hand, it includes "means of satisfaction," specifically the services of persons, logically including one's own services, and also services of "things," whether "owned" by oneself or by someone else. On the other hand, it also includes any accretion during the time interval for which it is measured, in the total productive capacity belonging to the individual affected. The relation between income in the form of satisfaction-yielding services and income in the form of growth in productive capacity is further complicated by the relation first noted between services rendered to oneself—by one's own person or by things which one owns—and services rendered by other persons and instruments owned by them. And even more serious complications arise from the relation between accretions to productive capacity incorporated in the individual's

own person (labour, power, skill, knowledge) and that which is incorporated in external things which he owns (capital goods). All that it is in point to say on this problem here is that the use of resources actually owned at any moment in any form is subject to the control of the individual, who, in so far as he behaves in accord with the principle of economic rationality, apportions all his available productive capacity, without regard to its form, among all the alternatives of use open to him, in such a way as to "maximize" the total "return" in all forms, reduced to common units in terms of his own value-scale. (In economic jargon, his value-scale is represented by a "utility function" or satisfaction function or system of indifference curves, including investment as well as consumption.) Opportunities for exchange with other persons (which must in some degree increase the total income of both) count to any one person as alternative modes of use to be considered in apportioning whatever resources he "owns." The result of intelligent apportionment, according to economic theory, is the maximum provision, to each individual, under the given conditions (especially the similar maximum for all others), of "means of life," realized either in the form of momentary satisfaction or in further addition to productive capacity; allocation between these two fields and among all the subdivisions of both should accord with the economic principle of a maximum, i.e., equalization at the margin. Beyond this maximum provision of *means,* the ideal of freedom as qualified by mutual consent obviously has nothing to say.

8. An outstanding ethical consequence of the theory of productive organization through freeing the urge to self-advancement is a new and sharp division in the field of conduct, a new ethical dualism (there are many such dualisms) or at least a bifurcation of the ethical problem. The situation is suggested by the vernacular expression, "business is

business," meaning that business is one thing, and "charity" another. There is a strong feeling that it is "right" to "play the business according to the rules," to make exchanges at the ratios objectively set or made possible by the market. That is, it is assumed to be ethically legitimate and even positively virtuous, to *desire* to maximize one's "income," as defined above, and to act in such a way as to do so, subject always to the sweeping reservation of mutual free consent in all relations with others. (Some problems in the nature of this freedom of consent, especially as regards "persuasion," and effects on persons not parties to a transaction, will come up presently.)

The question of what is to be done with income when obtained, or the reasons on account of which it is desired, not only receive no answer or illumination from the social-ethical principle so far discussed; there is even a certain tendency to deny their reality as ethical problems through emphasizing the right of every individual to do as he will with his own and his duty to live of his own and to make it fruitful. In any event, liberalism was emphatic that exchange dealings involve no obligation beyond honesty and non-predation—both primarily negative, but their meaning will call for further consideration later. In the political connection the payment of taxes and assumption of a fair share of the "proper" obligations of society was added. But at that point it would seem that the ethical theory of liberalism as a distinctive principle stops. Certainly the use of income, or specifically the matter of obligation in its use, belongs to a completely separate ethical problem field, and constitutes a different branch of ethical science or inquiry. This branch of ethics tended to be a stepchild.[4] We must keep in mind that

---

[4] One senses a certain hollowness, for instance, in Spencer's exhortations to and praise of charity, so strong is the balance of emphasis on the repudiation of any properly legal obligation.

in the ideal market economy of theory the individual has economic power only in the form of income and also that his income represents his own productive contribution to the aggregate social output.

However, the public mind or conscience of the civilization which in general accepted the liberal principle has never been clear or at ease on this question of obligation outside of and beyond the business code. Worse still, liberal thought has been much confused about the relations involved, and has never been happy even about the separation, the business-*versus*-charity-dualism which we may call the second axiom or principle of liberalism (the mutual-consent principle being its first axiom). The issue raised is one of the most important factors in the current situation of unrest and crisis. A little headway may be made in the illumination of the problem by considering it briefly in the light of history.

What we call primitive society, as known, and back of which knowledge cannot penetrate, presents as one of its most fundamental phenomena the notion of *equity* as a normative ideal and pattern of individual relationships. The most pungent example of "primitive" equity is the *lex talionis,* "an eye for an eye," etc., which of course represents an almost inconceivably long development of legality and civilization beyond the really primitive anger reaction. The bulk of primitive law is, moreover, law of tort rather than criminal law; it prescribes "damages" to injured parties, rather than punishment for wrongdoers. In our own society the notion of equity is still largely that of the preliterate tribal stage; we try to get away from it to what we consider higher ethical norms, but make slow progress. "Reciprocity" in all our emotional and social life, the return of cordiality for cordiality, snub for snub, if not blow for blow, affection for affection, and the "repayment" of gifts, visits and entertainments in kind, seems as inevitable as a precise calculation and explicit negotiation of terms (or compounding in money) is repugnant, so that one wonders about the realism of any ethical teachings which pretend to get very far away from this level, especially through discussion. But of course there are exceptions, a sort of fringe around the blanket of *quid pro quo* which moral progress may gradually extend from generation to generation.

Primitive equity also includes what we vaguely think of as economic reciprocity, the "exchange" of goods and services, but under very different conditions and forms from those of modern commerce. For the most part trade is foreign trade, and in general is highly ritualized; and the ratios of exchange, the prices, are very rigorously fixed by traditional standards. Much intertribal exchange is a pure ritual, without economic significance, though involving a substantial "cost." When conditions change and the amounts of any ware or token which will be supplied and demanded at the traditional prices become too unequal, other forms of interchange, especially gifts, largely take the place of exchange before prices yield. We find the same phenomena in "backward" areas today.[5] One of the great historical-anthropological problems is that of the development of markets in the modern sense, with flexible prices responding freely and accurately (more or less!) to changes in supply and demand conditions. It can be said with confidence that this happened first in the field of foreign trade, trade between groups, and was introduced into intra-tribal relations much later.[6] Exchange of services is a late development, and it is an important fact that labour is a commodity

---

[5] Cf. a paper by John H. Sherman, "Some Observations on Custom in Price Phenomena," *American Economic Review*, XVIII (1928), pp. 663 ff. It may be noted that at times of catastrophic change, either in the direction of shortage or demoralising superabundance, the price system tends to give way even in our own culture and be replaced by rationing, price-fixing, governmental absorption of "surpluses" and the like.

[6] See Brentano, *Die Wandlungen der wirtschaftlichen Einheit;* Hoyt, *Primitive Trade*.

which—apart from the trade in slaves—can hardly be a subject of international trade, and even with slavery can never give rise to a highly perfect market. The factual point to be made clear now is that the business-ethics principle of exchange of equal values is an obvious modification of primitive economic equity; the difference is that the value equivalence itself is subject to free adjustment in the market instead of being fixed by tradition at a specific figure.

But it is vitally important that, due largely to the survival of primitive notions of personal equity, modern civilization in general has never wholeheartedly accepted the dualism of "business *versus* charity," in business itself, or accepted its sharp dichotomy between standards of formally organized behaviour and the ethic of personal human relations. The notion of "fair price" and even of a considerate or humane price has persisted with varying strength in different connections, depending in part on the actual effectiveness of competition, in greater part on the public's conception of its reality and effectiveness, and in large part on more subtle factors of "psychology."

In any case, one of the main factors in the present crisis is that the public has lost faith, such faith as it ever had, in the moral validity of market values. In large part, as suggested, this is due to the failure of even the educated public to understand the mechanics of exchange relations, and to the existence of monopoly and of friction in price and production adjustments. It is especially in the field of wages, the price of "labour," that the tendency to reject market standards is strongest. But the dualistic principle must be accepted wholeheartedly in relation to economic organization if the kind of civilization we call free is to exist.[7] Business must be separated

---

[7] Business must be allowed to operate on business principles in relation to its given and legally defined conditions and these must be clear and reasonably stable. Undesirable features and results of the economic order can be modified through

from "charity," meaning all personal considerations. The principle of business-is-business is on a par with that of justice-is-blind, though both must be sometimes seasoned with mercy. Moral obligation to persons in consequence of special relationships is the general principle of feudalism, and is anachronistic and disruptive in a commercial or enterprise economy. Yet it persists; and not only in connection with the employer-employee relation; it, or its conflict with business principles and with wide areas of law as a whole, remains a fundamental aspect of the ethical problem-situation in modern society. The mixture of intellectual confusion with value judgments in the discussion of problems of economic ethics, as it takes place, baffles analysis, and is of course most sinister in import.

9. It must be kept in mind that the main immediate driving force back of the liberal revolution in political thought was a technological revolution which could only work itself out, and yield the enormous increase in economic efficiency potentially available, through economic transactions between individuals spread over a vastly greater geographical and social area than that of the primary social group, or any natural community, an area within which "social" relations in the ordinary sense become physically impossible.[8] The natural

---

taxation and public expenditure, and perhaps changes in the laws of inheritance, but only within the very narrowest limits through price fixing and other arbitrary interference with the workings of the markets. In these fields general laws mean a strait jacket and administrative discretion an intolerable fog of arbitrariness and uncertainty.

[8] And they still are for the most part. Development of instantaneous communication has changed this somewhat and may change it more if television develops sufficiently. But there is another and especially sinister aspect to mechanico-electrical intercommunication itself. Mechanism may make it possible for any number of individuals, even the whole population of the world, to listen or attend at the same time to the words and perhaps the facial expression and gestures of any one individual. But no invention can ever increase the efficiency of communication in the converse sense in the least degree. In spite of all science and technology it will remain impossible for one person to listen or attend at the same

result was "economic" conflict and the necessity of legal regulation of economic relationships, in this larger area, where "social" problems inevitably take a "political" form. But the contrast between social and political is a vague one. These wide-area relationships involve just as much conflict of interest and opportunity for clash as, say, a card game or neighbourhood social rivalry; but the conflicts take a special form, which we tend to call political because of the character of large-group psychology and behaviour. It is, however, a fallacy to view them as economic, which is no more true than it is of personal dislikes or family feuds. There always have been rivalries and wars between groups formed on every conceivable basis, local, political or religious, or even purely artificial or partisan. In modern times the somewhat special form of nationalistic rivalry tends to predominate.

10. The next point has to do with the nature of political coercion, beyond its negative role, and with the nature of the state. It is of the essence of liberal doctrine that action by the state is not action by individuals, although of course it is carried out, in the concrete, by human beings, officials of some kind. The liberal state is essentially "The Law."[9] In the liberal view, the individuals who implement state action do not act as individuals, but are the agents of the law, and the law is the creation of society as a whole, of the "sovereign people," and not of individuals. The same principle applies to legislators as to other officials. Of course this is an ideal, which no conceivable machinery could realize at all perfectly; but it is an ideal of fairly definite and intelligible meaning, and surely is one of ethical character and import. Undoubtedly

time to more than one! The whole tendency is to increase the effectiveness and power of "leadership" and to multiply mob-mindedness.

[9] This was not true genetically; the state was originally the military system, and law was a social phenomenon of a non-political sort. The state gradually assumed legal functions and at first only on the side of law enforcement; conscious law-making, or legislation, came much later.

it received its purest and classical formulation in the eighteenth century, at the hands of the political theorists in the British colonies in North America, and in the United States as a nation during its formative period. It is embodied in the principle, or slogan (of older date), "a government of laws and not of men." Much, of course, might be said about this ideal, as regards its practical consequences, in relation to various circumstances and conditions; notably the contrast between the conditions of frontier settlements, on a virgin continent peculiarly rich in natural resources, and those which obtain in the United States (to say nothing of Europe) toward the middle of the twentieth century. But our concern here is with the ideal.

The primary difficulty with the notion of law as an ethical principle or norm is that the content of the law itself can never be taken as simply "given," or beyond dispute, even at a given moment. In the liberal doctrine in its original form, this problem did not seem serious, because of the limitation of law itself and of its functions to the negative role of suppressing coercion. But even under this restriction, there was always and inevitably occasion for "interpreting" the law, in enforcing it, and also for making law outright, i.e., changing it, in consequence of changing conditions and standards.

11. We should next consider the meaning in liberalist thought of that coercion of individuals by individuals which it is the primary function of the state, i.e., of legal coercion, to prevent. To begin with, this was taken to mean simply "force and fraud," concepts which it was assumed could be fairly easily defined by legal process and in words, with sufficient definiteness and accuracy for practical purposes. This view now seems naïve, to the philosophic student of the problem; a very little perusal of a legal encyclopædia

under the pertinent headings ("duress" and "fraud") will show that the problem admits of no definite solution.

In connection with private coercion we must also deal with the distinctively economic category of monopoly. For the liberals of the nineteenth century, and even earlier (notably in England, and notably those classed as economists) clearly recognized that monopoly is a form of coercive power, and inadmissible in a "free" state. As is well known, at least among students of economics of the present day, the liberals, and specifically Adam Smith, tended to assume that monopoly would not require coercive repression, that it would not arise to an important degree in the absence of positive support, aid and abetting, on the part of the state itself. This indeed is still a "moot" question, one on which the writer has no very positive opinions, but on the issue of which he is by no means so optimistic as, for example, Professor von Mises, and Professor Robbins of the London School of Economics. However, it must be admitted that governments have never given the original liberal position any fair trial, and do not seem in a way to do so, in the visible future, even in the United States or Great Britain.

12. The observation next in order, as a sort of footnote, is that the "individualism" of liberal doctrine by no means excludes, but rather expressly includes, guidance of the activities of one individual by another, in the interest of increasing efficiency through more competent direction. It means only that the individual must be "free" to place himself under direction and guidance or not to do so, and hence to choose his own counsellors, and to follow their advice or not to follow it in any particular case, and to discharge a counsellor at will, with or without replacing him by another.

A peculiar and important consequence of the freedom to accept and to give advice or counsel (by free mutual consent) is that in many fields advice or counsel becomes a commodity in the market, subject to competitive purchase and sale. In fact the separation between direction and execution is one of the most important cases of the division of labour. Professions which tell others what to do include among many others the law, medicine, and business management. But expert counsel or leadership is a commodity unique in the absolute logical impossibility of standardizing it or even describing it objectively. This means that the market is peculiarly imperfect; and this fact helps to weaken popular faith in market values, and has wide ramifications.

13. We come now to consideration of certain elements of vagueness and ambiguity in the liberal principle of mutual free consent. Three examples call for notice. The first, and logically most puzzling, has to do with contract, the freedom of an individual to alienate his own freedom—for any consideration which appears satisfactory when the contract is made—for some specified period of time in the future and with respect to some specified scope of activity. Freedom to dispose of one's own freedom is evidently something of a paradox; it obviously has in practice to be allowed within limits but just as certainly has to be limited if freedom as a general condition is to be maintained.[10]

Liberal doctrine, according to my own impression, which is based on limited knowledge of Anglo-American law, has never had any clear position on this matter. In America, the problem receives a peculiar twist from the special emphasis of our founding fathers on "inalienable rights," from the fact that our government rests on a set of written constitutions, including national and state bills of rights—also from the

---

[10] The problem is somewhat akin to that of free exchange in dangerous drugs, weapons, etc. and it is still more closely related to the problem of lending and borrowing at interest, which are universally prohibited in primitive society—though gambling is usually less stringently dealt with!

circumstance that chattel slavery as an institution became established under peculiar conditions and was abolished only at a very late date in history, in consequence of a long and hard-fought civil war, the results of which, again, were incorporated in the federal and state constitutions. It is evident that freedom of contract, i.e., the extent to which the law will enforce contract binding anyone for the future (or permit any other enforcement), must be restricted to narrow limits if anything like individual liberty, in a practical common-sense interpretation, is to be maintained (if it is not to run into "involuntary servitude"). But on the other hand, this inalienability of control over one's own person, meaning especially over its economic powers and capacities, though based on the peculiar sanctity of such control, results in placing in an especially weak position anyone who owns productive capacity only as embodied in his own person in the form of labour power. For what cannot be sold cannot be pledged; and the man without "property," in the usual meaning of the term, is dependent upon a practically continuous opportunity to market his services, as well as upon continuous possession of capacity to render service (for himself and dependents) the means of livelihood. For these means must of course be had in almost completely continuous flow—"three meals a day," or some other number. This "would be" the case if "society" made no provision for "relief," outside the system of exchange relations; but of course some other provision is necessary for many categories of the population, who do not have "productive capacity" to sell of sufficient value to afford a socially acceptable scale of life, and this obligation on the part of the state has always been a feature of liberalism.

14. The second element of vagueness is of a different kind but of equally vital importance. It arises out of the fact that a large part of the goods and services which are subject to exchange cannot be effectively standardized, because their

relevant qualities and characteristics are not a matter of common knowledge and direct observation, or of physical measurement, but are very largely a matter of judgment and there is wide diversity of opinion. In such cases, market dealings inevitably become affected by *efforts to persuade,* on the part of the seller or buyer or both. As it works out, also inevitably, it is ordinarily the seller who immediately sets the price, and marketing becomes a literally "competitive" endeavour or struggle on the part of sellers to influence buyers. (The Economic man neither competes nor higgles—nor does he cooperate, psychologically speaking; he treats other human beings as if they were slot machines.) In a sense, what is involved here is a coupling with physical goods and services of information about them, which the buyer purchases, and of course pays for, along with the physical entities themselves. The social problem involved theoretically comes under the head of fraud; but the field in which, and range over which, assertions about wares cannot be viewed as objectively true or false is so limited that, from the standpoint of common sense, what is involved is rather the exercise of a kind of coercive force, or at least a struggle between opposed "forces," and not an exchange. The problem ties up with the general fact of uncertainty as a limitation on rationality. This is an infinitely complex and subtle problem; uncertainty itself is subject to uncertainty; we do not know how much we know, or how accurately; there is no visible boundary between knowledge, opinion, and ignorance.

The crux of the matter, from the standpoint of the workings of an enterprise economy, is the fact that the machinery of law, the formulation and enforcement of criminal statutes or precedents, cannot deal satisfactorily with these phenomena in terms of either coercion or fraud or the two combined. To the extent that there is no objectivity in the matter at issue there can be none in the law. At the same time and for the same reason, the machinery of the market also fails to evaluate as information or counsel the persuasive or "selling" activities of parties to transactions. The role of middlemen whose whole business it is to buy and to sell the same wares, presents especially interesting features. The whole arena is one in which, *prima facie,* high ethical standards and sentiments might be expected to produce results beyond those possible for any formal social machinery; and, in fact, ethics plus certain considerations which tend to make honesty good business policy, probably has more weight than legal action, though it remains necessary to treat as fraud and as criminal such persuasive efforts as go too far and fall "reasonably" within that category. The factor most neglected by critics of the enterprise economy is the irrationality and greed of the consumer himself; but outside the highly organized markets the whole system is saturated with "sentiment," rivalry and suspicion, and "strategy"—a polite name for trickery.

15. The third of the qualifications referred to is that the primary principle of liberalism, free mutual relations, takes no account of inequality in economic position. The ability of one party to bring to the market a vastly greater quantity of saleable service value than another, coupled with imperfections in the market mechanism, may amount to the exercise of coercive power by the stronger party over the weaker. From the standpoint of pure theory, it is the market imperfection which is primarily in point, and this may operate in special circumstances to place arbitrary power in the hands of the "weaker" party, the party possessed of less economic power as measured from a long-run point of view. The outstanding case, in the popular mind, is, of course, the "bargaining" between employer and employee. But the popular notions regarding the intrinsic superiority in bargaining power of the employer are very largely false. This is true even apart from situations where there is effective monopoly in one form or

another; and the monopoly factor itself may operate on either side.[11]

Freedom of accumulation not only carries with it the possibility of cumulative increase in the inequality of *economic* power, and creates a strong tendency in that direction; in addition, economic power confers power in other forms, including the political. And freedom of association is equally important in the same connection, since association may be for the end of power as well as that of efficiency. Freedom of association also raises questions as to the meaning and limitations of mutual consent, questions which cannot be taken up here.

16. Before turning to considerations of a somewhat different kind, it may be well to consider the general meaning of the principle of freedom, in the light of the points already made, but from a somewhat different point of view. Politico-legal freedom, i.e., the restriction of organized social action to the prevention of force and fraud, means that within the sphere of Freedom, i.e., outside the sphere of legal control, social relations are left to the control of "social forces" other than law as deliberately enacted and enforced. That is, all relations not covered by the concepts of force and fraud, as defined in the terms of the law and in its actual enforcement, are controlled by other, less formal and deliberate modes of action or social processes. Further investigation and analysis of what is involved in these other forces or control processes would have to inquire into the philosophical problem of "free" activity, first in the individual, in "private" action, and secondly in social behaviour under "free" mutual consent. Free activity would have to be compared and contrasted with

---

[11] It seems necessary to refer in various connections to the failure of economic teaching to give even the educated public any conception of the actual workings of competition as a mechanism of control, which failure and lack are one of the most serious causes of the failure of the system to work effectively.

such other categories as (*a*) the exercise of control by one free agent over another, by innumerable means and methods; (*b*) control by society over individuals; and (*c*) "positive" cause and effect, physical, mental, "moral" and cultural. In such an inquiry methodological and philosophical problems step into the foreground. Any pure cause-and-effect relation means that the social-human unit is an incident in an inevitable flow of cosmic process in some conception. All notion of effective purpose is excluded and all discussion—such as the present effort—and likewise the efforts of the advocates of natural or dialectical cause-and-effect—is reduced to meaningless physical or metaphysical process. But the main point is simply the fact that the hands-off policy on the part of the state means leaving the course of events to such other causes or controls as do and will actually operate under the conditions present. Its opponents are right, as far as they go, in insisting that inaction is also a policy. These other forces or controls, apart from politico-legal action, cry for classification and analysis, but the task, the main problem of sociology and social philosophy, cannot be undertaken here.

17. It is to be emphasized that acts most freely assented to and actually advantageous to parties immediately and directly affected almost always have effects for evil or good on others, whose consent is not obtained. The liberalism of the free market provides for the consent only of parties to transactions. Where either good or ill effects accrue to others, such a system cannot protect the interests of remote persons in wider circles, or motivate action which "radiates" beneficial effects. This, however, is rather a mechanical than an ethical weakness in the mutual-consent system, and its detailed consideration is outside the scope of the present article. As already noted, liberals have always believed both in political action for protection of important unrepresented interests and for "public works." But theory must recognize that a most intricate and

subtle combination of public and private enterprise would be required to secure anything like a maximum utilization of resources in terms of purely individual interests. And the problem of community interests would call for separate consideration.

18. These reflections naturally lead up to the most important single defect, amounting to a fallacy, in liberal individualism as a social philosophy. The most general and essential fact that makes such a position untenable as an exclusive principle of organization is that *liberalism takes the individual as given,* and views the social problem as one of right relations between given individuals. This is its fundamental error.[12] The assumption that this can be done runs counter to clear and unalterable facts of life. The individual cannot be a datum for the purposes of social policy, because he is largely formed in and by the social process, and the nature of the individual must be affected by any social action. Consequently, social policy must be judged by the kind of individuals that are produced by or under it, and not merely by the type of relations which subsist among individuals taken as they stand.

From the economic point of view, both this fact itself and its vital importance are especially obvious. The economic individual is a complex of three main sets of factors; namely, wants, physical capacities (of himself and all that he owns) usable in satisfying wants, and knowledge of the processes involved in the direct and indirect use of means in rendering want-satisfying services, i.e., in ''production'' and ''consumption.'' It cannot require more than a reminder and a moment's reflection to make any person interested in the facts realize that all three elements in the individual are very largely built up in and moulded by the social traditions, institutions,

---

[12] We reserve for later and extended consideration the fact that the other commonly accepted systems of social ethics make the same mistake, notably the Christian ethic.

and processes of the culture in which the individual grows up. More specifically, they are largely the product of forces operating in primary-group life, in which the "primary" primary group, the family, is overwhelmingly important. It is chiefly from and through the family that the individual is formed and endowed in all these respects.

Indeed it is evident (as we have already remarked) that liberalism never really meant individualism, and could not do so, in view of unalterable facts of life. From the standpoint of social policy, as well as that of scientific history or sociology, the "individual" is an evanescent phenomenon; he comes into the world destitute and helpless, and necessarily remains a liability for a large fraction of his life-span, before he can become an asset to himself or an "individual" with capacity for membership in an organization of responsible units. In the nature of the case, liberalism is more "familism" than literal individualism. Some sort of family life, and far beyond that, some kind of wider primary-group and culture-group life, of a considerable degree of stability, must be taken as they are, as *data,* in free society at any time, until they change or are changed, by action in accord with policy, into other forms. This is true not only because primary groupings and institutions are in fact "there," but because no society could possibly exist without them; and to safeguard them where it is necessary, and improve them where it is possible, must be the first concern of any intelligent social policy—on a level with the preservation of physical life itself. "Man is a social animal." And the social philosophy of freedom and mutual consent is finally tenable only in so far as it can be shown that there is a natural harmony of interests between individuals and between the individual and society as free behaviour affects the social structure at the level of primary-group life, as well as harmony of interest between individuals in their individual interests. For the most part, liberalism, in taking the individual as given, took society for granted also. It recognized, indeed, the right of "the people" to change their political constitution, and to make laws touching property and the family. But this could only mean the people of an existing political unit, or in fact, far more narrowly, the existing control system in such a unit. The revolutionary liberals were, as opponents have again pointed out, excessively rationalistic; they did not seriously consider the problems involved in the relationship between freedom of transactions and political freedom on one hand, and freedom of association in these wider institutional contexts of family and primary-community life on the other. Social policy in terms of action (beyond the merely preventive) means law-making; which is to say law-changing; and only to a very limited extent do individuals act independently in their efforts to bring about changes in the law. They act chiefly as members of groups, either previously existent, or spontaneous and *ad hoc,* or deliberately organized, or combining these characteristics in various ways and degrees.

19. From a practical point of view the naïve faith in the power and benevolence of the non-political and non-legal social forces which is logically presupposed in *laisser-faire* individualism, is questionable in connection with all three of our economic factors in the individual, but in connection with the third—his endowment with economic or "productive" capacity—it is palpably untenable. In free society, in the legal sense of a society which does not tolerate slavery, productive capacity falls into two main divisions—(*a*) the physical and mental qualities and endowments of the individual himself, and (*b*) earning power embodied in the properites of external things "owned" by the individual.[13] In the popular mind and

---

[13] Under the individualism of pure theory one individual has no power or control over the productive capacities of another otherwise than through purchase from moment to moment in a free market. In reality there are considerable exceptions. The case of minor children is perhaps the largest; but the serious imperfections of the market for "labour" (really markets for innumerable kinds of labour) give

in the propaganda of reformers, there is a sharp ethical contrast between these two forms of earning-power, between "property" and "human rights." It is very hard to find much foundation for this view in the facts. Both forms of earning ability are alike in being largely created and conferred on the individual by the social-cultural process, and primarily in and by the family. Both forms of capacity are partly inherited and partly built up by the individual. They are built up by "investment" in the individual himself or in external things, as the case may be. The investment in both cases is made partly by the individual himself and partly by others ("parents") or by society—on the basis of an inherited nucleus or "start." Ethically considered, both forms or sources of income seem to be more or less equally affected by the same complex of factors—inheritance, intelligent and conscientious effort, fate, fraud and "luck."

In a "free" social-economic system there is every presumption that movement will be away from and not toward fundamental human equality. It "tends," more or less effectively, to realize "commutative" justice, but "distributive" justice is completely ignored. And real human equity seems clearly to include a right to "be" equal as well as to "have" equal "rights." Freedom, again, means the right to do what one is able to do, i.e., to use power, and has content only in so far as one possesses power. Equal right to use unequal power is not equality but the opposite. The difference illustrates a fact which will concern us especially as we go on to a comparative consideration of ethical systems; namely, that social ethics must look to the distant future and take into account the unborn and the whole character of culture, and not merely relations between given individuals.

Moreover, even commutative justice or equity—quantitative

---

rise to more political discontent. It should be noted that all intangible property, including "goodwill," represents claims against or control over the productive power of persons or of things owned by them.

equivalence between what the "individual" puts in and what he takes out—has meaning only for the independent recipients of income. The effective social unit in consumption is the family, and for other members of the family than the head, at least for all "dependents," there is little or no relation between reward and contribution, or desert in any form. The position of wives is quite anomalous—their economic status being a "reward" chiefly for their wisdom in choosing husbands—and the injustice to children cries out to heaven. But these matters for the most part go with the family as a social institution; and it is doubtful how far they can be altered by any change in the economic organization, particularly because the changes proposed mean substituting politics (competitive or monopolistic) for economics (property and the market).

In an economico-ethical or political view, property is simply power to render saleable service, in a form which is itself saleable or exchangeable outright. But purchase and sale of property is an incidental feature of economic life or economic organization. The essential thing is exchange of services, by whatever agency they are rendered. Nothing fundamental would be changed in economic society if all property except the most perishable consumption goods were "entailed" and could not be alienated. Investment and accumulation would persist, and the interest rate would have the same economic significance as "now." Moreover, none of these things would be substantially changed by establishing "socialism," with property ownership and the control of enterprise a monopoly of the government.

As suggested at the outset, the principle of *quid pro quo*, of equality in exchange, defines a power system as regards relations between individuals. It has moral significance only in so far as the individual's contribution, what he brings to market, has moral significance as a measure of desert. There is, indeed, a moral factor (universally regarded as such) in the mode of use of resources, though this "intelligent efficiency" in pursuit of one's own self-interest, seems ethical in a rather "low" and even dubious sense. But the individual's economic status depends altogether on his *possession* of economic capacity, and this is justified in moral terms only in so far as it has come about through the intelligent use of pre-existing capacity, and of course only in so far as the efficient use of capacity in one's own interest is an ethical virtue.

The meaning of freedom is freedom to act so as to make changes in the course of events, as it would be or occur in the absence of such action. That is, it is freedom to use power, possessed in some form, to this end. Any intelligent defence of freedom as a principle, or effort to discover its proper limits, must consider the long-run historical consequences and must be based upon knowledge of what men will do with freedom and what effects their acts will have on the social life as a whole. It is not merely a question of the conflicting individual interests of different individuals. Market dealings leave wide circles of contemporary individual interests unprotected and fail to give others effective expression in motives to action and this fact alone calls for compulsory co-ordination of activities by some inclusive group organization. The individual cannot possibly know the effects of his acts or transactions even upon living persons and their interests, and still less upon "civilization," beyond an extremely narrow segment of space and time, and even then usually neither accurately nor at all completely. He does not "know" their effects upon himself but always *takes chances* in various ways and degrees.

20. We are not at the moment concerned with the question whether or under what conditions some organ representing the group and acting or ordering action on its behalf may be

able to see farther or more correctly (and may be relied upon to act in the general interest). The point at the moment is simply that society has strong reasons for maintaining powerful brakes on departures from the "beaten path." Primitive society was wise in its conservatism, for it knew at least that the group had previously lived somehow, both as individuals and as a group. And liberal society, it now seems, has acted frivolously in switching over quite suddenly to an extreme opposite set of assumptions, that the new is better than the old, that the good consists in change, or at least in freedom of the individual to make changes, rather than in stability. This emphasis on the necessity of an *onus probandi* in favour of conservatism, and against change, must stand as our last word at this point.

II. Idealism and Marxism

In this paper we shall consider, in their relation to the problem of economic reform, two of the three general ethical methods or approaches which seem to be most important in Western civilisation as bases for the criticism of liberalism, and possible successors to it as the ethical basis of a social order. The three viewpoints referred to are Idealism, Marxism and Christianity. For a discussion within the scope of an article, the respective viewpoints or conceptions must naturally be taken in a rather general interpretation, without any attempt at precise definition or references to the literature, or an adequate polemical defence of the view presented as to what constitutes the essential and distinctive principle of each. They will be considered more or less comparatively, in relation to liberalism, which, as the accepted moral basis of social order hitherto in our culture, seems to be entitled to the advantage of the *onus probandi*.

A. *Idealism*

In the academic and speculative ethical tradition of the modern world, the most important view of ethical problems and principles alternative to liberalism (utilitarianism, economism—and, we may add, pragmatism) in terms of which the latter has been criticised, is what may be referred to as rationalistic or idealistic ethics. It is represented philosophically by the Hegelian and neo-Hegelian school or tradition. The contrast between liberalism and idealism may be provisionally indicated by the terms, "individualism" and "groupism." The task of the discussion is to show what these concepts really mean for the purposes of our problem. It will be recalled as the main thesis of the previous article that the crux of utilitarian liberalism did not lie in the theory of hedonism, or any theory of the content of the good, but simply in the doctrine of individual autonomy, with mutual consent—assumed to be in general a criterion of mutual advantage—as the ethical ideal in all dealings or relations between individuals.[14] The central tenet of idealism, in contrast, is that

---

[14] The main difficulty in this whole field of discussion is the vagueness in the meaning of terms, which is partly due to the efforts of the advocates of every position to treat some compact verbal designation of it as a slogan and to interpret it in a question-begging way to include as much as possible of all that is accepted as good by ethical common sense (especially that of the particular culture to which the discussion is addressed). This is particularly true in connection with the pleasure principle, which can be used to interpret and to defend practically any ethical position. It is a familiar fact that its advocates have never found it inconsistent with ascetic ideals and practices, and indeed have not found suicide a serious intellectual difficulty for their doctrine. To the present writer, it seems to be an essentially meaningless idea, a dogmatic psychological verbalism. If the term "pleasure" is used by definition as a general designation of all motive, the hedonistic principle is true by definition. And if this is not done, if it is admitted to be possible for men to desire anything else than pleasure, then the principle is axiomatically false, or incomplete. It is possible to argue that what men desire is always a mental state, and to call "desired mental state" by the name of "pleasure." But it is as certain to common sense as anything can be that men

"society" is the real repository or locus of value, and the real choosing subject or moral agent. The idealist considers the individual as existing "for" society, much as an organ or cell exists for the organism, instead of the converse, or instead of viewing society as having no reality except as an association of individuals for mutual individual advantage. Of course both of these positions are untenable in any extreme version. Any simple either-or dichotomy of viewpoints in social philosophy is necessarily wrong. In this case it is especially clear that there is validity in both positions and that both are partial truths in various meanings, along with many other conceptions of society. (Among these other conceptions that of a part of the members of society exploiting or using others must not be left out of account.)

From the standpoint of a critical survey of principles advocated for the guidance of social action or policy, the elementary difficulty of definition or clear formulation arises out of the relation between theories of what is, and theories of what ought to be—assuming that the word theory can properly be used in this second connection. As regards idealism in particular, the first point for emphasis is that in the statements of the position by its advocates it is primarily a metaphysical theory of the nature of society and derives most of its appeal as a programme from its merit in this regard. Its implications, or the ostensible deductions from it, for the guidance of action, are much less cogent, either logically or ethically. That is, the social policies advocated are open to question, both as to their actual relation to the premises from which they are ostensibly deduced, and as to whether they are valid

---

rarely if at all think they are desiring pleasure, until they are asked (by themselves or someone else) to give a "reason why" they desire something which they do immediately desire. And when this issue is raised, the form which the answer takes seems to be chiefly a matter of the cultural traditions or education, including self-education, and habits of verbal usage, of the individual in question.

on any grounds, either as axioms or as deductions from any axioms which are acceptable as such.

The philosophical problem as to the nature of the empirical social and political reality is properly in question here only or in so far as such truths or postulates can be validly used as premises for the inference of principles of a distinctly ethical sort. On this point, it seems necessary to take a negative position, with one important qualification. Moral ideals, in the strict sense, must be either axioms of moral common sense, or deductions from such axioms. This problem is almost purely one of ''critical'' thinking, and relative to norms rather than facts. Its relation to any question of fact in the meaning of sense observation is very indirect. The qualification is that there is not really much meaning to moral-political speculation in a vacuum, i.e., without reference to what is possible and practicable in the real world. (The human significance of descriptive essays on ''Heaven'' is a question about which the writer has puzzled a good deal, without reaching any very satisfactory conclusions!) From this practical point of view, it is certainly necessary to keep clearly in mind that the question is one of changing an existing situation, beginning with that situation as it is ''here and now,'' and using means and procedures which are actually available as elements in that situation.[15]

---

[15] The negative proposition that statements about facts do not contribute to the solution of the problem of the end or ideal, really contains but half the truth about the philosophical difficulties of the relation between facts and values. There is a sharp contradiction between the world-views involved in approaching human data from the standpoints respectively of the intellectual or explanatory interest and of the practical interest, the interest in action. (This is true whether the interest in action is taken in the form of personal desire or objective value judgment.) The conception in modern thought of a ''theory'' of any subject matter is descriptive or positivistic. Positive science excludes any notion of ''real cause,'' which is to say any notion of activity or initiative on the part of the subject matter treated as cause. But in human phenomena, a subject is always in some sense and some degree being acted upon by itself. And for social phenomena we have also to

In spite of their divergent metaphysical premises, both utilitarianism and idealism have a common general conception of social action, which is the real essence of each position from the point of view here in question, the discussion of policy.[16] In terms of a first approach, the difference seems to be, in short, purely metaphysical. Both systems conceive of society or the state in terms of law, and of law as the expression of a "general will." The difference has to do with the relation between the individual will and the general or social will. Idealism defines its concepts in such a way that the two are always identical, while utilitarianism, in the "moderate" version of liberalism, recognises both harmony and conflict.[17]

---

recognise group self-action in the degree to which the society is "democratic," in contrast with a dictatorship, taken in the "absolute" sense that a single individual would own all the rest of society and treat his subjects as things. Thus the difficulty becomes two-fold; for even individual freedom is to the scientific intelligence "transcendental," mystical and unintelligible or simply illusory, but group freedom or self-determination is far worse in this respect.

In addition, liberal social thought has tried to straddle the world views of positivism and of individualistic voluntarism, utilitarianism, economism or pragmatism. These are inherently contradictory even between themselves, while both reduce to nonsense any conception of intelligent group decision in belief or action, because they make discussion, or meaningful utterance unreal. And Hegelian idealism reaches by a different route essentially the same impasse for thought, as far as human interests and activities are concerned. Its preservation of some kind of freedom or initiative for the "Absolute" (if it does preserve any) is of interest only to the speculative philosopher. (In fact, as far as this writer can see, the role of speculative thought itself, as a real activity, as "problem-solving," is just as effectively excluded by the notion of the Absolute as it is by that of universal mechanism.)

[16] This refers to one interpretation of utilitarianism, i.e., the ethical interpretation, which is just as contradictory to the psychological interpretation as it is to positivism, mechanistic or culture-historical. The psychological interpretation, whether in the form of hedonism or any purely individualistic conception of motive or interest, lands one in solipsism.

[17] In the more extreme versions of utilitarianism, such as that of Hobbes, the notion of primitive antagonism, as a feature of "human nature," is carried so far that there is not much left of the unity, or the social nature of man, *à la* Aristotle, or *à la* Hegel. Yet even Hobbes's notion of the primitive contract with a "dictator" (dynasty) for the purely negative purpose of preventing the "war of all against all" may be said to preserve some vestige of it.

The essence of Liberalism was, or is, the conception of a legal state with law or legality as a moral-religious concept—in spite of the pose of hard-boiled individualism—and with absolute and "sacred" equality of all individuals before the law. This equality, moreover, holds both in the passive sense of the treatment of individuals by the law, and in the active sense of their equal participation in "making" the laws (equality of voice or vote). Government officials in particular are supposed to have no "power" (and hardly any existence) as individuals, but to act exclusively as agents of the law, both when they enforce law and when they make (i.e., change) laws. This includes a theoretically equal voice in the selection of officials, and equal opportunity to be elected to office (both under the law) through the suffrage of all. Thus ideally all political decisions in a liberal state represent the best possible compromise between the (more or less conflicting) interests of individuals—a composite, or centre of gravity, or "equilibrium of forces," force being the form under which interests are conceived as operating.[18]

Differences between this ideal result and the way things work out in practice need not be considered in detail here. The "worst" features of the reality are no doubt two: First, the general conception tends to get to be that the majority has the "right" to rule the minority, which is an utterly different matter than the conception of the general will with voting as the best method of ascertaining or expressing it. (Also the vote which decides a concrete issue need not in fact be a majority, or even a very large fraction of the total, and need not be cast with much reference to that issue.) Secondly, and perhaps worse still, the machinery operates through campaign-

---

[18] The relation between interests in a purely individual, egoistic or selfish interpretation, and "opinions" as to what is "right" in some objective sense is a question to be mentioned here as of the heart of the problem, but one which cannot be discussed at the moment.

ing and partisan organisation designed to influence the electorate, and in the nature of the case campaigners use any procedure or device which "works," which brings victory to the user. Public political discussion under actual conditions very frequently works in the opposite direction from that of forming a real intelligent general will or consensus, giving rise to hostility, bad blood, and partisanship for the sake of partisanship.

Mere competitive persuasion of the masses is not generally, if it is under any conditions, a good test of truth or of the real merits of a question. The saving grace of liberalism lay in the assumed moral and constitutional commitment to minimising the functions of government and the sphere of its activity, i.e., to "freedom" as the fundamental ideal, and the use of coercion negatively for the most part, to prevent coercion by individuals and private groups. This means using it to enforce the ideal of mutual free consent as the basis of social relations, plus only such regulatory measures and "public works" as are not seriously questioned. Apart from this ideal, as an accepted constitutional principle, the notion of majority rule would probably never have been seriously defended by competent thinkers as essentially better than other forms of tyranny.

Turning to consider idealism as a contrasting political conception, with "society" as the unit instead of the "individual," we confront in the first place the rather mechanical but vital question of the definition of "society" in the concrete sense of physical boundaries. To this question there are two main possible answers. The first is to accept as "given," once for all, the existing political map of the world—divisions and subdivisions!—as it stands, at the moment when the question happens to be raised.[19] Now it is a glaring matter of

---

[19] We take for granted the definition of political units primarily in terms of territory, and omit any discussion of the exceptions, which are by no means unimportant.

fact, however unpleasant, that the political organisation of the world, or lack of it, at any date in history is a product of the historical processes of the past, which present a mixture of "brute force and accident," lying and trickery—the "horrid tale of murder and spoil, etc.,'' of the poet. The result is satisfactory to no one who views it with any impartiality. As an ideal it would be accepted only by the furious partisan of some glutted imperialism which could not hope to get more and would be certain to lose rather than gain by any change.

The question of a possible redefinition of political units, a redrawing of the political map of the world, is usually discussed in terms of the unity and diversity of "culture," which is the second conceivably possible solution of the problem of definition of "society." But this solution is in practice hopelessly ambiguous, whether referred to populations them-selves and their will to unity or separateness, or to "experts." In much of Europe, in particular, it would be physically impossible to draw the political map in such terms, by any interpretation. The European (and African-Islamic-Asiatic) settlement of 1919, after the first World War, with the aftermath, renders superfluous any detailed discussion of this topic. Besides the vagueness of the principle, in relation to the facts, we must also recognise that cultural unity and divergence are also, and nearly to the same extent as legal boundaries, the product of the same largely non-moral or immoral historical forces.

The position as to "real" or ideal boundaries of societies which is, quite naturally, taken in practice, for the most part, is one which mixes or combines the two possible solutions in such a way as largely to get the worst consequences of both.

The difference between the treatment, by states, of citizens by birth and of resident aliens and of travellers, and the claims of states over citizens abroad, and their descendants, and everything having to do with freedom of movement of men between states,—all these things are rapidly growing in importance under our eyes.

Most of the interpreters are partisans of some existing state, and draw the boundaries of that unit to include everything actually included at the moment and as much more as any plausible historical reason or justification can be found for doing. There are hardly any limits to the extension of most of the greater states on this principle, if one goes far enough back in history (and not too far). But in fact the process does not stop even here. The notion of "natural superiority," racial or cultural, is called in to support a "right" to include any strongly desired slice of the territory and population of the globe "inferior" in culture, either on the basis of incorporation or of permanent retention in a more or less servile status. (Nor is this a mere manifestation of wickedness; the problem of backward peoples is real.)

Thus the physical question of the boundaries and the inclusiveness of the state merges into the ethical question of the nature of the social end which is set over against the individual ends (individually judged) of liberalism. It is natural to assume that the end of political policy is itself political; and this runs naturally if not inevitably into the conception of the end as aggrandisement of the political and/or cultural unit as such. And again, political aggrandisement inevitably takes chiefly the concrete form of military power. A glance at modern history is enough to show that in particular the economic policy of states has aimed at military strength practically to the extent that it has been "socialised," i.e., has departed from the liberal ideal of allowing each individual to pursue his own well-being in his own way, subject only to the principle of mutual consent, enforced by law.[20]

---

[20] The essential ethical and hisotrical-psychological problem or problems brought to mind is (or are) why men wish to preserve and to propagate their culture and political institutions, and what is the human right and wrong of culture differences and their preservation, propagation or extinction, by various processes in both cases. It is not clear what are the actual desires back of the urge to cultural expansion beyond "material self interest" on the part of individuals and groups

The considerations just noticed have to do with the meaning of society in relation to other societies, or concretely with "international" affairs. With reference to the internal problems of any group, the fundamental issues may again be raised by the question "who is the state?" but with a different interpretation. The crucial fact is that when a society has occasion to "speak" at all—to declare itself on any matter, internal or external—it necessarily speaks through some individual human being, or at most some very small group; and when a society acts, either on any of its own members or externally, it acts similarly through human agents. The tendency in philosophical formulations of the idealistic theory is to ignore the social-problem side of this whole matter, to explain what happens by assuming that a social group acts as a whole and spontaneously, either directly in dealing with concrete situations affecting group life, or at least in designating agents to act for it. That is, the theory tends to abstract altogether from power relations within a social group and the problems which these involve. (Or if there is a contest, one side is naïvely taken as representing the society, the other as subversive.)

Now this view is in accord with fact in some divisions or aspects of social life, such as language, and social usages, in so far as these do take care of themselves "automatically," without giving rise to any recognised problem. In a small primitive group, the activities of various kinds, economic, religious and "social" in the narrow sense, may be reduced to a routine or ritualised to such a degree that this view is valid over most of the field of activity. It may even hold for the enforcement of the criminal law—if the concept of law is

whose power-status will be improved; and that, while important, is certainly not the main factor. The facts of culture rivalry are especially puzzling, because the basis or nucleus of it all is so largely language, and linguistically educated people do not think of one language as being substantially superior to another in a utilitarian or aesthetic sense, to say nothing of moral value. Latin-American nationalism is especially puzzling. But such topics would lead far afield.

taken to apply under such conditions; that is, the "law" may either be enforced by "mob" action (as we should call it) or by functionaries selected by ritual and proceeding in strict accord with ritual. It is conceivable, at least, that in nearly any connection the general will may be a plain matter of fact and may present no "problem" of discovery, interpretation or execution.[21]

The idealistic theory of society as an "organic" unity, or "whole," applies very well, in short, as long as there are no problems. A social problem arises out of difference of opinion, and/or clash of wills, within the membership of a group. A clash of wills, it should be observed, does not of itself give rise to a social problem; it does so only if there is a difference of opinion connected with it in some way—at least as to what "society" is to do about it. It is in connection with problem situations that the difference between liberalism and idealism comes to light. Such situations have arisen especially in connection with war, which resists ritualisation, and with demands for *change* in the law. In the face of a real problem, idealism tends to advocate the "traditional" solution in so far as one can be found; first, in the literal sense of following tradition on the concrete issue; and second, when tradition gives no direct answer, it tends to emphasise the traditional distribution of authority in the group. Thus the whole bias and tendency of idealism is *conservative,* in both the natural meanings of the term, adherence to any established practice, and leaving all matters of social action or change to the decision of the parties actually established in positions of authority. And under conditions where the need for action is

---

[21] The close connection between the idealistic social philosophy and the historical jurisprudence and the *Kultur-Historismus* in general is well known; also its relation to the Romantic Movement, with the latter's idealisation of mediaeval conditions. The sociology of the "social organism" should also be mentioned, especially because it was promoted, in a very different sense, by the individuals (and positivists) Spencer and Comte.

recognised, the latter tendency predominates, meaning that an extreme concentration of power in the hands of irresponsible persons as functionaries is favored; or, in everyday terms, it means aristocracy and monarchy.[22]

This view finds cogent argumentative support in the theory of division of labour. One thinks at once of the fable of the quarrel between the bodily members, hand, stomach and brain. The doctrine of evolution has contributed to strengthen its appeal, especially as to the progressive centralisation of control functions in the organism in the brain ("cephalisation"). Philosophically, or analytically, speaking, the issue between aristocracy and democracy (idealism and liberalism) is largely a question of the relations between knowledge and will, or of their relative importance. The social interest is naturally thought of as pertaining to the population as a whole. But knowledge, both of the precise nature and content of that interest, and even more, of the technical means or procedures adapted to promote it, is naturally treated as a speciality of selected individuals or circles. In practical affairs, the question of the relation between individual interest and group interest tends to drop out or become "academic," the issue being joined on the *method* of determining the best interest of the group and its members, which both parties virtually (and ultimately no doubt quite properly) assume to be harmonious. There is no possible issue on the fact that a group of any size must act through agents, officials, including under modern conditions the activity of law-making (i.e., law changing). Thus the concrete issue becomes that of the "responsibility," or irresponsibility, of officials, and of concrete means for getting officials really to act for the interests of society rather

---

[22] An undemocratic, traditional, and authoritarian organisation of religion naturally goes along with a similar conception of the state, the two being supposed to work together, but with one or the other predominating, depending on the "school" of idealism which is speaking.

than in their own interests, as individuals or as a "class." On this point, there is much to be said on both sides, but this essay is not the place to say it, except for one point.

Our concern is with ethics, and specifically with remedies for the basic ethical defect of liberalism or individualism. This defect, it will be recalled, has to do with the preservation and improvement of culture in those aspects which are not adequately taken care of by individual self-interest or the interest of the private family, or other private or voluntary associations. It is a question of fact and of factual analysis to determine what these are, since it is presumably admitted that there are moral and social interests of many sorts which will in practice be *better* promoted by "society as a whole," which means the state, or specifically the government, than they will be if left to voluntary action on the part of individuals and spontaneous free groups.

At bottom the problem is obviously two-fold—assuming that we do not accept a rigid ruling-caste system in which the rulers either use the mass of the people for their own ends or treat them as little children. First, there must be provision for adequate *discussion* of questions of social policy from the standpoint of the ultimate long-run or of fundamental values as distinct from individual interests, leading to the formation of a recognised general-will. Second, provision must be made that the results of such discussion shall be carried into effect, as fast as genuine results are reached. As regards the first issue, there is relatively little difference of opinion that leadership in discussion needs to be the work of specialists, of men of "leisure" in the sense of freedom from routine economic cares and ability to devote their entire energies to the "intellectual life." (The relation between this and "education," in the narrow sense, is a question.) In practice the question has to do with the selection of the individuals to perform the function of intellectual leadership, specifically whether they should be a hereditary class or caste, or a profession recruited from the whole population; and if the latter what is to be the method of selection, and the method of their training and remuneration or support.

The final question of application or execution, perhaps most crucial of all, is whether the class or group of intellectual specialists should have *power* to effectuate their decisions, or should have to act by persuading either political officials entirely distinct from themselves, or the masses. These questions cannot be discussed here. We may remark that the "commercialisation of culture" is one of the most sinister phases of liberalism as it actually works. On the other hand, the idealistic alternative to liberalism, while, viewed in the abstract, it does seem to offer some solution for the weaknesses of the latter in the way of a more adequate consideration of those interests of the distant future which seem to form the content of the concept of group interest, yet presents equally fatal weaknesses in practice. In particular, as already pointed out, idealism means in practice, first the deification of the state and the interpretation of the interests of the state in terms of political aggrandisement through military power rather than in terms of cultural values; and secondly, it means either traditionalism or authoritarianism in the constitution of the state.

A few words are called for in relation to the current historical development in the direction of social stratification and dictatorial leadership, or "corporativism." Superficially, this presents important differences as compared with a traditional-authoritarian system such as obtained in the later Middle Ages, the period of feudal monarchy. One detail, which will not be gone into here, is the tendency of the political state to absorb or even to replace "the church"; in reality, this is only a continuation of a tendency which has been going on in the national states throughout their history, and which, one must say, is a logical development, probably an inevitable one if national states were to survive and not give place to a world political order corresponding to the teachings of the accepted world religion. As to the corporative dictatorship itself, the essential fact may be stated in three words: it is new. This means, in the nature of the case, that it is not traditional. But it does not mean that, from the moment it becomes securely established and accepted, it will take the location of ultimate political power any less as "given" or a given basis for its further extension, than would be true in the oldest and most stable system under any ideology. It is also obvious that prior to the establishment of any dictatorial regime, in so far as it appeals for popular support, its promoters are in essentially the same position as the candidates for office under any democratic regime. (In so far as a political coterie is struggling to get or keep power through conspiracy and force, this of course does not so fully apply.) The special feature of the position of a group publicly campaigning for dictatorial powers is that they virtually announce in advance, to all who are intelligent enough to understand the simplest political situation, that once in power they will do as they please, as far as they "can," that the people are being asked to write a political "blank check" valid for all future time.

It is also in the nature of the case that any new power organisation, while it is organising and stabilising itself, will present much of the appearance of co-option, on a "merit" basis. In this respect, the most important question regarding the new dictatorships—"communism" in Russia as well as "fascism" or national socialism, or whatever name any ideological dictatorship may have given itself—cannot be answered for a generation or two, at least. That is, we cannot tell to what extent, or in what form, such a system will settle down into a "class" structure in the only proper sense of the word, a stratification in which position is determined primarily by birth. On general grounds, such a stabilisation is what one would expect to happen—as feudal relations and guild privileges tended to become hereditary in the Middle Ages.

B. Marxism

During the better part of a century—since the publication of the Communist Manifesto in 1848—economic reformism in the European world has been coming more and more to mean the philosophy and movement known as Marxism, ostensibly a development from the Hegelian form of philosophical idealism. As hardly needs to be said, it is impossible to discuss it briefly without seeming both superficial and dogmatic. This impression will undoubtedly be aggravated by the content of what the present writer has to say. For the movement presents an especially aggravated case of a large part of the world being "out of step with me." Especially interesting is its relation to Christianity. For where the latter seems to involve romantic oversimplification of a sentimental or moralistic sort, Marxism seems romantically immoralistic, destructive, diabolical. Sombart has somewhere remarked that Marx was a man of two souls, a thinker and a hater; I should say that as a hater he was undoubtedly entitled to a very high rank. If the gospel of love will not solve our problems we must admit the fact and turn from it in sorrow, but we can both confidently and joyfully reject the gospel of hate.[23] Marxism is not merely a romantic oversimplification; it is intellectually self-contradictory and ethically nihilistic and monstrous.

To intellectual analysis Marxism presents two main elements

---

[23] There is a natural causal connection between these two positions in spite of the superficial antithesis. Love for the downtrodden plus superficiality in diagnosis takes the form of hatred of the privileged, and belief that their wickedness is the cause of poverty and their destruction its cure. There are many Christian Marxists.

or aspects, a philosophy of history and a social propaganda; and the two meet and fuse in the highly ambiguous doctrine of the class war.[24] It is hardly possible to take the class war seriously as a theory of history, or even to form a judgment as to how seriously it was "really" taken by Marx and Engels, or is taken by their followers. The essential meaning of the notion is obviously its pragmatic significance. The class war idea was put forward as a theoretical view of what happens; but the aim, conscious or unconscious, obviously was to use the theory to make it happen, to foment a class war—which of course had not previously existed, at least in the desired form and degree, or there would have been no occasion for the propaganda. What is ominously as well as profoundly significant is that human nature and human mentality are such that a theory of what does and must happen—and especially such a theory of "inevitable victory," annihilating all opposition—will tend to make people act in accord with it, and so to bring the facts into accord with it. But this is largely the case. The doctrine that social life has been and is a war between classes has proved so effective in promoting a class war that it begins to seem doubtful whether there is an effective preventive, i.e., any effective mode of resistance except war, in which other classes will take up the challenge of the "proletariat" and its sympathisers and fight the thing through

---

[24] This sketch will not go into questions of critical interpretation. Marxism, which is like a religion in many respects, is so also in this, that the problem of what it means is a question of orthodoxy, the "party line." We shall discuss the materialistic or economic interpretation of history and the class struggle as a version of that doctrine, and as an ethical position. If Marxism does not mean that, there is nothing that it can be said to mean. For a survey, the reader may consult: M. M. Bober, *Karl Marx's Interpretation of History* (Harvard University Press, 1927); Sidney Hook, *Towards the Understanding of Karl Marx* (John Day, 1933); Henri Sée, *The Economic Interpretation of History* (Adelphi Co., 1929); E. R. A. Seligman, *The Economic Interpretation of History* (Columbia University Press, 1902, 1924); on Christianity and Marxism, John Lewis (ed.) *Christianity and the Social Revolution* (Gollancz, London, 1935, 1937).

to a finish. This is what current history seems to show; where the Marxists have shown serious strength but without being able to carry through their programme for seizure of power, Marxism is being suppressed and all the liberties of the masses along with it.

At the time when the propaganda became active, in the later nineteenth century, the social situation clearly was not one of class war. But the propagandists hoped to develop a political movement of that form, by which they would in the first place, of course, ride to power; afterwards, they would (presumably) use their power to effect certain political objectives and social changes which they considered desirable. The nature of the ultimate programme will be briefly noticed later. The interrelations and relative importance in the minds of the promoters of Marxism, as of any movement, of these two motives—getting power, and using power to achieve particular results—it is useless to attempt to unravel.[25]

Underlying the historical theory of the class war, the intellectual basis or content of Marxism is in the first place "dialectical materialism." This is a supposedly materialistic

---

[25] But it would be impossible to overemphasise the fact that such an analysis of the relations between individual motive and social purpose, and between both and action, individual or social, would be necessary as a foundation for any significant or genuine social philosophy. In these essays, there is no effort to go very far beyond demonstrating the necessity of such a philosophical viewpoint, through exposure of the self-stultification involved in any theory either of positive causality or of purely individualistic voluntarism—which two positions, though contradictory between themselves, have both been assumed in the social-philosophical literature of modern liberalism.

The connection in which the psychology of motivation most requires careful consideration, but is most neglected, is the motivation of social reformers themselves. Much light could undoubtedly be thrown on this psychology by an investigation of the mentality of inventors of perpetual motion machines. They usually "know" that they can produce the general result striven for, but are not committed to any particular method to a degree that causes any inclination to give up their project when it fails experimentally.

interpretation of social process, arrived at by inverting the Hegelian idealistic or dialectical world-view. There would be no point to any extended examination into the meaning of "materialism." As every student knows, it dissolves under critical examination into phenomenalism, sensationalism, conceptualism, or field theory, or some sort of non-physical conception of the ultimate nature of matter itself. The essential fact is that Marx and Engels never gave the matter any competent or serious critical examination. What they seem to have meant by it can be best expressed by some such designation as naive empiricism, positivism or sensationalistic phenomenalism, really involving an injunction against any effort at definition of content that would go beyond the common sense of the man in the street. The crucial matter for practical purposes, in line with the general standpoint of these articles, is that the position reduces all discussion to nonsense, all utterance to noise or physical configuration of some sort. The statements of the propagandist himself, like other utterance, are also social and historical phenomena. And to assert that they are merely the physical effects of physical causes amounts to saying that one is not saying anything, a self-contradiction which seems to surpass any other conceivable example of the species self-contradiction in self-contradictoriness.[26]

---

[26] In spite of the absurdity involved in using any form of historical determinism as the basis of a propaganda for action, it is obvious to the most superficial student of history and politics that the device has proved effective in many hands and in many connections. Confident insistence that a course of events is inevitable is typically an excellent procedure for securing wide and active support in bringing it about. The election theory of salvation in Calvinistic theology is a conspicuous case in point and is especially interesting as an interpretation of Christianity widely accepted by the best people and the greatest minds of the "Christian" world. And they have been perhaps the most effective as well as the most active Christianisers, from the apostle Paul to Calvin and Knox. Moslem and other Oriental fatalism, with its effect upon soldiers, is another case in point.

In interpreting all these facts, the objective student must keep in mind the ambiguity of his own role, or at least face the question whether he really means

In the second place, the Marxian historical philosophy is called "economic." This concept is so ambiguous as to involve confusion of most of the irreconcilable conceptions of the nature of social reality which the human mind has recognised or invented. On one hand, it may refer to a doctrine or thesis that all individual behaviour is economically motivated, meaning fully accounted for in terms of use of means, or effort to use means, with maximum efficiency, in realising given ends. But even this statement is ambiguous, since the assertion that men do act in such a way as to maximise something and the assertion that they attempt to do that, and nothing else, themselves belong in two incompatible philosophical systems. All treatment of motives on the analogy of mechanical forces, tending to establish equilibrium (or perpetual oscillations) involves abstracting from the factor of possible error, and consequently from that of effort, in human conduct and the elimination of any problem-solving character and denial of the reality of problems. If behaviour is really economic it cannot be "perfectly" economic. It is in fact and undeniably problem-solving, which is to say that it involves effort and the liability to error. Any other conception, excluding effort and error, destroys its economic character and is clearly untenable.

The third meaning which the concept of the economic has, or is assumed in Marxism to have, is a form of historical causality, or historical law, or cultural positivism. This is a conception of cause and effect in cultural phenomena as such, without reduction to physical terms on the one hand, or to

---

to be purely objective, or thinks also of influencing social change by his own activity as a student. If he wishes merely to achieve intellectual clarity—presumably for other members of some intellectual community as well as for himself, since otherwise he would not publish his analysis or give any utterance to it—he must make conscious and careful provision against exerting such influence, by keeping his work a secret outside the circle of "intellectuals" for which it is intended. Publication in any society of any discussion of that society and its activities must be expected to have some effect on the future course of events.

psychological terms on the other—i.e., without ascribing human conduct to motivation of any sort. This third meaning forms the natural and best interpretation of historical dialectic. It is the sort of methodological assumption ordinarily made in the study of linguistic change, and of which linguistics furnishes the best example. Languages are supposed to change in accord with their own laws of change and the changes are explained when the laws are discovered and stated. And the same interpretation can be applied to law, and other social phenomena. Marxism applies it first to "economic" process— somehow defined, or left undefined; it then explains other phases of the historical process by treating the "economic" element or factor as an independent variable or cause, which proceeds thus in accord with its special laws and controls all other elements in the historical process as dependent variables or effects. As to the meaning or content of the economic element itself, it would seem that the best interpretation of the Marxian conception is to take it as meaning technology, in an inclusive sense, and to view the whole position as a technological interpretation of history. This view cannot be derived conclusively from the writings of Marx and Engels, which do not indicate any one view unambiguously. But it seems to be more defensible than any other interpretation. A technological interpretation, again, amounts to looking at history in "Darwinian" terms, and accepting a theory of biological determinism. At the human level, biological efficiency as a variable may be considered to be a matter of technology, and historical change viewed as the "survival of the fittest" in a competition between groups on the basis of technical efficiency, taking account both of growth in numbers and of military superiority.[27]

---

[27] This interpretation seems to be advocated, for example, by the American Marxist A. W. Calhoun. See his review of M. M. Bober, *Karl Marx's Interpretation of History*, American Economic Review, Vol. 18 (1928), pp. 275–6.

Darwinism, in turn, is ordinarily thought of in terms of "natural selection" in a "struggle for existence"; and this struggle may verbally suggest the class struggle, or war, of Marxism, already referred to. But a little reflection will show that if Darwinism is made to support a culture-positivism interpretation of history, in the way just indicated, it cannot at the same time support, or even leave room for, a class-struggle theory. A criticism of the class-struggle concept requires consideration of the two notions, struggle and class. The first question is, how far and in what sense human history is an affair of struggle at all, as opposed to cooperation, or some other form of motivation, or of unmotivated action. Now the concept of struggle is really a new theoretical category of behaviour entirely distinct from all those hitherto mentioned, and in addition is itself a highly ambiguous notion. It clearly cannot be reduced to cultural positivism or "dialectic," although that is the meaning which must be given to it in the connection just considered. If it is a positive category it is not struggle in the meaning of ordinary usage in connection with war or any contest between human beings, whether individuals or groups, for this is or involves purposive behaviour, and at a very high level of complexity.

The notion of biological struggle, either against the environment or as "competition" with other species, is very difficult to interpret. We raise the whole question of the nature of biological phenomena and of evolution in particular. It seems to be impossible to think of the facts entirely apart from some idea of struggle and competition. But it is competitive in a sense in which competition is completely foreign to the behaviour of the economic man, and which yet is essentially teleological, and not reducible to positive process. In any event, the class struggle, if it is to serve the purposes of the Marxian interpretation, must be taken in a sense categorically different from both. This must be a real fight.

It is competitive in a far deeper sense than is, for example, a foot race. In the first place, it is like those games in which it is as much a part of the player's objective to impede and thwart the efforts of his opponent as it is to achieve his own positive aim of "scoring." But there is a third degree of difference from individual economic effort which itself, in so far as it is economic, is not competitive at all in the psychological sense. The Marxian class struggle is not merely a duel *à outrance* but is a duel without rules of any sort. There seems to be no intellectual bridge between such a notion and any form of historical determinism.

This brings us to the second element in the class struggle notion, that of classes, social or economic. But any effort to define the notion of class and to identify classes, as defined, in any actual historical situation will make one more than hesitant in treating historical conflict as a class struggle. In history, both individuals and groups in infinite variety of kinds, and changing in character almost from hour to hour, are constantly pitted against each other on an infinite variety of issues. And very largely there is no issue at all except the struggle for power for the love of power or even, in no small degree, for the love of struggle, or of victory.

For one thing, a matter of detail but fatal to the theory, if a class struggle or war is to be realistic, the lines must be drawn between two factions; even a three-cornered war is hardly thinkable. A final or crucial struggle must be between those who are "for" and those who are "against" something or other, some leader or programme of action. On the political arena, to be sure, there may be maneuvering and jockeying for power among a number of conflicting parties or positions, apart from any issue except that of power itself. But the effort to interpret any important historical struggle, especially in modern history, in terms of classes and class interests seems to reduce the idea to absurdity. Political parties do not correspond to classes, and neither does the line-up on particular issues. And this is a most fortunate and praiseworthy circumstance. For if political divisions did take place on the lines of particular but conflicting economic interests, or of sharply conflicting social philosophies, it is hardly conceivable that free society would continue to exist. In other words, the result would be a real class war, in which some class would win and all others would cease to exist, politically at least, if not physically.

Before leaving the intellectual confusions of Marxism and turning to its ethical aspect, and particularly the ethics of the class struggle theory, we may repeat once more our main point in this whole discussion of the ethics of reform. It seems to be a first and "absolute" requirement for any ethical discussion that it rest on philosophical premises implicit if not explicit, which make discussion possible, meaningful. But all the interpretations of the economic interpretation which have been mentioned have the characteristic in common that they violate this elementary requirement; they all make all social discussion of social policy unreal. Every one of them embodies either some form of positivistic premise or some form of egoistic voluntarism. And if anything whatever is self-evident, it is surely self-evident that the members of a group cannot carry on a discussion of group policy using exclusively propositions beginning either with "in fact" or with "I want." There must be recognition of some "objective value judgment," recognition that questions of policy for the group are problems, and have better and worse solutions. In so far as any discussion on the basis of any of the philosophical positions so far considered is thinkable at all, it is thinkable only in and for an intellectual community completely segregated from the society whose phenomena are the subject of the discussion, and the phenomena must be regarded as presenting problems only in the sense of intellectual problems for the discussion group, not problems of action for the society itself. This hypothesis would raise the philosophical question whether it is possible to believe in the reality of a discussion group without believing that other societies, taken in relation to other phases of activity, have the same fundamental character to some extent, i.e., that in human society in general problems of action are to some extent settled by real discussion.

If discussion itself is mechanically or culturally determined, or if it can be adequately accounted for (causally) in terms of individual interests alone, whether these are thought of as being essentially economic or of whatever kind, then discussion simply ceases to be discussion. The completely candid Marxist would have to begin every statement with the observation that the noise he is about to make is to be regarded as the effect of appropriate causes, or (really also, at the same time) that the proposition he is about to utter is purely an expression of certain (economic) interests of his own ego. Even this is not the whole story. A slightly more persistent and penetrating philosophical critique would show that without both individual problem-solving and real discussion between individuals, it is impossible to believe in facts, in the plain man's sense, to say nothing of the facts and principles of science; utterance itself becomes unreal and illusion an illusion. Ultimately there is no categorical difference in intellectual status or objectivity, in the general sense of validity or verity, between judgments or statements of fact and judgments or statements of value. Truth itself is finally a value, and the will to believe the truth, rather than anything else that one might for any other reason wish to believe, is the foundation of all morality.

Before we can take up the ethics of the class struggle theory, we have further to note that the theory violates the premises of its general position by its conception of classes. These are taken as given, as real, but as purely self-seeking entities, though without moral principles of any sort. They are unified by pure individual self-interest or some purely unconscious force. The Marxian economic class carries to a higher power the inherent unreality of the economic man. In the first place, given such classes, if any one of them entered into negotiation of any sort with any other, the activity would necessarily be regarded as purely a technique of manipulation, or essentially of combat, to be employed only when and as it should seem likely to be more effective or "cheaper" than any other procedure, and to be categorically dropped and all past results ignored, the moment these conditions ceased to apply. No agreement, commitment or promise made by such a class would have the least validity, and no statement it might make would have any status as truth. As Kant pointed out, if assertions and promises are recognized as having this character, they cannot be either effective or meaningful; the very notion is a self-contradiction. Negotiation in such terms can be meaningful only as deception; but the Marxists make this impossible by openly declaring their position in advance. The clear implication is that the only rational procedure is a literal fight or war from the outset, one which recognizes no rules and gives no quarter. Any utterance is a pure inanity, unless possibly of the nature of a war-cry intended to terrorise and unnerve the enemy, or to heighten the courage and energy of the partisans by and for whom it is employed.

In the second place, it should be superfluous to elaborate upon the absurdity of the notion of an economic class. The historical unreality of the category, already pointed out, is no mystery. It is as impossible for a social class, containing a minimum of two individuals, to be perfectly homogeneous in interests as it is for a society in any sense whatever. That is, there are "class" distinctions within any class, different in degree at most from distinctions between classes. Any group which is able to hold together and to function in any way as a group must be unified either by moral ideals or by a possible predominance of a common interest in the attainment of some very specific objective over the conflicting interests of the members. It cannot be held together by literal force, unless it is composed of a single individual possessing sufficient power in some form to dominate all others, who must be weak enough and few enough to be so dominated, both individually and in any combination which they are able to effect. For any ruling group or power group is again a society, necessarily more or less heterogeneous and with its own conflicts of interests. Under realistic conditions, the only possible common interest which, apart from some ethical unifying force, is conceivably able to predominate over divergent individual interests, is the conflict interest, a "war" against some other group or groups. And this is in conformity with the Marxist conception itself. What is overlooked, or purposely not mentioned, is the obvious fact that if any such combat group succeeds in its objective of destroying the enemy power, it must either in turn be held together by the interest in keeping power and exploiting the defeated enemy or it will immediately disintegrate along some lines into new groups or "classes" of some form, struggling for power.

We come now to the ethical ideals of Marxism, its critique of existing society and its programme of social change. Viewing it as a social phenomenon, and ignoring, as we have to do to consider it in that light, all its facade of philosophical hocus-pocus, we find an interesting variant on the not uncommon theme of romantic destructionism. Its philosophy of social action reduces to a variety of the doctrine popularised if not invented by Rousseau, that men are naturally good except as they have been corrupted by society and its institutions, but that these are entirely wicked, and consequently, the formula for the reform and regeneration of society is to destroy its institutions. The advocates of such a programme are oblivious to the fact that to destroy social institutions would be to destroy society in any possible human sense. They are victims of a naïve theory of social contract, according to which all social arrangements have been thought out, discussed and agreed upon, and consequently are subject to change, without limit as to extent or speed, by the same process. The view is completely unhistorical and essentially fantastic. There is no need to deny that men have any power at all to change their institutions; but it is certainly limited with respect both to the amount and the kind of change which is even "possible" for any society at any time, to say nothing of costs. To any competent mind, dissatisfaction with existing institutions should suggest as the first question the critical formulation of ideals, and then, and not really separable, the possibilities, methods, and costs of change.

The contribution of Marxism to this theme is its discovery and identification of a particular supposed source of social corruption. This of course is that some selfish "class," varying more or less in character through history, has taken possession by "force," in some form which is left unanalysed, of the virtuous masses of society as a whole and is "exploiting" them for its own purposes. The recipe for salvation through destruction in our own day therefore takes the particular form of "liquidating" the class which is said to be performing the role of devil in modern European civilisation, namely the "bourgeoisie." All political opposition to this programme is assumed as a matter of course to derive from the bourgeois class itself, either directly or through paid agents or dupes. (Non-Marxist economists are allowed to hover more or less between these two classifications, paid agent and dupe.)

What is really significant about such a theory is the fact that it is taken seriously, and not only by its proponents and by the masses, but even by so many students of recognised competence and presumptive freedom from conscious and crude political bias. As already remarked, this acceptance of the class-struggle programme is highly indicative as to the prospect of intelligent and moral political action by human beings. It not only does not seem to occur to the masses, or to the intelligentsia, who are taken in—to say nothing of the propagandists themselves—that the allegation of selfish interest which is glibly pinned on the opposition applies even more obviously to the promoters of the class war themselves. They are assumed to be free from any taint of self-interest! They are merely soliciting for themselves the role of absolute monarch over their country and the world, or of some satisfactory position at court or in the administration—the details to be worked out after the revolution. Their devotion to society and to humanity is so great that they offer to serve in the highest capacity, up to the unconstitutional imperatorship of the world.

The doctrine itself—that all that need be done in order to awake the next morning in, or on the way toward, an idealistic Utopia is to destroy the admittedly crude and imperfect civilisation which the race has developed through history thus far, by destroying its institutions and power relations and turning over all power to the promoters of the destruction for the purpose of reconstruction—has an evident if mysterious appeal to elemental human nature.[28] How such propaganda, and the romantic appeal of destruction in general, is to be effectively combated, is perhaps the most serious of practical social problems. And the most serious as well as most puzzling phase of this situation is that in their manners and conscious intentions the promoters are for the most part ''nice people,'' and ''honorable men,'' and will readily, and often artistically,

---

[28] Marx probably did not teach exactly this extreme form of revolutionism, and his followers have tended away from it to a considerably different position, especially with the rise of modern communism, as will be noted presently; but the fact does not invalidate the substance of this paragraph.

"with reasons answer you." Not only that; they are morally earnest, even to a fault—in fact, to a degree which makes it a serious ethical problem whether moral earnestness can be assumed to be a virtue at all. For in a plain factual appraisal, what they are doing is more catastrophically evil than treason, or poisoning the wells, or other acts commonly placed at the head of the list of crimes. The moralisation of destruction, and of combat with a view to destruction, goes with the kind of hero-worship that merges into devil-worship. Such phenomena show that human nature has potentialities that are horrible, in full match for all those which are noble and fine. Which qualities spring the more from original nature and which from social institutions is a question of little meaning. Man is a social animal, a product of history. All that is good in him is obviously a reflection of social discipline and the product of the age-long travail through which has developed that civilisation which our romantic destructionists purpose to sweep away by violent revolution.

As suggested above, Marx himself (or Marx-Engels) did not unambiguously expound any doctrine of an immediate and complete establishment of the ideal Utopia through a single revolutionary act. At least as early as 1852, he began to make vague references to a "dictatorship of the proletariat" as a transitional stage between capitalism and ideal socialism or communism. As the professed followers and interpreters of the highest recognised authority in the Marxist parties have never reached any agreement as to the concrete meaning either of this transitional state or of the perfected stages which follow it, or the process of transformation, there would be little point in the present writer setting forth any extensive speculation on these matters in the present essay. In fact, he makes no pretence to extensive Marxian scholarship or to any of the qualifications required for achieving an authoritative position in this particular branch of exegetics. On the basis of an admittedly brief and unsympathetic study, it would appear that what is really meant by the revolution is simply the seizure of political power through a *coup d'état* on the part of the leadership of some working-class party. And the dictatorship of the proletariat would be the dictatorship—over the proletariat and not by it, as well as over anyone else whom they might choose to allow to continue to live—of these same people, and their successors in the positions of power, however the latter might come to power, as long as they called their system by that name and were able to "get away with it." The ultimate "classless" society has never been described in the least detail. It is simply the bright vision of an anarchist Utopia, a society in which there are no problems or issues, especially economic issues, on which people at all seriously disagree. This is the only meaning which the writer can attach to such slogan-phrases as, the withering away of the state, the administration of things without authoritative control over men, and production for use and not for profit. Historically most notable is the fact that in Russia the dictatorship has not only become progressively more dictatorial over everybody, and more ruthless, and less equalitarian, but has obviously tended more and more to put off to the Greek Kalends the removal of the dictatorship and establishment of the classless communistic society.[29]

In extenuation for Marxists—though hardly for Marxism—it would be possible to bring forward a *tu quoque.* (This famous "argument" has an embarrassing way of seeming to provide a sort of defence for the advocates of any position, however bad, morally or intellectually!) At least it should be understood that there is practically nothing in Marxism which

---

[29] The main texts from Marx and Engels (and Lenin) bearing on the topics mentioned in this paragraph are to be found in Lenin's *State and Revolution,* and *Critique of the Gotha Programme by Karl Marx* (ed. C. P. Dutt); N. Y., International Publishers, 1932 and 1938.

is not either copied from or equivalent to older contemporary doctrines and widely regarded statements of position.[30] The Marxist ethical doctrine—meaning (*a*) anti-ethics or ethical nihilism, absolute egoism or moral solipsism—is identical with the theoretical position of the early nineteenth century utilitarians, who were practically the classical economists under another name. For this purpose it does not matter whether we consider the utilitarian position to be that of psychological hedonism or give any other theory or interpretation of the actual content or "object" of individual desire. The other form of ethical nihilism which is represented in Marxism, namely "dialectical determinism," has already been shown to be practically identical with positivism, in the sense of culture-historical positivism, which was the "first philosophy" of nineteenth century liberalism, usually combined, to be sure, with egoistic voluntarism, in spite of the fact that the two are palpably contradictory.

Of course this line of argument "defends" Marxism at the cost of the complete sacrifice of his originality. If there is any main element in Marxism which is new, to any substantial degree, it is the class struggle theory. That also is well known to every student to have a long history prior to Marx, but the Marxian version of it may perhaps be defended as substantially

---

[30] In this essay, we have had no occasion to refer particularly to the "economic theory" of Marx, because it seems to have—or to be especially conspicuous for having—nothing at all to do with the problems of social action or change. Of course it does pretend to afford a "proof" that all income except wages (at some level) represents "exploitation" of the workers. But since Marxism itself makes no pretence of defining exploitation, and cannot possibly give it any meaning which is at all consistent with the other features of its general philosophical position in any of their possible interpretations, this may be passed over as a detail. In any event, practically all the elements of Marxist pseudo-economic analysis, and especially those which are most screamingly absurd, could have been copied out of Ricardo or other acknowledged authorities on the Ricardian economics who wrote before the publication of the "Critique of Political Economy" in 1859, in which Marx's system may be said to have taken on something like its final form.

different. In any case we are not concerned here with the details.

In a recent pamphlet entitled *Warning to Europe,* Thomas Mann refers to the bitter thought that to a degree the crisis in which European civilisation finds itself is the consequence of the fact that the nineteenth century was too generous to the masses. Perhaps it might be said in defence, or extenuation, that the liberal reformers of the nineteenth century did not allow for the fact that members of the cultured class itself would make careers for themselves by preaching to the masses the annihilation of the cultured classes and their culture, as the way to a just, humane and more highly cultured order of things; or perhaps they did not allow for the readiness which the masses would show in listening to such preaching and following it. Proclaiming to the unfortunate and under-privileged that workers have no stake in civilisation, "nothing to lose but their chains" and "a world to win" through "violent revolution sweeping away all former social order," was a political technique to which the naïve Victorians perhaps did not think responsible men would stoop, or thought that, if one occasionally might do so, no considerable number of sane men, though uneducated, would listen receptively.

III. *Christianity*

The bearing of its most generally accepted religion upon problems of social-economic reorganisation in a modern "Christian" nation is obviously a difficult subject to discuss objectively, or, especially, briefly. Not merely is it almost universally affected by emotional attitudes—"prejudices," religious or iconoclastic as the case may be—or by a more mundane prudential regard for religion as a supposedly vital element in social order. Even from a strictly scientific point of view, we confront virtually unanswerable questions as to the causal relations between religion and morals, or *mores*, or other controlling social forces in culture and conduct. The two difficulties overlap; for there is no doubt that the belief in religion as the foundation of morality, and of social order and peace, is itself held as a prejudice or a tradition far beyond any possibility of justifying it by social-psychological analysis. Many earnest scholars and thinkers who both profess to be Christians and are recognized as such have considered the question whether modern civilisation is Christian, or if so in what sense, and have admitted themselves puzzled as to the answer.

But it remains an important fact that a large majority of the people living under West-European civilisation call themselves Christian in some sense of the word, and at least profess to believe both that moral progress since ancient times has been chiefly due to the influence of Christianity and that the New Testament writings (and/or the teachings of "the Church" based thereon) afford an answer, in principle, and in large part, to all the moral and social problems faced by mankind. It is the purpose of this article to subject this idea, especially the second aspect of it, to a brief critical examination.

Our thesis will be two-fold. First, we point out that the teachings of Christianity give little or no direct guidance for the change and improvement of social organisation, and in fact give clear *prima facie* evidence of not having been formulated to that end. On this point there is relatively little disagreement, even on the part of Christian apologists. It is indeed common for the promoters of nearly any "reform" to lay claim to the support of these teachings. But this may be explained by a desire to capitalise upon the esteem in which they are held; and the wide divergence among movements for which such support is claimed is rather an argument against the view that the teachings really support any particular social change. Real differences of opinion—likely in fact to be more or less violent—arise in connection with the second part of the thesis; this is that even indirectly there is also little to be found in Christianity in the way of moral principles or ideals which can serve for the ethical guidance of deliberate political action. The question whether any proposed measure is in harmony with the "spirit" of Christianity commonly admits of no clear answer or at least none of a sort which will be accepted by Christians as a solution for practical political issues. Indeed, evil rather than good seems likely to result from any appeal to Christian religious or moral teaching in connection with problems of social action. Stated in positive form, our contention is that social problems require intellectual analysis in impersonal terms but that Christianity is exclusively an emotional and personal morality; and this, while unquestionably essential, does not go beyond providing or helping to provide the moral interest, motive or "drive" toward finding solutions for problems. This is not only a very different thing from furnishing the solutions or even indicating the direction in which they are to be sought, but the teaching that it does furnish solutions has results which are positively evil and decidedly serious.

As already noted, the first thesis is generally accepted, and it need not be discussed at any considerable length. There is relatively little in the Gospels or other New Testament "Books"[31] which seems to refer directly to politics or the

---

[31] Christianity is, of course, a "scriptural," or "book" religion. It goes without saying that some Churches or spokesmen for Churches claim divine authority to "interpret" the sacred writings, and that, in this case as in all similar cases, interpretation requires no long time to change fundamentally or even to reverse an original pronouncement. But since theologians rarely hold explicitly that the New Testament Scriptures have been superseded outright by the dicta of later authorities, we are justified, in a brief sketch, in limiting our attention to these. Moreover, consideration of the Catholic Fathers and Saints or of the great Protestant leaders would only enforce and intensify what is said as to the indifference or positive conservatism of the Christian doctrine on political and social questions.

general structure of social relations. But there is enough to make it clear that the intent of the teachings was to have these conditions accepted and recognised as "given" factors in the world in which individuals and groups have to live their moral and religious lives.[32] Besides the much quoted injunction to "render unto Caesar the things that are Caesar's," found in all three synoptic Gospels, there are even more pointed passages, such as the categorical command (in Matthew only) to obey the Scribes and Pharisees (though not to imitate their deeds!). The epistles repeatedly enjoin obedience and respect to political rulers, and command servants to be obedient and respectful to their recognised masters. This last injunction appears in at least a half-dozen places, in as many Books in the New Testament. The word for "servant" covers, if it does not specifically mean, slaves, and it is a familiar fact that the Church never condemned or officially opposed slavery.

---

[32] In this respect the political environment was placed on the same footing as the physical-natural; there is no more suggestion of transforming the former in the interest of greater fitness for a higher type of human life than there is of the desirability of transforming the latter through promoting science and technology, or medicine. And it is superfluous to note that the numbers and qualities of human beings were similarly taken for granted, as well as the general framework of non-political social institutions. Indeed, it is clear not only that to change these given conditions of social life is no part of the Christian's duty, but that he is enjoined against such activities and the critical attitudes which would prompt them. Such interests would distract attention from the real or "spiritual" values. Except for purely moral-spiritual attitudes and sentiments, "the world" expresses the will of God, or natural law; and if conditions are hard, this is presumably deserved punishment or at least useful discipline for the soul. As to political or economic revolution, the mention of such a thing is hardly less than sacrilegious.

The position of Christianity on all these matters is roughly that of the contemporary stoicism, particularly Roman stoicism, of the first Christian centuries. It is not asceticism, but rather supreme indifference, plus, perhaps, and to an uncertain degree, "faith" that "God will provide," that "all these things will be added unto" those who diligently seek "the kingdom of God and his righteousness." It should be noted that the whole spirit of the Sermon on the Mount is very different in the two versions we have, in Matthew and Luke. And in general, there is the greatest diversity in the spirit of the teachings as between the different Gospels and the other Books of the New Testament (chiefly Pauline writings); but such questions cannot be taken up here.

Slavery, and then serfdom (in numerous grades) gradually disappeared in Europe, for reasons various and obscure. Before the process was complete, the African slave trade, and the exploitation of slaves in European colonies (and in part in Europe itself) developed. The defenders of Negro (or Indian) slavery found no difficulty in justifying it from scripture.

We turn now to consider briefly the ''spirit'' of the Christian teachings and its possible implications in the way of providing ideals which might serve as a moral leaven and indirectly work for the transformation of social institutions and relations, and ultimately furnish guidance for conscious social action. Passing over the limitless problems of disagreement among the sources themselves or among authoritative interpretations, and looking only for agreement on some ultimate essence, we undoubtedly find the latter (in so far as it is to be found) in the acceptance by students and by popular opinion of the ''gospel of love'' (*caritas, agapé*). This is embodied especially in the parallel passages on the ''greatest commandment'' in Matthew and Mark, and in the answer in Luke to the question what one must do to inherit eternal life. ''Thou shalt love the Lord thy God . . . and thy neighbour as thyself.'' Loving one another is also the main theme of the teaching in the Gospel of John, and there is the famous paean to love occupying I Corinthians 13, and further extensive documentation is familiar. If Christianity does not mean this, there is nothing that it can be said to mean. It is no doubt justifiable to take as either interpretation of the Great Commandment or an equivalent exhortation the ''Golden Rule'' of the Sermon on the Mount, found in closely parallel wording in Matthew (7:12) and Luke (6:31).[33]

---

[33] The wording in the King James version of Matthew is: ''Therefore, all things whatsoever ye would that men should do to you, do ye even so to them: for this is the law and the prophets.'' It is worth noting that the final commenting clause which ends the verse is closely parallel to the verse in Matthew which follows

In connection with the two texts suggested, the question, what is the spirit of Christianity (leaving the application to social reform for later consideration) becomes, what is the meaning of "love," or what do men want "others" to do to them.[34] The "love" doctrine, in the abstract, is certainly an appealing idea. It seems natural to believe that if people "liked" each other better, or enough, a large part of the problems which occasion strife, hatred and suffering in the world would not arise, or would not be acute. Conflicts of material interest would perhaps not arise at all, or at least would not matter so much, and envy, contumely, etc., could hardly exist. But the least critical examination in the light of facts will show that this view cannot be maintained. Even between friends in the narrowest and most ideal sense, conflicts of interest would by no means disappear; and while different in form, these do not necessarily "hurt" less than in the case of strangers.

But the more serious question is, how far ideal friendship intrinsically admits of generalisation over, say, the population of a modern nation,—and, of course, it must ultimately be over the world, since, for a world religion, national boundaries have no moral significance. Considering love in terms of the Golden Rule, it is clear that men do not want from many "love" in the special sense of ideal friendship. If it is not a contradiction in thought that one might give the same quality

---

the Great Commandment: "On these two commandments hang all the law and the Prophets" (Matt. 22:40). We are naturally concerned here only with the second part of the Great Commandment, which indeed Matthew tells is "like unto" the first.

[34] In Luke, the question, who is my neighbour, is asked and is answered by the parable of the Good Samaritan. This may be briefly dismissed. In the context, the significance is uncertain, and any general implication is doubtful. Taken as an injunction to render humanitarian assistance to the helpless victim of a calamity, on the part of anyone in a special position to give aid, there is nothing distinctively Christian about it, to say nothing of any indication as to how laws ought to be made or society organised.

and intensity of affection to all human beings, good, bad, and indifferent, to the most callous criminal or the farthest Eskimo or Patagonian as well as to one's "nearest," and still "love" any of them—if this idea can be formed, it is surely neither attractive nor helpful as a moral ideal. It would seem that a "Christian" who tried to practice such love would have no friends—being in that respect like the famous economic man. He would not be human. Hospitality as well as friendship would lose its meaning, to say nothing of "love" in any accepted interpretation.

Such universal love quite clearly is not the meaning of *agapé* in the New Testament writings. It evidently refers to some intimate association, not to human relations in general. In most cases, perhaps especially in the Gospel of John and the writings of Paul, the reference is clearly to the "brethren" in the religious group. The material as a whole strongly suggests the fraternity idea, which is such a familiar and important phenomenon virtually throughout history and anthropology. Any attempt to universalise this attitude is obviously contradictory to its nature. We have to keep in mind that Christianity was originally a gospel or cult of "brotherhood," in much this sense, and only gradually became a world religion. Moreover, its message was first addressed to the lowly, the weak, and especially the politically helpless, living in a world where they had no outlook, no future, no "hope." And the sex limitation of the concept, though not as extreme as in many other cults, can by no means be overlooked. In Paul's churches the women were distinctly silent partners. Again, an essential feature of the teaching was the conviction of the imminence of the "second coming" (*parousia*) and the establishment of the kingdom of God (or the Millennium). And even without this feature, the interpretation of Christianity as escapism, emphasized by Nietsche, unquestionably has a large degree of validity for the early period.

That the existence of affection, in the sense of the most intimate and ideal friendship, still leaves problems to be solved, is obviously true where there is any disparity of circumstances between the parties. Perhaps it is true in rough proportion as such disparity exists. The romantic ideal of friendship seems to apply primarily to comrades in arms, or partners in adventure of some sort, hence almost exclusively to men, and men in the prime of life. Much of it is bound up with the concept of chivalry, which historically is neither Christian nor European. (But it was no more Mohammedan in the East than it was Christian in the West.) Chivalry is anything but democratic or equalitarian; it involves superiors as well as "brothers," and obedience as well as comradeship. The more prosaic but practically far more important modern conception of "live and let live," specifically as regards tolerance of differences, in religion and politics and in opinions and tastes, is for the most part the product of commercialism, of business, and not of religion. This is certainly more constructive with relation to social problems than the ideal romantic or mystical brotherhood, in the religious or any other form.

The general idea that love is no solvent of problems or reliable guide to conduct is perhaps best brought out by relations within the family. Certainly no amount (or kind) of "love" answers or removes the problems of conduct in the relations between husband and wife. And this is more poignantly true of the relation between parent and child—as the difference in "circumstances" is greater. Deficiency of love surely is not the most common or serious source of family problems. Loving one's children does not tell how to raise them properly. The problem is rather that of loving in the right way, or expressing affection in the "right," meaning "wise," conduct. Very commonly it appears that the presence of love complicates the concrete problems rather than contributes to their solution. Love may certainly clash with science in connections where the verdict rightly lies with the latter.

The family relation is also the best illustration of the undoubted fact that we are under a moral obligation to treat in different ways persons who stand in different social relations to ourselves. We seem even to be bound to feel differently toward them, though an obligation to have a feeling also appears dubious under critical scrutiny. Passing over the whole question of the ideal emotional relations between husband and wife, we consider only the relation of parents to children. The command to love one's neighbour as one's self may seem like a "hard saying"; but it is "nothing" in comparison with the obligation to love other people's children as one's own, as would be required by universal and undifferentiated or impartial love. This is not conceivably possible without destroying the private family and going over to some Platonic communism as the basis of social order—than which nothing could be more antagonistic to the accepted teachings of Christianity. And even if this were done, likes and dislikes within some kind of primary group appear to be quite inevitable. And in any case it is physically impossible to have organised social life with obligations diffused uniformly over the whole race without regard to nearness either of personal ties or functional connection.[35] It is clear that personal obligations depend on and presuppose some form of social organisation and that ideals of personal relations and feelings cannot be used as premises from which to deduce norms of

---

[35] The question of obligations bound up in the relation between employer and employee as individuals is of course particularly important in our world. One aspect of it will be mentioned later.

change in the social order. Conditions of effective action in daily life and of material progress conflict with any idealistic dream of universal freedom and brotherhood—even if that were really ideal in itself. Universal love or friendliness is only one aspect, one value, in the formulation of the ideal society toward which we must try to move.

We turn for a moment to consideration of the Golden Rule ideal of doing as one would be done by. In most real situations, intelligent people know that the ''other'' not merely does not want what we would want in his place, but also that what he wants is not what is good for him, or for the world, and that to give it is not the right course of action. And this is true even in the case of face-to-face personal relations, before we get to the problem-field of how to organise society. The solemn fact is that what people most commonly want for themselves is their ''own way,'' as such, or especially *power*. And the question whether anyone ought to have power must be answered with very little reference to his desire for it or his own (honest) opinion as to his fitness to have it. Indeed fitness seems to bear rather an inverse relation to desire—as Plato taught. The question of whom to love, and how, or specifically how to express love in action, under infinitely various conditions, is certainly not to be answered exclusively in terms of the desires or wishes of the ''beloved,'' though these are data which must be carefully considered. Love must be wise, and often stern. The New Testament scripture itself says that ''whom the Lord loveth he chasteneth'' (Hebrews 12:6).

What men want of others, as a matter of fact, is a question somewhat difficult to discuss without seeming to be cynical or satirical. What most of us actually want from most of the rest of mankind is pretty largely to ''mind their own business and let us alone.'' And on examination, this is found to be by no means a mere manifestation of original sin. It is in fact very largely the moral ideal! But it is not love. On the other hand, it is like love in that it answers no questions as to the social organisation; for the whole content of minding one's own business also depends on the social organisation, and takes this as given. Yet it helps towards a correct statement of the ethical problem. It helps to make it clear that the ethical side of the problem of social reform is not a matter of personal feelings, but that on the contrary, as we shall further emphasise later, positive effort is necessary to keep moral emotion out of the discussion or keep it from playing a direct role. The social problem is a matter, first, of attitude toward the law or the rules of the social game as they stand at any place and time, and second, of attitude toward higher general cultural and human values as a basis for changing such an existing setup. It is the second which is the social problem in the strict sense.

Before coming to that, however, a few remarks seem to be in place on the subject of personal feelings or emotions toward others. In the first place, the type of personal contacts and relationships which an individual naturally has, or as a matter of choice may have or avoid having, itself depends on the character of the social organisation. In any functioning social order, an individual undoubtedly has in some sense an "obligation" to be friendly toward others with whom he comes in any contact, and also to show special sympathy, compassion, and material helpfulness, on "appropriate" occasions. This is not the place for a detailed homily on that subject, but one or two further observations seem to be called for on the content which is to be read into the Golden Rule injunction to do as you would be done by, and presumably to feel correspondingly.

What we ought to wish for others is clearly what they ought to wish for themselves—with "due" regard for their actual opinions and feelings, of course. In this connection, the first general observation in order is in line with the principle of Puritanism—which is hardly suggested by the wording of the Gospels. Each person ought to want, and very largely does want, to stand on his own feet, to play his own hand, in accord with the rules of the game.[36] In this regard, it is clear that much of what is commonly said about "helpfulness" and "service," etc., is "mush," or worse. Not only does love, as concession to the other's wishes, often conflict with respect for the person himself, or with intelligent desire for his well-being; in addition, love of persons often conflicts with love of the higher values of civilised life. It is in this connection that the really subtle and difficult problems of moral conduct arise, and the great tragedies of life. Not all the persons whom society has to treat as enemies and whom individuals have to shun or oppose are morally odious.[37] It seems to be not merely

---

[36] In this respect, the "Pauline" letters are often much more to the point. See Gal. 6:4,5. "But let every man prove his own work and then he shall have rejoicing in himself alone, and not in another. For every man shall bear his own burden." It is true that verse 2 in the same chapter reads, "Bear ye one another's burdens, and so fulfil the law of Christ." There is, of course, no necessary contradiction. Even the Pauline writings which explicitly command men to work (even as a condition of eating! 2 Thess. 3:10) stop short of any clear injunction to economic efficiency or recognition of economic progress as a real good.

[37] "Love for the unborn" only partly removes such conflicts, even in an abstract logical sense; and it cannot be identified with personal love, and is more of a rationalisation than a reality. This meets the contention of those theologians who try to defend the Christian Ethic by *defining* love as identical with morality. It is fantastic to extend the concept to cover the moral urge or emotion as such; but even if that be done the whole intellectual problem of conduct is still left out of account. The facts may be brought out by asking any chance group of Christians— say ministers—what should be done in regard to any public question. There will typically be no more agreement than in any other group from the same social and culture strata, or if there is it can usually be accounted for in terms of specific idols of the tribe; and where economic analysis is involved the preachers and reformers or religious cast can be counted upon to advocate easy and pleasant-looking or romantically appealing solutions for hard problems. In practice, they are particularly given to advocating the programme of taking away (by force) from those who have and giving it to those who have not; and the pleasantness of this line of action is not at all necessarily a matter of pure love for the beneficiaries.

impossible, but actually undesirable and unthinkable, that living should not to a large extent take the form of contest relations and be impelled by the competitive or emulative interest. This is overwhelmingly the nature of play, recreation or "free" activity and it is clearly a large factor in the ideal social order to convert work into play, or give to it the psychology of play as far as possible. This side of life seems not to be recognised in the New Testament at all, even in the Pauline and other letters, which are much more realistic and disposed to emphasise purposive action than are the reported teachings of Jesus. It is hard to think of sport or sportsmanship in connection with New Testament personalities or teachings. But sportsmanship seems to be the best that modern civilisation has produced as a practical and effective moral ideal or sentiment. In a contest, what each one is trying to do and wanting to do is to win. (This *means* to win in accord with the rules, though many are often willing to win by breaking them, by "cheating"!) Moral goodness toward an opponent in a game certainly does not mean "letting" him win, either openly or secretly (with possible exceptions of course).

Moreover, it seems that helpfulness, in "material" or economic activities should ideally be mutual, as far as possible. Now mutual helpfulness is precisely the ideal result of economic organisation on the basis of free exchange. Yet the formal, and enforced, mutuality of the market is only a short first step toward the ideal society and, as must be emphasised on every occasion, it leads to ideal results only under ideal conditions, i.e., under the condition that the whole framework of economic relations is ideal, as well as the individuals who enter into these relations.

Viewed in the large and in ethical terms, what each and all should primarily help each other to do is to realise sound ideals of personality, which inseparably involves realisation of ideal social relations and institutions. But this again can only be done in the main by helping them to help themselves, together with striving cooperatively to provide the most favourable possible conditions of self-realisation. In this connection, as already suggested, the most difficult of all the concrete problems is undoubtedly that of the "right" kind and degree of impartiality, and of partiality, to those who stand to "me" in any special relationship. It is evident that love of one's friends, and especially one's own children, is not unselfish and that the conceptions of selfishness and altruism admit of no simple definition. Even devotion to a cause, even a good cause, is often more or less selfish.[38]

A general view of the whole problem situation in society may be secured by adopting the standpoint of our earlier observation that in the context of reality and of relevance to reality, all discussion of moral values and conduct in the larger social relations must take place in two main stages. The first step in moral behaviour in organised society is to obey and to support the existing legal order. The first and presumptive definition of what is right in any doubtful case is the answer to the question What is the Law? And the law

---

[38] When both are reduced to intelligible meaning, the principle of the Golden Rule and the Great Commandment is substantially identical with that of utilitarianism. In the latter the only doctrine which was either intelligible or effective was that "each should count for one and none for more than one." (As we have already shown—in our discussion of idealism—the pleasure principle is either nonsensical or anti-ethical, and the same applies to the notion of "the greatest good of the greatest number.") When we ask in what *respect* each is to count for one or what is the content of the good, Bentham—especially in his economic writings— interprets pleasure to mean freedom, and this is also the best concrete interpretation of doing as one would be done by. Yet, interpreted in an absolute sense, it yields the social philosophy of Herbert Spencer! The limitations of this have been pointed out in our first essay (*Economica*, February, 1939) on Liberalism. Freedom is relative to actual wishes, which may be wrong, and also to actual endowment with power in every form, which may be inequitable, or wrong in other ways. Extreme individualism has no place at all for the "helpless" except through their moral or romantic appeal to the strong as individuals.

must be interpreted to include all generally accepted customs or standards which create "legitimate expectations" on the part of others.[39]

But the duty of conformity with law is only a presumption, and is valid only within limits. Often there is no law which clearly applies, or there is a serious question as to how far the law itself is "right." In so far as the individual feels compelled to pronounce that the law does not apply, or is wrong, the question of what is right behaviour becomes exceedingly complex and difficult. It is not simply a question of what the law ought to be. It may be one's duty to disregard and break the law, because the particular case is clearly exceptional for some reason, a situation which law could not practically be made to cover. (This, of course does not militate against the theoretical validity of Kant's principle of generality as the criterion of rightness.) To the question how far one should give the law the benefit of the doubt, because of modesty of belief or of the value of maintaining the legal order inviolate, there is no general answer. And whether the decision is to obey the law or to break it, one confronts the separate question whether to try to get the law changed. In general, the social problem is that of changing the law, including both tradition and the public and constitutional law, which is the legal machinery for changing the law itself.

Thus our discussion brings us to the social problem as such,

---

[39] This seems to be the practical lesson to be derived from Rev. Reinhold Niebuhr's strenuous preaching. See especially *Moral Man and Immoral Society* (Scribner's, New York, 1932). For example there may be no moral gain from the liberation of slaves by an individual master in a slave-holding society. The act might both make worse the condition of the individual slaves affected and strengthen the hold of the institution. It might well be more intelligent and more ethical to treat one's own slaves as humanely as possible and to work for gradual rather than sudden improvement in the status of slaves as a class.—But this is not often the way moral sentiments work in history! They tend rather to generate strife and war, as happened in America over the slavery issue—in contrast with Europe, however, where slavery was not tied up with conspicuous racial differences.

i.e., the problem of law making, which always means law changing, and in general means *legally* changing an existing law.[40] Society itself is properly defined as the legal order under which any group of people live. Any society is bounded by the area (along various "dimensions" of size and of kind and degree of sociality) within which people are actually subject to the same law. The area is not necessarily spatial or geographic, though this is now typically true for law in the formal or political sense. But any accepted rules of relationship among persons define a society as to extent, and as to the sense and the degree in which it is a society. Social problems, then, root in the brute fact that all organised relationships, or relationships of any degree of permanence whatever, imply a common recognition of rules, or an accepted pattern of action. It is an axiom of sociology that *human* beings, especially beings capable of discussion, could not possibly come into existence or continue to exist apart from a culture, or set of institutions.[41]

---

[40] Revolution, and even violent revolution, is not absolutely excluded. But there is an "almost" overwhelming presumption against it. (Cf. above on the consequences of the American in contrast with the European process of abolishing slavery.) And it is to be noted that "real" revolution, a profound and sudden change in the legal system of a country, is a thing which practically does not and cannot occur.

[41] Historically, beyond doubt, societies, which is to say groups of men living under some common institutional or legal order, "grew"; they were not "made." No doubt there was a gradual transition from association by animal instinct, physically inherited, to culture, transmitted by unconscious imitation ("ritual" in the broad sense) and then to conscious ordering of relations through law-making. But in the long stages of unconscious evolution there were no social problems in our sense. Whether the institutional pattern under which a group lived before becoming critically conscious of its institutions, as a system of constraint, should be called legal or not, is purely a matter of convenience in verbal usage. Our point is simply that social problems come into existence when this critical consciousness develops to a certain point. And their content is institutional or legal change, advocated as desirable (not merely desired) and opposed as undesirable, in more or less rational discussion—or at least advocated as desirable by some part of the group, against resistance, perhaps through mere unthinking inertia, on the part of the rest of its membership.

The point here, and the main point of this discussion of Christianity as a whole, is the negative one, that the Christian teaching not only has nothing to say about this whole problem-field of change in social organisation, i.e., about law-making and constitution-making, which involve institutional change, but that it positively diverts attention both from a correct view of the problem and from the fundamental facts of social life out of which the problem arises.[42] The spirit of New Testament Christianity (passing over the politico-legal activities of organised churches in later times—for which, incidentally, there is no scriptural foundation whatever) points definitely away from all matters of positive social action, whether thought of as compulsion exercised upon individuals, or merely as the rational adaptation of means to ends. As already noted, it has little if any bearing on the rational adaptive side of even the purely individual life.

Since all organisation involves more or less compulsion, Christianity may be said to point toward an ideal world in which all organised activity would be absent, a society of antinomian anarchism. Even the type of constraint involved in public esteem and disesteem in relation to "good manners," can hardly be admitted into the picture. And it is surely beyond argument that such a social situation implies the

---

[42] Categorical negations are not only undemonstrable in the nature of the case, in the field of social phenomena, but they are rarely if ever entirely valid. In this case, one certainly could not say that the teachings of Christianity have had absolutely no influence on the development of law in "Christian" countries. No doubt, moral judgments and principles which the law-makers and judges have supposed to be Christian teaching, or implications of Christian teaching, have played an appreciable role in guiding the activities of legislators and of judges in courts of record. Whether the sources were really and distinctly Christian, or are to be found in stoicism and natural-law philosophy, would be another question, and the main historical problem. It would be extremely valuable to have a careful study of the problem by competent theological and legal historians, particularly from the standpoint of the influence, first of the Roman Catholic canon law, and later of the Chancery and Equity courts, in the formation of our Anglo-American jurisprudence.

complete absence of even individual economic problems and activities, to say nothing of organised economic life.[43] Possibly it may be useful, in some very attenuated sense, to have such an ideal held up before the world for contemplation, with no indication of the character of organised action required to move toward the ideal, and with the apparent implication that it can be realised merely by admiring it or by acting as if it already existed. This seems very doubtful to the present writer, but the question may be arguable. Such an ideal, we must observe, would involve not merely material conditions of life categorically different from any that are possible for any biological species living on this earth, but also a race of "men"—if they should be called men rather than gods—having uniformly very different characteristics from any known or any possible human beings, the differences reaching far down into their biological endowment. The kind of "goodness" that would be involved is certainly not "good" for actual human beings living either in the actual world, or in the world as it can be imagined to become, as the result of any reasonably possible process of transformation, however long, by human agency. The social value of the role of parasitic saintliness in the real world is a question too long to argue, but the amount of it which can be defended as valuable, or which the world can afford, is certainly limited, and its value is highly indirect. It would seem that the situation is picturable in imagination only for disembodied spirits very different even from the "gods" of which we have anything

---

[43] On the other hand, it would be wrong to assume that if all economic problems (in the ordinary meaning) ceased from troubling, a "Christian" social order would become easy. A little reflection will show that any group activity,—in play or the pursuit of culture, as well as in "work" (even in psalm-singing!) involves power relations and differences in status. The "politics" of organisations in these other fields, and specifically in churches, do not actually differ significantly from the politics which relate to economic relations and problems—or they seem to be worse as often as better.

like a concrete picture in any extant religion or theodicy. Certainly the deities of either the Greek or the Teutonic mythology would not fit into the picture.

The intellectual problem underlying any project of social reform or transformation, i.e., the "scientific" sociological problem, is in the first place the relation between good men and good institutions or laws. Within some limits, undoubtedly, the one implies the other, and either may result from the other; better men will make better institutions, and better institutions will make better men. That is, the problem of action centres in the order of priority, or of emphasis on the two lines of action, preaching or educating, and legislating. Perhaps the first phase of the question to be distinguished, approaching it from the standpoint of Christianity itself, is that of how far it is possible to perfect human nature simply by preaching good will, by "converting" individuals.

Logically prior, however, to the problem of action in the concrete sense, is always the problem of deciding upon the results to be achieved by action. This is the problem of formulating ideals, the particular problem which these essays are written to emphasise as an intellectual problem. It is not even seriously discussed in most of the talk and writing about social reform, and it is no wonder that utter confusion reigns with respect to it. Recognition of the problem of ideals as logically prior to the problem of action does not in the least imply that it is necessary to have a detailed picture of the ideal society, the ultimate goal of action, agreed upon and blue-printed in advance. On the contrary; in the writer's view, all activity is more or less explorative. Perhaps no proposition about purposive behaviour needs more emphasis than the fact that goals of action are probably never completely foreseen when the action is begun or decided upon. A certain element of uncertainty as to the result of action, a certain amount of curiosity as to what the result is to be, seems to be a necessary factor in motivation. The end is always more or less redefined in the course of the action itself, and an interest in this process of redefinition is inherent in the interest in action. The end or ideal which functions in advance of action is rather a sense of direction than an end in the concrete sense. Moreover, there seem to be no ends which are really final (no *"summum bonum"* in the classical sense) or which are not more or less consciously recognised in advance as means to further ends, and as becoming means to the extent that they are realised.

But on the other hand, ends, even in the proper limited sense of a direction of change, are not simply fabricated by creative thought. They arise out of the criticism of what is, and rational reflection on the possibilities of improvement. This means that the question of ideals takes the form of "sound" criticism of the existing situation, and hence that a logically still prior requisite is knowledge, including understanding, of what the existing situation is. This is especially important not merely because all activities looking to change begin "here and now," but because they must operate entirely on the basis of means (in the most general sense) which themselves exist as a part of the existing situation. All these knowledge data are rather a part of the process of formulating ideals than temporally prior or prerequisite.

In Western culture in our own day, the criticism of what is and the proposals for change of a reconstructive sort, have come to centre very largely on the economic organisation of society. From the standpoint of the intelligent student of the problem of reform, this fact is itself one of the essential features of the existing situation. And it becomes in a sense the "very first" step to inquire into the validity of this belief. This is particularly important because relatively little objective examination is necessary to show that the belief that life is to be transformed for the better by changing the economic system, has only a very limited amount of truth.

This fallacy is a feature in the confusion of prevalent "common sense" assumptions about the social problem. It is at least closely related to the doctrine of the "economic interpretation," the falsity of which has received brief consideration previously.[44] It could be argued along several lines that the Christian teaching is more or less responsible for the spread of this idea, especially in the sense that it is undoubtedly in part a reaction from the indefensible notion that economic facts and interests are of no real or moral importance.

In the present connection we can only sum up the situation very briefly by pointing out that a rational attack upon the problem of social change is to be envisaged under three main heads or topics which in a sense are largely steps to be taken in the order indicated, but in a deeper sense are aspects of one process. The first topic, or step, must be the understanding of the "existing" economic situation, especially the mechanics of organisation of the enterprise economy (usually miscalled "capitalism"). As pointed out in our first article, on Liberalism, this inquiry itself again necessarily falls into two steps or stages, the understanding respectively of the general theory of such an economy, and of the divergences between the concrete reality and the theoretical picture, with the reasons for these divergences. As was also previously emphasised, this analytical order of attack is practically necessary because the first question of policy looking toward change is whether the undesirable features of reality are inherent in the general principles of the system or are primarily due to the divergences, and consequently whether the main principle of policy must be to make the system "work" more in accord with the analytical theory, or to replace this general type of organisation machinery with another type embodying different principles.

The second "stage" in the analysis is the formulation of

---

[44] See "The Ethics of Liberalism," *Economica*, February, 1939.

ideals, and in the first instance ideals of economic relations, and choice of directions of change, though this process cannot be carried very far ahead of the exploration of possibilities. The real difficulty is that the notion of possibility cannot be taken relevantly, if at all, in a strict yes-or-no sense. It is rather a matter of costs, and costs again are measured by values, or ideals. Thus we are plunged at once into the third aspect of the problem, or stage in the analysis, the problem of the means or processes of social change, meaning conscious (social) self-change or self-determination. Change must obviously be taken in a transitive and active sense, or the discussion has no meaning at all. There is literally no "sense" in arguing purely in terms of causal analysis, either that changes in one phase of culture are treated as independent variables and regarded as "causing" changes in other phases, or more generally that an antecedent state or condition of culture as a whole causes or determines its subsequent state or character as a whole, from moment to moment.[45] We have to assume that there is real action, initiative, on the part of "individual minds." Moreover, all action has to be pitted against a resistance of some sort to be thinkable. As already suggested, a social problem originates either in a difference of opinion—not merely of interest—between different members, or groups of members of the society itself (either as to the end of the change or as to some detail in the process) or at least in an opinion on the part of some member or members that change is desirable (not a mere desire for change); and the effort to effect the change must be resisted at least by "inertia."

If we consider the economic aspect of society as the main

---

[45] It is doubly nonsensical, proceeding from the standpoint of economic problems, however defined, to adopt the economic interpretation of history, i.e., to take the economic phase of social life (defined in the same way) as the independent variable which causes or determines everything else.

field in which problems arise and change is called for, we face two main questions. The first has to do with the way in which the individuals who advocate change can act upon economic relationships. This suggests the alternatives already mentioned, that they may act either directly as individuals—in their own economic conduct, and by influencing the economic conduct of other individuals, through moral and intellectual persuasion—or they may act through the politico-legal organisation of society, by changing the laws and/or the methods of enforcement. For the most part it is, of course, the latter method which is chiefly in point (whatever ought ideally to be the case). The immediate question then is one of the efficacy of law in changing men's economic behaviour, either by its very existence or through the machinery and process of enforcement. This refers chiefly to the "criminological" machinery of punishment, though the use of rewards may also be an important possibility.[46]

More generally, the problem of culture mechanics is that of the possibility of acting—meaning the ability of the proponents of action to act—either by preaching or by legislation, upon the economic side of life without at the same time affecting other phases or elements in the social and cultural life. More accurately, it is a question of social action that will effect a *net* improvement, an excess of good over evil in the economic sphere considered by itself, and either without affecting other social-cultural values, or without producing in other spheres a net damage which equals or exceeds the gain in that of economics. Even a summary outline of the main items of probable gain and loss through

---

[46] The working of reward and punishment is formally equivalent to exchange and a notion of equality or equity obtains in both. But we do not think of the imposition of a specified fine for being drunk and disorderly as an offer to sell the privilege for that amount! The psychology of exchange is very different from that of punishment even when both are in the hands of the state.

various possible measures of social action, in the economic sphere itself and in other spheres, would far exceed our space limits here. It should hardly need to be emphasised that as Bentham perpetually urged, there is a heavy *onus probandi* against legislative action, which is an intrinsic evil, because it involves compulsion, and also entails moral as well as material costs and uncertainties in enforcement. This is particularly true because the compulsion must always be administered by human beings politically selected and oper- ating in a political setting, and—perhaps practically most important of all—because it tends in numerous ways to strain the resources of government, which are limited, particularly those of free government, and need to be conserved for indubitably necessary and possible tasks.

Perhaps the feature of the situation which most calls for emphasis, because it is certain to be inadequately considered, is the general fact that any economic legislation—even if it were wise from its own point of view, which experience gives little ground to hope for!—inevitably has widely ramifying and serious effects on other phases of culture and social relations. This is particularly vital in connection with the family as an institution. On one hand, it is in the family system that the problems very largely arise, because, as merits constant reiteration, it is through the family that the "indi- vidual" comes into being and acquires most of his economic endowments and characteristics—because, in short, an indi- vidualistic system is necessarily very largely familistic and not individualistic in a literal sense. But at the same time, it is also through the family that the individual becomes what he is in all other respects and that culture in general is perpetuated. The economic individual is not really an indi- vidual, for the purpose of any social action, not even the administration of the crudest and most essential features of the criminal law. Any possible action by political society upon its members as economic units involves some transfer of functions and of responsibility from the family to the state and tends to aggrandise the latter at the expense of the former, and morally to weaken both. As already suggested, what we carelessly call egoism is in reality as much family egoism as it is individual; the basic conflicts of interest lie as much between families as between individual persons.

One of the most appealing economic reforms is the reduction of the ''artificial'' advantage or disadvantage in the competitive struggle which individuals receive through the ''accident'' of birth. (And, we should add, through either the ''accident'' of marriage, or the influence upon marriage of economic status and prospects of prospective or possible partners in that relation.) Inherited handicaps can be dealt with to some extent by such measures as inheritance taxation on one hand and by the provisions at ''social'' expense of educational opportunity—and conceivably also other elements of a fair start in life—on the other. But all such measures are subject to limits and to grave dangers if carried to extremes, unless we are prepared to contemplate the abolition of the private family altogether and the establishment of some kind of Platonic or ultra-Platonic communism. (This idea is no less un-Christian because Plato is supposed to have intended his proposal of property and family communism only for the governing classes of a society stratified almost to the ideal of caste.)

The teachings of Christianity, as a basis for the discussion of ideals for the guidance of economic reform, present in the first place the same general and essential weakness or defect that was emphasised in the discussion of liberalism. They look at morality as a matter of ideal relations between individuals who are taken as given. But from the standpoint of any discussion of organisation, individuals are not given, and in fact are not really individuals at all. For the purposes of any formal or legal action directed toward rational change (in contrast with preaching), society is a thing of institutions far more than of men. And at the head of the list of institutions, transcending in importance all others combined, is the institution of the private family—or whatever institutions might take the place of the private family in any other type of social order.

It is to be kept in mind, too, that there are fairly narrow limits to the theoretical possibilities of replacing the family by any large-scale political unit. There seems to be no way of preventing any administrative group from being more or less of a "clique," and indeed, the matter of personal harmony in the staff is one of the primary features of effective administration or management in any enterprise. How far it is conceivable for the teaching of Christianity, and/or any possible educational system (whether itself based on the spirit of Christianity or on compulsory discipline, as the Marxists seem to contemplate) to reduce the importance of this factor, is an open question, as indeed is that of how far it is abstractly desirable to do so.

But the heart of the difficulty of Christianity as an approach is not merely in the fact that it ignores the concrete problems of the moral-legal order in any possible world of social relations conceivably realisable by any biological species living on the earth. It lies not even in the fact that the Christian type of moralistic teaching tends to distract attention from the real problem by clearly implying or actually saying that "love" would solve all these problems, or what is still worse, that it is practically possible to solve them by preaching love. The concrete effects of envisaging the problem in terms of any sort of individual rights or individual obligations to any other individuals, are positively evil in a more concrete sense. It implies—and as far as it is effective at all, tends to bring about—a social order which is definitely contrary to fundamental moral ideals, and not merely to our ideals but to the general character of moral ideals which is necessarily implied in the fact that they are discussed at all. The direct effects of "preaching" about economic relations and obligations are in general bad; and the kind of legislation which results from the clamour of idealistic preachers—and from the public attitude which such preaching at once expresses and tends to generate or aggravate—is especially bad. All this is the natural consequence of exhortation without knowledge and under- standing—of well-meaning people attempting to meddle with the workings of extremely complicated and sensitive machinery which they do not understand.

The paradoxical results in real life can be sufficiently indicated by a little consideration of the worst concrete cases, namely, religious-moralistic pronouncements about the obli- gations of employers to employees, particularly in the matter of wage-rates. An adequate example is at hand in the doctrines of the papal encyclical *Quadragesimo Anno* of Pius XI in 1931. And the Report on Christianity and the Economic Order of the Oxford Conference of World Protestantism (non-Roman Catholic Christianity) of 1936, is similar; it is better, or not so bad, in that there is less of it in content and less self- confidence and authoritative dogmatism in the expression. The least familiarity with the "laws" of economics—a much abused term which properly means only the general *facts*— will show that any general pressure on the employers to pay wages appreciably above the market value of the service rendered is in the first place certain to be injurious to the interests of wage-workers—but more especially to those wage- workers who are already in the weakest position. The argument in proof cannot be elaborated here.[47]

---

[47] The writer happened to be invited to speak to a conference of liberal ministers in the early days of the "New Deal," and specifically of the N.R.A. One of the items on the programme of the meeting was an almost hysterical protest by a

But even this is by no means the end of the evil that naturally follows from such ignorant if well-intentioned tinkering with the machinery of economic organisation. A very little, and very elementary, analysis would again show that the general implication and natural result of making the payment of wages in excess of the value of the service a moral or legal obligation of the individual employer is in the first place to establish a feudal or quasi-feudal relationship between employer and employee generally. But under modern conditions of technology and other factors involving (ultimately worldwide) economic relationships in production, exchange, and distribution, such a feudalism is itself not generally or permanently possible. The natural political consequence of such interference must be either to segregate whatever elements in the population are not economically worth the wage set, and make them permanently wards of society, or else to cause the reorganisation of society itself under some kind of all-inclusive bureaucratic despotism. In the long run, the latter is much the more probable, or some combination of the two, involving much of the evil of both.

In conclusion: We come back to our initial contention that Christianity affords no concrete guidance for social action,

---

Negro minister on the way in which the wicked employers were tending to replace Negro workers with white as a consequence, or by them pretended consequence, of the legal fixation of minimum wages. It was, of course, entirely useless for an economist to point out to the assembled highly intelligent and liberal brethren that such results are in fact the inevitable consequence of such action, that in fact, given the action, replacement of inferior by superior employees is actually desirable; for if there is to be unemployment, it is better to have it concentrated on the least efficient. This is in the interest both of increased production and of reducing both the public burden and the amount of avoidable suffering and discomfort in connection with relief. All that they could see or imagine was that here were some unexpected detailed effects of the nature of evasion, to be met by further restrictions and more punitive measures of enforcement. They could not be envisaged as indicating anything wrong with the general policy.

beyond an urge to "do good and avoid evil"; and this is not Christian in distinction from any other religion, or from secular morality. The problem is, what is good, and what is evil, in political activity. In the first centuries of its history, the appeal of Christianity was to the lowly strata of society, not to persons holding any sort of power. The lowly were clearly exhorted to accept the existing structure of status and power relations, to obey constituted authorities, and not to try to "do anything about it." When persons in positions of power, and particularly rulers of states, came to be Christianised, they found little if anything in Christian teaching to guide them in the use of power. There was no doubt an implication that they should be gentle and humane in the performance of their "duties"; but as to the content of these duties, it could only be inferred that they consisted in enforcing the laws, and perhaps gradually "humanising" them—whatever that might mean. Surely it was not their function to introduce any important changes into the political or social constitution.

By that time, however, the Christian movement itself had become highly organised along authoritarian lines, and the official interpreters of Christian doctrine regarded it as the first and main duty of the political authorities to support, and defer to, the authority and power of "the Church," i.e., of these officials themselves. And in performing this duty, political functionaries were by no means supposed to be either gentle or humane. At least, it was made very clear that heretics and blasphemers who did not promptly yield to admonition faced the most cruel punishments that could be devised, culminating in death by torture. In fact, the Church more and more demanded political power in its own right, to be exercised by its own administrative and judicial appointees.

In consequence, down to the time when the power and unity of the Western Church were broken by forces partly religious but largely secular, the meaning of Christianity for

political action would be read less out of any moral pronouncements than out of the acts of the Church itself, in its
courts low and high, and in its political and even military
struggle for power. The general verdict of history is that,
where its own power was not at issue, the policy of the
Church as a political system was simply utilitarian, in accord
with highly conservative standards. It may be argued that—
again, where its own power was not in question—it was a
humanising force, in some degree. But it certainly cannot be
shown that the humanising of political power and of ordinary
morals and manners went on more rapidly than would have
happened under different religious conditions. It is not implied
that the contrary can be shown; we do not know.

If we turn to the "scriptures," the one recognised source
of Christian teaching now generally recognised as authoritative, it seems impossible to read into the text any exhortation
to, or ideal of, rational efficiency, or progress, in any form.
On the contrary, we find quite definite statements that such
things do not matter. But we know, if we know anything,
that if they do not matter, civilised or human life does not.
For civilised life under mundane conditions simply cannot be
pictured without quite extensive power relations between
human beings, in addition to power over nature. A defensible
ethic doubtless condemns overemphasis on power; but it must
include both the right use of power and the quest of power—
by right methods—for right uses. The concrete relation
between amount and kind of power in both these senses and
its various uses, and the quality of culture and of human life,
measured in moral terms, is indeed a problem; but it is merely
one of the most important phases of the general problem of
social action on which the teachings of Christianity shed no
light, or even tend to be definitely misleading. Indeed, with
the possible exception of some aspects of face-to-face personal
relations, scriptural Christianity gives no more guidance for

individual action in fields where power plays a minimum role than it does for individual or social policy in relation to power itself. It makes no place for either the intellectual or the æsthetic side of life, or for either the appreciative or the creative aspect of either of these realms of value. By implication it condemns all these interests. The Church has indeed found a place for intellectual speculation and for art,—but only in the service of the religious life and of the Church itself, as an organisation, a power system.

Moreover, the practical result of the teaching, in connection with the material and cultural progress which modern history has exhibited, is paradoxical, morally disconcerting, and largely evil. In large part, religion seems merely to sublimate any moral urge which people have, giving it expression and release in more or less æsthetic ritual, and leaving them entirely free, except for an hour or so in the week, to pursue worldly objectives by worldly methods. And when the urge to action persists, and the "Gospel of love" ceases to mean merely a mystical, almost cabalistic, emotion among the lowly, a consolation for the lack of more substantial life advantages, a mental-spiritual escape from its evils and deprivations—and perhaps a formula for salvation in a future world—and when it comes to mean active love for the lowly and down-trodden on the part of more fortunately situated persons, it quite naturally tends to become both a gospel of hate toward the "privileged classes," and a conspiracy to seize and use powers to effect a social revolution in which these classes will be "liquidated." Thus, in good Hegelian style, extremes meet and antitheses blend. Not only does love turn into hate as the effective social attitude, and submissive renunciation of power into resort to violence, but the gospel of peace turns into a call to arms for the proverbially most brutal sort of war, civil war, class war. The tendency of Christianity to join hands with revolutionary Marxism is one of the conspicuous trends of the times, in countries where all social movements and public discussion of social problems have not been suppressed by a dictatorship, either of the (self-appointed spokesmen for the) exploited proletariat, or of the (self-appointed leaders of the) advocates of preserving civilisation—as the case may be. And in any event, as we have emphasised, the approach to problems of economic inequality and unfreedom (or what appears to be such) in terms of "moralistic" judgments of personal rights and duties, in the absence of careful economic and politico-legal analysis, is virtually certain to have consequences utterly different from the intentions of the reformers, and predominantly evil.

But it is usually easy for the Christian apologist to escape from any unpleasant implications, by alleging wrong interpretation of the meaning of the doctrine. It is perhaps better to leave this problem-field with the observation made at the outset that the actual role of religious professions and beliefs, to say nothing of religious "practices," in the working lives of men is one of the profound mysteries of history and of social life. Indeed, mystery—or plain ignorance—seems to be the last word in the discussion of all the main elements in the political-economic problem. We do not know, either what are right ideals, or how the social-economic process works and what it can be expected to bring forth in the absence of interference, or how to interfere "intelligently" with its "natural" operation and development. At least there is little evidence of a consensus of the competent or unanimity in the mass on any of these main elements of the problem of reform. Only on that part of the second and third problems which is the subject matter of price-theory economics can it be said that any great headway toward satisfactory treatment has been made, and that is but a limited aspect of the total problem of action. Without an adequate ethics and sociology in the broad sense, economics has little to say about policy.

V

Socialism: The Nature of the Problem

I

*T*he discussion of socialism affords an opportunity to kill two birds, or indeed several, with one stone. Apart from the importance of the subject in itself, socialism and prevalent thinking about it present an especially interesting case study in the nature of social problems and social thinking, and hence in the methodology of a social science relevant to social action. The writer, at least, is more interested in the character of economic and political thinking as illustrated by the discussion of socialism than in socialistic schemes or even the general concept; for the nature of most of the thinking about the problem seems to be the most important datum in connection with the problem itself. The present sketch, written from the standpoint of economic theory, will attempt no more than a partial analytical indication of the character of the problems and the methods of attack. Its content will lie entirely within the field of the obvious, not to say the trite.

We start from the vague conception of socialism as a

Reprinted by permission from *Ethics,* vol. 50 (1940), pp. 253–289.

proposal to replace the organization of economic life through markets or to replace the enterprise economy (which socialists and others miscall "capitalism")[1] with a political system for the organization and control of economic life. The revolution and transition would also be worked out through political process. Intelligent discussion of the problems involved obviously calls for clarity of conception as to the character and mode of operation of the enterprise economy itself and also as to the nature of political phenomena and processes. The question or problem of socialism as a policy is one of comparison between two social-economic patterns, plus the question of the feasibility, and costs, of the change from one to the other—if the comparison results in a judgment in favor of socialism. Thus any solution of the problem involves use of facts and principles from the two social sciences of economics and politics—and beyond these of the more fundamental disciplines of history, sociology, etc., and also, in particular, of ethics, from which all final criteria of judgment are to be derived.

At the outset we encounter an interesting contrast between economic and political thought. Economic thought runs almost entirely in terms of the obvious and commonplace, while political thought is almost as exclusively inchoate, indefinite, and inconclusive, and in consequence political opinion is a matter of wish-thinking and romanticism in overwhelming variety. The most interesting feature of economic theory is that its larger and more important questions are generally self-answering when explicitly and correctly stated—in so far as they can be answered at all. Indeed, the problem of social

---

[1] The word was popularized, if not invented, by Marx, to characterize modern free enterprise economy, on the ground that the capitalists as a social class are in power and in a position to exploit the workers in a sense formally but not fundamentally different from that which fitted the hereditary aristocracies of slaveowners and feudal lords of earlier economic civilizations.

action, from the economic standpoint, is chiefly that of getting people—those in control of social policy, which in a democracy ultimately means the electorate—to act in accord with principles which when stated in simple and set terms are trite even to the man in the street.

A hoary illustration of this methodological dictum is the problem of international trade. Everyone understands—or at least admits without question—the economic advantage of geographical division of labor. And no one contends that the economic gain is reduced, or the situation affected in any way, by the existence of boundaries between political divisions. (We abstract here from political interests based on political antagonism, and also from the possible effects of war, even on a country not a party to it; for the most part, these qualifications are not in question in the actual political discussion.) Yet the overwhelming mass of civilized and educated mankind today insist on social-political action which is rational only in terms of the precise antitheses of these truisms. And the same general situation confronts us in connection with problems of internal economy, where emotions such as patriotism and antipathy to foreigners cannot be called upon to explain the irrationality. No one who is not definitely *non compos mentis* thinks that the economic prosperity of a country is increased by reducing the production of goods and services. Yet leading features of the policy of the most advanced nations today aim precisely at that result, under the leadership of their most eminent statesmen and with the overwhelming approval of the people at large and the enthusiastic co-operation of practically every important economic group. That raising the price of a commodity will decrease its sale is one of the least disputed laws of economics; but to apply it to the labor market is likely to brand one as an enemy of the workingman. And more generally it is assumed both in passionate propaganda and in action that the way to improve business is forcibly to raise wages, the main element in its costs; this is called creating purchasing power. The reasons for such paradoxes in the relation between thought and action in the field of social-economic problems seem to the writer to constitute much the most important subject for investigation for social science at large, in so far as it aspires to illuminate practical social questions or to be of service in bringing about any improvement through political action.

The situation in the field of politics is similarly paradoxical, though the superficial character of the paradox is strikingly different. In connection with political problems there is disappointingly little scientific basis for believing in one principle in preference to any other or for formulating any communicable principles which can serve as a basis for prediction, even in the hypothetical or "if-then" sense in which sciences in general do predict—to say nothing of absolute or historical prediction, such as is achieved by a few sciences, exemplified by astronomy. The natural result is, as already suggested, that even the most intelligent people— perhaps these especially!—typically hold and advocate political opinions (if they should be so called) which have no discoverable basis in fact and reasoning and even run sharply against historical experience. This is undoubtedly the most important general observation to be made in connection with socialism. There being no way of effectively disproving any political proposition which does not palpably violate recognized laws of physical nature, men first imagine and then believe in political processes of any character, and working in any way, which appeals to any individual's particular variety of romantic fancy.

Two examples of this romanticism really must be mentioned. One is the belief, expressed on every hand by the "best minds," in the unlimited possibility of changing human nature through passing laws or remodeling the political constitution.

This possibility is supposed to be proved by the fact that human nature has changed. Now, whether human nature has changed in historical time is still a matter of dispute even among the most competent students and is very largely a matter of the definition of words. One might say that it is changing human nature to teach men to read or to ride a bicycle! In any case, the fact that human nature had changed, even in its fundamental features, even if true, would certainly not prove that it could be changed—i.e., that anyone could produce changes according to plan. And it is a still more glaring truth that no one would want any human being or group to have any such power—no one with a minimum of modesty or good sense would want to have it himself. The other example, equally pertinent in connection with the problem of socialism, is the facility with which so many people explain anything that seems to them wrong in the world by finding an enemy and then find the simple cure in liquidating somebody. The reference here is of course to the idea of the class war. The essential fact seems to be that political man is a religious animal and that the most fundamental principle of his logic is *credo quia impossibile,* or at least *credo quia mirabilis.* It is a striking fact that the outstanding feature of the gods worshiped by men in all times has been power joined with caprice, or at least with enormous and unpredictable partiality. The conception of a God who could reason with anybody—even with himself—is so foreign to human thinking as to seem quite absurd.

It is not implied that political beliefs really stop with what there is no good reason against believing. They are in fact, even in the case of the same individual, largely a tissue of contradictions as palpable and demonstrable as any propositions can be in a problem field in which both the data and the objectives of action are so resistant to clear definition and classification. Regarding socialism specifically, perhaps the most important fact is that no definition of it can be given which combines any degree of definiteness or concreteness with internal consistency. The conception actually lies in the realm of prophecy as well as in that of vague ideals or wishes well designated as "cloud-cuckoo land." In the absence of any real science to serve as an adequate basis of prediction, and in disregard of such science as does exist, men exercise their freedom to believe almost anything and to promote almost any line of action. They even advocate ideals which have neither conceptual content, self-consistency, critical defensibility in themselves, nor any visible connection with any line of action sufficiently concrete and definite to make sense. In particular, it is easy to imagine and to believe (as shown by the fact that intelligent people regularly do so imagine and believe) that the (supposed) evils in the world or in any particular society (*a*) are economic in basis, (*b*) more specifically, that they are consequences of the form of economic organization, and (*c*) can without serious difficulty be corrected by replacing the economic organization with a system of control by politicians. The combination of these beliefs is the essential content of socialism, defined in accord with the beliefs and propaganda of most of its proponents. It is imagined that the state, i.e., the government, conceived in the abstract as a benevolent and all-powerful agency—essentially as God rather than realistically as a group of politicians—could order economic affairs rightly without generating new evils or incurring serious social costs; that humanity would with approximate unanimity approve and like the result; that no other serious problems would remain; and, finally, that everybody—or nearly everybody, apart, perhaps, from a few criminally minded recalcitrants—would "live happily ever after."

But we hasten to add, with all emphasis, that what has been said involves no condemnation of socialism. The reasoning on the basis of which it is condemned is commonly no better than that by which it is supported. It would be as irrational to condemn it as it is to advocate it in the absence of any intelligible definition. The main intellectual task of a discussion of socialism is that of investigating the possibility of definition and of what can really be said for or against it after such a definition (or definitions) is formulated.

One common misconception in particular must be corrected at the outset. Economic theory, as such, involves no disproof or rejection of socialism. Rather the contrary. Theoretical analysis of the mechanism of economic organization as worked out through free exchange and free contract, operating under the control of market competition, reveals many indisputable weaknesses which could, in theory, be remedied or avoided by an all-powerful, wise, and benevolent political authority. The problem of socialism is the practical one already suggested. It has to do first, with the possibility and probability of such an authority, or some approximation to it, being created on earth and among human beings, by political process, and the means and cost; and, second, with the question whether, in view of human interests and values other than those of economics, the citizens or subjects would really approve or like this consummation if it could be realized. The problem is, in the first place, political, not economic at all; and, in the second place, it is a problem of what human beings really want and/or of ideal values in relation to desires. The economist, as economist, has nothing to say about any of these questions. Only within fairly narrow limits, and subject to explicit hypothetical postulates, can economic science make any pronouncement as to conditions as they would exist under socialism or give any picture of the socialistic state or world. And economics has even less to say on the questions as to whether human beings would approve or like the pattern of social life according to any hypothetical picture or whether it would be good or better than the world as it is, was, or would be under capitalism at any place and time.

With reference to the first question, as to what society would be like under socialism, it is easy to show that the change in the form of economic organization might involve no substantial change whatever in the concrete character of economic life. Under socialistic forms every human being might be doing the same thing, in an economic sense, and reaping the same remuneration or reward as before. Socialism presupposes an all-powerful government enforcing its will on its subjects or at least an authority whose edicts are enforced on those who do not obey them without enforcement.[2] In consequence, the problem of prediction, or prophecy, as to what socialism would be sets the question of what the state, however constituted, would actually (*a*) wish to do, (*b*) try to do, and (*c*) succeed in doing, either on the basis of the will of the people or more or less in opposition to this will, and of what the will of the people itself would be after socialism became established in any country or area. The main fact is, to repeat, that socialists themselves have made little effort to put any intelligible concrete content into the picture or ideal. It is in order to suggest that this may be one of the main sources of strength in their propaganda (though this is another question on which the economist, as economist, has nothing to say).

One thing economic analysis can do: it can show the character of the economic problems with which socialism proposes to deal. And if these are not at all of the sort which

---

[2] Socialists of the nineteenth-century liberal stamp have tended to assume an ideal democracy, with a unanimity of public opinion bordering on the ideal of anarchism. This is one of the important romantic simplifications of reality and of the problem involved in the position as a whole. This view has of course tended to be replaced by the communistic theory of a proletarian dictatorship, as a transitional stage, to reeducate humanity for the ultimate classless society the nature of which is anarchism pure and simple.

socialists assume or represent them to be, no special political competence is required to reject the socialists' appeal for supreme power (and the perquisites thereof).[3] We do not turn our bodies over for major surgery and hygienic management to persons who in place of knowledge of anatomy and physiology have ingenious theories, even though they profess the best of intentions. Very recently—since the World War, and chiefly in the past few years—very few socialists have made a beginning in the way of discussing the concrete problems of a strictly economic sort which would confront the socialistic state and the organizational policies which would be appropriate for dealing with them.[4] The assumptions made by socialists in general, and by these socialists in particular, as to the character of economic problems, and specifically the problems of economic organization, afford the

---

[3] There is another aspect of socialism which is patent to any person of good sense (including economists) but which strangely enough is so generally overlooked that it may be mentioned. This is, that in promoting socialism its devotees are seeking political power for themselves. In view of this fact, their contention that opposition is based on economic self-interest and is to be overcome by revolution through class war and the fact that the contention is taken seriously by others are interesting phenomena of social psychology.

[4] Most notable in this connection are undoubtedly Professor Oskar Lange and Mr. A. P. Lerner. See especially Lange's two articles, "On the Economic Theory of Socialism," in the *Review of Economic Studies* (Vol. IV), with a critical note by Lerner (*ibid.*) and reply by Lange (*ibid.*). The Lange articles, somewhat revised, are republished in the volume *On the Economic Theory of Socialism* by O. Lange and F. M. Taylor (University of Minnesota Press, 1938). Mr. Lerner has given a penetrating analysis of the problem of natural monopoly under socialism in his article "Statics and Dynamics in Socialist Economics" (*Economic Journal*, June, 1937), though he fails to recognize the limited character of the problem to which his treatment is actually relevant. Several books and articles by Mr. Maurice Dobb might also be mentioned, but they are not so notable for rigorous economic analysis. But even these writers seem oblivious of the main problems. They treat management as mere administrative routine, ignoring innovations and substantive changes, where the real problem of control lies. And they also ignore the fact that any important change in economic life must be based on transformation of its given conditions, which means a revolution in social institutions, beginning with the family.

only concrete basis for discussing socialism at all. Since the practical proposal is one of substituting socialism for a pre-existing capitalistic organization, the concrete question to be considered takes the form of what are or would be the main similarities, and the important differences, between the two systems. In this connection it is the similarities which especially call for emphasis. In order to define any problem which can be discussed at all, it is necessary to begin with the economic problem; and limits of space, as well as the intrinsic difficulties of political discussion, already mentioned, will force us to confine ourselves chiefly to that phase of the issue as a whole. As already emphasized, it is not at all the main problem which lies in the field of politics and social psychology and ethics. But it is at once the aspect of the general issue which can be treated by an economist (or at all definitely by anyone) and the first aspect to be considered in a logical order of analysis. A summary examination of the economic problem will carry its own implications as to the more general aspects of the broader and really fundamental issues. We begin by noting briefly some of the main similarities, features of social-economic life which would be the same under socialism as under capitalism.[5]

---

[5] The more general principles of economic theory would be valid under any conditions possible on earth, regardless of the form of society as a whole and of the social philosophy accepted in it. They would be valid in a Pharaonic dictatorship, a society in which all people, outside the personnel of the ultimate governing class, would be the property as well as the subjects of the latter, i.e., would be slaves in the ultimate sense of beasts of burden, and where consequently the only ends or values considered at all would be those of the rulers, regardless of what possible character or content these ends might have. (Much of the body of theory is also valid for a Crusoe economy or a society made up of individuals or families purely self-sufficient in their economic life, i.e., with no economic organization whatever.) In any possible human life limited resources must be utilized to realize a plurality of ends and must be apportioned among different modes of use. Hence there is always a problem of so apportioning means as to realize to the maximum extent, with the means available, the abstract end or common denominator of all concrete ends recognized and pursued. Moreover, a large part of the resources in

II

The first major characteristic of socialism, in the conception of its proponents, in which it would be identical with capitalism—say as the latter existed in the nineteenth century in England and in the United States—has to do with the character of the ends to be realized by the organized use of means. Socialists accept the social philosophy in accord with which ends are individual rather than social. This is really expressed in saying that society is viewed as an organization rather than as an organism.[6] Socialists (in our sense) have agreed with the proponents of liberalistic individualism in

---

any possible society must necessarily be employed in meeting the economic needs of individuals and must be apportioned among the various needs. Thus there must be some apportionment of resources between meeting individual needs and other purposes treated as social. It makes relatively little difference for the problems of abstract economic theory what the concrete ends are or who estimates their relative importance or makes the decisions through which the apportionment and use of means is carried out. That is, the general character of economic theory is not dependent on social forms or institutions or on any historical accidents. This fact reinforces the observation already repeatedly made that economic theory as such has nothing to do, one way or the other, with the problem of choice by a society as a whole, either of the ends to be realized or of the general principles of the organization of the use of means in realizing them. More concrete problems of economics do, indeed, call for solution in terms of theoretical principles of less general applicability relative to more specifically defined conditions. Economic theory is a generalized description, first, of economic behavior, which means the principles of economically correct apportionment of limited means used to realize ends and used in accord with some given body of technological knowledge. And, second, it states certain principles of economic organization, in a social sense, of the use of means. It is not a description of actual behavior or organization and has nothing to say as to how far either is economic, or would conform to economic principles, under any hypothetical set of social conditions. Its main content has nothing to do with the actual machinery of organization or with the character of either the ends recognized or the means or the technology employed in any particular situation.

[6] Thus the socialism which we are considering is distinguished, more or less sharply and completely, from totalitarianism (secular or theocratic-ecclesiastical), in which the individual is treated as a means to social ends, on the general analogy of the position of the cell in the human body or other biological organism. Totalitarianism might be said to be socialistic in a categorically higher sense.

viewing society as essentially an organization of individuals for mutual aid, or cooperation, and specifically for economic cooperation in the interest of increased efficiency in the use of means (to realize individual ends). In both systems or philosophies, moreover, ends or values inhere in the individual rather than in society—or some transcendental realm to which society itself may be a means; and in addition, ends are defined, in both cases, by the free choices of individuals. Ends are individual, and each individual is accepted as the best judge of his own ends.[7]

A detailed examination, impossible here, would show that, in fact, socialists have typically been more individualistic in the philosophical sense than have their liberal opponents, whose position is often distinguished as individualistic. Economic socialism, socialized production, or planned economy has often been advocated, in opposition to free enterprise or economic individualism, as a means for the more perfect realization of the ideal of social and ethical individualism. And in the abstract, this is entirely defensible. This might be both the aim and the result of socialism. The question raised is twofold: First, is economic socialism itself feasible? and, second, could or would a state which socialized economic production be individualistic or free in the economic and other fields of activity or aspects of life? It will also be seen that liberalism—a synonym for individualism, in so far as the latter includes the second element noted above (that the individual is the judge of his own ends)—is subject to the same ambiguity. Socialism may claim to present the conditions

---

[7] It should be noted that this conception of ends is a theory or form of social ethics. Contrary to many common statements, no system of ends which forms the basis of any social policy is or can be mechanical or objective, or merely quantitative, in a sense which does not involve social, ethical evaluation. Any society is necessarily ethical, in so far as it has any consciously accepted social policy whatever. Under capitalism or liberalism, as under socialism, realization of individual ends is conceived and treated as right.

of maximum individual liberty, even true economic liberty, and hence to be the true liberalism.[8]

More particularly—and the fact is vitally significant—socialists have gone much farther than liberals (or than other liberals) in treating the problems of individual and social life as essentially economic. This is perhaps ultimately the most serious of the gross oversimplifications, amounting to an evasion of the main difficulties of the program from which socialistic propaganda derives its plausibility and its appeal. The truth seems rather to be that in the ultimate and essential problem the economic factor is relatively superficial and unimportant. If we imagine all individual economic problems solved once for all—say by giving to every adult the power to satisfy all his economic wants by magical procedure (say, again, by rubbing a copper lamp and wishing, or merely by wishing)—it seems probable that the conflicts which cause strife and unhappiness among men and give rise to problems of social policy would be intensified rather than ameliorated, and even that they would not be essentially changed in form. The deeper motives back of human activity and struggle center to a minor extent in concrete results to be achieved because of any inherent significance which they possess. They center rather in the desire for freedom and power for their own sake, associated with the more fundamental want for interesting activity. It is true that rational activity always seems to aim at some results, in play as well as in work. But it is not

---

[8] In order to have the record straight and complete it is in order for the writer to record his positive conviction to the contrary. It seems to me certain: (*a*) that the governing personnel in a socialistic state would be in a position to perpetuate themselves in power if they wished to do so; (*b*) that they would be compelled to assume permanence of tenure and freedom from the necessity of seeking frequent re-election, as a condition of administering the economic life of a modern nation, even if they did not wish to do so; and (*c*) that they would wish to do so—that we cannot reasonably imagine political power on the scale involved falling into the hands of persons of whom this would not be true.

necessarily instrumental to the result or dependent upon the value of a result for its own value or interest. Rather, the situation in play seems to be the ultimate nature of most economic activity also; the result is set up to make the activity interesting and, in the deeper view, is instrumental to the latter.[9]

Acceptance of the individual's choices as the final criterion of economic value has, as its first concrete consequence or meaning for economic organization, freedom of consumption. Each individual—really each family or some equivalent primary social unit—must be allowed to choose freely among final products the particular goods and services to be used to satisfy his (its) own wants. The only possible way of granting people this freedom is to give them their total economic income in the form of abstract purchasing power, i.e., money of some sort, to make final products available at prices uniform for all, and to allow each purchaser to select products at will as to kind and amount. Thus the socialistic economy will necessarily be a pecuniary organization in this sense. And since the prices of products will have to be set, or the relation between price and supply in each case adjusted, so as to clear

---

[9] The utilitarian rationalization of freedom—the theory that freedom is good because, in general, individuals will manage their own affairs better than they will be managed for them by the government—seems to be but a small part of the story even so far as it is true. The liberal social philosophy itself seems to rest not merely on recognition that men want freedom for other reasons than because it is a condition of economic efficiency, but also on the view that, within limits, they ought to be free, whether they may wish to be or not. This is clearly the meaning of the doctrine of inalienable rights, a moral-philosophical belief that it pertains to the dignity of man to lead his own life as a responsible person, even to making his own mistakes.

Considered objectively, the type of society advocated by Utopians and radical reformers usually bears a striking resemblance to a model penitentiary or asylum of some sort. One must question both whether that is a mode of life which men would like (or pronounce good) and the likelihood that under the conditions of the real world the asylum would be or would continue to be a model one.

the market, it follows that in the whole field of the final distribution of products the mechanism of socialism must be identical with that of capitalism. And in fact this has not been questioned by socialists or any other arrangement adopted or attempted in any of the quasi-socialistic economies, whether communistic or totalitarian, which have been set up in recent years.[10]

But the essential and necessary similarity by no means ceases at this point. Socialists also accept the view that the individualistic criterion of values also includes freedom of choice of the role to be played in production by the individual, i.e., his occupation. The clear implication of this freedom is that the money income of the individual must be received in the form of payment for services, at a level measuring the economic value of the service rendered, which is the amount which other persons as consumers are willing (freely) to pay for the contribution made to production by the services of the individual in question. It may not be apparent that it is necessary under socialism for wages to be equal to the service rendered. But a fairly simple economic analysis suffices to prove that no other rate of remuneration will apportion the laborers most economically among different occupations, that is, will apportion them in such a way as to secure at the same time the best relation between income and sacrifice for the worker and the maximum output as measured by consumers' choices.[11] In any case, payment at any other level than that of productive contribution is equivalent to payment of all at

---

[10] Some exception should be made for the use of ration cards or equivalent devices. But these have been treated as exceptional and temporary by the authorities. (The effective difference between rationing and accomplishing the same result through setting appropriate prices is important but cannot be taken up here.) It is not abstractly necessary that prices be uniform to all—say to those with large and those with small incomes. But the effects of differentiation could be much more simply achieved by taxation and subsidy.

[11] On this point see Lerner and Lange, *op. cit.*

this level, modified by taxation and subsidy to produce any other distribution desired; and it would be much easier to carry out rationally the second policy—if indeed the first is possible at all. The effect on efficiency of either mode of distorting payment away from the productivity level is the same. Thus only at a cost in loss of output can a socialistic government redistribute income toward greater equality or according to any criterion of need as between individuals of divergent earning power. [12]

It is now evident that the general pattern of organization in a socialistic economy, if it operates efficiently and in accord with individual choices as the norm of value, must be essentially the same as that of capitalism. It should go without saying that production is assumed to be carried on on the basis of modern technology. That is, there would be production units of the familiar types—factories, farms, railways and ships, stores, and even banks or some equivalent financial agency. A large proportion of such units would involve the organized cooperation of a large number of human beings and

---

[12] This does not imply that it should not be done. It is a question of how far efficiency is to be sacrificed to other values. It is unquestionably necessary, in any society, to bring about distribution with some regard to need, in contrast with the strict value of services rendered. Every society must have some provision for relief of the destitute and incapacitated and of persons normally dependent upon others who fall into this class. The question whether the difference between consumption and economic earnings should be called wages or charity where it is positive, and wages or taxation where it is negative, raises serious ethical and social-psychological problems and, hence, serious political problems. Any rational formulation of policy must face this issue, and this is not usually done in socialistic or popular thinking. A socialistic state would have of necessity to keep its accounts and manage its business in terms of productivity, i.e., for labor, wages actually earned. If it were democratic its accounts would almost necessarily be open to public inspection, with the consequence that the individuals taxed or given bounties of any sort, and other individuals concerned, would know of the difference between remuneration and productivity. The situation calls to mind one of the most fundamental conflicts in popular common-sense conceptions, as to whether one deserves and ought to receive what he earns or a share fixed on some other standard.

would presumably have managers. Each production unit would, as a unit (whatever its mechanism of control or management), buy productive services and make and sell a product or products of some sort; and in its buying and its selling operations each would compete, in the economic sense, with all other production units in the same industry and in different industries. Prices of products would measure marginal utility and prices of productive services their marginal productivity. All production units would be organized and managed on the basis of profit-seeking, just as under private capitalism.

The only important difference in this respect arises in connection with monopoly. Natural monopolies would in theory be conducted so as not to earn monopoly profit; but this has also been the aim of public policy under private enterprise, achieved or attempted either through regulation or through public ownership. In theory, socialism would not allow the existence of artificial or predatory monopolies. Space limits exclude any adequate discussion of monopoly. It would show that socialists and the general public have both a much exaggerated conception of the magnitude of the monopoly evil and a gross misconception of the character of the problem. (It is largely the problem of profit in a particular aspect, since in terms of correct analysis all profit is monopoly gain; the role of profit will be considered later in connection with progressive change, and it will be found to be inevitable under socialism also.) The further course of the argument should at least suggest that the establishment of socialism would in itself afford no solution of the monopoly problem, where it is a real problem, and that it is problematical how much difference the changed form of organization would make.[13]

---

[13] Socialists themselves generally assume that there will be very much more monopoly under socialism, even in particular industries, to say nothing of the fact that all production would in the nature of the case be one gigantic monopoly in

The discussion of the necessary similarities between socialism (if it is to be an efficient organization) and capitalism leaves, up to this point, two major questions unanswered. The first has to do with the internal organization of the productive units or enterprises. The general theory of socialism requires that management be in the hands of salaried appointees of the government. That is, socialism would prohibit the specialization of risk-taking, which is the essence of the entrepreneur function under private enterprise. It should hardly be necessary to point out that this would involve a restriction of individual freedom. Under the laws of modern liberal states the participants in enterprise can have any form of organization they prefer. Specifically, it might be that of a producers' cooperative, with the fruits of operations apportioned among the participants in any manner whatever upon which the parties might come to agreement. As between management and labor, the familiar relationship in distribution might even be reversed, management receiving a fixed share and the workers, the contingent share; and any functionary or arbitrarily chosen group might also be the legal owner of the business with the others in a position of employee. Ownership of an enterprise has no necessary connection with ownership of wealth, which may be borrowed or leased for use, and this is typically the case, in large part, in business enterprises.

Any serious attempt to answer the question as to why the managerial function and the receipt of a contingent remuneration or residual have been associated in the manner actually familiar would have to start out from the fact that this is the arrangement which has in general seemed most satisfactory to the parties concerned. The main reason for this satisfac-

---

the hands of the government—but of course all are assumed to be managed purely in the public interest. The idea that large-scale production is more efficient than small-scale, beyond fairly narrow limits, is another fallacy taken over into socialistic theory from popular thinking.

toriness, in turn, is that it is the arrangement which has been found to involve greatest efficiency and the larger returns all around. (More harmonious and agreeable conditions of work are undoubtedly another reason, partly distinct from the factor of efficiency.) No reason has ever been suggested, to the knowledge of this writer, why any of these facts would be different under socialism. The contention that the owning entrepreneur, individually subject to loss or the recipient of gain, according to the success of the enterprise, can be replaced by the government, *assumed* to have no such interest, without loss of managerial efficiency, surely rests more on the will to believe than it does on inference from experience. But this is not impossible; it *might* work out in that way! It is a political or psychological question, not one of economics. And the main problem will only be reached at a later point in the essay when we come to discuss changes in conditions.

The second unanswered question is essentially a different aspect of the first, just considered. It is the question of the disposition of the profits—or losses, negative profits—i.e., of the margin of contingency in the fruits of operations, the excess or deficiency of the earnings of an enterprise above what can be safely predicted in advance. It is one of the familiar and essential principles of the competitive economy that, in so far as the magnitude of the result from any productive activity can be positively foreseen, it will be imputed to the productive services participating; that is, these will be so valued and priced so as to exhaust the product, and there will be no profit. Of course, the participating productive services include non-human agencies or property, and the participants in distribution include the owners of these; and that would also be the case under socialism. Socialists, and the public generally, almost universally confuse the earnings of property with profit; but correct analysis, and rational policy, actually require their separation. The nature and role of property—what socialists regularly call the means of production, in contrast with human beings or their services—will come up for consideration presently. But it should hardly be necessary to point out that, for the purposes of the rational management of production, human beings (or their services, i.e., labor) are also a means of production in essentially the same sense, economically speaking, as any other useful agencies or services.

Unless it is assumed that under socialism both the managers and everyone else concerned will have perfect foresight of the future, there will be profit, including loss, in connection with most enterprises. It would be impossible to organize and control production without making a separation between the amount of productive result which can be anticipated with reasonable certainty, and with reference to which fairly definite plans can be made, and both an excess of uncertain magnitude to be hoped for and a deficiency which may arise. The amount of the contingent share will depend on the accuracy of the foreknowledge on which plans are based. Its distribution between positive profit and negative profit or loss will depend on the degree of conservatism with which expectations are formulated and definite plans made for the distribution and use of the product. The more conservative the plans, the more likely it will be that the departure of the actual results from expectations will be favorable—a profit in the ordinary sense rather than a loss. All this, again, is identical with conditions under private enterprise.

The question of what would really happen under socialism—i.e., what the authorities in power would actually do—carries us at once, and obviously, into the field of political prophecy, where, as sufficiently explained at the outset, objective discussion is practically hopeless. We may take it as obvious, if any assertion in this field can be made at all, that, on one hand, the individual participants in production in any situation

173

will desire, and strive in any way in their power to get, an income which is (*a*) as large and (*b*) as certain as possible; while, on the other hand, mere prudence on the part of management (in a particular enterprise or in society) would call for conservatism, i.e., for not guaranteeing or assuring to anyone a larger income, or to any use a larger allotment, than the planners can reasonably count on realizing. The political conflict generated, and its probable results, are again matters on which most students will form opinions on grounds too vague for discussion. But since some assumption has to be made, if the discussion is to proceed any farther, we shall assume that the management is prudent, i.e., conservative, at least to the extent that the profits earned in some enterprises— above distributive commitments in one form or another involved in the social-economic plan—would be at least sufficient to cover the losses incurred in others. Under this assumption the first use to be made of profit, where it occurs, must be to cover losses which occur elsewhere. That is, the profit made by any production unit must necessarily go to the state; it cannot be retained in the enterprise where it is made. If there is a profit in the aggregate, in excess of aggregate losses in the system as a whole, it will be available to the government for any use which it may choose to make of it.

III

It should be obvious that all management is largely a matter of prediction, and that the accuracy of prediction in economic affairs, and hence the possibility of planning and acting in accord with any plan, depends upon the amount of change in the conditions of economic life as a whole. Change may be deliberately produced or accepted as desirable or tolerated as unpreventable. And the relation between change and accuracy of prediction is not simple. If conditions were unchanging, and known to be so, prediction could be accurate and presumably would be. On the other hand, it is not theoretically impossible to predict the future when it is expected to involve change. And change deliberately brought about will presumably be foreknown, in so far as it is under control, and other changes may be more or less accurately predicted. But it will hardly be disputed that in practice the accuracy of prediction will be correlated directly and closely with the amount of change expected or recognized as probable.

It is also self-evident that any problem of action is a problem of making some change in a natural course of events—a course which events would take in the absence of action or interference. Intelligent action accordingly requires knowledge of two general kinds. The actor and planner of action must know (*a*) what the course of events would be in the absence of any action and (*b*) what changes will result from the various possible lines of action or interference. Knowledge on the second point includes knowledge of the means or power in any form at the disposal of the planner and director of action and of his actual control over available means of action.

These observations really bring us finally, and for the first time, to the heart of the problem of socialism. Relevant discussion calls for analysis of the natural course of events in economic life, how far it involves change, and what kinds of change, and how far changes of the various kinds are predictable in the absence of action; and consideration of possible lines of action for preventing undesirable, and bringing about desirable, changes, and how far the results of the various kinds of possible action can be predicted. Beyond all this lie the political problems: how far the hypothetical planning agency, which would be the central feature of the socialistic state, could be expected to possess or to acquire all these different kinds of knowledge and what it would actually do about it and with what actual results. And before any final judgment could be passed on the desirability of socialism we should have to have and to apply correct criteria for comparing and judging all the differences which the analysis would show between the course of events under socialistic planning and the course of events as it would be in the absence of planned action, i.e., under competitive individualism. The utter hopelessness of any such a task and the futility of attempting it in any detail—and hence the unfathomable presumption (if it is not sheer ignorance and simplicity) involved in passing any judgment about socialism in general—is the main point which this article is attempting to drive home. It may be noted, too, that the problem of socialism, as a conceivably real or practical issue, is purely one of degree, with respect to every detail in the complex of changes proposed. No one has attempted or proposed, or conceivably will seriously propose, anything approaching absolute economic individualism or absolute socialization of production or of any feature of economic life.

It is possible, however, to carry the investigation a few steps farther, to give some further indication of the character of the problems. To do this we turn from consideration of the principles and facts which are necessarily identical for the two systems—i.e., for all systems of organization which accept individual judgment as the final criterion of value and which aim at maximum efficiency in the use of means to create or produce such values—and inquire briefly into the differences between private enterprise and socialism. In this connection also the content of the discussion must, to the writer's regret, chiefly take the form of pointing out palpable errors, and especially vital omissions, in the theory of socialism as propounded by socialists.

The proposal of socialists is, in brief, to transfer from individuals acting in their own interest (individually or in voluntary groups) to society as a whole, meaning to the government, and concretely to politicians of some type, the management of production and the ownership of the chief means of production. By means of production, as already indicated, the socialist understands the nonhuman means or property; human beings themselves (as workers) are to remain each under his own private ownership. Socialists lump together and treat as a unit, as essentially identical, the ownership of property and the management of production; and the identity is assumed to hold under socialism as well as under capitalism. The fallacies must be indicated in brief outline, without the extensive discussion which would be necessary to prevent our own statement from seeming merely dogmatic at many points.

As a beginning it is necessary to note explicitly a few of the essential facts as to the nature of economic organization and the problem of its direction or control on a social scale. We have seen that the general form of the twofold system of markets and prices is largely inevitable under any form of economic organization, and it is entirely inevitable, in so far as the result to be achieved is efficiency in the use of resources in terms of individual choices. The general pattern of organized production must be that of enterprises buying productive services, using them to make products, and selling the products at prices determined in both cases by competition over the whole field of production.

In such a system it is a sheer fallacy, in contradiction with the postulates, to speak of any individual or human agency exercising any considerable amount of control at all. Every individual in the economy exercises an infinitesimal amount of control over production in making his choices as a consumer in expending whatever money income he has to spend, i.e., in allocating his expenditures among products at the prices which he finds marked upon them. And the prices of products must be set at the level which will clear the market of the actual supplies brought to the market in any short period of time. (In a competitive market all the talk about bargaining power is sheer nonsense; bargaining is possible only where both buyer and seller are monopolists.) In the second place, if production is to be directed in accord with the choices of consumers, productive services must be allocated to the industries making the various products by setting prices of productive services in every case to measure the value of the productive contribution of each. The only alternative is direct coercion, through the machinery of the criminal law or through process without law. The owner of any productive resource (whoever he may be and whatever the resource in question) can only choose between modes of use on the terms set by prices of productive services determined in this way. Each resource owner, including explicitly free laborers as owners of their own labor power, also exercises an infinitesimal amount of control, in so far as he has any preference on other grounds than the money return, between different occupations or modes of employment. The rest of the organization process follows automatically under socialism as under private enterprise. There is room for social control or planning only in so far as the market machinery may fail for one reason or another to work ideally and without friction; and under the assumed conditions the only action which is desirable is to facilitate the achievement of the results of theoretically perfect competition. Natural monopoly may be mentioned again, as one of the important situations calling for action in the social interest. It is worthy of note also that the main cause of imperfection in the working of the market mechanism is error in productive adjustments due to the fact that individuals will not plan and adhere to announced plans but expect the machinery of organization to make provision far in advance for their possible wants while they reserve decision until the last moment.

The entrepreneur function, identified by socialists with the ownership of a particular kind of productive resources, not only has no connection with ownership of resources but has no real existence, except in the limited sense indicated. It disappears entirely in so far as the market machinery works effectively; managerial decisions can only be in accord with the choices of consumers and resource owners, or fail to be in accord with them, which involves a loss of social efficiency. The essential feature of the enterprise economy is that it theoretically and to a reasonable degree in fact places managerial decisions, i.e., production planning, in anticipation of consumers' choices, in the hands of functionaries so situated that the major loss consequent upon any failure to make correct decisions impinges primarily upon the individuals responsible for them—those who make them, either directly or through agents whom they appoint and control.

In the second place, the categorical distinction made by socialists—derived as usual from the fallacious notions of common sense—between the ownership of property and the personal freedom of the individual as a laborer is fallacious economic analysis. The substance of the matter is that any individual "owns" whatever productive capacity he does actually own! This is a matter of brute fact in any society at any time. The kind of resources owned, and specifically whether they happen to be located "inside the individual's skin" or outside of it, is merely a technical matter and of limited importance for economic organization. Personal productive capacity or labor power is in the same position as earning power embodied in external things, in all respects which are important for economic theory or economic policy. There is no general difference in relation to economic mechanics of cause and effect except for certain consequences of the laws affecting the two kinds of property and the individual's freedom of choice with respect to them, which will be noted presently. In general, both personal capacity and property in the usual narrow sense are simply forms, or congeries of forms, of economic power; any property effectively possessed is properly regarded as an attribute of the personality of its owner, along with his personal qualities; or, alternatively, an individual may properly be said to own himself, his person with all its attributes, viewed as a productive instrument.

More interesting and important still, the categorical distinction in ethical terms between property and labor (power) which in popular thinking is universally accepted as axiomatic, and which is a cornerstone of socialistic propaganda, will not stand critical examination either and turns out to be equally untenable. The ethical questions as to whether an individual deserves to receive and enjoy the income produced by any productive capacity in his possession may be divided into two parts. The first has to do with the source of the economic power in question, or how the individual comes into possession of it, and the second with the manner or conditions of its use. In both cases—property in the narrow sense and personal capacities—possession originates in a similar list of facts and processes. These include in both cases, first, inheritance, and, second, the working of social-cultural and legal processes over which the individual has no control. Beyond this causally given basis or nucleus, productive power is created in the individual by a process of investment—in education and training in the inclusive sense—which is neither economically nor ethically different in any important respect from the investment which gives rise to any other productive agency. All these factors are affected to a large if not overwhelming extent by all sorts of imponderables and contingencies which may be lumped together under the head of "luck."

There is no visible reason why anyone is more or less entitled to the earnings of inherited personal capacities than to those of inherited property in any other form; and similarly as to capacity resulting from impersonal social processes and accidents, which affect both classes of capacity indifferently. And in so far as the creation of either form of capacity is due to motivated human activity on the part of the individual concerned or of his parents, or to anyone else, the motives may in either case be ethical or unethical in any possible sense or degree. And, finally, the use of productive capacity of either type may similarly be more or less intelligently motivated in accord with ends or ideals which are ethical or unethical in any degree and in any meaning. The grounds for the distinction generally drawn so sharply and so confidently seem to present a major problem in social psychology. The "labor theory of value," which has been the most important source of corruption in economic thinking through most of its history, is an unanalyzable mixture of fallacious causal analysis and false ethics.

A part of the reason for the idea commonly held is, no doubt, that the poor usually get what income they do get chiefly from the sale of personal services. But there is no close correspondence between the size of income and the character of the source.

The major difference between incomes from the two types of source is, as suggested above, a consequence of social institutions and law. The individual who is dependent upon the sale of personal services for his living is subject to a peculiar disadvantage in the way of security, which is a paradoxical result of the legal sanctity of freedom. Since an approximately continuous flow of some economic goods and services is practically necessary, such a person becomes dependent upon access to a continuous market. This does not apply to owners of property. The latter may derive an income for a time (though it is not really income) from the sale of assets or from a loan based on these as security. But the sanctity of personal freedom in Western legal systems, the doctrine of inalienable rights, makes it impossible for a person effectively to pledge his future earning power in exchange for present resources. This weakness, again, exists irrespective, in principle, of the magnitude or value of the earning power itself.[14]

The most important question in connection with the socialization of property is that of what would be gained from the change. Critical investigation of this question in terms of the statistical magnitudes the general order of which is known will show that the results would certainly be disappointing. In the United States, under the relatively normal conditions of the middle twenties, about three-fourths of the national income represented the value of personal services and one-fourth represented the yield of property. This fourth was about equal to the sum of the costs of government (all units) plus the annual saving added to capital. (Under the depression, governmental expenditure has soared and property incomes have shrunk far more than those derived from labor.) The maximum amount which a socialist government would have found it possible to seize out of property income would never have been as much as 10 per cent of the total labor income. Out of this it would have to pay the greatly increased expenses of government involved in administering the economic life of the country. (Some of this might conceivably be saved by

---

[14] One ground which might be given for socializing the more important nonhuman means of production, while leaving the laborer his freedom or ownership of himself, is that, even if there is no theoretical difference, it is easier or more practicable to socialize property. A very little critical reflection would show that this is not the case, when we think in terms of economic value, which is the only significant point of view. It is undoubtedly true that the government could not very well separate the labor power or any part of it from the individual in which it is embodied, while it could readily seize physical things and retain control over them. But what is relevant in both cases is the earnings, and with reference to these no such difference exists. And far more important is the fact that the development of earning capacity in an individual depends on investment in him, and the conditions determining the amount and character of this investment in any case are social facts and theoretically subject to political control.

cutting down high salaries paid to executives by private enterprise, but detailed analysis would show that this is very doubtful.) Moreover, in any sweeping process of income equalization much income would simply disappear through the downward revaluation of rare luxury products. The ultimate resources which produce a thousand dollars' worth of champagne or diamonds, or the services of a highly exceptional medical genius or portrait painter, would not yield a comparable value in products in demand from persons of average income, at prices which such persons could pay. In general, the "choice cuts" would fall in value much more than the ordinary ones would rise.

The discussion has come around again to the point we had reached a while ago. Under the accepted postulates as to the general objectives of economic life, and under any set of given conditions—wants, resources, and technology—as they stand at any given time, the changes or differences that would be made in the concrete nature of economic life could not be great and would be highly problematical as to both magnitude and favorable character. (In saying that they are problematical we mean to reiterate that within the physically possible limits they are a matter of political prophecy.) In other words, the power of a government committed to socialism to make any considerable difference in the economic lives of its citizens or subjects, i.e., in the production and distribution of goods, would depend upon its bringing about some fundamental change in the given conditions (wants or resources or technology) or upon its employing coercion or substituting some altogether different objective of economic activity, replacing individual want-satisfaction, and freedom of choice. We have seen that the "expropriation" of the "more important means of production" from their previous private owners involves no very important exception to this general statement, even with respect to distribution and even considering only the state of affairs immediately following such a confiscation of wealth, accumulated under a different system—i.e., without raising the question as to the probability of a socialistic administration effecting its revolution and "taking over" without extensive destruction and dislocation. Mere change in the form of organization, without sweeping changes in the given conditions, holds great potentialities for loss and quite limited potentialities for improvement, even taking the latter in accord with the estimates of the proponents of socialism in so far as they can be reconciled with objective facts.

Considering in positive terms the differences between socialism and free enterprise, the establishment of socialism would involve two general changes. The first is the appointment of the managers of business enterprises by political process and the second, the socialization, expropriation, or confiscation of private property, or whatever portion of it the socialist regime might actually think it expedient to take over. All objective inquiry into the effects of either or both these changes tends to minimize their importance—except for the possibility of catastrophic loss in case the political administrations should behave more in accord with the expectations of the gloomier prophets than with those of the optimistic votaries.

The chief statement which can be made objectively is that if the new administration seriously attempted to fulfill the expectations suggested by socialists themselves—and on the basis of which they would probably come into power, if at all—the consequences would certainly be disastrous. We should note in particular that the realization of the theoretical possibilities of socialism in the way of equalizing the distribution of income—if extensive change in that direction were seriously attempted—would call for a sweeping reorganization of the productive system from top to bottom. For, as just noted in another connection, no great redistribution could be effected without changing the character of the physical output. Any attempt to replace at all rapidly the production of luxury goods with the production of things that would be demanded by persons of something near average income would create a task for any organization machinery which it could not be expected to perform without producing large derangement and loss; it would be comparable to the task of shifting national production from an ordinary peace footing to what would be required for total war, or the converse change. (Again, both the ultimate limitations—the sheer disappearance of a large part of the value of luxury items consequent upon specificity of ultimate resources, and the serious political consequences to be expected as a result of impossible promises made for campaign purposes—should be kept in mind.)

Socialists commonly believe in the possibility of a great increase in the efficiency of production, merely through the change in administration. But it is quite certain that such beliefs rarely if ever rest either on any quantitative study of the facts or on any objective analysis of the organization problem. The judgment of students who emotionally are entirely sympathetic with socialism has generally been that the political administration at best would be doing extremely well if it maintained approximately the general level of efficiency achieved under capitalism, without estimating this standard very near the ideal. A feature of the whole discussion situation is the fact that even educated people, inclined to radical criticism—and the disposition is a trait of human nature closely related to moral idealism—have wild ideas as to the amount of loss and inefficiency in the modern economic organization. The best-known study of facts is that made by Nourse and Associates of the Brookings Institution[15] for the

---

[15] *America's Capacity to Produce* (Washington, D. C.: Brookings Institution, 1934).

United States in the 1920's. Their results, estimating achievement under normal conditions at about 80 per cent of what could reasonably be regarded as possible, is, in the opinion of the writer, a fair estimate, though the statistical quantities involved have no definite meaning, to say nothing of accuracy.

The point for emphasis is that socialists grossly oversimplify the organization problem which would confront the political order under their system by treating it as one of routine administration. In fact, it would necessarily be one of revolutionary reorganization. It is merely absurd to think of socialism being established in any visible future for the purpose of freezing a pre-existing state of life and preventing change.[16]

Thus the third major confusion involved in socialist theory has to do with the nature of the problem of management. In the few brief remarks which are possible here on this topic we shall continue to assume that the general objective of maximum individual want-satisfaction remains unchanged—as far as possible.[17]

---

[16] It is true that the original theory of Marxism involved an apparently more logical evasion of this difficulty. It is assumed that the socialist state would come into being through a fairly simple process of taking over a ripe economic society, one in which the problems of organization would have been worked out to an approximately final solution by the dialectical processes inherent in the evolution of capitalism itself before the revolution. The difficulties of that view are two: First, that the dialectical processes, in the two or three generations which have followed since the publication of the Communist Manifesto, did not work in close conformity with the Marxian prediction, to say nothing of the speed of change in comparison with the expectations of the early scientific socialists. In particular, socialism came, where it came at all, not in a ripe industrial economy but in the economically backward country, Russia—following upon disastrously destructive wars, foreign and civil. And, in the second place, Marx and his followers overlooked the fact which we have emphasized, that the redistribution of income cannot be viewed as a simple matter of taking money away from some recipients and giving it to others, but itself involves a fundamental reorganization of production (in which a large fraction of the distribuend would disappear and most of the famous surplus would prove illusory).

[17] In fact, this seems extremely improbable. The course of recent world-history indicates rather that socialism is much more likely to establish and maintain itself on the basis of some transcendental or totalitarian conception of the character and

The fundamental changes in the given conditions of economic life which the socialistic state must make to bring about any important change at all fall under the three heads of wants, resources, and technology. These are the three classes of conditions which, in the nature of economic activity, are actually given at any time and place and which determine everything else. For our purposes these may be reduced to two, resources and technology being combined under the head of productive capacity, over against the wants to be satisfied, as the two more elementary sets of economic data. Inventions and technical improvements of other sorts, whether patentable or not, are in fact private property under the law of modern industrial nations, or they certainly are such for the purposes of economic analysis as long as the person who makes an innovation is in a position to derive any income from it in excess of the necessary remuneration of the productive agencies employed in putting it into effect. (As already suggested, the major fraction of the profit in an economic system consists of this inherently temporary monopoly gain in connection with innovations, the prospect of which is the chief economic motive leading to economic progress.) In addition, inventions and other forms of property are genetically similar in that they all (including personal capacity—see above) result from investment, mixed with natural process and "brute force and accident."[18]

---

ends of social life, most likely military power and conquest, and abstract considerations of social psychology derived from history as a whole point in the same direction. These indicate that man is a religious animal and that the prospects of individualistic utilitarianism establishing itself as a religion are remote indeed. But we must follow the conceptions of socialist propagandists as to the nature of socialism if we are not to get "clear off the earth" into idle speculation.

[18] It is true that the results of activities—i.e., the use of resources—in making innovations are less predictable than some other kinds of economic activity. But the importance of the gambling or the aleatory element in different kinds of economic activity is a matter of degree, and no simple classification in this respect is possible. In particular, the results of exploration and development, which are

In consequence of these facts, all the different elements in productive capacity would present similar problems to the overhead control system, the government of the socialistic state. Productive capacity has traditionally been classified into three divisions or kinds: the "holy trinity" of labor, capital, and land. The classification is open to fatal objections from the standpoint of any accurate and thoroughgoing analysis, but the reasons cannot be elaborated here, and it may be followed for the purpose of a topical survey.[19]

Only one or two major facts or principles can be touched upon, by way of characterizing the problems which would confront the government of a socialistic state. In connection with the given conditions of economic life—wants or other ends, resources of all kinds (and however classified), and technical knowledge (if that is separated from resources)— two facts stand out as overwhelmingly important for general social theory. The first is that, in the absence of change or the possibility of producing changes, no problem can arise, while any activity directed to change involves uncertainty as to its results and is inherently a gamble. It is in connection with initiative that management has meaning. An obvious consequence of the uncertainty of results is that managerial activities cannot be evaluated until after they are performed— and often a very long time afterward, and most vaguely and doubtfully even then. This is the fundamental reason for the

the real source out of which natural resources (so miscalled) come into economic existence, are similarly unpredictable (as the activities are similar in other respects), and the investment which results in the productive capacity of human beings— rearing and education—is almost as much of a gamble. In fact, technology might very logically be treated as an attribute of human beings, and the social and individual problems connected with it, as a detail of education in the broad sense.

[19] The essence of the confusion involved lies in the fact that all these forms of productive capacity, and inventions as well, theoretically result from the same elementary causes or processes, i.e., more or less rationally and more or less ethically directed investment, superposed on the processes of physical nature, human biology, and social culture—as we have already had occasion to observe.

specialization of entrepreneurship or risk-taking, which is the central principle of the enterprise economy and the real meaning of the profit motive or principle. The socialistic state would have no objective or rational basis for fixing the remuneration of managers, the indeterminacy of their value being proportional to the degree in which they exercised initiative.[20] To secure a moderate degree of efficiency, along with adaptive flexibility, the socialistic state might well find itself compelled to revert to the enterprise principle of leaving the remuneration of all final management—i.e., of innovators—to be determined by results actually realized. If so, the last important economic difference between socialism and capitalism would disappear, and with it all chance for any approximation to economic equality. Making innovations is a gamble, and a lottery cannot function without large prizes. In any case, it is certain that the problem of selecting, motivating, and rewarding real management or planners with power to make substantial changes is one which has no solution. Such matters can only be ruled either by the "pull and haul" of free individual bargaining or by that of political and social forces.

The second fact referred to is that under the economy of free enterprise, the primary agency for perpetuating the various given elements or factors and for bringing about changes in them is the institution of the family. This proposition surely does not need defense or elaboration. In practically all forms of society known to history it is primarily through the family that the individuals of each new generation receive their

---

[20] Thus the contention of Professor von Mises, and other opponents of socialism, that there would be no objective rationale for the organization of production under socialism, while adequately refuted by Professor Lange (and others) for the routine operations of a stationary economy, is after all essentially correct for the really serious problem of organization. This is the problem of anticipating substantial changes in the given conditions of economic life and in making necessary adaptations and/or of bringing about such changes.

equipment in all these respects—and the statement applies to the group as a whole in so far as the phenomena pertain to society as a whole rather than to individuals. No society can possibly be really individualistic. In a world in which individuals go through the biological life-cycle, and especially where they do not inherit acquired knowledge, training, and habits, the minimum ultimate unit is the natural family; what is called individualism would be far more descriptively designated as "familism." It really makes little practical difference whether the ultimate mechanics of continuity be that of biological heredity or culture inheritance, i.e., tradition perpetuated by some mixture of unconscious imitation and more or less deliberate education. It is true that in modern Western civilization the biological and subjective individual has come to play a much larger role in culture continuity, and especially in culture change, than was true in primitive society or earlier civilizations. But there are fairly narrow limits even to the possibilities in this regard. The individual cannot possibly be other than a social product, a social or domesticated animal. The more important peculiarity of what is called individualism is the greater role assigned to the private family, meaning to parents; and "parental individualism" might be a still better designation for the most important distinguishing characteristic of modern free or competitive society.[21]

The general conclusion which follows from the type of consideration suggested, and which is important for the purpose in hand, is that the effective changes which are possible under

---

[21] It will be evident that any real discussion of the problems under consideration would call for a sociological and historical analysis of the relations between the individual and society, which in turn is an almost infinitely complex system of groups—political, traditional, and voluntary. Perhaps the most important feature of all in modern liberal civilization has been the greater freedom of individuals to form voluntary groups, including the much more free and voluntary character of marriage, as against the control of tradition and authority (meaning largely control by religion).

socialism and which would make up any important difference consist overwhelmingly in the transfer of functions from the private family, or from individuals as parents, to the political state. Reflection will show that, in addition, both voluntary groupings of all kinds, and also of the smaller political divisions, must very largely lose their functions and their very existence in favor of the nation. Whatever socialists may wish or intend, and whatever they may think, effective socialism must largely mean, in practice, "the omnipotent state."[22]

The importance of this for the ultimate problem of social control is twofold. First, the selfishness or self-interest of the family, as against other families, is far greater than that of the individual against other individuals. Or, the selfishness of parents for their children is greater than that for themselves. The ethical injunction to "love one's neighbor as one's self" does not get to the heart of the problem at all, either as to what is important or as to what is really difficult—as an obstacle to equalitarianism. The crux is rather the necessity for loving one's neighbor's children as one's own. In the second place, it is not merely the sanctity of the family relation and family institution which is at stake. If the family were consigned to limbo—as some socialists have been quite willing

---

[22] The form of the state itself is a political problem, and especially of a sort to be solved by wish-thinking rather than by rational discussion. Liberal socialists, of course, believe that it is realistic to think of their state as being democratic and to advocate socialism on this assumption, especially because it is thought to mean the preservation of individual liberty. On this point the main comment which it is pertinent to offer has already been made, but we may add the suggestions that the difficulties of any real democracy are increased in large ratio with increasing size of the contemplated unit and also that even if theoretical democracy could be realized, its meaning to the individual becomes correspondingly attenuated. To the writer, both recent history and general considerations point strongly toward the conclusion that not only would the socialistic government necessarily be of the authoritarian type, but that to maintain the social-psychological unity necessary for effective functioning it would have to substitute some totalitarian ideal for individual freedom and individual liberty.

to do—its place would inevitably be taken by some other primary group in connection with which essentially the same problems would arise.

The abolition of inheritance of wealth would tend both to weaken the family and to shift the family interest into other modes of creating and passing on to heirs a favored position, a position of power. The abolition of ownership of productive property would by no means close all opportunity for families to strive to give their heirs a preferred position as a start in life. Many channels for such activity would remain open, but the most important would be that of politics. Indeed, the program of socialism seems to consist primarily in transferring from business to politics the whole competitive struggle for power and the fruits of power—the things which men want and for which they scheme and struggle in life. To ask whether the results of such a change would be desirable or what the concrete results would actually be would merely carry our discussion into fields where, as sufficiently pointed out before, and for reasons sufficiently indicated, discussion cannot be expected to establish any conclusion.

The most important general result with regard to the ethical aspect of the social problem which should follow from the foregoing exposition is, stated in negative terms, that it is a fallacy to think of the problems of large-scale social organization—and specifically of large-scale economic organization—in terms of the relations between given individuals. Stating it in positive form, the problem is rather that of creating or producing the right kinds of individuals. Given individuals with the requisite endowment of capacity and disposition, the general principle that freedom is the only basis of ethically defensible relationships among men and the essential condition of all moral or personal life calls for leaving such individuals to work out and establish such relations as they themselves deem most conducive to economic efficiency, to personal and cultural well-being, and in general to their mutual advantage in their pursuit of the good life. Sound policies of social improvement must be based on a sound analysis and appraisal of personal and cultural values, taken in relation to a sound objective comprehension of the mechanics of economic organization and of cultural phenomena, as studied in the various social disciplines. Moralizing about the problems, in terms of the sentimental values and obligations appropriate to intercourse in small face-to-face groups, can lead to no good results and is certain to do harm rather than good.[23]

---

[23] The most important aspect of socialism which it has been impossible to consider at all in this overlong essay is the problem of business depression. It is probably in this connection that the most plausible case for the centralization of the control of production can be made out. Indeed, it is quite easy to prove that in a socialistic economy, under able, wise, and benevolent government, assumed all-powerful or without serious opposition (or disharmony within its own personnel), cycles and depression and unemployment would altogether cease from troubling. The difficulty with this argument is that it can about as easily be proved that a capitalist government could also abolish these evils, without the need of any legal or constitutional powers beyond those already unquestionably possessed, even under the eighteenth-century written Constitution of the United States—if only it had sufficient wisdom, internal harmony, and support from the public in taking the necessary measures. Economic depression is a phenomenon of the mechanics of money and presents an especially interesting and significant problem—a sort of test case on governmental action—in that it does not rest upon or involve conflict of interest. Practically everyone loses by depression and would gain from its abolition. The problem is merely one of knowledge of causes and appropriate remedies and of administrative competence on the part of the political organization. The import of these facts for the discussion of socialism can hardly need underlining.

Religion and Ethics in Modern Civilization

I

Zealous Christians and skeptical or antagonistic critics agree that modern society is by no means Christian; they differ as to attitude, of deploring or rejoicing. Its spokesmen commonly teach that a general and thoroughgoing acceptance of Christianity would solve all our social problems. On the other hand, extreme critics hold that Christianity is reconcilable with a high level of civilization only because it is not taken seriously, because in practice its content is always defined in terms of the current ethical "common sense."

The common line of criticism is that Christianity presents a beautiful and lofty ideal, but that it is "impracticable." This is often coupled with the view that, while it was appropriate to the situation in which it was promulgated, the vast changes in "conditions" between first-century Palestine and twentieth-century Europe or America make its suitability for the earlier setting a presumption against its fitting the later.

Reprinted by permission from *The Journal of Liberal Religion*, vol. 3 (1941), pp. 3–22.

It is also pointed out that the early Christians themselves expected the immediate Second Coming of Christ, and the establishment of the Kingdom of God on earth, which would end all mundane problems, and hence they were not dealing with problems of distant times. The aim of this essay is to develop a more thoroughgoing version of the theme of historical change and "culture lag" in its relation to religious ethics. The thesis will be that the important difference between the modern situation and that of the Roman Empire—or any other culture situation known to history—goes far deeper than a change in social conditions, in any usual or reasonable interpretation of the words. It is true that differences of the latter sort are very great, particularly in the fields of economic and political life, where what we think of as modern problems chiefly arise. But these changes must be passed over. What we shall emphasize as important is the revolutionary change in man himself, in his deepest ideals, his conception of himself and of the Cosmos, and in his conception of God and his relation to God—any God in whom he cares to believe, or can believe. In the broadest terms, we have to contrast the liberal philosophy of life with that of religion in the traditional sense.

However, our aim is neither mere analysis for its own sake, nor mere negation. Our purpose is rather to point out the futility of attacking the moral problems of our culture in the manner actually characteristic of the spokesmen of Christianity, and of others who discuss these problems in explicitly ethical terms. And the argument should indicate something as to the moral attitude and line of action really called for. It should indeed be understood that our task is by no means purely to attack traditional religion. We are not attributing the "crisis in modern civilization" to the excessive application of the principles of Christianity. But it does not follow that neglect of religion has been the cause, nor that a return to any orthodoxy is the remedy; and too much looking to religion, rather than to intelligence and rational ethics, may be a definite evil.

II

Religions, with all their vast differences, are fundamentally alike in the way in which they meet both the social needs and the spiritual cravings of men. The social function of religion is rooted in the fact that man is a dissatisfied animal, a critic of other men, of society, of the world, and even of himself. He has intelligence, in varying amount and kind, but is more conspicuous for egotism, boundless imagination, and manifold romanticism. Roughly in proportion to his human development, he finds nearly everything to be wrong, and for this he is disposed to blame other people and social institutions; and especially he lays the blame for the institutions on particular individuals who seem to be beneficiaries of their wrongness, those who are, or whom he imagines to be, in power. Nearly any intelligent and energetic individual thinks he could reconstruct society according to a far more admirable pattern, if his fellows would only follow his advice or obey his orders; and the natural disposition is to try to find some way to force them to do just that. Between such people and Utopia stand the stupidity and traditionalism of the masses of men, and the "vested interests." The sinister character of such traits is manifest; for in order to live a human life, men require organized society with a high degree of stability. The social function of religion is through appeal to supernatural sanctions—hence to prudence and fear—to suppress the destructive tendencies of romantic human nature, to force men to accept the established order of things on which life is dependent.

At the same time, man, the romantic fool, craves, or thinks he craves, a life without frustration or uncertainty, or antagonism or strife with the world or his fellows; in short, he yearns for "peace." Obviously, there are two possible ways for securing harmony between man's restless spirit and his world. One way is to change the world. This way is emphasized by the liberal philosophy of life, and more or less by liberal religion. It could not be followed prior to very modern times, for under earlier conditions it would have been fatally destructive. The other way of reconciliation is for man to find the wrong in himself and to change his own nature, to suppress and extirpate his restless cravings and "accept the universe." This is the religious way. Different religions have different formulae for the reconciliation. Hinduism and Buddhism represent the extreme of acceptance and repression, and similar was the Stoic ideal of reabsorption of the soul into the world-soul, parallel to the commingling of the body in the world of matter. The Jewish-Christian formula is "Love"—love of God and of one's fellow men.[1]

---

[1] We must pass over other factors in religion, notably the whole category of magic—no doubt as important as the factors referred to.

Space limits also exclude any real discussion of the obviously vital topic, the actual meaning of Christian ethics. We can only use, with a somewhat dogmatic or question-begging interpretation, the "stock" words and phrases of the New Testament, which Christians agree in citing and accepting as authoritative, if they agree on anything. The bracketing of Judaism and Christianity as Love-religions should suggest several perennial problems as to the relation between love and other key concepts such as faith, grace, and especially the law. (The primary reference is of course to the "Great Commandment," of the Gospels, the two parts of which are quotations from Leviticus 19:18 and Deuteronomy 6:4 respectively.) Faith may be disposed of rather simply as an implication of love, not distinct from it. The concept and doctrine of Grace may be passed over, from our point of view, along with all strictly religious or "eschatological" matters.

The "Law," however, calls for a word, because an ambiguity in this connection is central for our argument. The teaching of Jesus carried a somewhat "liberal" interpretation of the Jewish law, in contrast with Pharisaic literalism. The teaching of Paul called more emphatically for disregard of the purely ritualistic element in the Jewish law. But both assumed the ethical content as divinely ordained and eternally valid—and as complete and closed. The last is the main point; Christian teaching as a whole regarded "the law" as *given*, including the commands of all *de jure* authorities. But the serious ethical problems of our time center in the

The problem of religion arises largely out of the relation between its social and psychological functions. The simple and obvious solution of the second problem, of escaping conflict and securing peace, would seem to be suicide. Life without struggle would merely be death. Yet men find an abundance of "good reasons" for not adopting this solution. One of these is the fear that it will not work—"for in that sleep of death what dreams may come?" The "real reasons" cannot occupy us here, but one is certainly the antithesis of the fear that death may not be the end, i.e., the fear that it is. Of course "homo romanticus" does not know what he wants, but it is easy to see that he rarely wants "to die; to sleep; no more." Hence, some compromise must be found between peace and activity, between death and life, with its toil, struggle, and defeat, but also with some romantic adventure, and occasional triumphs. At a minimum, "the machinery must be kept going," in the individual body and in society, at some level, and as along as possible.

This dilemma confronts the Judaeo-Christian gospel of love, as well as any other formula for the reconciliation of man and the world from the "spiritual" side. In the Christian teaching, and specifically in the characteristic text of the Sermon on the Mount (Matt. 6:25–34, Luke 12:22–31) the theory seems to be that, if men will really embrace "righteousness" (love, including faith), God will at once establish his Kingdom on earth, and all environmental (economic) problems, as well as

---

making and enforcement of law by democratic process. If the New Testament means what it says, it excludes the Christian from participation in political activity, except obedience to the law as he finds it, in the above inclusive sense. This applies particularly to law enforcement, which would be a clear violation of the injunction to "resist not evil." (Hiring policemen or soldiers to do the "dirty work" for us will hardly clear our own skirts.)

In a notable and widely read volume on *Christian Ethics and Modern Problems,* Dean W. R. Inge cites from Augustine the principle, *ama et fac quod vis,* and expresses approval, but adds the "assertion" that Christianity is not antinomian! (*Op. cit.,* p. 390 of popular ed. of 1932; p. 410 in earlier edition.)

problems of human conflict, will cease from troubling. With reference to economics, we meet here with an extreme development of magical ideas, though it is a peculiarly "white" magic. The same general view might be rationalized without appeal to the supernatural by transferring the faith and trust from God as a personal being outside or inside the world to "social forces," such as custom, including religion. Or, it might mean trust in men as individuals, or possibly even as rulers. Or the view might be that, no matter whether or not his problems are solved, the individual believer should practice faith and love *à outrance,* even at the cost of suffering, even martyrdom. In this case, the individual would undoubtedly have to be supported by the belief that "God" will grant adequate compensation in a future life of immortal bliss; the "Kingdom" would be transferred from this world to the next (which actually happened when the Parousia failed to materialize).

Considerable support may be found in the New Testament for all these interpretations. And apart from the doctrine of immortality, about which we have unhappily no knowledge, there is undoubtedly much to be said for all of them. But they all practically have to be dismissed, or crippled with reservations, for present Western Civilization. Modern men simply do not believe in any of them to a point where they will practice the love-gospel *à outrance*. Moreover, we must face the fact that modern men neither care for a life of peace and quiet nor ethically approve of this ideal. They want life, as action, effort, adventure and achievement, and they believe in a moral ideal of self-realization and self-development, through work and play and cultural activity, involving effort, risk and conflict, and calling for energy, intelligence and courage. Men believe in these things for their own sake, for what they mean in terms of "character," and also because of results which they are confident will flow from such conduct in the way of better conditions and opportunities of life for future human beings. Moreover, we moderns frame our conception of God in accord with these beliefs, as a worker and a co-worker with man.

On the other hand, we think we know that any thoroughgoing acceptance of the gospel of world-acceptance in any form would abolish not only progress but all civilization, which is to say all really human life. And we are sure that, while the life of savages, or brutes, may have some idyllic features which are absent from civilization, it is on the whole not merely unappealing to us, but falls short in its possibilities for the good life, even more seriously than does civilization, with all its shortcomings. At the same time, primitive social life does not afford that peace, security and freedom from anxiety which is the object of the religious craving itself. To achieve this state, men would have to cease to be men; and we believe it is "better" to be men than to be vegetables, even lilies of the field.

III

Looking back over the history of the Western World since the first century, we find these beliefs confirmed, as far as history affords a test. Christianity had a reasonably fair trial at ordering the world and individual life for a "millennium" or so, and the result was very different from the Kingdom of God on earth. The period is, in fact, commonly referred to in history text-books as a "dark age" between two civilizations. The Christian Church itself, from the time of its secure establishment (specifically in Western Europe) progressively ceased to practice the doctrines of original Christianity, such as love, non-resistance, and taking no thought for the morrow. It taught others to obey, while it commanded; it aspired to be, and without scruple used all its power to become, a political power system, an authoritarian, imperialistic state.[2] And this is what it apparently had to do to live; and churches, like men (or more so) seldom yearn to die. Moreover, its spokesmen took and enjoyed the usual perquisites of power, notably wealth and luxury. The differences between the medieval Church and other state systems, in consequence of its theocratic basis, do not impress the modern student as great, or where they are real, as being conspicuously good. At the time of maximum religiosity in Western Europe, human life fitted, about as well as has ever been the case, the famous formula—nasty, brutish and short. Medieval society was no more outstanding for equalitarianism, or justice, or peace, than it was for comfort or beauty in the everyday life of its typical member, the peasant.

The historical changes which caused or constituted the transition from medieval to modern Western Europe are of course a topic too large even for summary here. We need only note that an integral and vital factor was a revolt against the Church and destruction of most of its power, chiefly to the advantage at first of a new authority, the territorial state. With reference to their frankly political objectives, the new states exercised a large measure of control, in "Catholic" as well as "Protestant" lands, over both religion and economic life. But in view of the underlying cultural and moral forces at work, political autocracy contained in itself the seeds of its own destruction. In the course of time, no very long period historically speaking, the struggle of the individual for both religious and economic freedom led progressively to victory.

---

[2] The change from a new, reforming religion to an old, established one, meant the loss of the original character of Christianity as a continuation of the prophetic tradition in Judaism and transformation into the priestly type. The mixture of forms was further multiplied by various degrees and kinds of rationalization under the influence of modern science and philosophic thought, until the content of "Christianity" today is practically anything that is considered respectable in any community which in the course of history has come to call itself Christian.

The victory carried with it, as what we seem justified in calling an inevitable consequence, the establishment of political freedom or individualism in the shape of democratic government, representative in structure and committed to the ideal of maximum individual liberty. The role of government, even in the freest, most democratic form, was to be minimized.

The story of the "Renaissance," and of modern history, must be taken as familiar matter. The revolutionary change was that men's minds were released from the medieval monkish ideal of poverty and submissiveness and turned in the direction of freedom and self-respect. The cult of obedience—to men who "obeyed God" and lived on the choice cuts—was replaced in the masses by that of free activity, individual and associative, in work, play and culture, and specifically in the form of the progressive conquest of matter by him or spirit.[3] We must emphasize the plurality of values involved in this ideal. It is considered good not merely because it is pleasant or interesting to the individual, or because it leads to "useful" results, or to "material," or even cultural, progress; but also and even primarily because such activity is the only way to develop human personality in the modern, positive interpretation of that concept.

IV

As to the "results" of this change in outlook, we may first mention what is in itself least important, the vast rise in the standard of living, particularly of the masses. In view of the flood of nonsense which is current regarding the "materialism" of modern liberal culture, it should be emphasized that the

---

[3] The third member of the monkish trio of virtues, "chastity," was not, of course, abolished; but it was fundamentally reinterpreted, in terms of esthetic and rational conceptions and the requisites for a worthy family life.

main difference in content between a high standard of living and a low one lies in the field of esthetic and social values; "decency," and indeed cleanliness, is only a very low level of beauty. One great difference between liberal civilization and religious barbarism roots in the recognition that beauty is a good in human life (not only in religion—see Note 5 on p. 208) and that it is frightfully expensive.

It is equally necessary to emphasize that the great achievement of modern civilization in the scale of living lies in the diffusion of standards of decency, a minimum of beauty, among the masses of the people, which is properly a moral rather than even an esthetic achievement. The living standards of the potentates, political or religious or economic, have, in essentials, been far less affected. It is a relatively simple matter for a society to provide the amenities, and even a high level of beauty and culture, for a small élite, if the lives of the masses are used as a means to that end, through an appropriate system of power and servility relations. The courts of the more prosperous Pharaohs probably had a real standard of life about as high as has ever been achieved. The complaint as to the materialism of our civilization reflects the interest of beneficiaries of power relations in our own society; one main root of it is the fact that the "lower classes" have come to demand a fair share in the benefits of cultured life, and to show a degree of independence and self-respect.

It is more defensible to designate as "materialistic" the achievements in the field of health, which affect the upper classes as well as the lower, if in lesser degree. Only in a civilization dominated by the modern spirit would it have been possible to eliminate the great epidemics which so frequently decimated—and constantly terrorized—the population of medieval Christian Europe. But not many who pine for a supposed golden age in the past want to exchange rational medicine for the practices of savages or pre-scientific society.

Other fields of civilized achievement in the Western world are commonly less emphasized, and when mentioned are nearly always *wrongly* treated as non-materialistic, in contrast with the higher standard of living. First, as to scientific knowledge and understanding of the world in which we live, and of ourselves as a part of it. It is true that these have proven to be "useful" in the ordinary, naïve meaning of the word; they are inseparably bound up with the growth of "wealth" as components in the "power" of mind over matter. But on the one hand they are ends, in any defensible conception of ends, and on the other they are, like beauty, very expensive. And again, the diffusion of education, in the broad sense, among the masses is a more important achievement of modern civilization than is the reaching of higher peaks of learning or intellectual insight.

What is back of the wail about materialism, as already suggested, is that some people abuse their freedom—"other" people, of course—and usually in ways which inconvenience "us," the élite who do the complaining (and who typically make our living by judging others, and selling the product). But this is not the whole story. A free and highly organized society does afford wide opportunity for the abuse of power; and it is inevitable, while men are imperfect, that many will yield to the temptation. In modern liberalism the emphasis on freedom has also tended to be extreme and uncritical and this has encouraged irresponsibility; and it has also encouraged undue emphasis on getting power, in comparison with reflection on the ends or values for which power is to be used. These facts define a major problem and task of free culture. Society must educate and restrain, must make men intelligent and moral in such a way and degree, and create such a social order, that they can be trusted with the freedom, which means the power, required for the good life.

V

We turn now from esthetics to ethics or morality, in the narrower and more usual connotation of terms which are used with little regard for critical definition, partly because this field of discourse is still so largely dominated by a tradition which was established under religious influence. It is true that "love" in the mystical-emotional sense of New Testament *agapé* is no longer accepted or professed as the substance of goodness. The question is whether this is a loss or a gain. It is almost superfluous to remark that it never was the real basis of the moral code of everyday life in a civilized society— not even for life in a convent or monastery, where order was always based on authority. Organization on a basis of "love" alone could hardly be approached in a self-contained society, i.e., without fraternalistic segregation, and moral, as well as economic, parasitism. (The difficulty, as will later be suggested, is far less in everyone's loving his neighbor as himself than in his loving his neighbor's children as his own, or treating them as if he did.) In modern society, personal relations rest on the ideals of mutual respect and friendliness, and especially on the "bourgeois virtues" of competence, foresight, and reliability, which are not conspicuous (to say the least) in New Testament teaching. "Love" in any reasonable meaning, is now recognized as a highly selective attitude, with its proper as well as its actual content varying infinitely from one situation to another. Or, in modern usage, love as a moral virtue means love of the "values," truth, beauty and goodness (fairness and generosity) and especially— because they are so likely to be overlooked—competence and its correlate, good workmanship. If men and life are to be made better, it will surely be accomplished by cultivating these ideals and attitudes, and not by trying to teach everybody to love everybody else in the world with undiscriminating fervor.

Nor do we moderns generally think of goodness as "helpfulness," apart from the special situation of people in distress (as in the Good Samaritan story!) due to some calamity, or to serious inadequacy. And in such situations "sympathy" is rather the appropriate emotion. Of course we still talk much of "serving others" and "doing good"; but again, this is largely because explicit discussion takes place under religious or fraternalistic auspices or is sentimental bubbling. Modern ideas and ideals assume that "others" are also self-respecting human beings, and hence neither desire nor expect to be "served" but, within the bounds of their capacity, to stand on their own feet, to "play their own hands" in the game of social relations, and also to carry their share of common burdens. On the other hand, sympathy and helpfulness, in situations where these are called for, as well as friendliness and the absence of hostility and suspicion in ordinary human relations, have certainly been developed under modern "ma-terialistic" and "commercialistic" civilization, far beyond the achievement of any other known society in which human relationships have extended beyond the scale of a small face-to-face group.

In positive terms, modern ethical ideals center in the concept of *freedom,* as indicated by the word "liberalism." Freedom means two things: First, maximum freedom for the individual, i.e., on the whole, for all individuals, as against coercion by anyone or in any form, specifically by law and the enforcement of law. This does not mean literal, "isolationist" individu-alism. Associative and specifically "organized" life, of a scope and intricacy undreamed of in the first century, is taken for granted, including freedom to consult advisers believed to be more competent than oneself. It means that association is to be, as far as possible, free, voluntary, not compulsory; the functions of government and law are to be minimized. In the second place, freedom means that such politico-legal coercion as is necessary in the interests of order—and hence of maximum freedom itself—is to be "democratic." The enactment and enforcement of law are the exclusive task of a political order made effectively responsive to the popular will, in the only possible way, namely, by the machinery of representative government and the electoral process.

It is (we repeat) particularly to be emphasized that in modern liberal thought freedom is an ethical value, and not merely instrumental to the end of economic efficiency, as a superficial reading of the literature of utilitarianism often suggests. It is assumed both that human beings, as moral, wish to be free, even at some sacrifice of efficiency, and also, that they *ought* to be free, even against a possible impulse or wish to the contrary. Modern legal systems do not permit the individual to contract himself into servitude either through error or through deliberate choice. The ethical principle of free association was well stated by Herbert Spencer—a thinker whose undoubted limitations currently tend to obscure his sound perceptions. It is the principle that each individual shall have the right to judge and to choose his own ends and the best course of action for realizing them, as long as he does not infringe the similar and equal freedom of others.

VI

These last remarks suggest the relations of "cooperation," and bring us to what is the most distinctive and in a sense the most fundamental characteristic of modern civilization, namely, the technology, capitalism and large-scale organization of "economic" activity.[4] This is the sphere or aspect of life which naturally comes to mind when we speak of modern problems; for it is in this sphere that those conflicts of interest arise which threaten order and peace, as well as progress. Any rational discussion must first of all clearly recognize that what we mean by "economy" is the effective use of means to realize ends, meaning any ends whatever. There are no distinct economic ends. All purposive activity, including play, is directed towards ends and calls for the use of means, a fact completely ignored by primitive Christian teaching; and the significance of activity in realizing value, either in the result or in the activity itself, depends on its efficiency. (Within limits, as always; the qualifications which many of our generalizations call for cannot be noted here.) As we have already emphasized, and as should be evident, the "higher" values, truth and beauty, and their diffusion or sharing are *especially* dependent upon the use of means; and such values constitute the real difference between a high and a low "standard of living."[5]

In the second place, the modern mind recognizes that in consequence of the given and unalterable conditions of man's

---

[4] The enormous development of organized play and of organized cultural activities is nearly as characteristic of modern society as the organization of "work"—and the lines which separate these categories are extremely vague. One thinks of Greek democracy in this connection. These things should be mentioned because reference to them is so conspicuously absent from New Testament teaching, while their value is so great and so unquestionable in the modern ideal of life. But only bare mention is possible here.

[5] Religion is no exception to the principle that it is the higher values which are costly, and illustrates the treacherous relation between our "talk" and what we really admire and strive to do. According to the talk, God is a spirit and is to be worshipped in spirit, even in secret, and in temples not made with hands. In practice, religious people go as far in the opposite direction as they can afford. Moreover, the temples and trappings of religion (including Christianity, especially in its medieval heyday) have often been purchased with wealth obtained in corrupt and dishonorable ways. The costliness of religious practice is connected with the fact that the religious experience is largely esthetic, in a narrow or a broad sense.

life upon the earth one indispensable requisite for even minimum productive efficiency, and hence for any civilized or good life, is specialization, which involves the *organization* of the use of means. Moreover, this organization has to be on a vast scale, especially because of the way in which necessary "raw materials," and climatic conditions controlling the character of production, are distributed over the globe.

Hypothetically, or in imagination at least, economic organization might be carried out and might achieve efficiency and progress under many forms or patterns. In modern history, it actually developed on the pattern called "free enterprise." The reasons cannot be investigated here. It can in fact be shown that *if* human beings conformed to appropriate specifications, and governments likewise—operated by the same or similar men, or by a special race of men, or by angels or Gods—the ends could be even better accomplished under a system of centralized control, i.e., socialism or collectivism. Even pure antinomian anarchism is imaginable, without violating any established law of nature. However, there are very cogent reasons for believing that with men at all as they are— and with governments as they will be, if staffed by such men—neither socialism nor anarchism in any approximation to the ideal pattern is a practical possibility.[6]

With respect to the ethical aspect of organization, one important proposition can be stated as a fact. The enterprise economy, with all the main features of cooperative action worked out through the purchase and sale of goods and services by free individuals, in free markets, on terms (prices) set by market competition, is the only possible method for

---

[6] This is a question of political, social and moral facts and principles; it is not a question of economics, in the sense of the subject matter of economics as a recognized special science or discipline. Of course, the revolutionist assumes that "human nature" will be completely different after the inauguration of his scheme; but this proposition does not call for serious consideration.

realizing at the same time the practically infinite gain in efficiency to be had through organization and a reasonable degree of individual freedom in economic life. A socialistic state with any regard for the freedom of the individual must retain the general pattern of the free market organization; and even ignoring personal liberty, the difficulties of administration are insuperable in a large organization without price relations, especially if it is in any degree progressive. The totalitarian states, communistic or nationalistic, keep this general pattern. And even in the most democratic organization, on the scale necessary to utilize modern technology, the infinitesimal voice of the individual in the government would be no compensation for regimentation in the affairs of everyday life.

Under "ideal conditions," described by economic theory— corresponding in a general way to abstraction from friction in theoretical mechanics—the enterprise or market organization also leads to maximum productive efficiency. That is, both total product and the income of every individual are the largest that is possible with the available means and without uncompensated transfers—robbery or gift. This conclusion, however, rests on three important "assumptions": (a) Individuals must know their own interests and act intelligently in their own interest but without exercising coercion of any kind—force or fraud or "over-" persuasion (i.e., any real persuasion, as distinguished from communication of facts); (b) Perfect competition must exist; resources and products must be minutely divisible, and there must be no monopolistic action, either by an individual in a position of power or through collusion between individuals; (c) Transactions between individuals must not substantially affect, either for good or for ill, other individuals whose interests are not represented.

The ethical character of the result is, however, subject to the further reservation that in the mechanical operation of the economy the individual is treated as "given," particularly in

210

his three economic components. These are (1) his wants and (2) his productive capacity, which in turn comprises (2-a) personal endowments, original and acquired, and property owned and (2-b) technique, or knowledge of productive methods. The content of freedom is relative to what one wishes to do and is dependent on the possession of power. In exchange relations, moreover, effective freedom requires power not too far inferior to that possessed by the other party to the transaction; hence freedom implies some limitation on inequality. In any case, the individual cannot possibly be treated as given. For it is a simple fact, not merely that his nature is largely determined by social action, but that determining the character and endowments of the individual members of society is the supreme problem of social policy. It is particularly indefensible in the case of dependent persons to treat economic performance as the measure of individual moral desert, or of socially imperative income. As already hinted, the family is in many respects more real as a social economic unit than is the individual.

Every one of the mechanical conditions listed is likely to be more or less violated by the facts, and to that extent there is occasion for intervention by the state or some other agency, without violating the principle of maximum freedom. In addition, as has always been recognized, social action is called for in many fields where the future of society as a whole is involved, or where the beneficiary at the moment is the community rather than a particular individual, and also where technical conditions lead to "natural" monopoly. (The importance of monopoly as an evil is grossly exaggerated in popular estimation.) These considerations map a large area in which market competition needs to be supplemented or modified by other forms of relationship—legal compulsion, or special forms of cooperation, or "charity." There is no implication of *laisser-faire*, but the detailed facts and the action appropriate under each head cannot be taken up in this essay. However, infinitely more important problems of social action arise in connection with the creation or formation of individuals fit for freedom, in economic relations as usually conceived, and in all relations. Christianity and liberalism have both erred in taking individuals too much for granted and viewing moral problems in terms of right relations between given individuals. But while Christian teaching ignored the problem completely, liberalism has progressively recognized it and sought to provide and to enforce proper training and a reasonable start in life for the young.

VII

We come finally to the question as to the cause and possible remedy for the dissatisfaction with modern civilization which is so widespread and so acute that it threatens to engulf that civilization and all its achievements in a "holocaust" of destructive conflict. The particular question for us here is the merits of religion as a remedy; but it is proverbial that diagnosis must precede effective treatment. And diagnosis in turn, to continue with the medical figure, must rest on adequate *knowledge* of the anatomy and physiology of the body in which the disease occurs. But knowledge and understanding with a view to action are no part of primitive Christian morality. Indeed, they are implicitly condemned, for they come under the category of means or power, and elementary consistency requires that the Gospel condemnation of wealth be extended to include all forms of power—material means, organization, and intelligence itself.

In connection with remedial action, the medical figure is particularly significant. The history of medicine reveals the striking fact that what "human nature" prompts men to do, to themselves or to others, when they are sick, is predominantly injurious or at best harmless because completely irrelevant. Curative elements in prescientific procedure have crept in by some accident, or perhaps by a kind of Darwinian selection of spontaneous variations. And the same pathetic situation is met with in connection with the malfunctioning of the "body politico-economic." Objectivity compels us to admit that "intelligent" procedure, looking at the facts and analyzing them down to principles, and acting in ways which there is some reason to believe will "work," is not at all a natural trait of man, the "romantic fool." Our natural impulses, even (perhaps especially!) where our intentions are good, run toward finding somebody, a supernatural entity, or preferably some human individual or group, to *blame* for anything that seems to be wrong, and to proceed by way of magical coercion, or by punishment, or "liquidation." This may not seem to be a natural consequence of Christianity, but as will presently appear such is very largely the case—if modern religious and moral attitudes are derived from Christian teachings.

In any event, no other action which seems to be a more natural or proper expression of love for individual human beings (or for God) is likely to be more effective, or much less disastrous. Let anyone reflect as to how far love will carry us toward a solution of the problem of money, the business cycle and unemployment! Economic depression profits practically no one, hence it cannot be due to exploitation; but it is the main source or center of the whole culture crisis, including the war. However, it is all this chiefly because of the kind of remedies which are proposed and tried—beginning with war, or perhaps ending with it.

The conclusions of the preceding section, which contain in substance the correct diagnosis of our economic ills, and indicate the lines along which curative action must proceed, follow from quite simple analysis, familiar to any fairly competent student of elementary economics. Of course the content of that discipline cannot be recapitulated here. The most important principles are not really economic in any special or scientific sense, but are at the level of simple arithmetic. A society cannot (in any moderately "long run") distribute or consume more than it produces, or have more by producing less. Yet exactly this is the obvious effect, if not the direct intention, of the measures which are typically advocated by "reformers," on moral and religious grounds, for alleviating poverty, whether by reducing inequality or by increasing economic prosperity—specifically in the United States of America at the date of this writing. Any such remedies can only be destructive of progress and ultimately of civilization.[7] Since free exchange must benefit both parties, it follows that any arbitrary dictation of any price, against free market forces (apart from force and fraud and monopoly), must injure both parties; and this applies specifically to the price of labor.

Two anomalies in particular are so outstanding as to appeal to any well-developed sense of humor. The first is the destruction of intellectual morality by the primitive natural prejudice already referred to. One of the most favored lines of action for alleviating poverty is to force employers to raise wages, without reference to the economic value of the service for which wages are paid, as judged by the ultimate consumer of the product. Most of those who advocate this remedy actually know quite well that employers cannot pay for services (on any general scale) more than this value, which effective market competition will force them to pay, without coercion. Forcing them to pay more must reduce production and employment. They know that employers in general have extremely little margin of discretion as to what wages they

---

[7] Renunciation of improvement, of progress, is not enough. Civilized life even at low levels will not even keep going without thought-taking of the same kind as that required for melioristic action; and it is doubtful whether civilization could exist without progress.

can pay and continue in business, and more specifically, that the particular employers who pay the lower wages are typically already bankrupt or on the edge of bankruptcy. As to the argument that in reality perfect competition is not present, the answer is that of course it is not, but that—apart from the gross exaggeration of the role of monopoly in the popular mind—this fact strengthens the argument against this kind of interference. In general, the "monopolistic" employers already pay the higher wages; and to force them to pay still more to their particular employees would be a palpable injustice to those less well paid and would produce new evils without curing the old.

The second anomaly is that such remedies should be advocated on the basis of "Christian" principles. This is clearly the antithesis of preaching the spiritual value of poverty, non-resistance to evil, and love of one's enemies. But the preachers of Christianity, and churches in their organized capacity, typically advocate both recourse to force and the use of force in ways certain to aggravate the evils, and in particular to injure the persons the measures are particularly intended to benefit. The limit of this tendency is "Christian Marxism," which, in spite of the contradiction involved, is a natural position, and quite logical. Love of the downtrodden seems a mockery if it does not lead to action on their behalf, which is naturally taken to mean liquidation of their oppressors. "Preaching at" employers and men of wealth along the same lines, or appealing to them in terms of "love" is better only in that it is relatively innocuous. But it is vicious in so far as it distracts attention from rational analysis and the discovery and application of effective procedures.

VIII

In the scope of an article, though overlong, it has been impossible to treat our topic fully. We hope enough has been said to show that the issues in modern civilization present intellectual problems, and cannot be fruitfully attacked in terms of the ethics of love, or any sentimental-personal morality. And this should indicate the type of religion and morality which are called for in order to develop civilization and forestall reversion to primitive savagery. Again, the comparison with individual medicine is profoundly illuminating up to a certain point. Effective medical practice depends upon science and workmanship; very much "love," or even sympathy, for the suffering individual is a serious obstruction to effective practice, a natural disposition which must be rationally repressed in favor of a highly sophisticated interest in science and craftsmanship. Of course, this does not mean that the doctor is not motivated by ethical ideals which have some ultimate relation to love of humanity—perhaps also to love of God, or at least to "religion." If more religious faith can create a greater degree of serenity and confidence, without sapping the springs of action, that is a consummation devoutly to be wished, both on its own account and as a condition favorable to effective action itself. But this does not mean that sound ideals can be identified with religious ideals, without a fundamental redefinition of the latter. *It is imperative to understand the relation between morality and intelligence, and the provision of adequate means.* The relation is one of complementarity. Development of any one of these three requisites for the good life calls for a corresponding development of both of the others, or the result will be evil rather than good. "True religion," we submit, is a matter of the right emotional attitude toward the problem as a whole, and an energizing faith that study and rationally directed effort will lead progressively toward its solution. Some of our liberal churches and ministers are undoubtedly working toward such an ideal.

On the other hand, our statement that the problems are intellectual must not be understood as implying that they are "scientific" problems. Undoubtedly, an excessive faith in science and the application of scientific categories to moral and social problems, where they have no application, has been one of the important factors leading up to the present crisis—far more important than excessive religiosity. *Science and technology tell us how to do, but never what to do.* Individual medicine itself is "scientific" only to the extent that men agree on the meaning of health and disease (in reality further qualified by the mental factor). In this field, the degree of agreement which is practically requisite may be taken for granted. In "social medicine," the case is distinctly to the contrary; the main problem in realizing social health is that of defining it, of agreeing as to what is to be striven for. The nature of ideal society is at once a moral and an intellectual problem. It is the general problem of values, in which the two modes of reality meet, existence and purpose. Science and religion both involve a high and austere ethic. But neither of them is directly relative to political problems; neither is an ethic of organized relationships. Scientific ethics is the grosser error, at least when science refuses to recognize that its own foundations and presuppositions are moral-evaluative, an impersonal devotion to objective truth, as against any selfish, or sentimental, interest.[8]

Finally, the practical problem of achieving any defined conception of a "healthy" (or an "ideal") society is still not a scientific or a technical one in the proper, instrumentalist sense. To begin with, it is the very different kind of problem involved in formulating, which means rationally agreeing upon, "rules of the game," which is not a matter of means and end. But right rules, in the sense of right relations between given individuals, is still a comparatively minor aspect of the problem. The major task is that of progressively creating

---

[8] Science is a close approximation to the pure type of democracy, free individual co-operation or "anarchy," settling all issues intellectually, by discussion.

"right" individuals, which in itself means a right cultural situation, one in which freedom, order, and efficiency are simultaneously possible to the highest degree. More concretely, the objective is such a society, made up of such men, that the individual can be trusted with freedom, meaning that he can be trusted with the *power* which is necessary to give freedom substantial content. Meanwhile, the issue lies between trusting men with freedom, and with the power over others which in organized society is inseparable from freedom, and trusting some small group of men with supreme power to govern, and to change, all others.

The greatest tragedy of the situation is that freedom has led men to conceive of their "rights" in terms which enormously overlap, and far surpass possibility, and that conflict of rights, while it is the only discussible form of conflict, is far more serious than conflict of interests. Only as rights can interests be discussed; interests are asserted, not argued, except as values, i.e., judgments about values. And discussion is the only way in which problems of conflict are really "solved"; force, which includes persuasion, yields no real solution of any problem. Yet in the discussion of rights, the very notion of their sanctity tends to result in an appeal from discussion to force.[9]

---

[9] Explicit mention should be made of international relations, especially since the immediate threat to civilization comes from war. It goes without saying that no country or nation can solve its problems or save itself alone. Some effective political world order is indispensable. But, as prohibition of usury, now recognized as a stupid policy, was the dominant principle of Christian economics in the Middle Ages, the most conspicuous result fairly attributable to Christian teachings in modern Western society would seem to be that "pacifism" which has made the peace-loving peoples so helpless and at the mercy of those who frankly worship force.

Social-ethical problems not centering in economic organization have had to be passed over here because of space limits. The general notion of "purity," for example, occupies a large place in moral ideas, from the most primitive beginning, and it is not implied that "morals," in the meaning conveyed by the quotation marks, do not present an important problem in modern society.

The Meaning of Democracy: Its Politico-Economic Structure and Ideals

*T*he prospect of saying anything about democracy, at this date in history and in the compass of a short essay, which will contain at once enough truth and enough novelty to be of value, seems to the writer to be small, and the attempt rather presumptuous. This article will merely attempt to present some notes on basic principles, which may possibly help thoughtful readers to clarify the nature of the ideal, and may shed some light on the problems which threaten the existence of democracy in this day of crisis.

Preliminary Definition: Freedom, Causality and Coercion

The popular, everyday conception of democracy is political liberty or free government. Another familiar definition is government by discussion. We shall start out from the former notion and proceed to explain it by use of the latter. We may

Reprinted by permission from the *Journal of Negro Education*, vol. 10 (1941), pp. 318–332.

note at the outset that the notion of free government presents a paradox, a seeming contradiction. For coercion, the antithesis of freedom, is of the essence of government. And to consider the notion of free government, as a reality, or something more or less approximated in reality, and as an ideal which is to be more closely approximated as well as preserved, we need to go still farther back and begin with some notice of the problem of freedom in the individual life. Freedom is a mystery, which, as everyone knows, has been discussed by philosophers and theologians through the ages. It seems to violate the principle of causality in nature, which is regarded as a presupposition of all science, and even of all knowledge.

We cannot, of course, embark here on any extended argument of this metaphysical problem. For our practical purpose, sufficient "proof" of freedom in human conduct is found in the fact that we raise the question and deliberate about it, and discuss it. Machines, we submit, do not bother, or argue among themselves, about the question whether they are machines, or beings with some freedom and responsibility. Human beings certainly *know*, more certainly than they know anything else, that they think and choose, and that it is the last word in contradiction for thinking to deny its own reality. One cannot say that one is not saying anything. Our conduct differs from purely mechanical process, ruled by cause and effect alone, in that we raise and answer questions, solve problems—with results which are more or less right or wrong.

In addition, everyone knows that conduct brings him into relations with other free persons, or selves, and that in these relations there is a difference between free association and coercion of one party by the other. The ultimate meaning of this contrast also is difficult to formulate; perhaps it is impossible to state it clearly in words, or even to form a satisfactory conception of it. But it is still literally undeniable. Again, the fact of discussion settles the matter. This article is a case in point. I, the author, am not coerced to write what I write and the reader is free to read or not read and to agree or not to agree. (Please note that coercion includes all persuasion, of which the essence is deception, and because the victim is not conscious of it, persuasion is the most dangerous form.)

It will be noted that we have already brought in, or come in sight of, the conception of government by discussion. It is in our intellectual life that we find what is perhaps the highest level of free association, a kind of "ideal type" for democracy. However, there is not much "government" in it, though there obviously is some, in any organized discussion, hence any which involves more than a very few participants. A main aspect of our task of explaining or illuminating the nature of democracy as free government lies in bringing out the contrast between political and non-political association. Either type may present widely varying degrees of freedom or coercion, but freedom in government involves special difficulties and more serious limitations.

Freedom in the Evolutionary Scale

We have found it necessary, for a starting point, to go back to mechanical process, where freedom and coercion have no meaning. Our "control" over the objects and processes of nature involves nothing of the nature of coercion or persuasion. It will be useful to think also of some of the changes which meet the eye as we contemplate the ascending scale of living forms. Even plants, to which we do not impute consciousness or intelligence, seem in a way to solve problems, to be adaptive or purposive; and problem-solving is the essence of free activity. But of more concern for the argument is the life of *social animals*. These are best exemplified in the elaborately differentiated and organized "colonies" of some insects, notably termites, and in a lesser degree, in the bees and wasps. The contrast between insect society and human society helps to bring out the nature of the latter. In a wasp's nest or termite colony there is highly organized behavior, hence "law and order" in a real sense. But since the behavior is instinctive, not intelligent, and from our point of view entirely mechanical, there is still neither freedom nor coercion, but only causality. Apart from the sense in which this is true of plant forms, the members of an insect community do not solve problems, either individual or social. Their behavior does not involve effort, or error.

It is of course the solution of social problems which is significant for our problem of democracy, but the crucial point is that the two sorts of problem solving, the individual and the social, are by no means inseparable. In contrast with such organized social life as that of the termites, the life of what we call the "higher" animals, and especially the higher vertebrates, is not socially organized, but quite individualistic. Even life in herds may involve relatively little organization. However, these species, especially those most closely related to man, are unquestionably intelligent, as bees and termites are not. The apes in particular show much capacity to solve problems of a considerable degree of intricacy. But they are purely individual and purely instrumental problems. Animals do not "discuss," and thus reach a group decision on group action, nor even individually deliberate about "ideals." From an evolutionary point of view, it is a very interesting fact that intelligence and social life evolved separately, in different branches of the animal kingdom, widely separated in biological characteristics, and in order and time of appearance, and that of the two, socialization appeared earlier and lower in the scale. It is as if nature's first effort to produce intelligent association—and that development of individual intelligence which is impossible without association—had first ended in failure in the insects, as if it had been found impossible to add intelligence to socialization on an *instinctive* basis. It was necessary to make a fresh start, and develop a considerable degree of intelligence in species living individualistic lives, and then "socialize" such creatures, and on this foundation to go on with the process of developing life on the pattern represented by man.

The distinctive character of human life is that it is both intelligent and social, with the two features inseparably connected. It is intelligently social and socially intelligent. To carry on the mode of life which we call human, i.e., to be human, men must solve problems, both individually and socially. In fact, very little if any, of the pattern, order, or "law" which is characteristic of human life seems to be instinctive, in the proper sense of the word. It is doubtful whether man is instinctively social, his urge or drive to association is so vague and inconsistent. The familiar adage that he is "naturally" a social (or political) animal is misleading. In sharp contrast with insect society, in which there is relatively perfect "law and order," but neither courts nor legislature, human society must in large part both enforce and make its "law." And it does both very imperfectly indeed! It is permeated with immorality, criminality, conflict and disorder, and would surely seem intolerably anarchic to a termite with intelligence enough to judge. Man is a social *being;* but his sociality is bound up with individuality, in a sense absolutely foreign to the "individual" member of an animal society. The latter is in a position more like that of a cell in an organism than that of either a citizen of a democracy or the subject of a despotism.

On the other hand, it is equally important that man is only to a limited extent intelligently social. For the most part, comparatively speaking, the organization pattern of any human society at any given time, and the forces or "laws" which govern it, belong to an intermediate category, between instinct and intelligence. They are a matter of custom, tradition, or institutions. Such laws are transmitted in society, and acquired by the individual, through relatively effortless and even unconscious imitation, and conformity with them by any mature individual at any time is a matter of "habit." Traditionalism was significant for evolution through greater flexibility, in comparison with instinct biologically transmitted. In so far as social life is a thing of custom and institutions, it is still "mechanical." It is not intelligent, and hence, like insect society, it involves neither freedom nor coercion. It becomes different, distinctively human, only as men become critically aware of their institutions, and deliberate, choose, and act with regard to their modification or preservation.

However, it is not at all certain whether this idea of men "becoming" conscious of behavior patterns already existing is historically valid or not. We do not know, and probably never can know, how human social life developed, particularly the comparative roles of gradual and more or less unconscious institutional change or drift on one hand, and violent struggle and ruthless domination on the other. No doubt both played a large part; but we cannot here concern ourselves with this speculative problem.[1] We do know that in present and historical human society men are more or less clearly aware of established patterns of action, often designated by the general term "usages"; and they have many different attitudes toward these usages, in different types of cases. Of many we are practically unconscious, while others are simply "there," and are taken for granted. We do not ask how they came into existence— unless we are anthropologists—and we conform habitually

---

[1] It is quite clear that despotism, deeply grounded in religion, was the first form under which human beings achieved reasonably effective organization on a large scale. Apart from extremely small and primitive communities, democracy, where it has existed, has always been established by a revolutionary overthrow of tyranny.

and more or less unconsciously, with no thought of what would happen to us if we did not. In other cases, we are conscious of a problem; we want to conform and know that we should feel much "embarrassed" if we ignorantly or inadvertently failed to do so, though no punishment would follow, except our own feelings—or that other people might be amused, or feel sorry for us. It is an open question whether the notions of freedom and coercion are meaningful in this connection.

But there are other "laws" which we know to be coupled with explicit provisions for enforcement through some penalty or punishment inflicted on those who break them, either by the group, as in some primitive communities, or by individuals acting as agents of "society," organized in the form or body which we call government or the state. Even most of these laws "we" would also obey as a matter of course—though there are some who would not! We should obey, either because the conduct prescribed is recognized as right, or merely because it is the law, and we recognize that it is right, and necessary, to be law-abiding.

In our attitude toward still other laws, the question of their actual content is closely associated with that of their source, or who "made" them, and how they came to be made. In some cases, we may think the law wrong, and conform only to escape the penalty, or may "take a chance" and not conform, or may even openly and publicly defy the law and the agencies of enforcement. (It is an important fact that laws practically cannot be changed without first being "broken.")

In thinking about law and government we inevitably form the notion of an ideal state, as (a) one in which no coercion would exist except in accord with law and (b) one where all law would be "right," and recognized as such by all right-thinking men. Hence, coercion would apply only to men who were not right-thinking, because of either incompetence or an immoral attitude. This definition of the ideal state does not logically imply democracy as a form of government, in the usual understanding of that term (and on the other hand democracy is conceivable, or is commonly thought to be conceivable, without law). Democracy as the ideal form of the state rests on two further considerations, which are familiar to all who have given much thought to the problems. The first of these is the instrumental consideration that democratic political institutions are believed to be the surest and best way, if not the only way, to secure that the laws, including procedures of enforcement, will be "right," or will come closest to conformity with this ideal. (Hence the relation mentioned above between right law and law made in the right way.) The second consideration is an intrinsic or "absolute" value judgment; it is held to be inherently right that men should themselves make the laws under which they live. In the familiar phrase, *free* government may be considered more important than *good* government—within some limits, and assuming that the two may conflict and that a choice must be made between them.

Freedom as an Ideal: The Meaning of Human Living

One general difficulty connected with defining democracy lies in the fact that it is inherently and so largely a matter of degree, both as a reality and as a normative ideal, as well as highly diverse in kind. In its ultimate meaning, democracy is simply the fact of consciously intelligent group life, or group action. Democracy consists in the fact that the individual members of any group recognize themselves and each other as a group, which faces group problems, and that they consciously act as a group in solving these problems. One of the first difficulties is that what we may call the pure abstract

idea of democracy, or democratic group life, does not necessarily have any necessary logical implication about either
government or "law," either law enforcement or law making—while the concept of government may also be separated
from that of law. Ultimately, to repeat, democracy is simply
group action, the decision of group questions by group process.
It is practically identical with discussion, the intellectual-
cooperative quest of right answers to questions. Right answers
are known by the fact of agreement that they are such. Hence
the very notion of a "right" answer implies some society,
and social recognition of truth or norms which have "validity,"
in contrast with merely individual opinion or preference. The
intellectual life appears again as virtually the pure ideal of
democracy, or *free* group life. Truth is established only by
discussion, in the absence of *coercion*, either by individuals
in their private capacity or in the exercise of authority, *or by
any majority*. An opinion really is not an opinion at all unless
it is "freely" adopted and held, on grounds of intellectual
conviction. Coercion also includes "persuasion," in the
distinctive and proper meaning of that term, the core of which
is deception (recognizing that any form of coercion may
proceed from benevolent motives).

Putting these considerations together, the ultimate nature
of democracy is simply that of *human* life. Men cannot live,
as human beings, outside of *free* society, outside of association
based on free agreement as to the nature of the society
(meaning its constitution and laws) and its activities, and free
agreement and disagreement within this framework. On the
other hand, the human type of association implies *differences,
conflicts*, which always combine conflict of interest and
difference of opinion. Mental life seems to be relative to such
differences; there is no conscious interest apart from conflict
of interest and no opinion apart from difference of opinion,
and these two aspects of mental life are inseparable. On one

227

hand, it is only in the form of differences of opinion that conflicts of interest are subject to discussion. Only "rights" can be discussed, not mere individual or subjective wants, which can only be asserted—and fought over! On the other hand men seem naturally to convert any feeling of interest which encounters opposition into an opinion that it is a "right." But to have any social (hence any human) life, men have to recognize the necessity and the possibility of reaching agreement through a social-intellectual activity or process. If they do not have some sphere of freedom, but are completely coerced, they are not men; and they cannot "agree to disagree," and go their separate ways "in peace" without destroying all society and human life itself. A "Crusoe" existence is possible only to an individual previously brought up in society. (But of course no tyranny can possibly suppress all freedom, individual or associative.)

Maximum Freedom

The principle of democracy as an ideal means that freedom is ethically good and coercion, evil—or that life is good in being human life—whether the coercion is practiced by one individual or one group over another, or by the majority in any organization over the minority.[2] It means that any interference in individual freedom, including mutually free relationships between individuals, even by the most ideally democratic government, is to be justified only on the ground that it increases total freedom, immediately or in the long run. This doctrine of *maximum liberty* is ultimately a deduction

---

[2] The most serious general problem in the practice of political democracy is that of the limits of majority rule. Some balance must be struck between complete individual irresponsibility and caprice—which, since men will not in fact agree spontaneously and unanimously, would exclude order and efficiency, if not peace itself—at one extreme, and the right of the majority to enslave any minority at the other.

from the principle already announced, that free discussion is the only method by which differences of opinion are settled "rightly," or any problem really solved. Either statement must stand as a moral axiom accepted as such in modern thought. The contrary principle, the alternative axiom, would be that it is intrinsically good for men to "obey" in belief and action, rather than to act as free agents. But a duty or ideal of obedience implies someone in the opposite role, to be obeyed. That is, it implies the division of the population into two classes—castes in the most extreme sense—born or called in some supernatural way to the respective rôles of authority and servitude. Such notions have indeed been accepted and believed in, at various times and places in human history, but in our modern world they no longer command respect.

The ethical ideals of modern Western man are not ascetic, or quietistic, or monastic. We, as modern men, believe (as we assume here) in material well-being, not poverty, as the basis of the good life. Moreover, our ideal of life is active, progressive, and individualistic, or libertarian, as against "community" in any mystical sense. We believe that personal relations should be on the basis of mutual respect and mutual consent, which carries a presumption of mutual advantage, and that association should be restricted within these limits. Freedom to refuse association, including cooperation, on any terms on which either may be offered, takes precedence over any conflicting "right." We believe in freedom of opportunity, and especially in freedom of the individual to get ahead, or improve his position, by his own efforts and means. We believe in freedom not only on the utilitarian ground that it is the best provision for efficiency and progress, but also for two further and deeper and more serious reasons. First, it is assumed that the typical human being, and specifically the man of intelligence and good will, desires to be free, to live responsibly, "stand on his own feet" and to "play his own hand," even at some possible material cost. And second, freedom is held to be an ideal value, a thing which men ought to want, even if they do not; it is an unquestioned principle of modern law and politics that an individual does not have the privilege of selling or contracting himself into servitude, either by error, or if he should deliberately choose to do so.

To be sure, none of these principles is to be taken in an "absolute" sense. Within limits, modern society recognizes the necessity of protecting individuals against themselves, against their own incompetence or prejudice. And individuals are given many rights or valid claims, both against others and against society as a whole—notably the right to education and to assistance or relief when in distress, either as a result of some calamity, or because of incompetence. Modern individualism does not mean antinomian anarchism! Moreover, it does not mean that each individual must always decide every question for himself, even within the limits of the law. He need not, for example, be his own physician when ill; he may consult with, and in a sense place himself under the orders, and even temporarily under the power, of an expert or specialist in the field of any particular type of problem. In this connection, individualism means a reasonable degree of freedom in choosing one's own physician, or other expert consultant— though even the most democratic states find it necessary to enforce some limits on the freedom of individuals to set themselves up as experts, or to advise and prescribe for others, in matters where special competence is obviously called for. The *primary* function of government is to *prevent coercion* and so guarantee to every man the right to live his own life on terms of *free* association with his fellows.

In the actual working of democracy, the activities of government itself are recognized to be tasks for individuals with special competence and special training. This means that in the making of laws, but more especially in their interpretation and application, the personnel of government at any moment, and particularly individuals in key positions, necessarily have considerable discretionary power. And it means that the concrete problems which are put up to the electorate take the form primarily of choosing officials, on the basis of their competence to decide special issues, or even more remotely, of their competence to select and appoint the officials who actually make concrete decisions. Only a limited number of questions of policy, and those typically in very general form, can possibly be decided directly by the people, in any election, and then chiefly by the selection of agents whose integrity and judgment must be trusted, within wide limits, in carrying out the verdict of the people, always meaning some "putative" majority. Government becomes highly "indirect," as to the content of legislation, as well as its interpretation and enforcement.

The Government and the State: Its "Just Powers"

Turning to the problem of government as such, we must retrace our steps a little. We go back to the observation made a few pages back, that the pure abstract conception of democracy, as exemplified in the intellectual life, does not of logical necessity carry the meaning either of group *action* or of *government*. And moreover, action or government, by discussion, does not necessarily imply law, i.e., any established or enduring pattern of action. It is doubtful whether it is actually possible to form a realistic conception of group life without some more or less stable constitution and laws, though men have thought that they formed the concept and even believed in it as a working ideal for society; the position has a name, antinomian anarchism, or simply antinomianism.

In any event, the notion of government, implying a constitution and laws, and generally law enforcement and law making, is far broader and more inclusive than the notion of the state. Reflection makes it clear that any group with any degree of permanence or stability whatever has some government in this sense. This is really true in some degree even of a casual social gathering or conversational group. And in proportion as any group has permanence and stability, it must have government (since men do not agree unanimously) and must exercise a degree of coercion over its members, depending on the amount of disagreement, and limited by their freedom to quit the organization. And more or less in proportion to the size of any group, the coercion exercised inevitably takes a more or less personal form, through the specialization of particular individuals for the functions of law enforcement, or law making, or both.

The difference between other societies or organizations and the "state" is ultimately one of degree. It is a matter of the degree of "compulsion" upon the individual to belong to the organization, or of his freedom not to belong. Yet the difference in degree is very important. The main peculiarity of the state as a society, among forms of organization, is that an individual has categorically less freedom and power of choice as to whether he will belong to it or not. He is not only born into some particular state—that is also true of other societies, notably churches and political parties; but in practice it is typically "impossible," or nearly so, for him to cease to be a member of the state in which he is born. This is a consequence, in the first place, of the fact that the state, in the modern sense, is based on "territorial sovereignty." Considerable organization on the territorial basis is virtually inevitable, since those who live near each other have, in consequence of that fact, a wide range of common problems. But the actual division of the world into states, and provinces, etc., with definite boundary lines, is of course largely the result of "brute force and accident," in the course of past history.

The existence of territorial states inherently sets narrow limits to the freedom of the individual. At most, he might have some freedom of choice among the different states, or jurisdictions, among which the habitable earth has happened to be divided up. But in addition, the states themselves have for the most part refused to recognize, or have destroyed, even "legal" freedom to transfer membership. (The qualifications which would obviously be called for are not in point in a brief survey.) These facts make the "sovereignty" of the state so different in degree from the coercive power or authority of any other organization that it amounts to a difference in kind. The state has virtually absolute power over the individual, except as it is limited, especially with respect to new measures, by *moral forces* (and other associations) and the fear of arousing revolt. At the same time, every state, considered as a "society," has inherited from the past a vast mass of law, and the conditions of modern life require constant and rapid growth in the volume of law. (Large scale technology is of course one of the main "conditions" referred to, but the matter cannot be taken up here.)

It is now possible to see what we must mean by democracy in relation to the state, or free government. A perfectly democratic state, as already observed, is one in which, first, there is no coercion except by authority of law and according to law, all other coercion being prevented by legal process; and second, the law itself is in accord with what normal, right-thinking men consider to be right. And we must add, and emphasize, that men must consider the whole body of law to be "necessary," as a condition of its being right. For law is coercive, and being a restriction of individual freedom, largely by the will of others, it is justified only when it really adds more to freedom in some way than it directly subtracts. Modern man does not believe that any existing law was supernaturally ordained, or that any living law-maker has divine authority. All law, therefore, is regarded as created or maintained by human agency; and the only condition under which law can be right is that it is made and enforced through some political machinery or organization by which the general consensus and will of the people as a whole is constantly embodied in law, through legislation adding to or subtracting from the existing body of law, or reformulating it. Consequently, where there is any serious difference of opinion as to any rule, liberty must prevail; no man or group of men, and specifically no majority, has a right to make law which binds others, beyond a substantial consensus that the rule in question is right and is necessary to the general good.

The Limited Significance of Political Forms

We are now ready, at last, to consider the specific subject of our study, the political and economic structure of democracy, in relation to the ideal. The political side can be quickly disposed of. A modern democratic society will typically present an almost infinite complexity of organization, with the greatest diversity from one state to another. We tend to think of "the state" as the national government. But on one side, the sovereignty of the state is limited by at least some formal and informal framework of international order or law. And on the other side, sovereignty is split up internally among jurisdictions in a more or less hierarchical order, such as "states" or provinces, counties, municipalities, and smaller local units. The concrete pattern of this organization may be indefinitely varied, and may change in any way in a given "country" from time to time, without significantly affecting the degree of approximation to ideal democracy. The only requirement in this connection is that the frame of government or constitution itself shall be in accord with the general wishes of the people, that it shall not be forced on any major fraction of the (non-criminal and mentally competent) population against their will. The form of government might be "absolute" monarchy, without violating the requirements of democracy, provided the "people" have effective freedom to change the monarch, or the constitution, at will. In practice, to be sure, this is hardly conceivable apart from some electoral machinery which is maintained by being more or less regularly called into use.

What is essential to democracy, then, is little more than this: that there be a real "will of the people," or public opinion, i.e., that there be a general consensus among the people on fundamental ideals or values, and on the major problems and issues confronting the society. If such a consensus exists, the form of governmental organization is *relatively* unimportant. Under this condition it is in the first place so unlikely as to be virtually impossible that the personnel of the government itself will desire to act contrary to the public will in any important way or degree. For the individuals who administer the government are members of the same society; they have their own opinions, and norms, molded in the first place, from childhood, by the same cultural influences or forces; and they associate, on duty and off, with ordinary citizens, and hence are certain to be continuously responsive in the same general way to changes of any sort which produce changes in the public opinion or will. In the second place, even if we assume, by a stretch of imagination, that the various officials of the government should be sufficiently united among themselves on a policy contrary to public opinion, and disposed to carry it out by force, they could hardly expect to be successful in doing so against a reasonably strong and unified public disposition to the contrary.

Of course these statements must not be interpreted in an extreme sense, particularly in view of the fact that governments constantly have to decide issues of varying degrees of importance with respect to which the public at large cannot have adequate information or even a substantially unanimous opinion and desire. It is by no means to be inferred that the machinery of government is a matter of little consequence. But its importance is much greater in connection with the formation of public opinion than in connection with conformity to it when formed, more important in connection with leading than with following. And in connection with freedom *vs.* despotism, the problem of form is vital chiefly for the maintenance of a dictatorship already established. It is still difficult to imagine a dictatorship replacing democracy in the face of any reasonably unified democratic will opposed to this eventuality. Apart from the unlikelihood of any conspiracy being able to control the army and the police, there are too many unofficial organizations with power to paralyze the activities of government, such as labor unions, churches, and various associations representing powerful interests.

Freedom and Economic Organization

The second aspect of our subject, the economic organization, or structure of democracy, brings us to the zone from which danger threatens. The great bulk of the issues discussed in modern political life, and dealt with by government, whether by the national government or some other political unit, are economic, in the broad sense of the term. Historically, democracy in the modern sense arose out of a successful struggle for the two main forms of freedom or individual liberty, namely, economic and religious.

These two struggles for individual liberty were closely interrelated, but the latter does not concern us here, since the religious structure of democracy is not included in our topic. We assume, as a matter of course, religious freedom, with complete separation of church and state. We may note that this issue was considered to be settled, at least in America, practically from the beginning of our national life. The issue of economic individualism was never settled at all so completely; but the main difference is rather that it would not "stay settled." Progress of *laisser-faire* individualism aroused increasing opposition, almost from the beginning of the movement, in that direction, both on the part of interests or classes, notably wage earners, which felt themselves disadvantaged, and in society at large, on moral grounds. It should be noted however that under present conditions the issue of religious freedom also tends to be revived, even in our own country; and it is doubtful whether any closely planned and controlled economic organization would or could do without some religious basis, or practice *complete* religious toleration.

What can be said about the form of economic organization is essentially a particular application of the more general political principle that democracy implies maximum individual liberty in all fields of action. Where interests conflict, the freedom of the individual must be limited by the free consent of other individuals affected by his actions. Relations of economic cooperation present in a somewhat special degree— or at least in a peculiarly obvious form—the combination of harmony or mutuality, and conflict of interest. The tremendous gain in the efficiency of action through association, and particularly through specialization and organization, forms a community of interest of great power. But the distribution of the fruits of collaboration, and the adjustment of the power relations which are necessarily involved, are potent sources of conflict. It is hardly a mystery that the major social problems arise in this field. But in this connection as elsewhere, the primary ethical principle is freedom, meaning mutual consent.

And the obvious meaning of mutual consent is free exchange, with each party in the position to deal with any other and hence to select the "other" who offers the best terms. Generalization of this relation yields the form of organization known as free enterprise, regulated by market competition.

The general theory of free enterprise, as set forth in any sound textbook or treatise on economics, shows that in such a system freedom for all is realized to the maximum possible degree—*for given individuals*. Under the "ideal conditions," described by general economic theory—corresponding in a general way to abstraction from friction in theoretical mechanics—the enterprise or market organization also leads to maximum productive efficiency. That is, both total product and the income of every individual are the largest that is possible *with the available means* and *without uncompensated transfers*—robbery or gift. The organization of the free market for goods and services is demonstrably the only possible way of combining effectiveness in cooperative production with individual freedom. It would, moreover, have to be employed by any socialistic state, even if totalitarian, communistic or fascistic, as the only feasible method of administering a large scale organization. But it would particularly be necessary for democratic socialism, concerned for the liberty of its citizens. Even in the most democratic organization, on the scale necessary to utilize modern technology, the voice of the individual in the government would be infinitesimal, and no compensation for regimentation in the affairs of every-day life.

However, this agreeable conclusion that freedom of the market leads automatically to both maximum liberty and maximum efficiency consistent with liberty, rests upon several "assumptions"—the theoretically ·ideal conditions—which must not be taken for granted in real life. (a) The individuals must know their own interests and act intelligently in their own interest, but without exercising coercion of any kind—force or fraud or "over"-persuasion (i.e., any real persuasion, as distinguished from communication of facts). (b) Perfect competition must exist; resources and products must be minutely divisible, and there must be no monopolistic action, either by individuals in positions of power, or through collusion between individuals. (There is no "bargaining" in an effective market.) (c) Transactions between individuals must not substantially affect, either for good or for ill, other individuals whose interests are not represented.

Moreover, the ethical character of the results is subject to the further and vitally important reservation that in the mechanical operation of the economy, the individual is treated as "given," specifically in his three economic components. These are (1) his wants and (2) his productive capacity, which in turn comprises (2-a) personal endowments, original and acquired, and property owned and (2-b) technique, or knowledge of productive methods. The content of freedom is relative to what one wishes to do—and men's wants must be "right" as well as "rational" if the result of action is to be "good"—and is also dependent on the possession of *power* to act. In exchange relations, moreover, effective freedom requires power not too far inferior to that possessed by the other party to any transaction; hence general freedom implies some limitation on inequality. In any case, the individual cannot possibly be treated as given, in any realistic discussion of society or of social policy. For it is a simple fact, not merely that individual attributes are largely determined by social processes, but also that determining the character and endowments of the individual members of society is the supreme problem of social policy. It is particularly indefensible to treat economic performance as the measure of individual moral desert, or of socially imperative income, in the case of dependent persons. The family is in many respects more real as a social economic unit than is the individual.

Political Intervention in Economic Relations

Every one of the mechanical conditions listed is likely to be more or less violated by the facts; and to that extent, there is occasion for intervention by the state or some other agency, without violating the principle of maximum freedom, but rather effecting its realization. In addition, as has always been recognized in liberal thought, social action is called for in many fields where the future of society as a whole is involved, or where the beneficiary at the moment is rather the community than a particular individual, and also where technical conditions facilitate monopoly or require "natural" monopoly. These mechanical considerations map a large area in which market competition needs to be supplemented or modified by other forms of relationship—legal compulsion, or public enterprise, or special forms of cooperation, or "charity."

There is no implication of *laisser faire*. If society is to remain free in the economic and other fields, it must in the first place act to maintain the general framework of free enterprise (miscalled "capitalism"). It must create and maintain the conditions of the free market. For one thing, this clearly means limiting the size of the bargaining unit—instead of encouraging the formation of interest groups with so much power that only the omnipotent state of totalitarianism can cope with them. (Much of what is currently preached as liberal doctrine leads straight to the destruction of liberty.) In the second place, the laws must allow sufficient incentive to induce free enterprise to venture and experiment. The actual amount can only be learned from experience, but the facts show that it has not been sufficient in recent years; and no experimentation should be needed to show that the individual will not play the game if the government fixes the terms of risk-taking on the basis of "heads I win, tails you lose."

Again, liberals have always recognized that many fields are unsuited for private enterprise, at least in the complete sense, some because the conditions are those of natural monopoly, others for other reasons. (The importance of monopoly as an evil is enormously exaggerated in the popular mind—and the most serious monopolies are those created or fostered by the government itself.) Here, also, experience and the analysis of situations are necessary to show where it is best to draw the lines between private enterprise, public enterprise, and regulation. Society must also set limits, through relief measures, to the effects of unsuccessful competition on individual lives; especially it must constantly safeguard the oncoming generation.

Comparatively speaking, however, all these mechanical problems are simple. Infinitely more serious problems of social action arise in connection with the creation or formation of individuals to enjoy freedom—in economic relations as usually conceived, and in all relations. The older liberal thought undoubtedly erred in taking individuals too much for granted and viewing the social problems merely in terms of free relations between given individuals. (Our traditional Judeo-Christian religious ethics, promulgated under far more primitive conditions, no doubt contributed to this error.) Modern democracies have at least made a beginning in the way of facing the larger problems and have sought to provide, and to enforce, proper training and a reasonable start in life for the young. It needs emphasis that education for freedom involves a large moral factor; free men must somehow be taught to feel and to exercise responsibility. Probably limits will have to be set even to freedom of expression, for those who love to trouble the waters to make better fishing for themselves, and regardless of whether such persons are self-seeking or well meaning but ignorant and romantic.

In spite of the difficulties, the writer must reemphasize the necessity of maintaining economic freedom, in the general form of free enterprise, as a condition and a prerequisite to other forms of freedom, as well as because economic activity, in the usual popular meaning, must be the main concern of the bulk of the population. Economic and other freedoms cannot be separated. The underlying reasons are not based on economic theory, which is rather on the other side, but are political, psychological, and moral. A very little examination of the political aspect of socialism will show that the difficulties of making competition work are multiplied many fold by throwing all the details of economic organization and management into the arena of politics. Reflection will also show that a government which controls the economic life of a modern nation must ruthlessly suppress opposition, and all conduct likely to lead to serious opposition. Hence it must suppress freedom of discussion and be a dictatorship. Even if the persons in power did not want this it would be necessary, to keep the machinery going and secure even minimum efficiency; and it is hardly imaginable that people who did not like power could get into the control positions.

Conclusions

In conclusion: The political and economic structures of society are so closely interrelated that they are ultimately little more than aspects of the same organization. The problems or issues with which modern society has to deal arise predominantly in the field of economic life, and particularly in connection with the terms of economic association and cooperation. The main function of government in the modern world is to provide and enforce a framework of rules for securing freedom, and the conditions necessary for effective freedom, in economic life. This means that either politics or economics can be regarded as a sub-division of the other. The ultimate ideals which must guide action are of course an ethical problem, and the fundamental requisite for democracy is a reasonable degree of consensus in the whole population as to the "right" meaning and character of life, individual and social. If this consensus exists, there is little danger that the society will be undemocratic in any large degree. And if it is absent, any large measure of democracy is impossible, and the eventuality will be either social disintegration or strife, perhaps war, between the proponents of different ideals— more or less closely associated with special interests—or finally, society may be held together and a kind of peace preserved through the establishment of dictatorship.

It follows that the ultimate task of society as a whole, and of government as the organization by which society acts as a unit, is to create such individuals, in such a total culture situation, that agreement on right ideals will be possible, and will be achieved, by nonpolitical processes. Finally, under modern conditions, and especially modern economic conditions, this is a task which no state or country can accomplish for itself alone; it is largely an "international" problem, or one for a world political order in some effective form.

Science, Philosophy, and Social Procedure

Discussion of this topic within the compass of an essay can naturally be no more than a sketchy survey of the problem and cannot avoid oversimplification and over-statement of generalizations and of distinctions necessary for analysis. As a starting-point, we must state, with little pretense of development, two main distinctions, yielding three levels of subject matter. First, "procedure" is a manifestation of *activity*, in contrast with "process," which is passive, mechanical—positive in the Comtian sense. Activity is an attribute of a purposive individual, a subject, or self. Process is persistence and change, in accord with cause and effect, or scientific law, in material which may be acted upon but does not act (unless we extend the term to include resistance to action, *perseverare in esse suo*). Second, individual activity must be contrasted with social activity, in which a plurality of individuals, a group, acts as a unit.

Social action, which is our main concern in this paper, is

Reprinted by permission from *Ethics,* vol. 52 (1942), pp. 253–274.

a conception fraught with difficulty, for several reasons. The individual himself is only to a limited extent active, or dynamic; the bulk of his observable behavior and of his mental phenomena is to be accounted for as mechanical process. (Mechanical or scientific dynamics, dealing with change in accord with unchanging law, belongs to statics, in a philosophical dichotomy.) Again, individuals act upon other individuals, and mutually interact, and act jointly with others, all in both the real sense of action and the sense of mechanical cause and effect or process; and no clear separation is possible, empirically, or perhaps even conceptually, between these categories among themselves or in contrast with social action. Finally, the human individual himself is "social" in a complexity of ways, and consequently the notion of purely individual action is an analytical concept reached only by quite heroic abstraction.

I

The essential nature of activity is, like any primary experience, indescribable, except by the use of synonymous designations. But this is true in a special sense of activity, for any literal description of it is not merely a failure but definitely falsifies its nature. To begin with, true activity lies only in thinking, in deciding, in solving a problem as to how to act in the overt sense. Overt or physical action is a physico-chemical process and presumably of the same character in the human body as anywhere else in nature. Moreover, much, perhaps most, of what goes on in the mind is of the same character—phenomenal process. It is amenable, as activity is not, to generalized scientific description, in terms of positive existence and sequence in itself and in relation to other phenomena. In true activity the self acts upon and uses its mind as well as its body. This is particularly important in connection with intercommunication between selves, which is necessary to the existence of a self, and takes place through the mind-and-body mechanisms of both parties. *Activity is problem-solving,* which is the primary ultimate or indefinable reality of thinking in general; the terms "activity," "problem-solving," and "freedom" refer to the same fact in different aspects or connections. It is "pragmatic" if the word is used in a sense as inclusive as the concept of a problem. The heart of the matter is that the solution of a problem cannot be predicted in advance of the "activity" of solving it (and the sequence of "events" in the solution is also unpredictable), and when the solution is found it is no longer a problem. We must start from the assumption that everyone knows that he acts, solves or tries to solve problems, in the various capacities mentioned: individual action upon inert objects; one-sided individual action upon others (which is coercion, including persuasion); interaction between individuals; joint or co-operative action for individual ends; and social action, which is carried out by some human group as a unit and is directed to a group end or purpose. The earlier items in the sequence can only be touched upon.

The relations between knowledge and procedure in individual action upon inert objects may be brought out by considering the situation of an isolated individual, a Crusoe. This analytical device is familiar in economic theory, and the essential point here is that Crusoe epistemology goes with Crusoe economics. The purely individualistic individual—a purely hypothetical and analytical conception, of course—is simply the economic man. He knows, or would know, only useful facts, about inert things and processes of change, and would solve problems only in the instrumental sense. He would be a "pragmatist" in the crudest meaning. He would deliberate—act, exercise freedom, solve problems, in contrast with cause-and-effect behavior—but only in connection with the use of given means to realize given concrete ends. The ends would be biological, or possibly psychological, in the phenomenal sense of experiences intrinsically desired. Ends, including their magnitudes, would be known immediately. Our hypothetical Crusoe would have no interest in truth as a value, no intellectual curiosity— and, of course, no moral interests or values. His knowledge would be exclusively scientific, at the instrumental or "economistic" level. Its content would be the useful properties of things, their responses to manipulative treatment, and the effects upon himself. His thinking would deal with the problems of such knowledge and the skills required for its application. The economic man may only in a rather unrealistic sense be said to work, and he does not play; he maximizes satisfaction, subject to the condition of the "resources" at his command.

With reference to action upon other individuals (and interindividual action) we can only note that, on one hand, it is still instrumental but, on the other, that the fact of mutual knowledge and interest makes profound differences. Knowledge of other persons is a very special kind of science, and its application in manipulation involves equally peculiar skills. Its employment is coercion, centering in deception; it is called persuasion when the deception is so complete that the subject is unaware of being coerced. Such notions as deception and coercion have no meaning in connection with action upon (or casual relations between) inert objects. The mutuality of instrumental interests inherently involves a simultaneous effort of each to control and use the other, which generates conflict. Conflict also arises in other connections, not all of which involve instrumental interests in persons or in external things, in any reasonable definition of instrumental interest. But conflict of some sort, or opposition of interests between individuals, is always at the root of any group problem.

Especially important is the category of joint or cooperative action between individuals for purely individual ends, with a view to increased efficiency through specialization. This does not involve either coercion or conflict, as long as the parties are in agreement as to the terms of the relationship. This type of behavior takes place in and implies individualistic economic organization, and its treatment is the main subject matter of theoretical economics. It gives rise to social problems, because if men are to cooperate they have to agree upon the terms, and here their interests almost necessarily conflict. Cooperation for increasing individual efficiency is in fact the main locus of social problems, in the guise in which they are currently so critical; social interests in the more strict sense, involving group ends, are actually far less serious as a source of danger to the social order.

II

Discussion of social action must center around the fact that human interests give rise to social problems in so far, and only in so far, as they involve a combination of harmony and conflict. But this is true of practically all our interests. It seems impossible to make any satisfactory classification of the interests of civilized man or to make a clear separation between those interests of any individual which involve other persons and those which do not. The interested and active self is social, through and through, a social individual; but, as will presently be emphasized, it is social in a way which inherently involves being also antisocial. It is apparently impossible for any human being to take toward another any simple or pure attitude. Instrumentalism, cooperation, helpfulness and rivalry, and love and cruelty are inseparable.

One of the serious defects of social philosophy is its relative neglect of play and romantic or "nonserious" interests and activities in general. Play is important in several respects. It is anti-utilitarian and even tends to be positively destructive. Human play is typically social and also competitive (in the psychological sense of rivalry, which is entirely alien to economic motivation). Most important for our purpose, play involves "rules of the game," which are felt to have the imperative quality of morality and truth and which form a bridge to serious law. Moreover, play exhibits in relation to its rules or laws the ubiquitous harmony and conflict of interests. All the parties to any game have a common interest in the game itself—hence, in general obedience to the rules. But they have conflicting individual interests in winning—consequently, in law-breaking or cheating. Similar consider-ations apply far more acutely to the improvement of the game by changing the rules. The notion of law and its enforcement—and improvement—will be found to be the locus of virtually all social problems.

Harmony and conflict, of instrumental interests—and of sportive and other "romantic" interests, which may be equally primary—all connected with law, have given rise to our distinctive human nature, including the three main levels already suggested. Superposed upon inert physical and mental and cultural process (the nature of culture process will be considered presently) is, first, instrumental, problem-solving intelligence in its human form; and, second, thinking and action in relation to a value cosmos. The core of the third level or category, for our civilized thinking, is seemingly the noninstrumental interest in truth, truth about facts, the con-ception of scientific truth as a primary interest or value. (Genetically, and perhaps philosophically also, personal fi-delity may be more elementary for critical self-consciousness.) Built around scientific truth are other objective values or ideals, and especially the conception of *development*, along "right" lines, of the individual personality, of any particular society, and of culture in the world as a whole. The heart of the philosophic problem seems to lie in the inextricable entanglement in our thinking of instrumental with cultural or developmental and romantic interests in conduct, and of causal process with individual and inter-individual and social action. The truth interest itself, when it is not instrumental and when it is more than the romantic appeal of novelty, is in fact largely competitive and involved with domination—the didactic urge and the disposition to force agreement. Yet it is a primary axiom that belief under coercion is not belief, is indeed a contradiction in terms. "Mere" truth is both unimportant and uninteresting, a bore. Again, it is doubtful whether there is any opinion wholly apart from difference of opinion. Yet truth is recognized only through agreement, and there must be an interest in agreement, a general aversion to having each individual simply hold his own opinion and "letting it go at that." And the obligation to believe the truth, because it is true as against any and all other reasons for believing, seems to be the foundation of all obligation, of "integrity" and of all serious thought or communication.

III

It is necessary to consider a bit more explicitly what is meant by the statement that man is a social being. What has been said should indicate how misleading it is to describe him as a "social animal." As far as we can tell, the social life of animals, where it is highly developed—as it is chiefly in certain species of insects—is instinctive and ultimately mechanical. It does not seem to involve "interest" at all; or, if interests are present, they are entirely conservative, useful, and harmonious, neither individualistic-instrumental nor romantic (both of which mean conflict) as human interests inherently are. Termites, for example, are thought to show some evidence of fellowship, but none of effort to utilize or dominate one another, or to shirk duties and sacrifices demanded by the community interest, or to compete, for sheer love of a contest. All this is far from being so true of the animals most closely related to man. While the special problems arising out of gradation of organic types and overlapping and admixture must be passed over here, one fact calls for notice. The higher animals which, in contrast with insects, show intellectual and emotional kinship with man, present little social organization, in comparison with the colonial insects. Human nature seems to have been produced by the subsequent socialization, in a unique way, of a species which first achieved a considerable degree of individual-instrumental intelligence and which had also acquired an emotional equipment difficult to explain in terms of survival value.

But it is equally important to an understanding of human social life to recognize that it also is only to a limited extent based on intelligence or on conscious interests. The great bulk of what happens in human life, in the way of overt activity, social as well as individual (and mental as well as physical), is (actually and necessarily) process, not free, problem-solving activity. Our behavior is largely of the type variously desig-nated as social habit, custom, tradition, usage, or institutions. Such behavior forms are perpetuated by processes which sociologists call imitation and suggestion, acculturation and the like, and often refer to as social inheritance, in contrast with the biological inheritance of instinct. In man the instincts have become attenuated to vague urges or "drives," in which the emotion is the only aspect which is in any large degree specific. The behavior part, both stimulus and response, is vague and is given its specific form by the experience of the individual, especially social suggestion. The connection with biological needs is commonly not clearly traceable, and even in the case of food and sex behavior the traditional-institutional element is so large as to make the use of the word "instinct" inadvisable. But traditional-imitative or institutional behavior is theoretically reducible to the mechanism of conditioned response, in contrast with activity, and is not social in the distinctively human sense, though institutions are nearly as distinctive of human society as is deliberative group action. It is not different in essential principle from the instinctive organized life of termites.

Custom or tradition is especially important as the basic form of law, in which, as we have noted, the social problems of civilized life almost entirely center. But law, in the sense of traditionalized rules and patterns, presents no problems, to the group or to its individual members. And to the extent that any behavior of the individual is determined by institutional mechanism, it presents no problem to the subject himself. Customary law, including the whole culture and life of a society living on the basis of such law, functions and changes automatically, as process, involving no procedure. For the purposes of analysis we seem compelled to imagine a historical stage or level at which law is felt as imperative or obligatory, and so is differentiated from law in the positive sense of scientific law, yet is never violated or even made the subject of critical judgment (however "willingly" or unwillingly it may be obeyed). Law becomes a problem, and there come to be social problems, only when men are not merely conscious of their laws and institutions and of the imperative to conform but are also critical and more or less defiant of them, and specifically in so far as there come to be conflicts of interest and differences of opinion with regard to the law. To the extent that such twofold disharmonies exist and are not resolved by intellectual-moral activity, group life is either impossible or it is coercive (always including persuasion), which is to say that it is not social in the sense that social problems are faced and dealt with by social action. To some extent social problems may arise out of unique situations and may have no connection with law. One thinks of war and natural catastrophes. But this is a matter of degree, both as to how far any action follows precedent and as to how far it is expected to set a precedent; the special problem of *ad hoc* action may be ignored here, and all social action viewed under the form of changing the law.

Of course, critical thinking and discussion about the law is in fact one of the most familiar features of social life. But its intellectual aspect, as thinking and discussion in the proper sense, needs to be distinguished from and correctly related to the various romantic or emotional attitudes which are as conspicuous in this connection as anywhere else in human mental life. Men seem to have an inherent disposition to erect instrumental interests into absolutes and a positive yearning for absolutes, even the most incompatible, if not for the impossible as such. They chafe at all restrictions, all given conditions of action, physical as well as human, those in themselves individually as well as those found in others or in society. They are interested both in harmony and in conflict as such, as intrinsic ends, for which other ends will be sacrificed to an astonishing extent. The urge to dominate, or craving for power, without regard to any use to be made of it, is more commonly a subject of comment; but a mystical craving for fellowship, in which individuality is lost, is comparable in frequency of occurrence and is perhaps equally inimical to sane living. Society would be impossible if the urge to self-expression, to attracting attention and leadership, were not counterbalanced by its opposite. In this connection situations of a more or less ritualistic character play an important role. Man seems to be inherently both a law-maker and a law-breaker. And if he has any traits which may rightly be called instinctive (i.e., inborn), one of them surely is an urge to enforce the law upon others.

It will probably never be possible to acquire much of that knowledge, which would be so valuable, about the long process of evolution from relatively solitary animal life to the really human level, to society as it is known from direct experience and from history and anthropological observation. We must largely guess at the course of change from instinct by way of individual intelligence (and emotion) to a complex mixture of tradition with coercion and with deliberative social action. We cannot describe the mixture of unconscious "drift" and brute force by which custom originated, replacing instinct, or by which it was changed and developed toward lawmindedness and morality, in the prehistoric millenniums during which *Homo* was being humanized. Struggle and selective survival undoubtedly set boundaries to the path of change, but the human reality which resulted is strangely resistant to explanation in those terms. Beyond reasonable doubt, institutions and law first emerged from causal process and became what could be called a social problem in connection with the enforcement of conformity against recalcitrant individuals, and this must have happened ages before "legislation," deliberate change in the law, was thought of by anyone. At the level of primitive culture, enforcement by impulsive individual and "mob" action presumably gave place gradually to more regular and organized procedure. From a very early stage more or less stabilized patterns were certainly under the protection of religion and religious authority, both of which rest on tradition, i.e., on the bare fact of their existence. (It is plausible to assume that feelings of purity and impurity played an extremely important role in the development of a sense of obligation to norms.)

Law-making was undoubtedly first achieved under authoritarian form—the authority being grounded in tradition and religion—and in small groups. It is hardly believable that there ever was a real stage, either of purely unconscious conformity to custom or of law felt and obeyed as obligatory entirely apart from crude coercion. Men cooperate, or even associate naturally and freely, only in the smallest family group, if indeed they do so at all, with any degree of permanence. Stable social life and organization, on an appreciable scale, must have been forced on the species by the exigencies of economic life and/or of warfare and must have been first achieved under authoritative leadership. Free society seems always to come into existence through successful revolt and the revolutionary overturn of an autocratic (always meaning oligarchic) system. Even today, in the most democratic society, compulsory enforcement is an essential feature of the notion of law, in contrast with custom which is followed unconsciously or voluntarily, or even usage enforced by "moral pressure." Yet social problems and social procedure, properly speaking, pertain exclusively to free society, to ideal democracy, in which there is no formal enforcement of law.

The nearest approach to the pure ideal of free social action or democracy which is at all possible in reality is undoubtedly the discussion community, or intellectual association at the various levels—art, science, and philosophy, and also morals and politics, apart from mechanical organization and ritual. This community has no definite membership or boundaries and very little formal organization or formulated law. Practically any individual is free to be a member, to participate in the activity, at will, subject to the momentary *de facto* consent of others. A similar degree of freedom is realized in small, spontaneous, and temporary groups, active in such fields as conversation, sociability, and play. In consequence of human individualism and its limitations, this is possible in practice only where the individual is free to "belong" or not to belong. (There is only an inner moral and emotional imperative to belong to the truth-seeking community, which is naturally world-wide.) In any formally organized group, which means in all groups having any degree of permanence, there is a definite and fairly stable line between members and nonmembers, and such a society must have some definite "laws," with a more or less distinct constitution, covering matters on which agreement is felt by the controlling members to be "necessary." The power of choice of the individual, to be or not to be a member of a particular society, may vary from practically perfect freedom to effective compulsion or exclusion.

IV

The subject of social procedure suggests especially the problem of action in political society, i.e., changing the laws governing individual behavior in some state or political jurisdiction. Political society is distinguished from other associations by the fact that the individual has relatively little freedom to belong or not to belong. This is partly because states are defined by political boundaries, or have "territorial sovereignty," and the habitable earth has been divided up among a limited number of states. But, in addition, culture differences and explicit politico-legal action set limits to the freedom of the individual to transfer allegiance. Thus the laws of any state are practically coercive on its individual members, and their freedom is limited to conduct not regulated by law and to participation in activity directed to changing the law (and to law-breaking). The concept of social action, or of a society as acting socially, being restricted to democratic process, persons are members of any society to the extent that they are actually free to participate in its processes of legal change. In so far as any society is autocratic, its formal membership consists only of the members of the ruling group. But others are really members to the extent that they may actually participate in the formation of public opinion which even an autocratic government has to respect in legal action. In large measure the problem of understanding and describing social procedure arises out of the fact that the legal forms governing participation do not correspond with the realities. Equal voting power does not mean equal influence, and individuals who are not "voting" members may have more influence than many who are.

Overt action in political society is always individual action, not group action in the philosophical meaning; this is limited to the unitary decision as to how to act in the overt sense. That is, social action, paralleling individual action, is the process of reaching a group decision, specifically for the most part as to law, i.e., as to presumptively permanent changes in the existing law. "Pure" social action is *discussion,* the joint intellectual quest for the solution of *value* problems. Overt social action is the "action" of individuals (a mixture of activity and process) in carrying out the law, including the enforcement of law by punishment of law-breakers and also including any action by an individual in performing any group function in accord with the law and under legally delegated authority. In a large society even the actual formulation of law—legislation in the concrete sense—is necessarily carried out by an individual, or a small group, legally selected and acting as agents of society, by delegated authority. In the case of legislators, and in general, the delegation of authority cannot be at all precise, and in fact both legislation and the execution of law are to a considerable extent a matter of the individual judgment and will, hence the authority, of the agent or delegate. Actual law, as formulated in words, necessarily runs chiefly in terms of general objectives or ideals, the "overt" action for their realization being left to the judgment of the appropriate agent. Thus social action in the concrete is largely the effort to select officials who will be competent, and trustworthy, agents of the group.

Political discussion properly so called, i.e., in its impersonal intellectual aspect, centers in the problem of what the law "ought" to be—how existing law ought to be changed, if at all—what law is "right," or most right, or best. As an aid to understanding, it may be contrasted with purely intellectual discussion, which centers in the question of what is "true," where truth is a group end, or value. As already noted, discussion can arise only through difference of opinion, backed up by conflicting individual interests in the various opinions, but accompanied also by a common interest in establishing the truth. Political discussion generally originates on the side of conflict of interests rather than difference of opinion; but discussion is possible only on the question of right—which is to say opinion as to the truth "about" what is right. No discussion is possible in propositions beginning with the words "I want," just as discussion is different from mechanical process. It must be a cooperative quest for truth—about facts or about values, including truth itself. (Unhappily, it is also over rights, chiefly, rather than over interests that men fight, individually, or by groups, as in war.) Both intellectual and political discussion are developmental. They look to cumulative growth and improvement, the one in a corpus of established knowledge, the other in a corpus of law. Both types of discussion may begin either with a question of principle or with a "case," but both use deduction and induction, together, interactively.

The problem of politico-legal change in its aspect of process is the province of "political science." The most important fact about formal political process is that it is relatively unimportant, or of secondary importance. The real social activity involved in democratic action takes place outside the sphere of explicit organized political behavior, and we have already noted that there is relatively little to be said in words about it. The important principle is the negative one that the main difference between forms of government lies in the degree to which they obstruct or control or facilitate the informal and intellectually mysterious processes, or procedures, by which public opinion is formed. The danger of autocracy, totalitarianism or dictatorship, is not so much that it will directly control the overt conduct of the people but rather that it may suppress or distort these informal and unorganized activities of free intercourse and corrupt their results. The existence of free society—meaning a legal social order in which the ordinary individual is recognized as an end rather than treated as a means and in which issues affecting all are settled by discussion open to all—depends chiefly on the ultimate moral and intellectual capacity of the mass of individuals themselves to reach by free discussion substantial unanimity on the scope and the general content of their constitution and laws. It depends relatively little, in a direct and positive way, on political forms.

V

All discussion is really critical and philosophical, even in the realm of facts. The decisive problems and discussions of science deal with method; for discussion of what is true runs largely in terms of the methods of inquiry and proof. In the field of law they deal with moral philosophy. Science is instrumental knowledge—knowledge of facts about the properties and behavior of things (including persons) with reference to using them as instruments for given ends. But "valid" science is social knowledge. As the deeper problems of science itself have to do with method, they are critical and philosophical; the noninstrumental interest in truth is a philosophical and an ethical interest. The problems of scope and method in the human and social sciences are too complex for treatment within the limits of this paper. We can note only that they must be very different from what is true of the natural sciences. An individual does not use "scientific method" in predicting or controlling his own thinking, and the same is true of groups. The task of positive science in connection with human data is to discover and formulate the "given conditions" of action, to ascertain and describe the course of events in the absence of interference and the consequences of possible courses of action in changing it. All this comes under the head of instrumentalism; an individual and a society uses both the world and itself as they are, at any moment, as instruments for changing the world and itself.

With regard either to the ultimate procedure of action as discussion of values, or to the content of values themselves, there is relatively little that can be said, in a positive sense, and at all briefly. On the second point, the content of values, this statement is true a priori. It is of the essence of any problem that its solution is not known or predictable in advance of the *activity* by which it is reached. And when we look at the matter objectively and critically, it is clear that little more can be said about the activity. The course of events cannot be foreseen. This indeed is true of individual thinking, or thinking in its individual aspect. All our methodologies and logics have limited and chiefly negative significance in practice, however great their intrinsic intellectual interest. Study of the rules of logic is only within narrow limits, if at all, of more value as training in clear or accurate thinking than the same amount of mental practice on "real" subject matter.

In connection with group thinking, or discussion, we know something about the organization of deliberative assemblies and their "rules of order." But it relates at best to rather superficial and negative aspects of the activity. The most important fact is the moral and sinister one of the rarity and difficulty of genuine discussion or of the discussion attitude. The inveterate human tendency is to turn serious intercourse into a contest, a debate, or mere verbal clamor and combat instead of a cooperative quest for solutions. The truth interest in men is feeble in comparison with various romantic propensities. (The relation between discussion and debate would call for notice if space allowed; it is not purely one of contrast or opposition.)

As to the content of values, we may briefly notice the traditional tripartite classification, "truth, beauty, and goodness." The relations between these categories are extremely subtle and complex. Any one of them in a sense includes the others, yet conflicts, even contradictions, are also apparent. For the purposes of a discussion of social policy the essential concern, as already indicated, is with moral value or "goodness," which from the standpoint of political discussion is a matter of truth about what is good in society. At the present juncture in history it is very important in discussing moral values to emphasize some factors in the intellectual history of our culture that lead to misconceptions which threaten disastrous consequences. Only the briefest indication of the issues can be given here.

VI

Historically, ethical ideas have been bound up with religion—in our own culture with the Jewish-Prophetic-Christian tradition. All distinctively religious ethics is primarily traditionalistic, especially in its relations to the social order, inculcating acceptance of and conformity with what is established in law and usage, and particularly enjoining obedience to established authority. As to general culture, religious teaching is likely even to press in the direction of reversion to more primitive conditions, where customs are followed more unquestioningly. It is conservative rather than constructive or progressive. Its most constructive side is emphasis on mutual helpfulness within the social group, however this is defined. In comparison with primitive and other civilized religions, Judaism and Christianity have added, or vastly broadened and deepened, emphasis on the emotional attitude of "love" (*agapé*) or mystical "brotherhood," under the Fatherhood of God. This lofty religious view unfortunately affords little help in solving the concrete problems of large-scale association. The working principle of Christianity is faith that "love" of God and one's fellowmen will translate itself into right action automatically, implying that there are no serious intellectual problems. Error, and acute differences of opinion, are rooted in "sin," and the religious attitude is antagonistic to that of critical inquiry. Historically, when a serious attempt was made to apply Christian principles in political life (in the Middle Ages), it was found necessary to give them a very strained interpretation, and the result was ecclesiastical authoritarianism and a civilization neither high nor progressive, as judged by the most objective standards. The Hebrew Prophets and the New Testament writers thought of morality as personal righteousness and of righteousness partly in terms of formal religion and partly in terms of personal relations at a level of primitive simplicity, and never in terms of democracy. Christianity has never actively condemned slavery or tyranny when established, if they were not cruel and did not interfere with Christian observances.

In the course of modern European history this conservative-conformist and personal-sentimental religious ethic came to be overlaid with a different and largely contradictory set of principles derived from science, from commerce, and from the requirements of large-scale industrial organization (combined with the influence of "frontier" conditions). The democratic ethic of liberal individualism, in contrast with our traditional religious ethic, is objective and rational, not sentimental, and progressive, not conservative. It centers in intelligent and effective action, not in thankful acceptance of the world, material and social, as one finds it; and its ideal of personal relations in economics and politics, and also in sport and the cultural life, is respect for the interests and rights of others rather than personal "love." It emphasizes cooperation, on terms of equity, established by free mutual consent, for the promotion either of individual interests, freely chosen, or of ends which are communal or even mystical; and it stands for individual liberty—limited by equal liberty for all—in work, play, and social and cultural activity, as an intrinsic good. It is hardly strange that the mixture resulting from this superposition has led to confusion amounting to chaos in the ethical ideas of modern man.

It is an especially important fact that the ethic of Christianity and that of liberalism, divergent as they are, embody a common error or oversight. Both systems look at social and ethical problems in terms of "right" relations between individuals, taking the individuals as given. Right relations are conceived in terms of love in the one system and in terms of free, equitable mutualism in the other. Neither system effectively recognizes the institutional character of society or the connection between changes in individuals and in institutions, which is in fact the locus of social problems. The New Testament teaching eliminates the problem by taking institutions as given and as a matter of ethical indifference; early and extreme liberalism eliminated it by reducing institutions to the vanishing-point in economic, cultural, and religious *laisser-faire*. Political discussion has tended to correction of this error, but the movement has been laggard. Progress toward solution of our critical present social problems requires recognition of the fallacy of treating either individuals or institutions as given. The evils of today are, of course, more directly a consequence of the shortcomings of the liberal philosophy and not of an excessive application of the teachings of religion. They are not so much a matter of wrong relations between given individuals as of "wrong" individuals, particularly with reference to their economic attributes, their endowment with wants and with economic capacity or power, and wrong opinions as to their rights and the manner or possibility of realization. But since the individual is largely made what he is by institutional processes—notably again with respect to economic wants, means and capacities—the immediate practical problem confronting society at any time is that of progressively remaking its institutional system. But this problem is to be solved in the light of the answer to two other questions; the first is one of fact as to what kind of individuals, and of inter-individual relations, different kinds of institutions will tend to create, while the second is the value problem—what characteristics in individuals and in culture are to be judged good.

VII

The crux of the practical problem of today centers, as everyone knows, in the economic life, in the loose everyday sense, and specifically in the large-scale cooperative organization of production which is absolutely necessary to modern civilization, as dependent upon the exploitation of modern technology. This is, in the first place, a matter of agreement upon "fair" terms of cooperation between given individuals. The analysis of economic theory (which, of course, cannot be gone into here) shows conclusively that "fairness" in this connection must for the most part be defined in the traditional liberal manner, as the exchange of equal values, determined by free competition in markets. But in the second place, the results of even perfectly free and fair competition may be ethically good or bad in any degree, depending upon the individuals between whom such competition takes place—specifically their economic attributes, their wants and their endowment with productive capacity. All these attributes are obviously created and constantly re-created by the working of institutional processes, under the impact of individual and social activity.

It must not be assumed that mere negative freedom necessarily results in free competition, as the opposite is clearly the case. But even under perfect competition the natural long-run tendency of the individualistic economic process, operating under individual motives and negative social control, is in many respects evil. To some extent it undoubtedly tends to the corruption of men's wants in the large sense. But the more important fact is that it tends to the cumulative growth of inequality in economic power. This is true in the span of individual life, and more seriously true in the long run, through the working of the family system. Obviously, the family is far more real, as an economic unit, than the ephemeral individual. The exchange of equal values between excessively unequal individuals may result in fundamental injustice in the distributive sense, in contrast with commutative justice, which alone is recognized in *laisser-faire* individualism. And it may reduce effective freedom to the vanishing-point. Of course, nineteenth-century political liberalism progressively recognized this fact and attempted to work toward distributive justice also and to maintain effective freedom, using such measures as progressive taxation and relief and the provision of public services, especially free education for the children of the poor. It is impossible to go further here into the problem of the content of value.

VIII

With reference to the relation between science and philosophy, the supremely important matter is the danger that social problems will be viewed exclusively or primarily in scientific terms, and effort be directed to solving them by "the scientific method." As we have seen, the nature and operations of science are instrumental and individualistic (or relative to the interests of a group taken as given). A "scientific" approach to the study of society, from the standpoint of action, proceeds on the assumption that the problem is one of finding the given properties of the "material" with a view to its manipulation and use for the purposes of the knower as manipulator. Apart from the question as to how far these purposes are likely to be wise and benevolent, this is the antithesis of the concept of democracy, or political freedom. And individual liberty must be the first principle of rational political ethics. It is a necessary requirement for complete human status to be a free judge of one's own interests and life-purposes and a free agent, possessing the necessary power, in promoting or realizing them. This may, of course, involve free consultation with others, under freedom to follow or reject their advice. And it is an implication of any public discussion of social problems (such as the present example) that they are "of right" to be solved by discussion, by all the parties concerned. The contrary principle, of one-sided control, is justified only to the extent that those subject to it are explicitly denied the full status of human beings. That is, it is justified in the case of "infants" to be educated, or that of adults objectively determined to be antisocial or undeveloped and subject to re-education, and of any who require overt control to prevent their acting destructively.

In the social field the natural function of knowledge and thinking, in the scientific meaning, is either to give every individual power over every other, which is a prescription for the war of all against all, or to give "the government," meaning some individual or group, power over the mass of the population. Even as a matter of correct definition, the social problem, as a problem for society as well as of society, is one of rational *consensus,* as to desirable change, not of *control* in the correct meaning of manipulation. The application of positive or instrumental categories by any subject to itself is a self-contradictory expression. As we have seen, science deals not with activity but with the given conditions of action. It is true that the determination of the existent in relation to the active in the individual and in society is one of the most baffling philosophical problems.

We may conclude by repeating two observations regarding the concept of "control," so commonly confused with the problem of social procedure. The first is that all "control" relations, in the proper meaning of the word, between human beings, are "ideally" immoral, though they may be necessary, and in that sense right, under the un-ideal conditions of real life, especially where biologically human units are real human individuals in variously limited degree. In the right view of the problem it is a matter not of control but of arriving at a rational consensus. Second, the knowledge used by any human being in controlling others, when his activities do take that form, rightly or wrongly, is descriptive and instrumental, and hence scientific, only in a highly abstract sense of the word. Positive knowledge of human beings is so different in origin and mode of application from the natural sciences, based on sense observation and used to manipulate inert things, that it seems more confusing than helpful to use the same word— "science"—to refer to both.

IX

Fact and Value
in Social Science

I

The problem of method or procedure in the social sciences is raised and emphasized especially by their failure to parallel the modern achievements of the natural sciences, either in startling discoveries of truths unsuspected by commonsense, or especially, in laying the basis of techniques for transforming the character of life. This paper is an investigation of the reasons for this "failure"—or of the question whether it is correct to apply the term.

The position to be taken is, in the first place, that because of fundamental differences in the subject matter, and especially in the nature of the problems, in the two fields, no such revolutionary results were or are possible, in the nature of the case. Consequently, in the second place, the great need of the hour in the social science field as a whole is for an understanding of the nature of the material, the problems and

Reprinted from *Science and Man,* edited by Ruth Anshen, by permission of Harcourt, Brace & Company. Copyright, 1942, by Harcourt, Brace & Company.

the possibilities. Only on the basis of such an understanding can we expect so to define our concepts and choose our methods as to avoid not merely waste of energy, but the production of consequences which are positively evil. In the field of social policy, the pernicious notion of instrumentalism, resting on the claim or assumption of a parallelism between social and natural science, is actually one of the most serious of the sources of danger which threaten destruction to the values of what we have called civilization. Any such conception as social engineering or social technology has meaning only in relation to the activities of a super-dictatorship, a government which would own as well as rule society at large, and would use it for the purposes of the governors.

In the social field, as elsewhere, knowledge is wanted both for its own sake and for use in the guidance of action. It is a serious reflection that the unsatisfactory state of affairs in social science has largely resulted from the very progress of science, the revolutionary development of techniques for acquiring knowledge, and applying knowledge, which is an outstanding feature and achievement of civilization in our own and recent time. It becomes the primary function of a discussion such as this to contend against the twofold fallacy which has been current, if not predominant, in social science circles. The root fallacy is that social science should be or can be a science in the same sense as the natural sciences in which the revolution referred to has occurred. It is argued that the problems of pure science on the one hand, and those of its application to life on the other, are to be solved by carrying over into the study of society the methods and techniques which have led to the celebrated triumphal march of science in the study of nature and the application of scientific knowledge of nature in technology. In other words, the philosophical basis of social science is held to be positivism, with respect to pure science, and instrumentalism or pragmatism when considered with reference to application in action.

In this connection in particular—more or less characteristically for social problems in so far as they can be solved—it would seem that a clear statement of the issue ought to be sufficient to resolve it definitively. It ought to be obvious that the relation of knowledge to action cannot be the same or closely similar, nor can knowledge itself, apart from the question of action, be at all the same, where the knower and the known are identical as where they are external to each other. In a genetic-historical view the fundamental revolution in outlook which represents the real beginning of modern natural science was the discovery that the inert objects of nature are not like men, i.e., subject to persuasion, exhortation, coercion, deception, etc., but are "inexorable." The position which we have to combat seems to rest upon an inference, characteristically drawn by the "best minds" of our race, that since natural objects are not like men, men must be like natural objects. The history of British-American social thought in modern times is particularly interesting in this connection. In general, it has represented the combination mentioned, of positivism and pragmatism—two philosophical positions with respect to the nature of man and his place in the cosmos, and specifically with respect to social action, which are at once contradictory between themselves, and equally indefensible as a basis of social action. For man, conceived in positivistic terms, could not act at all; and conceived in pragmatic terms, he could not act upon himself, which to do is in fact his most characteristic trait.

II

A survey of the problem of method in the study of society will naturally begin with the point of view of pure science, the achievement of knowledge and understanding without reference to any use to be made of them in action, and will then go on to consider the relations of science to action which, in one sense or another, are determinative in all fields, for theory as well as for practice.

The primary fact which limits the development of "science" in the strict "positive" meaning of the term, in the field of social phenomena, is the virtually infinite heterogeneity, and unpredictable variability in time, of the subject matter or data, i.e., human beings and their behavior, and social institutions. The basis of all science is classification, supplemented by the analysis and measurement of attributes, by which differences in kind are reduced to differences in quantity or degree. From the point of view of classification, chemistry is the ideal natural science, while from that of measurement, physics is similarly the ideal-type. With reference to classification, the mere naming of an "object" as a sample of a certain purified chemical conveys to an informed person most of the information that would ever be desired about that object. In contrast, the designation of an object as a "man," or, say, a family, or a deliberative assembly, serves chiefly to raise questions. (Data of botany and animal biology range themselves along a scale between these two extremes.) The natural way of meeting such difficulties is subclassification; but this procedure soon runs into the familiar dilemma between size and homogeneity of statistical classes. Where individual objects or instances are highly unique, classification can only be crude.

The effort to analyze and measure—especially to find quantitative correlation between antecedent and consequent, which is the meaning of causality in science, encounters at the outset the difficulty that there simply is no real measurement of distinctively human or social data. It is doubtful whether these phenomena should even be called quantitative, so different must be the meaning of the term from that which it has in connection with physically objective magnitudes or variables. Human and social phenomena unquestionably present differences of degree. But in the nature of the case these differences can only be estimated, not measured. The nature of measurement is illustrated by the simple case of thermometry. It is not men's feeling of temperature which is measured, but some physical phenomenon which, as we learn by a complicated theoretical analysis of experimental data, corresponds in some way to the feeling of heat and cold. But it does not correspond at all accurately, or measurement would not be called for, or would lose its meaning. What is called measurement in the social sciences, including psychology, is the averaging of estimates, and the use of the term measurement is a misnomer.

The difficulties of classification and measurement, amounting to impossibility, if the terms are to imply any high degree of objectivity and precision, suggests and indeed rests upon, the essential fact that the data with which social sciences are concerned are themselves not objective in the physical meaning—are not data of sense observation. They consist of meanings, opinions, attitudes and values, not of physical facts. It is these subjective data or facts which are at once social in nature and of interest, to scientific as well as to vulgar curiosity, and especially from the point of view of action. They constitute the "reality" into which it is the function of social sciences to inquire. To be sure, there is always some correspondence or parallelism with physical facts, but as the example of temperature is sufficient to suggest, the parallelism is of a sort which rather accentuates the difficulties and limitations of scientific procedure. Not merely is the correspondence crude and imperfect; in addition, there are two sets of physical facts involved, and they are not closely or quantitatively parallel between themselves. These are respectively physiology and overt behavior. Expression and communication are generally included in the latter though only by something of a *tour de force*.

From the point of view of science, the situation presents a paradox; our difficulty is not so much the absence or inaccessibility of knowledge, but rather that we know too much. Knowledge of these subjective data has to be obtained through observation of overt behavior, or especially through intercommunication, doubtfully to be classed as observation. Hence the problem becomes primarily one of *interpretation*, the uncertainties of which are notorious. The crux of the matter is the relation between *motive* and action. And as suggested, we not merely know this relation very inadequately, but we *know*—at least as certainly as we know the nature of physical data themselves—that there is no close or simple relationship, as a matter of fact.

The expression of motive in action, and specifically in language, gesture, etc., is subject to error. Men do not even at all accurately know their own motives, but in "fact" act in part experimentally, to learn what they want, and also deliberately change their own motivation, as will be emphasized later. All this is in the nature of man as a knowing and acting entity, or as in part "free" or problem-solving. Thus motives are analogous to the "forces" of mechanistic science, but not parallel. There is no such strict and necessary correspondence between the "force" and its "effect" as there is where forces are known only by inference from their effects. Motives differ in being also known from other sources, communication and interpretation. Moreover, as we also know, men do not always try to express their motives to others at all accurately, either in communication or in overt action, but very often explicitly attempt to conceal or to deceive. The contrast between physical objects and such a choosing, struggling and scheming emotional and romantic entity hardly needs explicit mention. The limitations in the use of physiological data as a source of knowledge of motivation, or of feelings and emotions as facts, or for the prediction of overt behavior, are equally familiar and call even less for elaboration. One need only think of this method of investigating the feeling of temperature.

III

As soon as we look concretely and realistically at the problem of knowing about man and society, and specifically that of getting the knowledge we actually want, either for its own sake or in connection with action, we confront the simple fact that our subject matter has to be interpreted in terms of a highly pluralistic system of conceptions or categories. The root of the difficulty is that we know, and are interested in, man, in contrast with "nature," not merely or primarily as known and acted upon, but also and especially as knowing and acting. It is hardly mysterious that this contrast between man and nature as known, or the identity and mutuality of relation between man as knower and man as known, makes a profound difference in the activity and results of knowing. Men "exist," so to speak, in several different universes of reality, between which philosophy has so far built no adequate thought bridges, and does not seem to be in the way of doing so.

It is an indisputable fact that man is a physical object, a mechanism, and that the phenomena into which he enters are in considerable part to be explained by the same physical sciences which we use in interpreting inert objects. And just as indisputably, man is a biological organism, more specifically one of the "higher" animals. Hence he is also in part to be explained by the biological sciences, in their whole range from the lowest plant life to the most highly evolved animal species. Of course this raises the issue whether unconscious biological phenomena might ultimately be explained as physical phenomena merely. The question cannot be argued here, beyond noting that biological science does constantly use teleological categories, such as struggle and adaptation, and that it is sheer dogmatism to assert that they could be reduced to purely physical or positive content.

Next, it is as indisputably a matter of "fact," in the inclusive sense, that man and human phenomena present characteristics which any discussion must and does recognize as sharply different from those of non-human biology. Man as investigated is, like man as investigator, a being who *thinks,* and who acts on the basis of thinking, who *solves problems* of many kinds, in a way which sharply differentiates him from any other organic species, and which we have to assume is not characteristic of inanimate nature at all. Other distinctions will be developed in the detail allowable, as we proceed. It should at once be clear that man is at the same time many different kinds of being or entity, which are not reducible to any one kind. The appeal of the contrary notion is readily explained. Man as intellectual inquirer is characterized by a craving for simplification and unification, for *"monism"* as against pluralism. And since "he" cannot deny that "man" is a physical being, this craving leads him to deny that he is anything else. And of course the "triumphal march" of physical science and technology, already mentioned, contributes largely to the strengthening of the prejudice. But why these considerations should actually lead men to accept knowledge of man as a physical being and deny to him the characteristics which he, the inquirer, exemplifies *even in denying them,* must remain in the status of mystery, as far as the present writer is concerned.

We enter upon the domain of social science when we name the next familiar distinguishing characteristic of man—that he is a "social animal." But the social nature of man is utterly different from that of the animals which are properly and distinctively called social, such as the colonial insects. It is misleading to call man a social animal, since it is not as an animal that he is social. The social phenomena of the termite colony, for example, are based upon *instinct,* which positive science interprets as mechanism. Man is social as a feeling, knowing, thinking, desiring and acting *individual.* He is an individual in a sense categorically beyond the meaning the term has in any other connection. His social life must be interpreted in terms of individual interests and social interests, and especially in terms of *conflicts* of almost infinite complexity between diverse interests of both classes. Man, we repeat, is a *problem solver;* and the distinctive character of human society, from the point of view of the significance of knowledge for action, is that it presents problems, both to any society as such, and to the individuals who compose it, closely inter-related with their individual problems. In this respect, it presents a virtually absolute contrast with termite society—as far as we know, and as science must assume. And this characteristic, this fact, is vital for science, as description and interpretation, as well as in relation to action. These facts throw us back upon the notion of man as a motivated individual.

But the relation of priority between individual and society at the human level is a mutual one; each presupposes the other and this fact accentuates the complexity of the problems. Human society presents another fundamental aspect, with respect to which it is in one sense similar to animal society, but in another sense sharply contrasting. It is largely "insti-tutional" (in Sumner's "crescive" sense) in its basis and character. In other words, human behavior, individual and social, is to a large extent "traditional." In this aspect, behavior is nondeliberative, not problem-solving, and is even largely unconscious, and mechanical, like the behavior of termites. But the character of the mechanism is very different. It rests upon unconscious imitation. The "social inheritance" involved is distinct from the biological inheritance of instinct, and has played a vital role in human development.

Turning again to the individual, the analysis of human emotions, attitudes, motives, and rational nature cannot of course even be surveyed in this essay. But one important detail of such an analysis imperatively calls for notice. Still another element in the pluralism of human phenomena is found in the fact that man as an individual, in one of his aspects, at one of the levels at which he exists, deliberately uses means, to realize ends which are given or are simply "there," while at another level he also deliberates about ends. The "possession" of individual ends, and of means, and of more or less knowledge as to how to use means to realize given ends, are the factors which make up and define the "economic man"; or, they serve to define economic behavior—two ways of saying the same thing.

Two facts need the utmost emphasis. On the one hand, every conscious subject is an economic man, and behaves as such in every conscious act. Every activity involves the use of given means, in accord with given knowledge, to achieve ends which are given or factual in some sense and in some degree. This is true of play activity, individual and social, as well as of work, and of the intellectual, esthetic, moral, and even the religious activities, as well as of those which we think of as connected with "subsistence." (This term has practically no meaning in connection with civilized life, for all human motivation is relative to *standards*.) The pursuit of all ends alike is "expensive," meaning that it requires diversion of means or *power* from other uses. And in so far as any activity is rationally purposive, it presents the problem of "efficiency," or the economy of power. That is, man is impelled to use power in such a way as to achieve the maximum possible realization of "ends-in-general," as given or desired, aggregated in terms of some common denominator of desiredness. (In all developed society, there is of course a conventional unit called money.)

The second fact referred to as calling for equal emphasis is that just as all activity is economic, none is purely or merely economic. For, while the three elements of economic behavior—means or resources, knowledge of their use, and ends for which they are used—may be taken as "given" for a given subject at any moment of action, in a larger view and a longer run they are not given, but changing; and the effecting of changes in them is commonly an essential and even a major factor in the motivation of the activity itself. This fact is especially important with regard to the "ends" of action. Under critical scrutiny, the given ends of action generally turn out to be not given, but themselves instrumental to *purposes*. And the essential character of purposes is not to be given or static, but to be inherently dynamic, progressive, looking toward indefinite growth in directions which are largely to be determined in action itself—action always including thinking.

IV

These facts serve in a way as a bridge between the points of view of science for its own sake and science as a basis for action, in the social field. On the one hand, if we are to tell the "truth" about man, the most important truth, or fact, is that he is a free or problem-solving entity or being, or in a word, is *active*. This means that his doings as behavior events are ultimately more or less indeterminate, and cannot even theoretically be exhaustively predicted or described in advance. It is abstractly possible to formulate "laws" which will fit any past behavior or course of events, to any desired degree of accuracy. But, as already observed, we *know* that man is a deliberating and choosing subject, that human behavior differs from that of inert objects in that it involves effort and error, in a manifold sense. This fact of freedom is connected with and accounts for the peculiar heterogeneity and unpredictable variability in time already emphasized as factual characteristics of human phenomena. But the problem-solving characteristic has itself to be subdivided and considered at different "levels." We *know* again that men deliberate and choose with respect to the use of given means to realize given ends, and that they also deliberate about and choose ends.

Such deliberation or criticism of ends gives rise to many problems which cannot be explored here, but especially to the problem of valuation and of values. In all the folk-lore to which human thinking has given rise, in connection with human beings themselves, perhaps the most false and misleading single item is the common notion that men "know what they want," or that there is no arguing about tastes. It would surely be much nearer the truth to say that there is no arguing about anything else, or specifically about "facts." The principal thing that men actually want is to find out what they do really want; and the bulk of what they want, or think they want, is wanted because they think that in some sense they "ought" to do so, that it is "right." They "want" to be "in the right," in an infinite variety of meanings which cannot be explored here. (They also want to explore for the sake of exploring.) Such factors are at least as important for concrete motivation as is the achievement of any given end. This is another way of saying that the given ends are only provisionally given; ultimately they look beyond themselves to purposes, which have the antithetical character to givenness. And problem-solving and choice at this higher level are correspondingly important as a source of indeterminateness in the phenomenal sequence of human events.

The distinction between personal desire and value, or

"ought" in the most general sense, is one which is made by every human being, at practically every moment in his deliberative life, and most interestingly in the effort to prove a theory that the distinction has no validity, i.e., in maintaining "positive scientism" as a position. Very little critical analysis is sufficient to show that other values have the same objectivity as truth, including scientific fact. As soon as any question is raised, the problem of fact is one of evaluation, and truth itself is a value. The distinction between individual wish or opinion and truth as a form of validity—indeed the most fundamental imperative or "ought," or "oughtness"—is presupposed in any serious utterance whatever (any but "conversation," which is perhaps the greater part of all actual utterance!). To say that there is no distinction, no *validity* beyond individual acceptance as a state of mind, would be to say, "I am not saying anything"; and this is surely a contradiction, an absurdity and an impossibility far beyond the familiar example of A and not-A in formal logic.

These considerations serve, as already suggested, as a sort of bridge between individual and social phenomena and problems, and also between science for its own sake and science as a basis for action. For, to begin with, valuation is inherently a social activity, in contrast with individual motivation as simple desire. Values arise out of conflicts between interests, and out of reflection and discussion about these conflicts—the essential and distinctive feature of human social life, as already brought out. It is only as asserted *rights* that interests in conflict can be discussed or treated as a *joint* problem—in contrast with a problem for each of the parties in conflict of overcoming the other party by some kind of force. A value is the solution of such a problem. Values are established or validated and recognized through *discussion,* an activity which is at once social, intellectual, and creative. No discussion can be carried on in propositions beginning with the words "I want" or even "I think"—without further implications which are their real meaning. And even these assertions themselves, in so far as they make any real sense, raise the question of their truth, which is a question of valuation, and one to be settled only by discussion as a social-intellectual-creative process. Truth is the fundamental type of value, and in an important sense includes all other values. For a "valid" valuation, in esthetics or morals (and in religion if that is recognized as a distinct category), takes the form of a "true" proposition. The general nature of validity is the same everywhere as in natural science itself, and the validity of valuation as a category should not call for discussion beyond "pointing" to any scientific discussion, or to what we are doing here and now, as an illustration.

This argument is fundamental for any "science" of human-social phenomena, apart from problems of action. Man is, in fact, a being who exists and behaves at all the levels indicated— to carry the process of making essential distinctions no farther than we have done. He is a mechanism, and a biological organism, and the "bearer" of a culture tradition. At all these levels, his behavior is to be described in terms of mechanism or scientific law, in one or another sense, the conception not being pressed too far. In addition, he is a being who solves problems in the sense of using means to realize ends. Even at this, the "economic" level, his behavior is not exhaustively describable in terms of science, for to assert that the solution of any problem, or result of any experiment or exploration, is given in advance is a denial of its character as a problem.

But man is also a problem-solving entity at the higher level of critical deliberation about ends, or free choice of ends on the basis of thinking, illustrated by the pursuit of truth. That is, he is a being who seeks, and in a real sense creates, values. The essential significance of this is the fact that man is interested in changing himself, even to changing the ultimate core of his being. This is the meaning of being active. It marks a categorical distinction between men and all other objects of knowledge. We cannot be sure that other objects are not conscious, or even that they are devoid of will; but if they have any conscious will-attitude toward themselves it is limited, as far as we can tell, to the *perseverare in esse suo.* They do not strive to change their own nature or character— or indeed to "convert" fellow-members of their species; and in so far as scientific categories apply, they do not undergo change at all, in their ultimate nature. In contrast with natural objects—even with the higher animals—man is unique in that he is dissatisfied with himself; he is the discontented animal, the romantic, argumentative, aspiring animal. Consequently, his behavior can only in part be described by scientific principles or laws.

Even at the level of economism, scientific description applies only to "perfectly" economic behavior, which both abstracts from all forms of error and also relates to motives assumed as given, but these in fact cannot possibly be accurately known, even to the behaving subject himself. These facts invalidate the common effort to reduce the evaluating process from qualitative to quantitative form, to a matter of "maximizing" aggregate fulfillment of desire, even for the individual. And of course such a maximizing theory completely eliminates any "obligation" to consider the interests of another subject beyond the point where the first person may happen as a matter of fact to be interested in the other, to a degree which takes precedence over any more strictly individualistic interest. Any social science which does not take full account of problem-solving activity at both these levels simply ignores the most important facts about its material.

V

We turn to explicit consideration of the relation between knowledge and action, and of knowledge as a basis of action.

It is in this connection especially that we encounter the categorical differences between social and natural science. The fact that there always is some relation between knowledge and action surely need not be argued or developed here, beyond noting, perhaps, that even the simplest experimentation is action, as is also all communication of knowledge in any form. Action may be instrumental to knowledge as well as conversely. Science itself, even, considered purely as an end, is a part of the social and socially purposive life of man. It is through intercommunication that most of any person's knowledge is gained, that all knowledge becomes objective by verification, and that the capacity for rational knowing is developed in the individual, or that it was developed in the race.

All action by man, including expression or communication, begins with action by a purposive subject, with a motive, on his, or its, own body; and its next link is the use of bodily changes to produce changes in the world outside one's own skin. It is through, or *via* changes in the physical world that one human individual acts upon, or communicates with, another. This is theoretically important especially because at virtually every step in any action, the physical processes involved consist essentially in the directed release of potential energy, and in such changes there is no quantitative relation between physical cause and physical effect. There is no minimum limit to the energy of a spark which sets off a conflagration and no maximum limit to that of the conflagration which it sets off. Hence, as far as physics is concerned, the degree of indeterminism needed for effective human freedom is infinitesimal and far beyond experimental detection.

The question of knowledge in relation to social action in the natural sense of "overt" action must be considered under two heads, action by man as an individual upon other individuals, and social action in relation to social problems.

With regard to the first, the essential mutuality of both the knowing and the acting relationship means that the procedure employed takes such forms as suggestion, persuasion, coercion, and especially deception—and beyond these the cultivation of affection and trust—or such forms as communication of information, the rendering of reciprocal favors, etc. None of these procedures has any meaning whatever in the relation of men to inert natural objects. (As usual, the animals, especially the "higher" species, are in an intermediate position.)

In the second place, action upon other individuals by any individual, or exercise of power over them, in so far as it takes the form or has the meaning of a one-sided manipulation and use of them, is regarded, in modern free individualistic culture, as the essence of immorality. And this moral judgment is at least closely connected with the "fact" that the consequences of violating the principle may be expected to be undesirable to the actor himself. Even where the action is performed on behalf of the party acted upon, serious questions are involved: first, as to the validity of the altruistic interest, and even more as to the presumption of knowledge of the other's interests superior to that of the other himself. And if the relationship is not ultimately mutual—as, e.g., between the doctor and patient—the person acted upon is at least treated as an inferior type of being, not as a human in the full sense (e.g., treatment of criminals, children and the incompetent).

VI

We come finally to the most important consideration of all, that of social action proper. After all the introducing that has seemed necessary, this must be disposed of so briefly that the treatment may well seem dogmatic. But it surely ought to be evident that social action is not a problem of manipulation of an inert object-matter, by any subject, and hence is not one of "technique" in the proper sense of the word. That is, instrumentalist categories do not apply. In social action—action by any group, as a group—the really social activity, the solution of a social or group problem, consists in the establishment of agreement or consensus among the individuals who make up the group, as to what action is desirable. Consequently, the process is essentially that of *discussion of values,* the nature of which has already been suggested. Indeed, social action is not merely of the same form as the pursuit of truth, but that is always its essential character. To refer again to the former illustration, social action is what we, the parties to this discussion, are doing, here and now.

Social action in the proper sense is the solution of a social or group problem. With reference to overt action, which is to say, in the field of politics in the broad sense, it consists in reaching a decision in and by the group in question, upon the desirability of some change in its own character as a group. Agreement as a quest presupposes a question, a conflict of interest, a difference of opinion, and an objectively right answer (or at least a better rather than a worse answer) to be found by joint intellectual inquiry. More concretely, a social problem always has the content as well as the form of changing the "laws" in which the character of a group as a group is formulated and contained. In practice, social change is usually carried out by voting upon general objectives of policy and delegating individuals as agents of the group to formulate and to enforce specific laws. Thus all concrete action is carried out by individuals—apart from mob or lynch law, more or less characteristic at primitive levels. But in so far as the action is really on behalf of the group these agents are "responsible" to the latter. Social action always looks forward to embodiment in new institutional patterns or to culture change, and to related changes in the nature of the individuals who make up the group. It is a matter of group self-change, an activity even more remote from technical or instrumental intelligence, not to mention mechanical process, than is individual self-change—and the notions of social mind and social will and choice are correspondingly more repugnant to the reducing and simplistic proclivities of our minds.

The little that can be said, i.e., stated in intelligible and unambiguous verbal propositions, about "method" in this field of value creation and self-change is vague and tenuous at best, and the meaning of essential terms is more or less figurative rather than literal. This is apparent in the literature of "criticism," in all the fields of value. It is especially clear in esthetics and ethics; but it applies also to "logic," including science itself, when it goes beyond the mechanical and more or less commonplace into issues which are really problematic. The problems of discussion or criticism or value creation by group intelligence cannot be taken up here. That is the task of philosophy, not of social science or its methodology. But social science must recognize and emphasize the reality of group action as well as individual action, and must attempt to say what can be said about it in terms of generalized description. Hence there can be no clear line between social science and philosophy. (In fact there is no clear line between natural science and its methodology, for at the growing point, where the really acute problems lie, these are essentially methodological and evaluative.)

These considerations would naturally lead into a discussion of the various positive—or more or less strictly and purely positive—social sciences, as sciences and in their relation to action, individual as well as social. Within the limits of this essay it is possible only to touch upon the problems raised. Discussion would re-emphasize the pluralism of categories required in the realistic treatment of human-social subject matter. The foregoing argument has shown that man must be described in terms of at least a half-dozen fundamental kinds of entity or being. He is (a) a physical mechanism; (b) a biological organism, with characteristics extending from those of the lowest plant to the highest animal in the biological scale; (c) a social animal in the traditional-institutional sense; (d) a problem-solving individual in the economic sense, an economic man; (e) a problem solver at the higher level of critical deliberation about ends; (f) a social being in the sense of the free association of individuals with characteristics (d) and (e). (He may also be to some extent a social animal, in the proper instinctive sense; but, if so, it is to such a limited degree that for present purposes it may be left out of account.)

It is evident that at least the first three of these types of existence can each be the subject matter of a distinct positive science or group of such sciences. And these sciences have already been more or less extensively developed. We do have more or less distinctively human physics and chemistry, human biology, and institutional science, sociology, or cultural anthropology. And of the last, in particular, there are many branches, including institutional economics and descriptive ethics and esthetics. Each of these sciences deals descriptively with an aspect of human phenomena which is isolated and treated in the positive terms of "uniformities of coexistence and sequence," on the general pattern of a natural science. At least one further distinction must be made—a fourth type of scientifically describable form of existence recognized. Consciousness is not necessarily or always active, deliberative, or problem-solving. And to the extent that it is not of this character but is merely phenomenal (or epiphenomenal), it is possible, in theory (and more or less so actually) to describe consciousness in positive categories. Such description is the task and subject matter of another highly developed science— that of psychology—in the meaning indicated by the statement, which is its original and proper meaning, in distinction from various special physical and biological sciences such as neurology, physiology, and "behaviorology."

It is also evident that all these sciences must in a sense take account of the social nature of man. Yet they are not social sciences, with the exception of culture anthropology. This is in a sense *the* science of society, if the word is restricted, as far as the subject matter allows, to the category of a natural or positive science. It will naturally be subdivided along the lines of the major distinguishable branches or aspects of cultural life, such as language, law, religion, technology, economic organization, social usage and recreation. But it should hardly be necessary to emphasize that the content of culture anthropology as a positive science—namely, institutions—is not learned like natural science data through sense observation merely, but primarily through intercommunication and interpretation. In consequence, the results must be far less definite and precise than those of natural sciences, particularly with respect to the vagueness of classification and the absence of real measurement already emphasized. And the science can have no direct significance for social action in the society of the scientist himself; for if it results in such action, its conclusions are no longer true. It does, however, need to be emphasized that the phenomena of our own society are very largely of the traditional institutional character, and this must be true of any society which is even intellectually conceivable, just as any real or possible society must involve human beings in all other "lower" aspects. The study of these phenomena may itself bring them above the threshold of social awareness and make them problems of social action.

A few words are called for regarding economics, at least as to the existence of a purely deductive quasi-mathematical science of theoretical economics or economic theory, in addition to the description of economic behavior patterns as institutional phenomena, already mentioned as a subdivision of culture anthropology. Economic theory as a branch of knowledge and inquiry deals with two main topics. The first is the abstract principles of individual behavior oriented to the maximizing of "want-satisfaction" through the correct allocation of limited given means among alternative modes of use. The second is the principles of *organization* of economic activity through the free exchange of services (or "goods" as the embodiment of future services) between individuals, giving rise to markets, and to the theory of the perfect market. Economic theory assumes—because it is an indisputable fact— that men do economize, and that economy is an ideal only partly realized in fact. They strive more or less successfully to achieve maximum efficiency in the use of means in realizing given ends. But these facts are and can be known only intuitively; they cannot be verified or established by sense-observation, as even the principles of mathematics can be— within the limits of accuracy and generality set by the labor and expense required.

The methodology, or logic, of various social sciences, in the abstract, and as far as they go as positive sciences, is not essentially different from that of the natural sciences, including that various mixtures of inductive and deductive procedure which these present. The main difference, as already noted, is in the large degree to which sense observation is replaced by intercommunication and interpretation. The relevance of the positive, or quasi-positive, social sciences for action, is essentially that of revealing and clarifying the "given conditions" of action—which again is true of the natural science also. The actual nature of the "given-ness" in this connection, and of action itself, and the relations between the two, belong, again, to philosophy rather than to social science as such. It is not the province of science to say what values society ought to strive to realize in action, any more than it is in the case of natural science as the basis of technology. Science does not even explicitly tell how to realize any values. But it is its province to show by implication, through description of real and hypothetical courses of events, what would be the results of proposed lines of action—or what lines of action may be expected to produce any results accepted as desirable.

VII

In conclusion, a few words seem to be in order as to the relevance of this discussion as a whole to the present crisis in Western culture. The predicament in which free society finds itself at the moment arises precisely out of the fact that any free society must, by virtue of its nature as free society, reach agreement, by discussion, on fundamental values, wherever "serious" conflicts of interest arise. For, as already pointed out, it is only as conflicts of values or of "rights" that conflicts of interest can be discussed, and any solution of such a problem is in the nature of the case a value or mode of rightness. Now scientific inquiry has, and rests upon, a moral code, or in sheer fact a "religion"; and it is supremely important at this hour that scientists recognize this fact, and even more important that society consider carefully the moral code and the religion of science, and its general applicability in connection with social problems.

As we have already emphasized, truth is a value, and science itself is the type of the pursuit and creation of value as a social activity. The basic principle of science—truth or objectivity—is essentially a moral principle, in opposition to any form of self-interest. The presuppositions of objectivity are integrity, competence, and humility. The combination of the three gives the essential principle of freedom, i.e., problem-solving through rational discussion, a social-intellectual creative activity, the quest and definition of values. All coercion is absolutely excluded, in favor of a free meeting of free minds. Three aspects or forms of coercion particularly need emphasis. The first is the exclusion of persuasion which, as appeal to emotion, i.e., to *wrong* emotions (emotions conflicting with the love of truth or validity) is a form of coercion, and perhaps the "worst" form because the most insidious and therefore likely to be misconceived and adopted or condoned. The second form is coercion of any minority by any majority. Truth, or validity, is not a matter of a majority vote. The third point is that only in the most extreme cases can coercion be justified by considerations of "sentimental" morality, such as personal love, or the desire to do good. In general, these things have no more place in the solution of other value problems than they have in relation to science and truth. This is not merely a matter of moral idealism, but a *fact,* as to the nature of problem-solving.

The writer does not need to be reminded that serious questions are raised. "Real" discussion is rarely if ever "really" and purely discussion. Even scientists acting in their own field are frail men, and affected by original sin. They can only struggle, and "pray," for liberation from wrong emotions, dogmatism, sentimentalism, and the will to dominate, overcome and coerce, and especially to persuade—even in the interest of truth. And in the fields of economics and politics, social order is admittedly impossible without much coercion, in the ordinary use of the term. (International relations present the most serious problem in this regard.) Practical politics is necessarily a matter of compromise, of balancing evil against good. At least, the use of force might be largely—though by no means entirely—restricted to the negative form, coercive prevention of coercion. This was the central tenet of the older and genuine liberalism, which is unhappily tending to be overshadowed by the romantic craving for action, involving "thinking with the blood," which even appropriates the designation of liberalism itself. Space limits preclude more than mention of these topics. But surely, competent scientists ought not to be—as they too frequently are—heard favoring and advocating the placing of "intelligence" in charge of social affairs, not recognizing that this means putting *politicians* of some breed and brand in charge of all other people, including scientists.

X

Some Notes on the Economic Interpretation of History

*I*t has already long been recognized that one of the intellectual vices of that far-off age, the nineteenth century, was the excessive "rationalization" of human behavior and human nature. The economic interpretation of history was a phase or product of this error. The modern rationalistic world-view may be said to have come in with the European Enlightenment; but it was given a special twist by the empirical-practical English mind in utilitarianism, of which the classical economics, the science of the economic man, was essentially an application, after considerable logical purification. Marry this to the German-romantic rationalism, or rationalistic romanticism, of Hegel, and the Marxian interpretation of history is the natural, reasonably predictable, offspring.[1] The doctrine of our title is already well on its way

---

Reprinted by permission from *Studies in the History of Culture*, Menasha, Wisconsin, 1942.
[1] It is notorious among critical students of economics that Marx and Engels got the main points in their position, and especially their most palpable economic fallacies, by copying from the Ricardian economics but paraphrasing in a somewhat more rigorous, and "consequent" or thorough-going presentation.

to the discard and might before now have become a topic of historical interest only, if it had not got into politics. In that field, almost as in religion, a theory retains its truth, and even a degree of untouchable sanctity, as long as a large number of people will abide by an agreement once made to believe in it.

A convenient approach to the issues raised by our topic is afforded by a well-known small volume of lectures by Professor G. N. Clark of Oxford University, entitled *Science and Social Welfare in the Age of Newton*. The third chapter, on "Social and Economic Aspects of Science" is explicitly a reply to an essay on "The Social and Economic Roots of Newton's Principia" by the Russian Professor B. Hessen, which is a polemical interpretation of the English seventeenth century movement in terms of orthodox Marxism.[2]

Professor Clark's work is also suited to bring out other relations between history and economics, and to illustrate the type of reasoning one may expect to encounter in this field of discussion. Writing as a historian, the author on one hand rather adequately demolishes the Marxist error but on the other hand himself falls into economic fallacies of equal magnitude, in addition to missing the main point (according to this writer) of the subject he is discussing. His economic reasoning is of a kind which is characteristic of historians and of educated people generally, a fact which is at once the main practical reason for teaching economics, and the despair of

---

[2] Clark, *op. cit.*, Oxford University Press, 1937. Hessen's paper is published in the volume *Science at the Crossroads* (Kniga [England] Ltd., London, 1932— see pp. 151–212), with other items presented by members of the Russian delegation at an international scientific congress held at London in 1931. The fullest and best discussion in English of our subject as a whole is probably the volume of M. M. Bober, *Karl Marx's Interpretation of History*. Cambridge, Harvard University Press, 1927. See also Seligman, E. R. A., *The Economic Interpretation of History*, 2nd Ed. Rev., 1924; and See, Henri, same title (Trans. M. M. Knight), New York, 1929. This last, as well as Bober's work, has extensive bibliographic notes.

those whose profession it is to do it. It would hardly be possible to imagine a "better bad example" than is afforded by a couple of sentences taken from the end of Professor Clark's second chapter: "Again, technological improvement was most active . . . in those industries in which there was international competition . . . the export industries, which each state now tried to foster in order that its dependence on imports might be lessened, and its exporting power increased." Obviously, the fostering of export industries would *increase* a country's dependence on imports—unless the exports were given away to foreigners, which is not customary. And importation is the only intelligible motive for fostering exports, as well as its natural consequence. There are other hardly less "flagrant" sins against facts and logic, such as the observation that a labor-saving invention is a "synonym for unemployment"; but we must turn to the main subject of the present essay.

In arguing against Professor Hessen's economic interpretation of the scientific movement in which Newton was the most dramatic figure, Professor Clark admits that the economic interest plays an important role in the activities of men, and hence in social change. But he argues that five other types of interest, distinct from the economic, have also to be recognized as playing roles, which are of comparable importance. The first of these is the *health* interest, underlying medical science. He admits that this is "utilitarian," but distinguishes it from the category of economics. Clark's second noneconomic interest, he says, is not even utilitarian, unless "everything is utilitarian"; this is the interest in the *fine arts,* particularly painting and music. The third is *war*. The fourth is the *religious* interest, to which the discussion centering around the life work of Max Weber has drawn so much attention. The fifth is the pure *intellectual* interest in science, the desire for knowledge for its own sake. The validity of the distinction between the scientific and utilitarian interests is explicitly argued in connection with mathematics and the motives and personalities of the leaders in that field; but a reasonable person must surely admit its reality in connection with any branch of inquiry.[3]

In attempting to build upon this analysis, and to get beyond it, we may start from the question which will undoubtedly be raised by anyone disposed to advocate the economic interpretation—the question whether these various interests or motives are really distinct from the economic. The thesis of this paper is that this question itself rests on a fallacy, so that no answer to it can be correct. Properly speaking, there is no distinctively economic motive, or end, or value. We may speak of an economic *interest,* but only if we are careful to understand that what we mean by it is not an interest in doing any particular thing or kind of thing, or in achieving any particular kind of end; it is merely the interest in doing "economically" anything that one does at all, i.e., in acting efficiently or effectively. These terms, "economic" and "efficient," which are closely synonymous, refer to the use of means or resources or "power" in any form, in the pursuit of any given end, regardless of its nature. Any activity or problem is, then, "economic," or is affected by the economic interest, in so far, first, as it involves the use of resources or power, and secondly, in so far as the problem is actually and realistically one of "economizing" the available means or power.

No yes-or-no answer can be given to the question whether any problem is economic or not; at most it is a matter of

---

[3] The story is often told that the great mathematician K. F. Gauss once closed a paper before a public meeting by giving vocal thanks to God that no one could possibly make any use of the theorem he had demonstrated.

Professor Clark recognizes a kinship between the scientific and esthetic interests, but still holds that they are different. He quotes Arbuthnot, a writer contemporary with Newton: "Truth is the same thing to the understanding, as music to the ear, and beauty to the eye."

degree, and at bottom even this form of the question embodies a misconception. Every human activity involves the use of means or power, and the degree of satisfactoriness of any activity is always in some sense a matter of success in achieving what is attempted, and hence a matter of the efficiency or effectiveness with which means are used. All human capacities, and time itself, a dimension of all activity, are, formally speaking, means or "resources." And all activity involves economizing human capacity or time, as well as more tangible means and resources which are practically always involved to a greater or less extent in any project or problem of action. This is clearly true of all the activities which are contrasted with the economic by Professor Clark. All of them involve the use of what we call material means, in the loose general sense of the word "material." This is apparent if one goes through the list; doctors, artists, soldiers, ministers of religion, and scientists have their economic problems, and so do institutions concerned with these fields of activity. Professor Clark must be aware that universities have them, and by all reports it is as true of armies, hospitals, art schools and museums, and "even" of churches.

To begin with, "one must live," as a familiar aphorism says, as a condition of pursuing any of these "higher" activities; and "living" is universally recognized as an economic problem. But this undisputed fact glosses over the deeper issues. Some of these are uncovered by asking what is included in a living, and attempting to relate that category in turn to the activities to which it is alleged to be prerequisite, such as health, art, war, religion, and the pursuit of truth— and others which, as will be noted presently, might be added to this list. The complexity of these issues may also be suggested by an aphoristic question regarding the means-and-end relations of eating: Do men eat to live or live to eat? It is obvious that they universally do both, and in a multiplicity of senses. And the same is true in every conceivable degree of curing disease, searching for truth, and of all the higher activities; they are both ends and means.

The question whether any activity is economic or not is, to repeat, the question whether, or how far, it makes sense to regard the *problem* involved as one of economizing means in realizing some end, given in advance. Living, in the large, does not seem to fit the means-end relation to any specific activity, but rather to *consist* of an indefinite aggregate of activities and interests, which are mutually means and ends to each other. In particular, it needs to be emphasized that that "living" which is prerequisite to any of the so-called higher activities cannot possibly be defined in biological terms. Human living is always a complex mixture of the higher activities themselves. Living, at the human level, means living in some way, according to some standard. This is clear if we reflect that in our own culture a relatively small fraction of what is nominally spent for "food," even by people classed as poor, really represents the cost of physiological nourishment, while a still smaller part of the cost of clothing, shelter and other budget items ministers to animal needs, to physical life and health, or to "comfort." The human value even of "subsistence" is esthetic and social.

It is possible, however, to make some headway in the analysis of the general problem of what is meant by the economic as a category, as a more or less distinct form of motivation. To begin with, there are two aspects of economic activity, or of economizing, in ordinary common-sense usage. The first aspect is "technical" or technological; there are various concrete, manipulative ways of using any means to any end, which are "effective" in various degrees. But economics, as a recognized special science or subdivision of knowledge, is not concerned with technological problems. These belong to the various branches of technology as such, including the fine arts and the crafts. Every art or craft has its technique—not merely the fine arts and the professions, engineering, etc., but also agriculture, business management, cookery and the most menial occupations, in the home and outside of it. Economics is not concerned with these techniques. It deals with another aspect of economic activity, which—putting the matter in crude, common-sense terms to begin with—is that of employing means or resources for more important rather than less important uses or immediate ends.

Refining the conception somewhat, economics deals with the *apportionment* of resources among various modes of use. The science takes its rise from the empirical fact that (in consequence of the principle of "diminishing utility") the effective use of resources commonly involves such apportionment. Hence there is a problem of "correct" apportionment, in order to secure the "best" results, or what is called in economic jargon, "maximum satisfaction of wants." Much of the difficulty of economic theory as a science inheres in this conception of a generalized end of activity, called "want satisfaction." It means simply the common denominator of the more specific and concrete ends of action, the perfectly abstract general end to which all concrete ends are means.[4] We do compare these prospective results as quantities, in so far as we choose "rationally," in deciding how much of our total expenditure, in money or productive capacity, is to be allocated to each. "Want satisfaction" commits one to no theory of motive or the good; it is merely the term which has

---

[4] Want satisfaction is not really the *summum bonum* of the moral philosophers, since ethical or other critical evaluation is excluded from economic comparison, which is quantitative only. But logical definition runs in much the same terms, and utilitarianism and pragmatism virtually reduce all ethics to economics.

become conventionalized to refer to *that which* any individual is trying to "maximize," to get *more* of in preference to less, in choices between different ways of using means.

It will now be clear that it is at best a vague question of degree, how far any problem of action, or the effective motivation in any human activity, is "economic." It is a matter of judgment, of one's feeling as to how far it is good sense, or is realistic, to view any type of action problem as one of economizing means. Of the five interests discussed by Professor Clark, religion and the fine arts are perhaps least realistically described as economic, in the problem they present; war and medicine would surely be "more" economic, with scientific activity somewhere between. Writing poetry surely is not primarily a matter of economizing paper, ink, and "labor," and neither is religious worship. The need is first to understand what statements about economy mean, and then to realize the vagueness and subtlety, amounting to sheer paradox, in the means-end relation. When we say, for example, that the ministry of religion, or musical composition, is not primarily an economic activity, we mean only that we do not ordinarily think of the problems involved as problems of the allocation or effective use of means. Under critical scrutiny, it is evident that we "could" do so; and sometimes and within limits we do. Thus the validity of usage or of our thought habits as a test of the nature of things becomes questionable. Worship and the creative arts certainly involve the use of means, and specifically of what are unquestionably classed as economic resources; and these can be used more or less "effectively." Moreover, economic resources certainly are apportioned between these activities and other (competing) uses, and a "margin of indifference" is determined upon. The apportionment of resources between "higher" and "lower" uses is presumably made, or people try to make it, in such a way that at the indifference margin all the different uses are "equally important." This makes the meaning of importance itself something of a paradox. But there is no escaping the logic which makes this equalization of the importance of all alternative uses of any means, "at the margin," the *meaning* of economy (in the aspect of apportionment; technical efficiency is another meaning).

Before leaving Professor Clark and his list of five interests, it must be emphasized that while undoubtedly useful for the author's purpose in making it clear—as against Hessen and naïve or dogmatic economic interpreters generally—that other interests than the economic must be recognized, this list itself will not stand scrutiny as an analysis or classification of the ends, motives, or interests which must be taken into account by the historian or other student of social life. It seems doubtful whether anyone can make a clear analysis of human motives, or one which will stand much critical scrutiny. It must suffice here to point out that this list has nothing to say about such fundamental interests as play, self-expression, and self-development; of activity and achievement for their own sake; or of social interests, including emulation and personal and group likes and dislikes, as well as sociability as such—all in highly various forms.

The play interest seems to be especially important, and seriously neglected in discussion. It seems to stand at the opposite pole from the economic interest, however defined, and is indeed largely antieconomic in principle; and yet it also contains its economic element. In play as well as in "work," one is always trying to do something, to achieve some objective, and to do it effectively. And yet, as someone has remarked, the first step in organizing a football game according to the ideal of economic efficiency would be to put all the men on the same side; it is wasteful and absurd to have half of them struggling with all their might in opposition to the other half. Moreover, an element of the play interest is probably universal in all voluntary activity. Reflection upon the meaning of these facts is sufficient in itself to reduce any economic interpretation of conduct as a universal principle literally to "foolishness."[5] In addition, all interests are suffused with a desire for *power,* dominion over men and over things. But power as an end, apart from any desirable result to be obtained by its use, is outside the concept of economy or economic rationality.

In sum: Economic thinking deals with the problem of using given means to realize given ends. Its scope is limited in one direction by critical reflection about ends, in contrast with the problem of getting wanted things, and in the other by the unconscious or mechanical cause-and-effect aspect of behavior. The means available to any individual (or to any group, considered as an economic subject) are at any time "really" given; but the end is not given or is given only in a partial and provisional sense. There is no final end in conduct, in any concrete and intelligible meaning. Such terms as want-satisfaction, or "happiness," or self-realization, as general ends, are little more than names for the fact that, for our thinking, activity is at any moment directed to *some* purpose beyond the concrete end immediately in view. All concrete ends are really means, as one realizes the moment any end is questioned; and the ultimate end is simply "the good life!" And "the good" must include many species, which resist analytical differentiation. Moreover, the means-and-end relationship is complicated by the indisputable fact that means—or more properly the procedures by which means are used, i.e., activities as such—may evidently be good or bad *per se;* they are subject to value judgments, about as much as are ends themselves.

---

[5] Sociability, of course, combines with more concretely directed activities, in which the play and work interests on one hand, and cooperation and conflict interests on the other, stand out as two sets of polarities.

Again, even the immediate, concrete end or objective, in a particular limited problem or project, never is fully given at the beginning. It is always subject to re-definition during the process of its realization. This is true in all degrees. In the limiting case at the opposite extreme from the concept of economic behavior, the end is not given at all; the essential motive of the action is "curiosity," it is to find out what the result will be. Such activity is *explorative*. And all activity seems to involve this motive as a factor. For example, we would never read a book or listen to a lecture if we knew in advance exactly what book we are going to read—its content— or what we should hear the speaker say, though to be moved to action we must have some idea of what is to be expected. And all creative activity above absolute drudgery is more or less explorative and creative. Worse still, reflection about play makes it clear that in a very large measure the end is really instrumental to the activity, rather than the converse. We deliberately set up an end for the purpose of making the activity interesting. This is also true, in all degrees, of "economic" life in the empirical sense, both in production, or "business," and in consumption. Activity in either of these fields may have as much the character of a competitive sport as that of satisfying wants, as a specific and final consequence of the use of means. Or, the motivation may be that of play in games of solitaire. There is no clear distinction between work and play, and the concept of economic activity has no clear relation to either. All economic activity is affected by the creative and explorative interests, which have much in common with play, and by numerous social and individual motives which do not enter into the make-up of the hypothetical "economic man." In short, the economic interest is an aspect of conduct in general, varying widely in importance relative to other aspects. It does not pertain to any distinct field of action or class of activities.

It is a particularly serious fallacy, associated with the economic interpretation, to think of economic activity as the only field in which conflicts of interest occur, between individuals or between groups, or as the only field in which conflicts reach the proportions of a major problem. Candid reflection will rather make it seem doubtful whether the abolition of all economic problems—say by a fairy gift to every adult of the power to work physical miracles—would ameliorate social conflict, or would even change its form in any important respect. All the "higher" activities are both competitive and cooperative, including religion and pure sociability, as well as science and philosophy, and it is doubtful whether the competition and power relations in other fields, and particularly in politics, are morally better or tend less to conflict than those of the business world, or whether they are essentially different.

The application of this brief and sketchy theoretical analysis must be briefer still. The quest of the historian, as a philosopher, or as methodology-conscious, is for causes, forces, laws, uniformities of sequence, or elementary concepts in some form, which will serve to make historical writing intelligible, to "explain" the past, and in some degree, as he fondly hopes, give an inkling as to what may be expected in the future. A classification of the possibilities in this direction should begin with a dichotomy. The first question is to decide as to the relative importance in historical process of motivated and unmotivated behavior, or deliberate action as against unconscious "social forces." Surely, this is a matter of degree; neither sort of causality can be excluded, or have fundamental importance denied to it. And the same will be true of numerous sub-heads under each of these general categories; especially on the side of motivated action, one must recognize many kinds of ends, good and bad, rational and irrational.

In teaching economics, and writing for economists, who are notoriously afflicted with a naïvely utilitarian, rationalistic, and individualistic bias, it is the unconscious and social element which needs emphasis. The writer's favorite procedure has been to insist upon some reflection on the part of students about language and the scientific study of language. Linguistics is recognized as perhaps the most "scientific" and intellectually satisfactory of the *Geisteswissenschaften*. The outstanding fact in the study of linguistics is that no one proposes to explain or interpret the evolution of language in terms of conscious or rational individual motivation. Indeed, it is something of a paradox that, although language is evidently one of the most important instrumentalities or tools of social life—and hence of all human life—and is consciously and purposively used as a tool, effort to increase the functional efficiency of language is found to play a relatively small part in linguistic change. Even the struggle for existence and selective survival among variations hardly seems to work toward the "improvement" of language.

In the respect indicated, language is only a somewhat extreme example of features in which all social-cultural phenomena share in greater or less degree. Next to language in this respect would doubtless come the law. In fact the same statements made about language would apply literally to the law through most of its history. It is only in fairly advanced civilizations that laws are "made," or changed, by "taking thought," or that they even become subject to conscious observation and criticism on the part of the mass of the people who live under them; and even here the historical school of jurisprudence denies or minimizes the effective reality of legislation.

We might go through any working list of departments or forms of social behavior, and show that custom, subject to slow, unconscious modification, is the basic element in all of them, though this is decreasingly so, in most fields, as we approach the conditions of today. Language still obstinately remains exceptional; we do indeed see efforts made to improve language or make it more "scientific," but they do not get far. In primitive society, conscious motivation seems to function almost exclusively in a conservative sense, in all fields; it acts to resist change, to enforce conformity to tradition.

It would seem that this unconscious and highly conservative form of change, called "drift" by the linguists, and custom or tradition by sociologists, is the proper meaning of the "historical," as a distinct type of causality or process, and as a category of interpretation. Thus it is largely antithetical to the category of the "economic," as understood by economic theorists, for the latter refers to behavior of a conscious, highly deliberative and "rational" type.[6] In this usage, a "historical" interpretation of history is the antithesis of the "great man" interpretation, to which the "economic" interpretation would be closely related.

But this is not the way in which the terms are commonly used; and surely the supreme need is for the removal of ambiguity in usage, and establishment of some consistent terminology. Most history, as actually written, is primarily biographical; its main problems and its method of explanation run in terms of individual motivation, though not, for the most part, of "economic" motivation, as defined by the economist. The chief motive recognized by historians is the

---

[6] But as we have seen, the economic is by no means the extreme antithesis to tradition or historical causality. The economic view of behavior assumes that the end of action is given, as well as the means and knowledge of procedure; i.e., it abstracts from deliberation about ends, and consequently does not apply to behavior as affected by problems of evaluation—"truth, beauty, or goodness." Thus scientific, esthetic, and moral activities, in which ends are not given but problematic, are rational in a higher sense than the economic. The latter, as already noted, is bounded in an upper direction on a scale by critical evaluative action, on the lower side by unconscious or non-deliberative behavior.

desire for political power.[7] On the other hand, what *historians* (and Marxists, in the dialectical aspect of Marxism) mean by the *economic* interpretation is a species of what we have called the "historical" category *per se*. The economic interpretation, commonly so-called, consists in selecting a particular field of activity, and thread of change, called the economic, but defined vaguely or not at all, and making that, conceived as a drift, the "independent variable" in historical process, and treating other types of behavior and threads of change as causally dependent upon it.[8]

In the field of economics, it is important to note, we find a situation which may be regarded as either parallel, in a sense, with that found in history, or inverse, according to taste. That is, we find a succession of "historical schools" of economics, beginning especially in Germany about the middle of the nineteenth century, of which the *"Neo-Historismus"* of Weber, Sombart, *et al.,* in Germany, and "institutional economics" in America, are current or recent phases. Thus, while historians have been running to an economic interpretation of history, many economists have been advo-

---

[7] It is true that in the "new" or "social" history this is less true than in the older and more exclusively political history. But it is perhaps still predominantly true, even in these newer writings, at least that the motives of action are conscious interests, though a broader range of such interests is taken into account.

The relation between political and economic power is an important topic, but must be passed over; it is obvious that each is in varying degrees a means to the other, with economic power growing in importance in modern times.

[8] The best meaning for the expression "economic interpretation of history"—if one were given the task of finding a definite, particular meaning for it—is surely to take it (as the American Marxist Calhoun has argued) as the application to human history of the Darwinian principle of selective survival on the basis of biological efficiency. This gives in effect a technological interpretation, which is the evident meaning of Marx and Engels in many passages, and undoubtedly has much truth in it. It also has limitations, among them its incapacity to explain decadence, which is a historical fact as real and as important as progress. The important but puzzling pretensions of Veblen to be the apostle of the Darwinian method in economics come to mind in this connection, but can only be mentioned.

cating an historical interpretation of economics. It would be interesting, if space limits allowed, to subject this situation to philosophical scrutiny. A combination of these two opposite views or approaches would make a good starting point for a real discussion of the general subject of social and historical interpretation.

Finally, there is space for only the briefest indication of the lines along which it would be interesting to develop a critical analysis of the economic interpretation of history as itself a phenomenon of intellectual and cultural history. We mean, of course, the theory—not really originated by Marx and Engels (who ever originated anything?!)— but which at least was forced upon the attention of scholars and of the public chiefly by their writings and the work of their followers. Marx and Engels, and the "scientific" socialists, shifted somewhat recklessly between the expressions, "materialistic" and "economic" interpretation or conception (*Auffassung*). The background is of course Marx's "flirtation" with the Hegelian dialectic, in which he more or less playfully, as he said, stood the dialectic on its head, or, in his own view, on its feet. "Dialectical materialism" is another stock designation of the position. It would be easy to show—in fact it hardly seems to need demonstration—that the three concepts, materialistic, dialectical, and economic, if clearly defined, are mutually exclusive, that they belong in different universes of discourse, with no intellectual bridge between any two of them.[9] All three undoubtedly have reality, and all three are

---

[9] A dialectical interpretation of history is "practically" equivalent to a mechanistic view, the difference being purely a matter of metaphysical theory. The "rationality" referred to at the outset has become in Hegel "absolute" reason, which is so far from human reason that they are antithetical. The same paradox is found in connection with economic process; "absolutely" economic behavior is conceptually identical with mechanical sequence; without liability to error, purposiveness is unthinkable.

valuable, even necessary, in the discussion of historical process, stability and change. But in so far as a phenomenon belongs in any one of these categories, it does not belong in either of the other two. This means that a highly pluralistic conception of history is unescapable, at least until philosophy and metaphysics have made enormous progress, beyond anything either yet achieved or in sight for the future, in the way of unifying the ultimate concepts used in our thinking.

But this is by no means the end of the confusion in Marxism. For the Marxian Scientific Socialists, all three of the categories mentioned are intellectual preliminaries to their real interest— one might even say a kind of smokescreen. What they have been trying to promote is, in the first place, a "class struggle" theory of history. But it is evident, first, that in "struggle" and "class" struggle we have two more categories, irreconcilable as principles, either between themselves or with any of the prior three. And second, even these theories of history are still preliminary, a part of the propaganda for the real objective, which is the practical political one of fomenting a conscious class struggle, which did not exist or predominate before, or it would not need to be promoted. Incidentally, critical examination would show the notion of an economic class to be so vague and shifting that it can hardly be used in any scientific discussion of *political* struggles.

The vital fact is that any single scientific or positive theory of motivation is self-stultifying, especially in connection with any sort of propaganda. For any general theoretical explanation of behavior or motive must apply to the activities of the (explainer and) propagandist himself, and any intellectually satisfactory explanation reduces his propaganda to nonsense, to selling talk, if not to mere noise. The suggestion of an economic interpretation of the economic interpretation is all that should be needed as an answer to it, if taken in a thorough-going and inclusive sense. The "victims" of the propaganda must be kept from thinking of that possibility—which in fact has an embarrassing amount of validity! For the real motive back of any political propaganda is largely the quest of power on the part of those who are carrying it on. The propagandist can usually see this clearly in connection with every propaganda except his own. To the Marxists, as to most reformers, it has been only their opponents who have been actuated by selfish or "class" interests. *They* are asking nothing for themselves—except supreme power and the perquisites thereof! From an impartial or objective historical and political point of view, perhaps the most interesting fact in connection with the Marxist theory of history is the paradox that, human nature—and specifically human political intelligence—being what it is, one of the most effective ways of securing active support for a cause is to "prove" that it will "inevitably" triumph, that in fact there is nothing that anyone can do about it. Predestinationism in religion (Islamic fatalism) is an earlier conspicuous illustration of the same psychological principle.

What seems most philosophically significant about Marxism is its bearing upon the problem of ethics. For what it primarily means in practice is the complete futility and even the unreality of any intellectual-moral discussion, especially of group policy. It teaches that economic self-interest is the exclusive principle of human action (except that of the teacher?), that all human conduct is to be understood in terms of such interests, backed up by force. It is essentially the repudiation of real discussion and of reason (except in so far as dialectical process means the will of the Absolute, really expressed in "my" will) and direct appeal to violence in behalf of group self-interests. Since the same phenomena of class division and struggle would undoubtedly reappear within any "class," however composed, as soon as it became dominant (by "liquidating" its opponents) the doctrine finally spells the *bellum omnium contra omnes,* or complete social chaos.

In conclusion: Any unique or monistic interpretation of history is a delusion and a snare. But the "economic interpretation" particularly needs to be combatted, above others because, while it contains a large portion of truth, this is so obvious, and so much in line with the dominant trend of oversimplification in modern thought, that it naturally tends to receive too much recognition and emphasis. The "economic factor" is both assumed to have a much more definite meaning than can properly be given to it, and is also assigned a far greater rôle in comparison with other principles than is possible, if it is separated from other principles in any defensible way. It is the limitations in favor of other principles, and the danger of oversimplification in historical analysis in general, which call for emphasis.

XI

The Rights of Man and Natural Law

*A*s a student of theoretical economics the writer constantly faces problems of "methodology," of the concepts and presuppositions involved in generalized description and interpretation of social phenomena, where motivation of behavior cannot be ignored. This discipline also stands in a peculiarly close connection with the problems of social action—i.e., of the procedure by which a human group acts as a unit—and the meaning of group objectives. All these are essentially philosophical rather than scientific problems, in the sense of ordinary usage, in which there is a contrast between the two. In this situation it is natural to seek help from specialists in philosophy, a discipline supposedly concerned with these issues, which was age-old when any of the social sciences now recognized began to be cultivated. But the results of this quest are disappointing. The philosophers typically seem ignorant of and indifferent to facts which are essential to any understanding of the problems. What they

Reprinted by permission from *Ethics,* vol. 44 (1944), pp. 124–145.

have to say is so remotely relevant to the issues that it is often fairly to be characterized as empty verbiage or sheer absurdity. The book which gives its title to this article[1] is such an excellent illustration of this situation, such a "good bad example," as to justify reviewing, and quoting, at a length disproportionate to its own, and using it as a basis for an attempt to sketch a serious discussion of the vitally important issues with which it purports to deal.

The author calls his book (in the first sentence) "an essay in political philosophy," and that, rather than a "review" is the intent of this paper. In context it is largely an abridged and in a sense popularized version of doctrine presented in earlier works, perhaps especially *Freedom in the Modern World* (New York: Scribner's, 1936), with elimination of the more explicit argument for Thomism and Roman Catholic apologetics. It impresses the reviewer as being not too carefully done; the English is much inferior; and, while the translation in this case contains absurd renderings of the French idiom,[2] the French text itself is strangely lacking in the clarity and aesthetic qualities typical of the better literary work in that language. However, the translator's main fault is the usual one of excessive literalness, of crudity rather than of changing the author's meaning. There are two chapters, entitled, respectively, "A Society of Human Persons" (pp. 1–49) and "The Rights of the Person" (pp. 50–114), and a four-page appendix giving the "International Declaration of the Rights of Man" put out by the Institute of International Law at a session at New York in 1929. Each chapter is divided into a number of sections (respectively, 11 and 9), which have titles

---

[1] Jacques Maritain, *The Rights of Man and Natural Law*, trans. Doris C. Anson (New York: Charles Scribner's Sons, 1943). Pp. 119. $1.50.

[2] E.g., in the second sentence of the book, *dans une guerre* and *dans la paix* are rendered "given a war" and "given a peace"; and on p. 66, *à voir* is translated literally "to see," with nonsensical results.

but no numbers. The author does not follow his subtitles at all closely, and at least three-fourths of the book logically belongs in the first chapter. The early sections of chapter ii expound the doctrine of natural law, and later ones take up named "rights," concluding with a résumé. Only in a general way will this review follow the author's order; our summary and comment will be organized around a few main issues. The main points which call for critical notice are the author's reasoning, his use of history, and his social-ethical position.

I. Logical Method

We may begin *in medias res* with an example of the reasoning, taken from chapter ii, and from a section entitled "Natural Law":

> Since I have not space here to discuss nonsense (you can always find very intelligent philosophers to defend it most brilliantly) I am taking it for granted that you admit that there is a human nature, and that this human nature is the same in all men [p. 60].

The reviewer would merely change the last part of this sentence so as to make the proposition "human nature is the same in all men" the example of the nonsense which is defended by "philosophers." Critical discussion must begin with the word "nonsense," because of its wide ambiguity and of the need to use it freely in discussing the book itself—the author having set the example. The term does not usually refer to mere collections of words without grammatical sense but rather to statements which convey a meaning which is viewed as "absurd." Here again, however, caution must be exercised. A proposition which in its literal meaning is absurd may still be significant and important. It may even express a meaning more effectively than one which is objectively scientific, and it may at the same time have other important values, such as humor or poetic beauty. M. Maritain's book will hardly suggest these qualities; and it is more pertinent to observe that a statement which is nonsensical, in nearly any meaning of the word, may be intelligently made and published, if the intent of the author is to arouse some emotion or to conduct propaganda to promote some cause or line of action, whether good or bad.

Various minor types of nonsense might be illustrated from the book before us. For example, the statement (p. 11) that "an unjust law is not a law," taken literally is a bald self-contradiction. But if it means that an unjust law is not a just law, it is nonsense in the meaning of verbal truism. What the author presumably does mean is that an unjust law carries no moral obligation to obedience. In this interpretation it begs one of the most important questions at issue. In the Christian tradition, for which our author explicitly speaks, both Plato and Jesus—undoubtedly high authorities—are on record in opposition to the view stated (cf. *Crito,* 50; Matthew 23:2–3; 5:17–18). Again, the book recognizes the distinction between natural law and positive law, and it is a truism that a law in one meaning of the word may not be a law in another meaning. However, the main use of the word "nonsense" in describing this book will be to characterize statements which are so ambiguous that they mean nothing in particular, being true in numerous interpretations and false in quite as many.

The statement "human nature is the same in all men" is, of course, true, to the extent that the word "man" is meaningful as a class name; and, in fact, its members are usually (though by no means always) distinguished without difficulty. In the same sense all living beings, including men, are alike, and all objects. But it is just as true, and as trivial, to say that men are all different—like the members of most important classes. Men (and the members of most other classes) are both alike and different in respects innumerable and impossible to list. A biological species is rarely distinguished from all others by any single differentia, and a biologist of standing is authority for the statement that no valid general distinction can be drawn between life and combustion; and this writer is not in a position to prove him wrong by stating the distinction. One of the most important attributes of man as a species is the extraordinary range of difference between different individuals as to personality and culture. It is these differences which both make men peculiarly interesting and give rise to the major problems of describing men, and also to the practical problems which men themselves face in their effort to live together satisfactorily in the "societies," also of boundless variety, in which they do and must live. The statement that all men are alike is not at all helpful in dealing with any of these problems. Furthermore, the innumerable differences which distinguish any class from others are largely a matter of degree in the possession of traits which in the qualitative sense are common to the classes and with respect to which the members of the same class also differ in degree. Consequently, classification is a matter of quantitative estimation, since measurement is usually impossible, and is a matter of judgment.

Finally, characterization of any biological class must both take account of the whole life-history of a "normal" individual and have special reference to the "normal" adult; and normality cannot be accurately defined. The last point is especially important in connection with the characteristic traits of "man." A careful expositor would hesitate to say without qualification that any particular individual is "the same" at any two moments of his life. And the infallible Roman church has had difficulty in formulating indicia to show at what moment in the biological life of a "human being" he actually becomes (potentially) a "human being." In short, it is about equally true, or illuminating, to say that all men are alike and to say that all are different; and there is a sense in which they have nothing in common. (We cannot take the space and impose upon the reader's patience to comment in detail on the idea that "intelligence," undefined and without recognition of differences in kind or degree, is "the" differentia of man as a species, the unique trait of that "human nature" which is always and everywhere the same.)

Real issues arise when we inquire into the significant differentiae of human beings, those relevant to questions beyond the relatively academic matter of classification. Immediately following the sentence first quoted, our author tells his readers that

> man is a being gifted with intelligence, and who, as such, acts with an understanding of what he is doing, and therefore with the power to determine the ends which he pursues [and] being constituted in a given, determinate fashion, man obviously possesses ends which correspond to his natural constitution, and which are the same for all, as all pianos for instance, . . . have as their end the production of certain attuned sounds. *If they don't produce these sounds they must be tuned, or discarded as worthless.* [Italics here added by reviewer.] But since man is endowed with intelligence and determines his own ends, it is up to him to put himself in tune with the ends necessarily demanded by his nature. This means that there is, by very virtue of human nature, _an order or a disposition which human reason can discover_ *and according to which the human will must act in order to attune itself to the necessary ends of the human being. The unwritten law, or natural law, is nothing more than that.* [Italics here in original; double emphasis by the reviewer; explanation hardly necessary.]

It should "leap to the eyes" of any reader of a philosophical journal that the argument is a tissue of self-contradiction. The simile of the pianos tells us that the end of all men is to serve as an instrument for a specific use by some purposive subject outside of man himself (under penalty of being "discarded"). Whether true or false, this is the antithesis of determining for himself the ends which he pursues. Further, our author ignores the fundamental facts of the relation between desires and moral ends, as well as differences of opinion about ends. Apart from differences it is probably impossible to think of anyone's having any opinion at all. In one view such differences are the root of all social and moral problems (since conflicts of mere desires cannot be discussed). In another view it is the similarity of men as to ends (desires, needs, or values) which generates conflict, by leading different individuals to seek the same things which they cannot all have; and our author's reasoning also ignores this aspect of social problems.

Also interesting for its reasoning is what the author goes on to say about our knowledge of the natural law. We are told that "the only practical knowledge all men have naturally and infallibly in common is that we must do good and avoid evil." But "this is the preamble and the principle of natural law . . . not the law itself. Natural law is the ensemble of things to do and not to do which follow therefrom in *necessary* fashion, and *from the simple fact that man is man,* nothing else being taken into account" (pp. 62–63). Yet "men know it . . . in different degrees, running the risk of error here as well as elsewhere"; "every sort of error and deviation is possible . . ." and our knowledge of natural law is classed with that of arithmetic and astronomy (p. 63). The later discussion of particular rights gives no example of necessary deduction from the simple fact that man is man, but only vague assertions that different rights belong in different degrees to natural law and positive law. In fact, the Encyclopedists are denounced for their rationalistic view of natural law as "no longer an offspring of creative wisdom but a revelation of reason unto itself" and for transforming natural law into a "code of absolute and universal justice inscribed in nature and deciphered by reason as an ensemble of geometric theorems or speculative data . . ." (pp. 80–81). The "logic" by which the validity of positive law, and the substance of particular rights, are deduced from natural law is that the duty of man to fulfill his destiny implies the right to do so, and to "the things necessary for this purpose" (p. 65).

II. Natural Law in History

A striking feature of our author's technique is his practice of repeatedly laying claim, without argument, to the natural law and human rights and everything good in European civilization or all history as due to and originating in the teaching of the Gospels, or the church, or of "classical" writers which was taken over by the church and somehow reconciled with its theology. As an early example, we read:

> All alike, Catholics and non-Catholics, Christians and non-Christians . . . recognize, each in his own way, the human values of which the Gospel has made us aware, the dignity and rights of the person, the character of moral obligation inherent in authority, the law of brotherly love and the sanctity of natural law . . . [p. 24].

And again:

> It was first in the religious order, and through the sudden pouring forth of the evangelical message, that this transcendent dignity of the human person was made manifest [p. 73].

(For other similar expressions see pp. 11, 46, 61, 68, 74, 80, 81, etc.) This is historically indefensible; natural law as custom is recognized in all human society, while modern ethical individualism is a product of a recent movement away from the religious view of life; and, as we shall see, the author practically admits the fact (cf. here the statement with respect to the views on slavery of the great thinkers of antiquity and the medieval theologians, p. 105).

In place of direct comment on the historical assertions

sprinkled through the book, it seems better to survey the main facts. The expressions "natural law," "natural rights," and "rights of man" are familiar to every student of politics or ethics. Phrases equivalent to the first have been bandied about since the earliest beginnings of the European intellectual tradition among the Greeks. (Outside this tradition the concept seems hardly to be met with.) The appeal to "nature" has always been a slogan or *Kampfwort;* it has been used to beg the question in favor of any position which a particular writer or school happened to wish to defend or promote—or against any one singled out for condemnation. The "state of nature" has been a symbol either for idyllic social life or for all that is horrible. The political state and positive law have been either primary dictates of the (benevolent) law of nature or man's punishment for sin. The form of the state ordained by nature has been everything from absolutism to pure democracy or antinomian anarchy. All men are "naturally" equal, and free, or naturally unequal, making slavery and social castes and rule by absolute authority a feature of the naturally right social and political order. Natural law has served as a defense for any existing order against any change and as an argument for change in any direction. Prior to the eighteenth century, natural law was chiefly a support for order and authority; since then, "natural rights" have played the opposite role, as the appeal of the individual against government. Finally, the "nature" from which laws or rights are derived has borne every possible relation to "God" or the gods.

While the central idea goes back to the early Greek (pre-Socratic) distinction between what is right by nature and by convention, the first general use of the expression "natural law" (*nomos physikos*) was that of the Stoics. These writers talked in general terms about reasonable ideals of conduct and of social relations on which they thought "reasonable" men would agree. But the Stoics were philosophers and held an essentially quietistic ethical world view. They addressed themselves primarily to philosophers, meaning Stoic philosophers, as their conception of reasonable men. They assumed that such men's interests are centered in the contemplative life, leaving them indifferent to such crass material considerations as practical politics and economics, even to physical pleasure and pain. They were also indifferent to beauty and to "knowledge," other than abstractions evolved out of the inner consciousness. Their ideal, if followed to its logical conclusion (which was sometimes done), means indifference to life and death, or is perhaps equivalent to "Nirvana." The Stoic social ideal is thus anarchy, in the philosophical meaning of the rule of reason, while their "relative" natural law accepted existing institutions. The classical source of the rule-of-reason ideal, for the individual and for society, is Plato. But, in sharp contrast with the Stoic theory of universal human equality and freedom (in an abstract spiritual sense), Plato's ideal society assumed that few men are even potentially philosophers and set up a hierarchical class system, with the philosophers as rulers. Aristotle largely followed Plato, specifically in defending slavery and Greek political hegemony on the ground of natural human inequality.

The teachings of Christianity are especially in point here. The original position was similar in the abstract to Stoicism, but with the inner life of freedom and equality interpreted in emotional or religious, in contrast with intellectual, terms, leading again to a social ideal of anarchy; righteousness, based on love, took the place of wisdom, as the controlling principle or law. But the "historical" Christian position was in practice analogous to Platonism rather than to Stoicism, though it confused love and knowledge. Only a few people are capable of supreme righteous love—or of apprehending the divine reason—and these should be the rulers of society. In fact, the righteous were soon divided into two groups, the religious orders and the church bureaucracy, the latter holding all power, the former theoretically segregated from the sinful world with its power relations and practical problems, for a role of vicarious atonement. This might well have happened under Platonism, if a serious effort had ever been made to bring its doctrine into any practical relation with reality, prior to its absorption in Christianity. The organized church became an authoritarian hierarchy indorsing slavery and a caste system of society, in line with the historical background of Christianity in Old Testament theocracy. But the Old Testament contains little or no trace of natural law; its law is positive and revealed, down to concrete sanitary regulations and military dispositions. Of course, modern research finds the laws given by Yahweh to Moses largely identical with those given by Shamash to Hammurabi centuries before and with those of the Canaanites and Israel's other enemies, who deserved death for their immorality and worship of false gods. The laws are crude, often barbarous, by modern standards (e.g., ''Thou shalt not suffer a witch to live,'' Exod. 22:18). In the New Testament there are a few suggestions of a moral law in the ''hearts'' of men; Rom. 2:14–15 is an example often cited, and the word ''conscience'' occurs a few times in a nontheolological reference.

Medieval Christian thought vacillated on the question as to how far natural law could be discerned by the reason, or conscience, of ''fallen'' man, how far he is dependent upon revelation, meaning the Bible. But, in sharp contrast with Judaism, the revealed word had to be ''interpreted'' by the divinely inspired church and was subject to amendment by law and fiat of the latter as God's spokesman on earth. In any case the law of nature became the law of God, meaning in practice the law, or will, of the church, and this is still the Catholic position (since there is no real limit to matters of ''faith and morals''). For the church, the end—beginning, of course, with maintenance of its own authority and prestige—has always justified any means; it was not bound by any law, and resistance or disagreement was blasphemy or heresy and called for suppression by torture or execution. Human reason was out of it, except possibly in some sense for the supreme authorities in the church and as prescribing agreement by others. The writers are not clear how far the church itself follows reason or revelation, or even love. As to the divine source of law, the doctors also disagree as to whether it comes from God's own reason, a reason prior to and above God, or God's arbitrary fiat.

While it would be out of place here to follow the history in detail, it should be noted that in the post-Renascence epoch, particularly in the seventeenth century, the idea of a natural or moral law (now practically separated from theism, as in the case of the Stoics) played an important constructive role in the development of an international law governing the relations between the new sovereign and absolute states. By the next revolutionary period, the eighteenth century—the Age of Reason, or the Enlightenment—the ideal had become thoroughly individualized as well as secularized. The function of natural law was now inverted (as we have seen); it was used to beg the question for what is called either liberalism or bourgeois class morality, according to taste or prejudice. It was now the "nature" of man (whether "created" or not) to be "free and equal," free from the shackles of custom and authority, in his economic, political, and religious and social life, free for the pursuit of happiness—and, it should be added, for actively promoting "progress," material, intellectual, and spiritual.

In its mundane working content, the law of nature has always been primarily commercial, centering in exchange in the market and specifically in contract. Scholars reasonably guess that the first working form, the Roman *ius gentium* (later fused with the Stoic idea of *ius naturale*) actually grew out of a "law merchant" or commercial law independent of governments which was prevalent in the Mediterranean region when the Roman dominion was established. Thus the content has been "natural" in the crude utilitarian sense of a set of rules necessary for orderly economic relations between individuals, or other units, possessing a considerable degree of freedom, and associating on the basis of mutual agreement or consent. In a large historical view, such a pattern of relationships is not "natural" at all, in any meaningful interpretation of the word. Only in a relatively advanced state of civilization—and a civilization of a particular type (historically the type called "commercial")—do people in considerable numbers act or think in such terms. And still more novel and artificial are modern natural rights, extended to include the various "freedoms" and claims of the individual at the hands of government, which are recognized in the legal systems of liberal society, or demanded through legal action.

III. Political Philosophy

An attempt to discuss our author's political philosophy encounters great difficulty in discovering any particular position that he holds to the exclusion of numerous other and conflicting positions. Roughly speaking, there are two ways of using language which has an apparent reference to morals and politics but which ends up by saying nothing or shedding no light on any question which might possibly be at issue. One way is to make statements so abstract that they can be interpreted as taking any side of any question, i.e., statements which amount to saying that their author stands for truth and high ideals and wishes other people to do likewise. This may not unfairly be characterized as the method of "preaching," in contrast both with objective argument and with propaganda, in which the speaker has something to "sell." The other method is to make strong categorical statements on both sides of issues, without recognizing the conflict and the inconsistency. In political discussion this is familiar as the principle of eating one's cake and having it or producing omelets without breaking eggs. The methods overlap; and those who use either may be serious and honest but naive, or they may really be engaging in propaganda, or their naivete may cover any combination of these. Our author's motives are beyond question, but the obvious fact is that he combines platitude with evasion and self-contradiction. And an obvious strain of propaganda also runs through his book, as well as preaching. This he probably would not entirely deny; perhaps there has to be some of both in any writing addressed to a public broader than a small group of specialists and dealing with this type of subject matter rather than with the most objective facts.

The mode of effecting this combination, in the book under review, is to deal only with abstract issues and in highly abstract and ambiguous terms and to remain blind to the contradictions which are involved in advocating any simple abstract principles of conduct. The subjects dealt with, by sweeping pronouncements, are primarily freedom, law—moral and positive—authority, and institutions, particularly the political institution of the state, and "the" religious institution of "the church." The "position" of the author is to come out strongly in favor of all of them, while avoiding such definition of any as would convey a suggestion of the essential fact, which is universal conflict of interests and "rational" ideals and of principles, with all real issues arising out of this conflict. Thus the essential character of the book is that of a political platform advocating a moral and social order in which there would be no such conflicts, or, in other words, a world and a human race utterly different from those of reality and which, indeed, are hardly in any concrete meaning philosophically imaginable.[3]

For a serious analysis of the real problems, the essential concepts and the relations between them might be brought out by a series of questions putting them in a serial order. Beginning with the ideal of freedom—with peace and order— the first question would be why there must be a moral law felt as constraint, hence a restriction of freedom in the most literal interpretation, and reflecting a cleavage in the will at the core of "human nature." Next would be the question of why there must be a positive law to supplement the moral law; and the third, why there must be authority or authorities. The essential meaning of positive law is a set of rules "sanctioned" or enforced on the individual by some agent outside himself, some human individual or group or some supposed supernatural power, or the former as an agent of the latter. The distinctive attribute of such an enforcing agent is authority; but, in addition to enforcing law, authority always has in varying degree the attribute or function of issuing

---

[3] One of M. Maritain's most obvious positions being Roman Catholicism, it is in order to observe that the pronouncements made under "liberal" religious auspices differ chiefly in following more largely the first of our two ways of saying virtually nothing, i.e., advocating high ideals with no concrete and hence controversial implications—though they are also by no means free from advocacy of clearly incompatible things. As an example we may quote the "seven points for peace" of the first American interfaith pronouncement on world order by more than 140 top-ranking Protestant, Catholic, and Jewish leaders: "1. The moral law must govern world order. 2. The rights of the individual must be assured. 3. The rights of oppressed, weak, or colonial peoples must be protected. 4. The rights of minorities must be secured. 5. International institutions to maintain peace with justice must be organized. 6. International economic co-operation must be developed. 7. A just social order within each state must be achieved" (*Pathfinder*, October 18, 1943). At best this could be defended as a beginning toward a breakdown of the problem or listing of its "aspects." We certainly do not wish to be invidious, and the significance of our criticisms is increased by the fact that other schools of thought exemplify the weaknesses pointed out. The religious writers are merely the worst sinners in this respect.

commands, by "fiat," outside the text of any established and recognized set or code of rules. These are only the most general analytical questions, leading up to the concrete issues which have to be decided in social life.

It is not too much to say that all real moral problems, all that are discussable, arise out of inherent overlapping and conflict among these different principles. (As already observed, mere interests cannot give rise to problems, to be settled by discussion, in contrast with force.) Men, as we know them, inevitably have some freedom (as do all animals, as far as they are conscious and intelligent). But this is inevitably limited, especially their effective freedom, which requires power, since power is limited. But (normal) men, as we know them, both crave more freedom and power than they have and also demand both as a "right," specifically at the expense of other men, as individuals or organized in the various social groups in which men have to live and want to live. (This demand is probably peculiar to men.) All rights, in the abstract, are rights to freedom and power, for some use; they are conceivable only in relation to other men and as generated by a combination of harmonious and conflicting interests. A "Crusoe," living in isolation, can hardly be thought of as having either rights or obligations or freedom in an ethical meaning, unless these are rooted in a relation to some supernatural being. Finally, all human groups are more or less institutional. Institutions are partly brute historical data, partly defined and enforced by law, including definitions of the rights and duties of agents—of rulers or the group itself or superhuman powers—who enforce law and, within some limits, make law and issue *ad hoc* commands.

The pertinence of these observations here is that the book under review (and the author's other writings, as far as known to the reviewer) contains no recognition of the nature of the social context of harmony and conflict out of which problems arise, or, *ipso facto,* of the nature of the problems themselves, or how they are, or should be, dealt with. To begin with, as would be expected, there is much talk throughout the book about freedom, the dignity of man or of the person, etc. The expression "freedom of expansion and autonomy" recurs with minor verbal variation (pp. 9, 34, 44), and slavery and bondage are condemned (pp. 45, 47, 68, 105). Much of this is quite laudable—from the standpoint of a liberal, i.e., one who accepts freedom as the fundamental social ideal; more accurately, it would be laudable if it could be taken out of its context.

There are three difficulties in the way of taking seriously these noble expressions about freedom and the dignity of man. First, in general, they are platitudinous in the abstract and ambiguous and contradictory in the concrete. The Christian view of freedom was never found inconsistent with slavery until after it was already abolished in any jurisdiction, and, in the writer's opinion, it is not inconsistent. On the other hand, the ideal does not now tell us who ought to have more freedom—practically meaning power—or how the increase is to be arranged. In the second place, the expressions themselves include equal praise of authority and the virtue of obedience. For example: "The common good is the foundation of authority [which] requires that individuals be charged with . . . guidance and that the directions which they determine, the decisions which they make . . . be followed or obeyed by the other members of the community" (pp. 9–10; cf. also pp. 24, cited above, and 56; and elsewhere). It is noteworthy that the authority to be obeyed is explicitly that of individuals, not of law. True, the author goes on, characteristically, to assert that it is aimed at the good of the whole, not the particular good of those who exercise it. Elsewhere (p. 21) we are told that God is its prime source. There is here no more recognition of the need for some mechanism to hold authorities responsible to the governed, in order to prevent abuses, than there is of the inherent moral value of free government, even at some cost in good government. We are not told anything about the relations between authority, positive law, and the state. It is true that in the latter part of the book we find sweeping assertions about the rights of the individual and the state, about universal suffrage and the people's right to choose their political constitution (pp. 85–87).

Reserving these ostensibly more concrete expressions for later comment, we must consider at this point a third difficulty in the way of interpreting the author's position on freedom. At least as important as his insistence upon authority is his reiterated reference to the superiority of the church over the state. His references to "the church," or explicitly to the Catholic church, leave little doubt as to the ultimate locus of authority and shed much light on its character and scope. A section on "Four Characteristics of a Society of Free Men" (pp. 20–22) lists these as "personalist," "communal," "pluralist," and "theist or Christian"; and this is followed by a section entitled "A Vitally Christian Society" (pp. 23–29). In these pages we are told that "the world has done with neutrality," that "states will be obliged to make a choice for or against the Gospel," and that "the Catholic Church insists upon the principle that truth must have precedence over error and that the true religion, when it is known, should be aided in its spiritual mission in preference to religions whose message is more or less faltering and in which error is mingled with truth" (pp. 23, 25–26). Also, the society of free men, as theist or Christian,

> recognizes that in the reality of things, God, principle and end of the human person . . . is . . . the prime source of political society and authority among men; and that the currents . . . sanctioned by

it, the feeling of responsibility before God required by it, . . . are the internal energy which civilization needs to achieve its fulfillment [pp. 21–22].[4]

To be sure, we could as usual cite numerous passages which seem to contradict much of the above. The society in question is not theist or Christian, "in the sense that it would require every member of society to believe in God and be a Christian" (p. 21). And one must "distinguish the Apocryphal from the authentic, a clerical or decoratively Christian state from a vitally and truly Christian political society" (p. 23). And earlier (p. 19), in discussing the need for "more limited groups or fellowships" within civil society, it is said that "these the person enters of his own free choice . . ." (cf. also p. 22). In the latter part of the book the discussion of rights—particularly the section on "The Rights of the Human Person"—indorses intellectual, moral, and religious freedom as absolute rights of the individual, but explicitly only against the state (pp. 75–77), and even here there is an interesting reservation:

> If this religious path goes so very far afield that it leads to acts repugnant to natural law and the security of the State, the latter has the right to interdict and apply sanctions against these acts. This does not mean that it has authority in the realm of conscience [p. 82 n.].

The reader is left to draw his own conclusion as to who is to judge when such action is necessary and to determine its

---

[4] There are many other expressions in the same vein: "Above the plane of civil society, the person crosses the threshold of a kingdom which is not of this world . . . a supra-temporal society which is called the Church, and which has to do with the things that are not Caesar's" (p. 19). "Other communities are of a rank superior to the State, as is above all the Church in the mind of Christians . . ." (p. 21). In a later section, among the rights which "belong to natural law in the strictest sense of the word" are included "the rights and liberties of spiritual and religious families," and specifically "the superior right which the Church invokes by reason of her divine foundation" (pp. 82–83); cf. also pp. 75–76, and elsewhere.

character, especially whether it is to be the state or the "higher kingdom" to which such frequent reference is made.

If one carefully balances all the author's confused and conflicting statements about freedom, law, and authority and about the rights of the individual, of the state, and of the church, it seems fair to conclude that the only social order which meets his specifications is an ecclesiastical authoritarian state. This would not be the theocracy of the Old Testament, in which there was at least a law which no one claimed the right to change or set aside; it would be the Roman Catholic church according to its own claims, substantially realized over much of Europe in the thirteenth century. For the content as of today, particularly the internal government of the church and the "freedom" implied, one who does not have the documents in mind may look up the decrees of the Council of Trent, the Syllabus of Errors of 1864, and the Acts of the Vatican Council of 1870. A careful and repeated reading of the book as a whole suggests nothing so much as the Marxian idea of an educational dictatorship, but with the church in the role of the party. However, the state would not "wither away," giving place to an anarchist utopia, but would be preserved as an administrative organ of the church (as in the ideal of the Middle Ages) in a social order in which authority and obedience would be the moral cornerstone.

This conclusion is in no way modified by the author's repeated condemnation of totalitarianism, with explicit reference to communism and fascism or National Socialism. Of course, he does not recognize and probably does not believe that his own system is totalitarian. Mortal enmity of any group with such aspirations toward other groups differing in ideology or even merely in personnel is to be taken for granted. (But this antagonism may be the means of preserving freedom.) The similarity between the platforms of Roman Catholicism and communism has often been pointed out. But an ecclesiastical authoritarianism is hardly to be preferred to other species of the genus; rather, its very claims to superhuman wisdom and virtue are likely to make it more arbitrary and ruthless than other forms, and this inference could be abundantly documented from the history of western Europe.[5]

The interpretation suggested is more or less confirmed by the social nature and function of religion in general, and in particular by the history of Christianity. The function of religion has been to sanction established morality, law, and authority, not reform, at least in any constructive or progressive sense. Apart from the naïve "brotherhood" ideal, embodied in "anarchist" propaganda, in a "social gospel," or in fraternities, some exception would be called for only in the case of theocracies in which the church has become essentially a state, with political and other mundane functions pushing religion into the background. The essence of the original Christian social teaching was literal acceptance of established political forms and obedience to established authority. This is a recurrent note in the New Testament. In the Middle Ages, of course, the church became a theocracy and played the game of political and economic power in the manner to be expected from an organization with absolute authority, direct from God, over this life and the next. Now that historical changes, which both "the church" and the churches set up by the "Reformation" opposed as long and as vigorously as they were able, have established "freedom," in place of obedience to authority, as an unquestioned ideal, spokesmen for religion are

---

[5] If the political principles of Catholicism present more of a contrast with fascism than with communism, the similarity in historical policy, in propagating their creeds, and in establishing their political authority by completely ruthless use of force, is striking enough. This again is a natural consequence of the religious basis, and the quasi-religious character of both fascism and communism is a familiar observation.

quite naturally in favor of that—or at least render lip service to it.[6]

We should observe, again, that the common notion of active freedom is also ambiguous. It confuses freedom in the literal meaning of absence of unnecessary or arbitrary coercion or restraint with possession of power or the necessary means to do what one wants to do. And a thoroughgoing analysis must further consider the possibility that the individual may not want to be free, because "conditioned" to obedience as an ideal. The will to freedom is adequately recognized in the book we are discussing. It also formally recognizes the individual's right to economic means, in a sense far beyond the original Christian ideal of charity and even beyond the traditional defense of property by the Roman Catholic church. Most of this is in the latter part of the book, in connection with economic rights, and will receive comment later. In chapter i, we also find a section dealing with "Progress," an

---

[6] General assertions about religion in this paper relate to recognized religions having a body of belief and practice, and usually an ecclesiastical organization. There is assumed to be a distinction between religion and philosophy or Weltanschauung, and space limits exclude discussion of "prophecy."

With respect to freedom, the Christian conception is that this, like truth, is achieved through a voluntary emotional self-surrender to another will, ostensibly the will of God (sometimes apostrophized as truth—cf. Matt. 26:39; John 8:32). But it necessarily meant in practice the will of ecclesiastical authority, where any problem was involved. This, of course, is straight totalitarianism in a theological formulation; but the philosophy of modern political totalitarianism differs from historical Christianity in being activistic, where the original form of the latter was strongly quietistic. The Christian conception of an all-loving and omnipotent divine will and divine love as the fundamental cosmic reality and the supreme and all-inclusive good cannot be logically harmonized with an ethic of action. Effective participation of Christians in economic and political activities merely shows that they do not believe what they profess.

This Christian conception of emotional freedom presents an interesting contrast to the more rigorous quietism of Hindu thought, in which the ideal is self-annihilation of the personal will, without reference to either a cosmic will or a political authority superior to ordinary men in its thinking and interests.

ideal inseparable from freedom in liberal thinking. It is notable for expressions which a liberal can commend, if he gives them a liberal interpretation, to which they are more or less susceptible. While there is no specific definition of progress, the political task is summed up as "essentially a task of civilization and culture" (p. 44); and it is even admitted that the political task of meeting the "aspiration of the person . . . towards liberty of expansion and autonomy" is conditioned upon material progress in techniques and organization and "supposes [presupposes] societies all the more strongly equipped and defended because they seek to be just" (p. 46). A liberal is inclined to ask, first, what else the common task could be and, second, when or where Christianity showed an interest in progress, other than progress backward to the Garden of Eden, with no problems to solve and only one negative duty— to remain ignorant of good and evil—and a life of bliss without effort. Moreover, the study of history raises doubts as to whether any authoritarian organization, or especially one of the ecclesiastical type, ever acts to promote cultural progress except for the benefit of a small élite, or material progress except for similar ends or as a basis of military power to be used for predatory action. Of course, it may be the alternative to chaos and make for cultural progress in the long run.

Finally, our interpretation of the author's position as some type of authoritarianism is confirmed by his repeated derogatory comments on democracy as it is, in the modern world.[7] This is referred to by such designations as

> the old disguised anarchic conception of bourgeois materialism, according to which the entire duty of society consists in seeing that the freedom of each one be respected, thereby enabling the strong freely to oppress the weak [p. 8].

---

[7] The words "liberalism" and "liberal" are not used in this book. But in the parent-volume, *Freedom in the Modern World,* we read (p. 63): "Liberalism is not merely false in theory; it is finished in fact, bankrupt by the turn of events."

The antithesis of this description, specifically the last clause, to the entire aim and practice of modern democratic government needs no comment. Again we are told:

> In the bourgeois-individualist type of society there is no common work to do, nor is there any form of communion. Each one asks only that the State protect his individual freedom of profit against the possible encroachments of other men's freedoms [p. 39].

It is obvious that what is really lacking in democratic society is a common task or form of communion of the type approved by the author, *imposed by authority from above*. It seems that what is objected to is the freedom allowed to the people to find these forms and tasks, or to interpret the common good, for themselves—as well as to have ends and enjoyments of their own, under a system of law designed by themselves to protect this freedom, to limit it where clearly necessary, and to facilitate and implement free association.[8]

IV. Natural Law and Natural Rights

We must run very briefly over the early sections of chapter ii and hasten on to the treatment of more specific rights. The first two sections deal with generalities of the same sort as found in chapter i, including the discussion of Aristotle's regimes, just cited, and further disparagement of democracy as "the old bourgeois individualism" (p. 55). The citations

---

[8] The three political regimes of Aristotle are contrasted in terms of their characteristic values. The democratic regime tends above all to freedom, the monarchical to strength and unity; it is the aristocratic which "tends above all to the differentiation of values and to the production of the noblest and rarest values" (p. 51). It is at once explained that to be faithful to Aristotle's terminology and also to designate properly the author's own "political humanism," or "commonwealth of free men," the democratic regime should be called "republican." No definition is given beyond its characterization as a "mixed" regime and a general statement of the vague and conflicting ideals which it should realize. It is also designated as a "new Democracy" (pp. 54, 86).

given early in the review to illustrate the author's logic are taken from the second section, on "Natural Law." In the next section, on "Natural Law and Human Rights," we are told that "the same natural law which lays down our most fundamental duties, and by virtue of which every law is binding, . . . assigns to us our fundamental rights" (p. 66). This is defensible in the abstract, in terms of modern ethical theory, but it is contrary to history (as we have pointed out), and it is not illuminating to quote or paraphrase alternately Thomas Aquinas and Thomas Paine. These sections contain many general assertions about human rights which are highly commendable, or rather commonplace, from the standpoint of liberal social philosophy, as long as they are viewed in the abstract and effectively isolated from the conflicts and problems to which they give rise in the real world. These rights formally recognized include the right to life; to keep one's body whole; to the pursuit of happiness and moral perfection; to intellectual, moral, and religious freedom; to marriage and family life; and to the ownership of material goods. (Interspersed are numerous derogations of democracy, some already cited, and statements in praise of authority and asserting the superiority of the church over the state.)

The section on "The Rights of the Civic Person" (pp. 83–91), in particular, contains (with other matter) a fairly good statement of modern liberal-democratic political principles. Universal suffrage for every adult human person, is "one of those rights which a community of free men can never give up" (p. 85), though it is not explicitly derived from natural law. It implies the right to affiliate with, or to form, political parties, though not in the totalitarian meaning and without the abuses and vices which have caused the degeneration of the European democracies. The qualifications are left at the plane of pious wishing—or to the care of the supratemporal society superior to the state. In the next section, the author refers to the natural right of association, sanctioned by positive law (p. 96; cf. also pp. 19 and 90). Again:

> The right of the people to take unto itself the constitution and the form of government of its choice is the first and most fundamental of political rights . . . subject only to the requirements of justice and natural law [p. 87].

Other rights of the civic person are

> summed up by the three equalities: political equality . . . equality of all before the law . . . equal admission of all citizens to public employment according to their capacity, and free access of all to the various professions without racial or political discrimination [p. 88].

Earlier (pp. 72–73 and note) President Roosevelt's Four Freedoms are approved as yearnings "to be fulfilled by positive law and by an economic and political organization of the civilized world."

> What we know as freedom of speech and expression . . . better designated [as] freedom of investigation and discussion . . . is a fundamental natural right, for man's very nature is to seek the truth. [But] freedom to spread ideas . . . , like freedom of association is subject to the regulations of positive law. For the political community has the right to resist the propagation of lies or calumnies [and] activities which have as their aim the corruption of morals [or] the destruction of the State and of the foundations of common life [pp. 89–90].

However, "censorship and police methods are in my opinion the worst way—at least in peacetime—to insure this repression"; among "many better ways," the only one named is the "spontaneous pressure of common conscience and public opinion . . ." (p. 90). In conclusion, we are told that this problem

> can be properly solved only by a recasting of society on an organic or pluralist basis . . . a regime no longer based on the self-propagating

power of money . . . but on the human value and aim of work where the class struggle introduced by capitalist economy will have been surmounted along with this economy itself. . . .

This last statement explicitly serves as a transition to the last and longest section, dealing with "The Rights of the Working Person," viewed as the locus of the most urgent problems of the social person in various functional relations. Half the space is again devoted to the same type of moral and political generalities that fill the early part of the book. One of the most remarkable passages in the entire work is the second sentence of the second paragraph of this section:

The principal phenomenon in this point of view, which emerged in the nineteenth century, is the *consciousness of self (prise de conscience),* achieved by the working person and the working community.

We have previously alluded to this. What is remarkable is, of course, the admission that recognition of those who do the ordinary work of the world as human beings with essentially equal rights "emerged in the nineteenth century" and, by omission of the author's usual contrary claim, the admission that this revolutionary moral advance was not due to the teaching of the Gospels or connected with Christianity. Of course, the doctrine "emerged" somewhat earlier, in the rationalistic age of the Enlightenment; but it became generally recognized in the nineteenth century.

Early in this section, the author warns against two "temptations." The first, "which arises from old Socialist concepts, is that of granting primacy to economic technique, and by the same token of tending to entrust everything to the power of the state. . . ." This "leads in the direction of a totalitarianism . . ." and is to be avoided through replacing the idea of planned economy with a new idea of "adjusted economy," and the idea of "collectivization" with that of "associative ownership of the means of production'' (pp. 97–98). The second temptation, ''which comes from old concepts formerly in favor in certain Christian circles is . . . paternalism . . .'' (p. 99). Still another is ''corporatism,'' moving toward state corporatism; but ''the notion of 'corporation' or rather of vocational body, as presented by Pope Pius XI,'' in the encyclical, *Quadragesimo anno,* of 1931, is of course ''completely free from these connotations'' (p. 100); but no difference is pointed out. The ''essential thing'' is that reorganization of economy on a structural and cooperative principle must establish itself

> from below upwards according to the principles of personalist democracy, with the suffrage and active personal participation of all the interested parties at the bottom, and as emanating from them and their free unions and associations [p. 100].

Beyond the advocacy of a radical economic reorganization in accord with vague idealistic principles, admirable enough in the abstract, it seems impossible to make out what the author has in mind. We are told that, ''aside from certain areas of altogether general interest, whose transformation into public services is to be expected,'' the proposal is ''an associative system substituting, as far as possible, joint ownership for the wage system, that . . . ought to take the place of the capitalist regime'' (p. 98). However, we have previously been told that the rights of labor include ''first of all . . . a just wage, for man's work is not a piece of merchandise subject to the mere law of supply and demand; the wage which it yields must enable the worker and his family to have a sufficiently human standard of living, in relation to the normal conditions of a given society,'' whatever that may mean (p. 94). It is hardly needful to point out that these statements are a tissue of contradiction. A wage is the price of a service, regardless of pronouncements by idealists or by the United States Congress in solemn (or cynical) convention; and, if it is not to correspond with the economic value of the service to the purchaser and beyond him to the ultimate consumer (the meaning of the law of supply and demand), some other word should be used. Moreover, we are given no light on the question of economic organization, how resources would be allocated, or how even the product of the single enterprise would be shared among the participants, when joint ownership has replaced the wage system.

It is probably useless to point out that "supply and demand" is the only possible way of apportioning men and other productive agents to their tasks, between different enterprises or within any enterprise, in such a way as to produce what consumers want or to produce anything effectively. It is the main reliance of totalitarian, as well as free or "capitalistic," economies. Whether or not consumers have any "rights" (to what they want or in the amount to be had through a sound administration of production), it is now impossible to organize production at all on the basis of any contrary assumption. Moreover, if the productive agents—including all kinds of laborers and of nonhuman instruments, natural and artificial— are not to be attracted into their occupations through the preference of larger to smaller earnings, they must be apportioned and organized by the fiat of some authority; and this would simply destroy all freedom of economic choice and substitute dictatorship, possibly but not probably paternalistic, in a benevolent meaning.

In connection with the rights of labor, we should consider the discussion mentioned earlier of the right to economic means. Apart from a "sufficiently human standard of living," we are told in an early section that *"redistribution"* is a first essential characteristic of the common good (p. 9). A right to the private ownership of "material goods" is said to be rooted in natural law and to be "an extension of the person itself";

but the explicit reason given is its necessity "to make up for the protection nature does not afford it"; further, it "supposes [presupposes] the conditions normally required for human work . . . according to the form of a society and the state of development of its economy" (pp. 71–72 and note). At this point the author refers to a discussion on private property appended to his earlier book, *Freedom in the Modern World*. A careful reading of this appendix, of some twenty pages, will leave any student with an elementary knowledge of economics mystified as to what the author thinks is the meaning of property in organized modern society. In the larger work, as in the one under review, economic rights and ideas are discussed entirely without reference to the most elementary facts of social life or the conditions under which it may be possible for a society to pursue intelligently the objectives of a sufficient production to support its people and maintain a culture, with as much regard as possible for such values as freedom, equality, and justice. Nor is there any more recognition of the fact that property, as things, owes its existence and its perpetuation to saving and investment—or that the same is true in essence of the laborer's capacity to work—than there is of the institutional facts of ownership, which in a free society comes about through production, saving, management, and risk-taking, or through inheritance. (Of course it would be merely immoral to entertain the thought that an excessive birth rate could have something to do with poverty and bondage.)

Finally, a few words should be devoted to the ideal of the "participation of the working personnel in the management of the undertaking," which is emphasized by our author as an essential feature of associative ownership. This is described as "*an association of persons* (management-technicians, workers, investors) entirely different from the associations of capital which the idea of joint ownership might suggest under the present regime'' (pp. 98–99). In this connection a few facts may be pointed out. The first is that what are called ''associations of capital'' *are* associations of persons; hence no other associations could be ''entirely different'' and perform the same necessary functions. Further, under the mechanism of the competitive market, everyone connected with any enterprise does participate in the management, including especially the consumers of the product, ignored by our author. The mode of participation is impersonal and indirect in various degrees and ways, but it is more effective than direct control has ever been made, for most of the participants in a vast, heterogeneous, and freely changing organization; this is the main reason the ''enterprise economy'' has developed as it has.

As anyone interested in the facts presumably knows, those who immediately direct operations in any business enterprise are not the owners but the employed agents of nominal owners; but neither managers nor owners nor the enterprise as a whole has any considerable degree of arbitrary power. Actual control is in the hands of those who sell to and buy from the productive unit, primarily the consumers, but also the various employees and the several categories of property-owners. It is true that voting-power is distributed on the basis of economic capacity, in contrast with the nominally more democratic principle of one person, one vote. The reasons underlying the arrangement lie in the conditions of efficiency on one hand, and debatable ideals of justice, on the other, including the merits of private property. They cannot be analyzed in detail here. A critic can only ask for some recognition of facts and confronting of issues and note that both are conspicuously lacking in the treatment under review. He may point out, as one pertinent fact, that if any group prefers, and can agree upon, any method of more direct control, or any other distribution of control, there is not and never has been anything in the institutions of "capitalist society" to prevent their having what they want, subject to their ability to achieve efficiency, with due consideration of other interests and values. The reason things are as they are lies in human nature and the given conditions of life on the earth.

This does not at all imply either that things as they are are abstractly ideal or that they "cannot" be changed or improved. It does imply, to some minds at least, that to be improved the complicated mechanism must be understood and that remedial action must be oriented to facts and to some critical regard for the meaning and relative importance of conflicting ethical principles. Our author seems oblivious to all such considerations, as well as to all the fairly sweeping measures which have been taken in modern liberal society with a view to remedying the evils and realizing the ideals toward which he points in abstract terms. The program has been carried forward as fast as specialists and the public have found it possible to reach agreement on objectives and methods and to act with a reasonable prospect of doing more good than harm.

Our main criticism of the book, to repeat, is that it cites principles that are true but truistical, with the air and implication of enlightenment. Let us repeat also that this practice is not peculiar to our author or his school of thought; it is met with in most political discussion, whether it aims at action or edification. One can always cite a principle—or a proverb or even a legal precedent—to support either side of any question which is seriously at issue. The task of the moral philosopher is not to emphasize ideals—that pertains to the preacher—but to define ideals with a precision not found in common sense or "wisdom" literature. Practical social problems, on the other hand, center in the political order which determines who is to make and interpret the positive law. Here the main question is whether such persons are to be held responsible to a public opinion and will, formulated through free discussion, or simply to themselves. It is a secondary matter whether men in power without this check profess to follow ideals or to be responsible to God. No one wholly repudiates freedom or law or authority or property or the family or any right named by our author. But what freedom, authority, and rights actually mean depends very much on whether those talking about them are in power or seeking power. This is true of political parties and leaders in a democracy, as well as of "the Church." The supreme paradox doubtless is that the anarchist ideal—the rule of reason and/or of love—works out in practice to mean authority, backed up by force. But the transition is simple. It is easily assumed that disagreement—with "us" or "me"—rests on some immoral motive, obstinacy, or incompetence, perhaps due to immaturity or defective education.

V. Absolutism and Relativism in Value Theory

We may now turn from the defects of M. Maritain's work to suggest what would be required in a more objective treatment of the central ethical problem. A philosophical discussion of natural or moral law, in the context of modern thought and in a way meaningful to modern minds, must begin by recognizing that it is a "historical category" in the large sense in which the major part of history is anthropology. The philosophical task involves formulating a workable conception of freedom and progress and of the relationship between moral and other value judgments. It is customary to think of these as the "triad"—truth, beauty, and goodness; but some place must be found for the neglected values of play and sport, and perhaps sociability and religion should be recognized as separate types. Play interests and relations have unquestionably played a large role in the genesis in our race of the ideas and sentiments of legality and fairness and of leadership; and the play spirit, including emulation, is obviously a large factor in aesthetics and morals and religion, and even in science and philosophy. History and all the main branches of philosophy must cooperate in the task of studying the development of the critical consciousness, in all fields of normative judgment. Further, any intelligent use of the word "nature" must rest on a critical interrelating of nonhuman and human nature, nature and art or artifice, cause-and-effect and purposive action, hence on a tenable conception of man's place in nature. The student must attempt to follow the thread of more and more inadequate knowledge, merging into speculation, back in time to a point where the biological forebears of civilized and reflective mankind were merely a part of nature, and to form some conception of the sequence of change by which "man" has become at once more and more artificial and more creative, in opposition to nature, in his individual and group life.

What such beings as we call men (normal adults) most conspicuously have in common, and in distinction from the other main recognized orders of existence—inert objects, plants, and animals—is the faculty of speech. Growth of this faculty undoubtedly went along with growth in "intelligence" in various meanings, but equally and inseparably with vast changes in emotional traits. The primary use of speech among civilized men today is doubtless the expression and communication of emotion, including playful and esthetic matter, and including also the formulation of unexpressed mental content. The "highest" form of mental activity, and use of speech, is in formulating and expressing reasons for judgments which combine discrimination of the various values, including truth, with the emotional attitude of approval or condemnation. Pure literature (and ornate oral discourse), culminating in poetry, involves this process in a form different from that of science and philosophy and with more emphasis on emotional qualities; but these are also clearly present in connection with intellectual discovery and belief.

These activities are "high" in the sense that they involve a distinction between high and low. What men actually say and think is in all degrees, and, indeed, in innumerable meanings, wise or foolish, beautiful or ugly, good or bad— in content, motive, and result. Moreover, the content is still largely determined by impersonal, nonpurposive processes of social life, backed up and modified by coercive force. Speech always means the use of some particular language, which has been created by a particular culture and learned in and through that milieu. The learning and use of language is inseparable from the acquisition of the content, also cultural, whether intellectual and emotional or merely trivial, which speech is used to express to others or to mediate to the individual in his thinking, and from the various ends which expression is used to promote. There is practically no sense in speculating as to what any man would approve or disapprove, in conduct, belief, or taste, apart from the context of some cultural background, some complex of social institutions. Even our beliefs about the most rudimentary "physical" facts are only to a limited degree an exception; and so, at the opposite extreme, are the most "original," romantic, and false ideas of the "crackpot."

The degree to which the attitudes and beliefs of the most independent and critical-minded individual of today are really determined by culture and tradition, "sanctioned" by various "forces," is a fact which one is reluctant to admit and which one comes to realize only through a process of education and self-discipline. At the level of "primitive" society, meaning through most of human history, intellectual and spiritual independence hardly existed. The mores made anything right (and true and beautiful). In the most primitive societies of which we have any knowledge and in any society we should call human, there is plenty of "difference of opinion" and even a kind of discussion, or proto-discussion. But, as far as one can learn from anthropologists, there is in known primitive societies no true critical discussion (or virtually none) involving an appeal from customary and established criteria to such "higher" norms as are represented by the idea of natural or moral law. (Discussion of morality and law undoubtedly emerged long before discussion of scientific or esthetic problems.) In any stable social order all norms generally recognized in practice at any time are necessarily traditional and are called in question exceptionally or not at all. The formulation of ulterior norms, as rational grounds for judging, approving, or condemning established and accepted criteria, goes with a high degree of cultural sophistication. This tendency to criticize what is established is obviously a force making for social instability, and one main function of religion, throughout history, has been that of suppressing or checking it. Criticism undoubtedly "began" in a very limited sector of a society already possessing a relatively high civilization in the sense of concrete achievement—among a few priests or lawspeakers or in some relatively functionless elite or leisure class. It has spread downward with the growth of freedom of discussion, and especially in consequence of democratic government (to be contrasted with the upper-class republics of antiquity), until in our own culture practically everyone freely judges what is in terms of what (he assumes) ought to be.

The general idea expressed by such phrases as "natural law" is that of supposedly rational principles used as norms to criticize law and tradition. (Criticism, of course, includes defense against negative criticism, as well as attack or condemnation.) Natural law is any general unwritten norm or principle which is cited or appealed to on any moral or political issue. In the nature of the case the issue must be one which is not thought to be settled "rightly" by the written law or by custom equivalent to law; hence the issue involves passing judgment on the law, written or customary. However, norms themselves are validated, or become effective, only by acceptance in some community of discourse, or possibly through the use of literal force by an advocate. An individual may, of course, take his stand upon his own opinion "against the world," like Athanasius; but this amounts to assuming he is "God" or stands in some unique relation to ultimate truth; and, again, such a position becomes effective only as it is accepted by others (and/or is backed up by force).

A moral law, in terms of content commanding respect, is clearly a phenomenon of moral progress, on the one hand, and, on the other hand, of the differential nature of progress, the "lag" of generally accepted laws or standards behind more advanced views. To be strictly objective, we should say "cumulative change" instead of "progress"; but, since there is no criterion of validity beyond the "verdict of history," men have to act upon the faith that the trend of change is forward, or upward, toward what is better. The "true" moral law is defined in any society by a "consensus of the competent"; but there is at any moment no objective or absolute test of competence beyond the consensus itself of the competent group and its recognition by wider circles. In this respect the moral law is in exactly the same position, in the abstract, as scientific truth and as judgments of beauty or of any value. All such judgments are forms or species of truth—truth "about" different kinds of subject matter. To the extent that any truth is subject to a supposed objective test, as in natural science, the issue is merely carried back to the validity of the test, which depends on the same social criteria. It is worth noting that the truths of mathematics and formal logic can be tested empirically to any degree of accuracy and universality which is considered worth the trouble; hence, only their "absolute" accuracy and universality is in at all the same position as moral and esthetic truth, i.e., directly dependent (without testing) on a consensus reached through judgment and discussion. The same reasoning applies, of course, to logical demonstration.

We must recognize an ultimate paradox in connection with all judgments. They are meaningless apart from some issue; and, as long as there is an issue, either party can affirm its position as truth only by asserting the incompetence of the opposition—or by backing up its own position with over-whelming force. On the other hand, when an issue is finally settled and no longer in question in any way, the matter of truth or falsity has lost all relevance and all meaning. It may be assumed that reasonable men now admit that force does not really answer questions in terms of truth. But this position, again, rests on the faith that force as expressed in the historical process is ultimately on the side of "real" truth. Through most of human history, truth has been a question of the morality or immorality of belief (or sanity versus insanity) or especially of religious orthodoxy versus heresy; and all these issues have actually been settled by force in the most overt meaning—and this is strikingly true in the history of "Christian" civilization.

It will be evident that "natural law," properly defined, is the opposite of "natural." To the extent that men are aware of it, it is a highly artificial product of social mental life, exceeded in artificiality only by the creative products—or mere aberrations—of individual minds. We may perhaps think of moral progress, in the etymological meaning, as occurring automatically and unconsciously, but such change can hardly be called moral in the higher sense to be distinguished as ethical. A true moral law rests on a recognized conflict between what is and what ought to be, or at least upon some conflict which is not resolved by established customs and norms and which presents a problem for solution. It reflects a threefold cleavage, in varying degree, within the individual (self-criticism), between different individuals in a culture group (mutual criticism), and within the group as a whole (group self-criticism). A moral law, with any content whatever, about which there is no disagreement or even no serious disagreement is essentially a contradiction; if not self-contradictory in the abstract logical sense, it is at least contrary to all historical reality.

The philosophical problem is one of interpreting moral progress, which, to repeat, involves interrelating this with other aspects of man's spiritual development. The familiar triad may be interpreted to cover the whole field. In all its aspects, progress means advance through effort, in which the activities of individuals and groups can be only partly distinguished, even in abstract analysis. When a society becomes conscious of its problems, these are tremendously complicated by the fact that, within limits, the primary consideration is social order and peace, hence the necessary degree of agreement, with less regard for the abstract merits of the position on which agreement is reached. This makes for conservatism. However, since agreement is the only test of truth, we must assume that the two quests coincide and that deliberate compromise is only a working approximation to a right answer to an unanswered question. Any forward step must begin with some individual digression, and this leads to real advance only through acceptance on intellectual grounds. Most incipient innovations are certainly wrong and never take root or are rejected by "history."

Progress is thus a matter of the two factors, innovation and critical discussion, leading eventually to a consensus (or to social division or disintegration or conquest). The first factor is freedom, under another name. It is an intellectual mystery or surd, yet the most certainly known of all facts, since it is a presupposition of all thinking and cannot be denied without asserting it. (That it is a mystery is itself hardly a mystery, since mind as subject clearly could not well adequately see itself as an object.) Moral freedom is not to be conceived as arbitrary whim or caprice or blind chance but as the active endeavor to get right answers to questions; it implies the possibility of error, to which (effortless) mechanical processes are not subject. Innovation, and particularly rational freedom, are both experimental and narrowly limited in scope. The critical mind itself is, of necessity, formed for the most part by forces antecedent to itself and, at any moment, by its own prior history; it can only in small part be self-created. Complete or absolute freedom operating *de novo* at every instant (as if the actor had no past) is unthinkable. It is equally essential to recognize historical determination and process and the fact that the spiritually developed individual, in a spiritually advanced social milieu, has the capacity to react critically, creatively, upon himself and upon the culture which has largely made him what he is. We must assume that all peoples, or publics, and their individual members, must experience the threefold cleavage of self-criticism, when they reach a certain stage in the historical progress of mental and spiritual development.

If men are to think critically and yet escape moral skepticism and a destructive relativism, they must have faith, on some ground, in the validity of thought and discussion and in the ultimate verdict of history, i.e., in the reality of progress. In the historical past and in our present Western civilization the majority of serious minds have viewed their faith as founded, first, in ultimate real norms which do not change but are merely progressively discovered and, second, in some idea of "God" as the ground of this reality. But there are enough examples to the contrary to prove that neither of these conceptions is necessary. To many competent minds (as to this writer) it is as reasonable to regard values as progressively created, or actualized, in a world in which they have been potential but not actual as it is to conceive of progress as the discovery of an immutable reality. And it seems to such minds more reasonable to view the nature of the cosmic ground of the distinction between the valid and the invalid in all fields, or the nature of the objectivity of this distinction, as an open philosophical problem. It also seems to such minds more reasonable and better to recognize that the validity of all accepted concrete judgments is only more or less provisionally established. This seems to be the only view which is reconcilable with the facts of historical progress, in which new insights have constantly superseded old knowledge or changed it by reinterpretation.

Nothing properly called absolute truth is possible for any principle or proposition, or even the simplest fact. The highest certainty, beyond the direct awareness that thinking is a free activity, is that it takes place in social beings living in a social milieu, i.e., in connection with discussion, and that discussion recognizes problems which are discussable. The precise way in which we conceive or picture ultimate cosmic reality—as far as we picture it at all—is largely a matter of taste and convenience as long as our conceptions make a place for the belief that the effort to solve problems is real and "makes a difference." Experience shows that men confront a real danger of arguing themselves into a world view which denies this essential fact, though ultimate denial would be madness. This fundamental requirement excludes both absolute mechanism and absolute will and makes absolute values tainted. One may believe in such values only under the explicit condition of admitting that he does not know what they are and that absolute knowledge would be identical with nihilism. The danger here lies in the psychological fact that one who believes in the absolute character of values in the abstract is likely to go on to use that proposition as a premise to establish conclusions which are highly relative.

This reasoning applies still more cogently to the belief in God. Again, a conviction that intelligence and moral will are operative in the cosmos and in human history is admissible and should be useful, provided that God is thought of in such a way as not to negate the essential consideration of human achievement through effort. But this is extraordinarily difficult. God must not be thought of as statically complete or "infinite," in any ordinary meaning. In fact the ideas of omnipotence, omniscience, and infinite goodness are self-contradictory; in the final analysis they negate the ideas of power, knowledge, and goodness. If God, or the ultimate cosmic reality, is to have any of these spiritual attributes—to which "taste" should certainly be added—he must be thought of in essentially human terms of struggle to achieve the several values. It is then necessary to think of co-operation, a working-together, between God and men, and this is where the greatest difficulty is encountered.[9] Those who try to make the will of God practically meaningful in moral and social life seem inevitably to fall into the error noted above in connection with absolute values, i.e., they think they know what God wills with respect to controversial issues. The idea or feeling of communication with God (even indirectly through a prophet or demigod or inspired organization) seems to have too much attraction for frail human nature, though neither the channels of commu-

---

[9] There is a scriptural reference to God as working—John 5:17—but in its context it has no intelligible meaning; and it is difficult, if not impossible, to give the idea any practically significant meaning. The use of the word "hitherto" in the saying of Jesus cited suggests the position known as "deism." This is an intellectually respectable position and was prominent in the eighteenth century. But the idea that God created the world and man and then turned both loose, the one to follow its natural-scientific laws, the other to struggle along as best he may, amounts for all practical purposes to leaving God out of the picture.

nication nor the content of the revelation stand up under critical examination. The common result is pride and bigotry, in a sect or people, though usually on matters of form rather than matters of substance.

What has been said should make it clear that the problem for modern thought and life is that of the validity or objectivity of values. The fallacies which men tend to fall into may be approached in two ways. From one point of view the error to be avoided is a false dichotomy between absolutism and relativism, with respect to all values, whereas these terms themselves should be used in a relative and not an absolute sense. From the other point of view it is the treatment of truth, where the error is treatment of scientific and logical truth as absolute and the relegation of moral and aesthetic judgments to the level of relativity. It is better to approach the problem by looking first at the fallacy in the second form. Here the essential fact is that even the truths of science are finally judgments of value. When there is any issue, it is a matter of weighing evidence and the cogency of reasoning; and, when there is no issue, any assertion is nonsensical. Again we confront the paradox of the inherently progressive or "dynamic" nature of intellectual life; truth is the answer to a question; and, when any question is definitively answered, there is no longer any question, and no truth, in any significant meaning of the word. Further, an objective answer to any question, in science as elsewhere, is a social judgment, dependent on verification.[10]

All questions are questions of truth or falsity, whether they relate to matters of "fact" or to "values" in the narrower

---

[10] We restrict our discussion to discussable questions, such as presuppose an answer that is valid for some group, some community of discourse. We leave aside purely private problems—if there are any such in the strict sense—in which an individual merely has to decide between conflicting purely personal values, no one else being involved. Even the answers to such questions may have a kind of objectivity, but we cannot go into that here.

sense of morals and esthetics. On the other hand, truth itself (*where any question is at issue*) is a value, a matter of what one "ought" to believe, of better and worse reasons for believing; and the obligation to believe what is true because it is true, rather than to believe anything else or for any other reason, is the universal and supreme imperative for the critical consciousness. All discussable questions come down finally to good judgment, including "good" taste and "right" moral discrimination versus "mere" taste or preference. It is true that moral questions involve a further imperative or obligation, that of *acting* in accord with true judgments as to what is good or right, but they are not peculiar in this respect. Esthetic judgments have their creative aspect as well as that of appreciation. And truth about "facts" is also expressed in action, giving rise to the imperatives of economy (versus waste) and of "workmanship," which also involves esthetic norms. None of these distinctions can be sharply drawn. In a special sense the judgment of truth is a moral judgment, since—truth being a social category—the obligation to believe what is true is inseparable from the obligation to "tell" the truth (apart from other grounds for this rule). Yet the different forms of value imperative also conflict. Literal truth in discourse must very often give place to other values, both esthetic and moral; and, while beauty may be viewed as a kind of truth (or conversely), the two may conflict as well as coincide. There are also conflicts within each category, conspicuously in the case of moral values or duties; but different truths also conflict, in spite of the logician's prejudice to the contrary.

Looking at all value problems, then, from the standpoint of truth, we return to the position stated above: that no such judgment can be "absolutely absolute" or "absolutely relative." Absoluteness or relativity is a matter of degree of certainty, the only test of which is the degree of agreement in a community of discourse, the consensus of the competent (and unbiased). The simpler axioms of mathematics and everyday matters of fact are "relatively absolute," in comparison with disputed rankings of works of art—or any matter which is controversial among competent and serious (honest) students. Of course, what any individual believes to be true is based chiefly on what he believes to be the consensus of the competent, a community to which he does not usually profess to belong for most of the field of knowledge. The only meaning of "absolutely absolute" truth or validity is a judgment on a matter about which there is assumed to be no possible question—a commonplace and a species of nonsense. When anyone makes an assertion as an absolute truth, in the face of disagreement, he merely sets himself up as an absolute authority or as a spokesman for such an authority. The meaning of the position is to forbid discussion by fiat and finally to claim the right to silence opposition by force.

At the other extreme an "absolutely relative" judgment would not be a judgment at all but would merely describe an individual state of mind. Thus both absolutely absolute and absolutely relative judgments negate discussion and all intellectual life, the first by asserting dogmatically that there is nothing to discuss, the second by limiting discourse to utter banality. In so far as any assertion of the absolute validity of a proposition is meaningful, it is so by raising the issue of the relative competence—or honesty—of those who assert and those who deny it or of some authority for which they speak. (The authenticity of the spokesman's credentials may also be at issue.)

The meaning of all values is rooted in a process of progressive sociocultural achievement, including resistance to change in wrong directions. A value is something sought rather than finally possessed. This is the meaning of the statement that man is a rationally social being, or "potentially" such. The determination of truth by free discussion is also the meaning of democracy as a social philosophy. Its antithesis is authoritarian society, which is a mixture in varying proportions of traditionalism and arbitrary dictatorship. In another view the issue is between a "liberal" and a "religious" ideal of social life and conception of belief. A dictatorship must be religious in some sense, and a democracy must be rational. However, the ultimate ideal of liberalism or democracy, government by (rational) discussion alone, is antinomian (in the sense of enforced law) and is inherently unattainable. But progress in that direction is the final meaning of social-moral progress. The ideal has the two aspects, free government and a minimum of government by enforced law or by authority, i.e., maximum freedom for individual disagreement and nonconformity. Where agreement is "necessary," i.e., where other values are more important than freedom (even if lower in ideal rank), it must, of course, be secured by some mechanism of compulsion enforcing the closest achievable approximation to a social will based on a common opinion.

XII

Human Nature and World Democracy

Abstract

*H*uman nature is a manifold paradox. Man is a social animal, in the sense of "conventional," with anti-social traits equally prominent. Intelligent morality is a product of social evolution, partly uniform or convergent, partly the opposite of both. Custom, authority, and deliberate consensus are three distinguishable "stages" above instinctive animal society; the last is peculiar to recent western European civilization. Our individualistic, free, or democratic social ethic is largely limited to relations between members of particular states by the facts of cultural and political differentiation. The place of conflicting economic interests in international war is highly ambiguous. The common idea of deliberately changing human nature is a tissue of logical confusion. The changes necessary to eliminate war without destroying freedom are largely undesirable, since war arises from conflicts between ideals and rights rather than mere

Reprinted by permission from *The American Journal of Sociology*, vol. 49 (1944), pp. 408–420.

interests. A peaceable and free world order calls for a combination of agreement and toleration, and both have ethical limits. The visible issues in war are relatively unimportant in comparison with the inherent clash between quantity and quality and between different qualities, in human life; and survival in a struggle for existence is, for the visible future, the final test of higher and lower. But some changes are clearly worth working for, while "we" defend our own cultural achievement.

I

To discuss this topic in the compass of a journal article we must limit our treatment closely to the practical problem. This means resisting the temptation to write a literary essay on human nature, which might bear such a title as "the low-down" or "the truth about human nature finally disclosed." The essential fact would be that human nature as we know it—the nature of man sufficiently advanced or civilized to think and talk about his own nature—is a tissue of paradox. It would be difficult to make any general statement about "man" which would not contain substantial truth; and this means that the antithesis of every statement, or, indeed, several antitheses, would also be partly true and, on the average, equally so.

The practical interest back of our discussion is a human aversion to war. This is partly because people do not like danger, suffering, and hardship; yet it is human nature to fight for interests of innumerable kinds and every degree of importance and for no interest except the fight. Man typically describes himself as the intelligent animal—*Homo sapiens;* but the main significance of this seems to be that man loves to compliment himself and considers this the highest compliment. "Intelligence" is a word of numerous meanings, and with respect to all of them man is both a stupid animal and a romantic, preferring emotion to reason and fiction to truth. He is the laughing and the weeping animal, laughing most often at things obscene or cruel and weeping for pleasure at the sorrows of imaginary people.

Man also proverbially calls himself a social animal. He is social in a sense entirely different from other animals, a sense which involves antisocial qualities—a love of privacy, even solitude, and innumerable antipathies and conflicts of interest with his fellows in any social group. One of his social traits is exhibitionism; yet he is the only animal that has physical modesty and conceals his body in clothes; and what he does to his body is a tiny circumstance compared to his parading, concealment, and dissembling of his mind, his thoughts, and his feelings. For this function he is endowed with the marvelous faculty of speech. In his social life, again, man is a lawmaker and law-abider, one who loves ritual, formality, and rules for their own sake; yet he is also a lawbreaker, for many reasons and merely for the sake of nonconformity and defiance. He loves what is established becuase it is old, and he loves novelty because it is new, and change for the sake of change. Civilized man is a capricious and perverse animal. He typically has no clear idea what he wants or which of obviously incompatible things he wants more. His acts often contradict his professed interests, which in turn are often contrary to any defensible notion of well-being. Even less, as this behavior proves, does he really believe what he says or thinks he believes. He progressively develops a repugnance for useful work and for any routine of settled, orderly life, preferring play, adventure, and excitement. He has a strong bent for fun, mischief, destruction, and cruelty, which is hardly found in any other species. Animals are not "brutal" as the word is applied to man, i.e., cruel or lascivious; and "inhuman" behavior is as distinctive of man as "humane" acts.

For our purpose here, the most important general truth about human nature is that man is a conventional animal—social in that sense. Of course, he is also unconventional; but this is true in the main in fields where it is conventional to be unconventional. Man is unique among animals in that he laughs at others but cannot endure being laughed at—except when he deliberately provokes laughter, which is one of his favorite sources of joy and pride. He cannot even stand it to be "looked at," except with looks of approval and admiration—though even less can he endure being avoided or ignored. Conventionality finds its extreme development in religion, a unique human interest. Yet people often welcome revolution, even in religion, and troop after the prophet of a new cult. One of the sharpest antitheses in human nature is the combination of the groveler and the power-seeker. But, on the whole, man is a conventional being, and this implies a preference for his own conventions over those of other groups. This bias, as we shall emphasize, is the primary root of war. But, even here, human nature is a paradox, since men also typically regard "foreign" people and ways and things as superior to their own; a prophet is not without honor save in his own country.

Another important fact in the study of war is that man is a discontented animal, and particularly that he is likely to grow more discontented as he becomes better off. But this is mainly because he is prone to think someone else is getting the best of it or is putting something over on him. The conflict between different systems of conventionality or "culture," different customs, traditions, mores, on the one hand, and, on the other, increasing mass discontent as a direct consequence of an unprecedented increase in mass well-being in the last two centuries or so of our civilization are the two main causes of war which must be considered today in any thoughtful study of the problem of eliminating it.

With reference to our practical objective, it is necessary to have a clear orientation to the type of action which is contemplated. The objective is a world order which is not only peaceful but free, or democratic, and also preserves other values of our civilization. There is a vast difference in the meaning of intelligent action where the intention is to change human relations, in contrast with changing the behavior of nonhuman objects. In the latter case we can find out and apply laws of behavior which are not affected by our knowledge or intentions or attitudes, because the objects acted upon do not have reciprocal intentions or attitudes toward "us." With human beings the contrary is true. But within the human field itself there is another distinction, fully as important. If we wish merely to influence the overt behavior of other persons, it is theoretically possible to do this by coercion or persuasion—really a form of coercion and typically based upon deception. But, if we wish permanently satisfactory relations with others, this procedure is rarely effective, even in the narrow practical sense; and in the present context we assume it to be excluded by our ethical norms of satisfactory relationships. Even if it were possible to abolish war by making ourselves so strong that no one would dare to oppose our will, the result would not achieve our purpose.

Thus the problem is not one of the use of means, or power, to achieve a given concrete end. We should rather think of changing the rules of a game, so as to make it a better game. It makes all the difference in the world that the problem cannot be treated simply as one of making others agree with us on ends and procedures by force or fraud or persuasion, but that agreement will involve mutual give and take. In a word, an essential feature of the problem is the presupposition of *democracy;* and it is necessary at the outset to recognize the historical uniqueness of this concept and its implications for human nature. Only in the past few centuries, and chiefly in the limited area of western Europe and its colonies, have men confronted this task or attempted to direct future history by intelligent mass action. Democracy is much more than a form of government. Its advent marks a transformation of man and of the meaning of a social problem. Entirely new ideals, of freedom and equality in place of status and authority, go with the revolutionary changes, dating chiefly from the seventeenth century, which established our free social order. Another unique ideal is that of progress, material and cultural. We must view human nature as active and self-changing and not merely as undergoing changes in response to outside activities or forces, and we must view social action as based on a rational consensus.

The essential fact is freedom, or creative activity. But freedom is like other traits of human nature in that it is created by a social situation or, in more technical terms, a complex of institutions. This also sets limits to freedom. The supreme paradox of man, in our civilization, is that he is an individual— unique, creative, and dynamic—yet is the creature of institutions which must be accounted for in terms of historical processes. Nothing could be more false historically than the notion that men are naturally free and equal, or even that they naturally have a right to freedom. In the light of history as a whole, the natural state of man is to live imbedded in a ''crust of custom,'' in which most of his activities, thoughts, and feelings are determined by established patterns. These are, or were, enforced upon him and also ingrained in his being, so that he hardly thought of departure from them and hence had little feeling of unfreedom. The existence of man as a free individual is a function of free society, which is the product of biological evolution and human culture history.

The familiar saying from Aristotle, that ''man is a social animal,'' is both true and misleading. That human beings can exist only in organized groups is true biologically and more strikingly true with respect to the traits which make us distinctively human. But the social life of man is different in principle from that of the animals, particularly those forms in which social organization is highly developed—the colonial insects. Man is social, but also naturally antisocial. His social organization always involves coercion, which he intrinsically dislikes. The capacity of coercing and being coerced is virtually peculiar to man, though we impute it in a certain degree to the "higher" animals, in domestication and in herd life. Men do not coerce the inert objects of nature and are not coerced by them, and the latter do not coerce one another. Furthermore, man's love of freedom and hatred of coercion inherently involve a craving for *power*, not merely over the objects of nature but over other men—an antisocial trait. Power is a factor or dimension in effective freedom; no clear separation can be made between "freedom from" coercion—by custom or authority—and "freedom to" act, which presupposes power. But men desire freedom and power in the abstract, as well as for the sake of any particular use which they wish to make of either. They also claim freedom and power as a moral right, against other individuals and the various social groups in which they live. And within some limits everyone admits the validity of this claim on the part of others; but their claims to freedom and power overlap, creating conflicts of interest, which are the basis of social problems. Such features seem to be entirely absent from insect society. There the biological unit is not an individual, in the human meaning. It is not motivated by interests or rights which conflict with those of others or of the group.

Human intelligence, in the primitive instrumental meaning—the use of means to realize ends—recognizes the value and necessity of group life, first, in the aspect of cooperation. But it also involves a tendency of the individual to use the fellow-members of his group for his own purposes or to try to make the terms of cooperation favorable to himself. In addition, man is endowed with a craving for "sociability," in other forms than cooperation, which have no clear biological function; and these forms also involve both harmony and conflict of interest. A typical sociability interest is that of competitive social play—and most play is social and competitive. Here the immediate object of the individual is to win, to defeat the opponent, individual or group; but the game itself is a common interest of all the players. Very early in the history (prehistory) of civilized life, men developed a third type of social interest, the pursuit of "culture," meaning intellectual and esthetic activity, in contrast with the economic and recreative. This "higher life" partakes of the nature of both "work," or cooperation, and play.

The "higher-culture" interests of man present a challenge to the student. They cannot be explained in terms of biological utility but are largely peculiar to man as a civilized being. From a natural point of view it is difficult to account for the development of the appreciation of beauty or a sense of humor or for speculative curiosity or the feeling of decency or that formal purity which is probably the ultimate root of the moral sense. It would seem that the civilized traits, taken *en bloc*, must somehow be useful, since the more civilized groups survive and increase at the expense of the less civilized— though again in the long course of history a high civilization seems to have been rather typically self-destructive.

From our point of view these interests are the heart of the problem, because among civilized peoples it is chiefly the right to civilized life, defined in terms of a particular civilization, which is at stake in war. The cultural amenities come to be regarded as "rights" by those who have them and by those who want them, and it is for such rights that men are most likely to fight. They do not, in general, fight for any mere "interest" and are likely to be generous and self-sacrificing in the face of disaster, as when a ship is sinking or even in a food shortage, giving up the basic right to comfort, security, or life itself. To say this is not necessarily to exalt the moral nature of man; for, on the one hand, the features of a culture for which men will fight are not necessarily good, even in terms of their own recognized standards. And, on the other hand, an important trait of human nature is the disposition to regard as a right practically anything which is intensely desired, and that largely irrespective of whether the individual regards the object as really important.

Human nature is a function of the nature of society, and both are historical products. Knowledge of the course of evolution of man and of civilization would be infinitely valuable for the interpretation of human nature and for dealing with human problems, but little information about it is to be had. It is worth noting that man did not evolve from social forms, such as the insects, in which the patterns of individual and group life are instinctive, but from species of a totally different biological type. At an early stage, these lived individual lives, except for mating; then followed longer and longer association for rearing the young; later they gradually formed loose larger groupings of the "herd" type, apparently a "harem," or extreme patriarchate. The mammalian herd as we know it presents a mixture of instinct, custom (imitation and habit), and authority or dominance. Its psychological basis seems to be emotional rather than rational, as is undoubtedly true also of human society. The development of the herd was apparently connected with important physiological changes in the sex life, fairly complete in the anthropoids, while the romanticizing of sex and family relations is one of the most distinctive traits of *Homo*. From the anthropoid herd to human society the great change is, of course, the development of speech, along with the brain capacities and mental dispositions, both rational and emotional, which are associated with articulate communication.

With reference to the course of development at the human level—though again only the most recent history is at all well known—we can discern some of the great changes through which advanced civilized man and society have become what they are and which help us to understand our situation and its problems. In "primitive" human society the most important principle of order is *custom*, as we have already noted. It is always associated with an elaborate tradition, a mythology suffused with "religious" ideas. The patterns of action and the traditions are transmitted by social inheritance through imitation and habituation, accompanied by some active "teaching" on the part of the mature generation and learning on the part of the young. The process of unconscious acculturation differs from biological inheritance of instinct, but it is equally mechanical, conservative, and opposed to individual freedom. Authority is also conspicuous in tribal society; but mostly it is not "real" authority, since those who exercise it get their position through inheritance in accord with sacred custom and tradition, of which they are the custodians, with their activities prescribed; and in this role they are viewed as the agents of supernatural powers. Their authority, or that of the traditions they enforce, is supported by the group as a whole, against recalcitrant individuals, though deliberate breach of custom is relatively rare. Thus the primary phenomenon is that of "culture" in the anthropological meaning, or of law as usage "sanctioned" by public opinion and religion.

In a summary view modern free or democratic society may be viewed as the product of an evolution from tribal life, involving two great stages of advance. First, "civilization," in our meaning, seems always to have developed out of barbarism under an authoritarian organization, a monarchy associated with a nobility and a priesthood. (Various forms of agricultural village and "city-state" doubtless mark the transition from tribal life to a kingdom or empire covering a wide area and including numerous "cities.") From the standpoint of the development of individual freedom, the transition from tribal life to monarchy is rather a step backward (except for the rulers), since "government by law" is replaced in part by "government by men." But it made possible a vast increase in power in all spheres and a great advance in "culture," the higher life, though only for a small elite.

The second step giving rise to free society, akin to modern democracy or accepting similar ideals and combined with a high civilization, has resulted from a revolutionary overthrow of despotism, autocracy or oligarchy, and "priestocracy." A democratic order may or may not preserve its culture, inherited from the preceding stage, or develop it further over a substantial historical period. It will be seen that this three-stage scheme is obtained by intercalating an intermediate stage of authoritarian society between "status" and "contract," in Sir H. S. Maine's well-known formula for the evolution of law. In juridical terms our first stage is that of customary law, including the authority and procedures for enforcement; the second stage sees the advent of a "state," with rulers exercising a greater range of real or arbitrary power to make law, in addition to enforcing law; the third stage is that of democratic legislation, expressing a more or less rational general will, social consensus, or public opinion.

Without ranging over world history, we may think of the past thousand years or so of European civilization. Conditions in northern and western Europe at this "beginning" may be regarded as practically those of barbarism, under customary law. The religious sanction was Christianity, in the form in which it had become established in the period of decadence of classical civilization. The later evolution was, of course, profoundly influenced by survivals of the older culture and especially by the "transit of civilization" from the East (including the Moslem world), where it survived in much greater degree, to backward regions with "frontier" conditions. The political transition occurred in northern Europe and is rather indirectly related to the cultural "Renascence" in the Italian city-states. (Even the latter was at least as much a unique new growth as a "rebirth.") The political movement manifests the two revolutionary changes mentioned: (*a*) the development of autocratic states in the Renascence period and (*b*) liberalization and democratization in the revolutions of the seventeenth and eighteenth centuries.

II

We come back to the point stressed early in the article— the historical uniqueness of the present social and political situation and its accepted ideals. What is referred to as democracy anywhere else in the panorama of history—in tribal life or in city-states or in the Middle Ages—was not democratic in anything like our equalitarian meaning of the term but was largely based on customary law, which sanctioned slavery, class distinctions and status relations. It also existed only on a minute scale, in comparison with modern states; and where it was associated with a high "civilization," especially in classical Greece, it was very short lived, running into tyranny at home and then into absorption by an imperial order. (These facts inevitably call to mind analogous tendencies in our contemporary world of western European civilization.)

Our modern social ethic is individualistic. Based on the ideals of freedom, equality, and progress, it repudiates the authority of custom and of individuals as political or religious rulers. It regards "society" as a free association of juridically equal individuals, for the pursuit of ends and ideals which are individual or freely chosen. Laws are viewed as rules, made or accepted by all, governing the association of individuals and voluntary groups. Groups are formed at will in response to any common interest of their members; even the state is viewed as ideally based on free association or "contract." Ideally, groups within the state exercise no coercive power over their members, and the state itself has a minimum of such power. The purposes or interests for which men form organized and more or less permanent groups within the state and across state boundaries (and states, in the liberal conception) may be loosely classified under the three heads of work, "culture," and play, previously mentioned.

The acute internal problems of states arise chiefly in connection with the work interest or, more broadly, the economic life. In modern thought this also is conceived in individualistic terms, as cooperation for efficiency in the pursuit of individual ends by the use of means which are either incorporated in the person of the individual or "belong to" him. In fact, of course, the individual is typically the head of a family, the natural family is the minimum possible unit in organized society as a going concern, and the system would more properly be called "familism" than "individualism." (Of necessity the family is largely traditional and authoritarian in structure.) The individualistic or familistic ideal in economic life implies that economic cooperation is worked out primarily through "free" exchange in markets, with its terms fixed by economic competition. (This has no relation to psychological competition, emulation, or rivalry, and strictly economic motivation excludes the latter.) In fact, again, neither the individual nor the family is the typical unit in modern economic life. Production and exchange (purchase and sale for money) are carried on chiefly by organizations which vary in size and internal constitution, but the business corporation is the characteristic form. Like all stable organizations, the productive unit actually has considerable power over those who participate in its activities (as legal members or on contractual terms); and this virtual "sovereignty," as well as that of other associations for economic purposes (labor unions, etc.), is an important source of internal problems in the state.

With respect to these internal problems, the general objective prescribed for the state in modern social-ethical thought is to secure the maximum of individual freedom, including free association. This ideal calls for minimizing the functions of the state itself; for even the freest state acts through law, which is coercive upon a large part of the population. Thus its main internal function is the negative one of "policing" the relations of individuals in direct association and in more permanent voluntary organizations. It is given a monopoly of coercion, chiefly for preventing individuals or groups from coercing others, through either force or fraud. However, liberal thought has always recognized a large range of positive functions for the state, to be determined by expediency, but limited to matters on which there is substantial agreement.

III

Our problem here, however, is not the "internal" problems of states but conflict between states, in which the immediately serious threat to our civilization arises. But it is of the essence of the matter that no clear separation can be made between internal and external political relations or problems; for within the state conflicts occur between institutional groups, especially families, far more than between literal individuals, and the state itself is merely one form of institution among a vast number. The state is peculiar in two respects. First, the sphere of its power or "sovereignty" is defined by territorial boundaries. (This delimitation is not at all precise, since political

371

allegiance does not coincide with residence, while sovereignty itself is of every degree.) Second, the state has a legal monopoly of military force, including police, within its boundaries—as long as civil war, or the threat of it, is absent.

As we emphasized earlier, human society has two aspects: it is an aggregate of individuals, enjoying more or less freedom, and also a complex of institutional groups. From the standpoint of social science, the second aspect is the essential reality. The "individual" who makes choices and figures in relations of harmony and conflict is the creation of an intricate complex of institutional groups of every imaginable character and degree of permanence, and he usually acts in the interest of some group. In modern culture the natural family and the state stand out for their relative permanence and functional unity. But we must recognize the role of innumerable other groupings of varying size, degree of stability, and formal organization. These are unified and separated by various common traits or common interests, and their boundaries have little relation to those of states or political jurisdictions. But modern social thought, on its ethical side, takes the opposite view, regarding "society" as an association of free individuals for mutual advantage. Any organization or group, including the state, is viewed as a sort of *ad hoc* affair, made voluntarily and to be remade at will, by any group of individuals to serve any end or purpose which may arise.

In our individualistic ethics, values and ideals exist in the free individual, who is taken as given. The student must recognize that this ideal view is largely contrary to unalterable facts. The ultimate possibilities of freedom are limited. Human nature is a cultural phenomenon, and the individual exists as the bearer of a culture. Viewing man in terms of civilized society, the self-perpetuating biological group plays somewhat the role of the soil which supports a particular species of plant. The nature of the plant is determined chiefly by its inheritance; and the case of man is similar, except that it is a cultural inheritance which is humanly determining rather than a physical germ plasm. The human being does not achieve individuality or freedom, or the idea of freedom, except through a culture made and continued by the various groups in which he lives. His interests and ideals, as well as his capacities, and the external means of life are derived in the main and in most cases from his cultural inheritance. But this inheritance is very different in different culture situations. In consequence the individual's interests and social and political activities are divided in uncertain and varying proportions between striving to change the various culture complexes in which he finds himself to accord with his desires and ideals and striving to preserve and defend these against the encroachments of others which he feels to be still more alien and repugnant to his spiritual cravings, nurtured by his own group life.

These facts give rise to social conflicts, in the dual form of conflicts between individuals within groups and conflicts between groups differentiated in innumerable ways. The groups in conflict may be states or groups of states, or they may lie within states or cut across state boundaries. The conflicts tend to eventuate in war between nations or alliances or in civil war or class war or simple "crime," as the case may be. Since groups based on economic functions or other common interests, including alliances between states, are indefinitely numerous and shifting, while war practically has to occur between two "sides," the parties must be vague communities of interest which are, in fact, highly heterogeneous.

Under modern conditions, national or world war and class conflict present themselves as alternatives. Political groups tend to strive for internal unity by appealing to, and manufacturing, suspicion and ill will toward other groups. Leaders whip up patriotism by accentuating conflicts of economic interest and the feeling of difference and opposition between cultural ideals vis-à-vis other nations. As everyone knows, modern states, as they have happened to come into being in the course of history, are by no means natural economic units. Economic differences show little correspondence with political boundaries. National interests are not unitary, and between nations as they exist on the map the relations are far more complementary than conflicting. Accordingly, the causality of wars between nations or groups or blocs of nations—the issues about which peoples fight—must be sought elsewhere than in real conflicts of economic interest. The economic policies of protectionism and autarchy, so characteristic of modern states, are patently antieconomic from the standpoint of the peoples themselves, and colonies are notoriously an economic liability.

National states on the political world map of today do correspond in a general way with major cultural differentiations in the human race as a whole. And every cultural unit which feels itself to be homogeneous and different from others has a "natural" tendency to strive both for its own preservation and for expansion or aggrandizement along numerous lines. These include population numbers, standard of living, culture, and control of territory—all sought as ends, as means to one another as ends, and as sources or symbols of power and "greatness." This endeavor leads inevitably to a competitive situation, which tends to generate antagonism and violence. This will be true even for a group which strives to be progressive without in any way injuring other groups.

This situation gives rise to conflicts of economic interest, in the broad meaning, overriding the mutual advantages of cooperation. All human life requires economic resources, both natural and artificial as usually classified, and the immaterial resources of science and technology. These are necessary for biological and cultural preservation and, additionally, for any form of growth or progress, including intellectual and spiritual culture. Moreover, the effective utilization of resources already possessed requires trade, with or without political control, as a means of access to other resources, physical and human, which are naturally complementary. But it seems to be "human nature" to seek political domination in place of free international trade. Little success has attended the efforts of modern economic teaching to get the general public, even in the most advanced and highly educated countries (specifically our own), to realize effectively and carry over into their political thinking the truism that in free exchange the advantage is mutual.

This fact is apparent in the protectionist sentiment which is manifested, not merely on the national arena but in our states and smaller communities, against one another. The predominance of mutual advantage over conflicting interests is largely true also of functional economic groups, such as capital and labor, agriculture, industry, and finance, etc. Even individuals, but especially organized groups, tend to take it for granted that in exchange relations the other party dictates the terms in his own favor, through "monopoly" or other unfair advantage—regardless of the extent to which such factors are actually present. This is particularly true when the other party seems to be better off; and there is a real difficulty in that modern ethical thought has not reached any general understanding as to the meaning of justice or fairness in exchange where the parties are unequal in economic status. While we all believe in cooperation, we usually mean that others should cooperate with us, on our terms. This particular animus toward group antagonism and conflict would be greatly reduced if "human nature" were changed, presumably by "education," so that men would carry over into political thought and action principles which they intellectually recognize as axiomatic, such as the mutual advantage to all parties from territorial and functional specialization and exchange. But there would still remain the problem of the one-sided obligation of the economically strong to the weak, or the rights of the latter against the former, which in the nature of the case are not taken into account in market dealings. Or we may think of attempting to remove or reduce inequality in economic capacity.

The two questions—(*a*) as to the amount of good which economic education might do in eliminating antagonism and strife and (*b*) as to the possibility of the education itself—must be answered or discussed in the light of still other facts. The first is that, entirely apart from economic relations, "human nature" is competitive and that men tend to form competitive groups, as well as to enter into individual competition. This is evident in play activities. When civilized people are freest to do what they want to do, they typically enter into some competitive game or participate vicariously as spectators. And games are usually contests between groups—and, incidentally, the contests tend strongly to generate ill will, running into strife and combat. The play interest is connected with a craving of "human nature" for power, victory, and dominance and for the admiration which "human nature" also awards to superiority and power.

The motivation of all human activities is largely the play interest and specifically that of competition, involving both individuals and groups. This is manifest in cultural activities—even religion—as well as politics and also in the reality of economic life. "Real wants" for subsistence or health and comfort for one's self and family and posterity obviously account for a small fraction of the economic activities of civilized men, even in modest circumstances, and these are readily sacrificed to less tangible considerations. The content of the wants for the goods and services for which people strive as producers and consumers is predominantly social, conventional, cultural, and esthetic; the urge or animus is very largely emulation and rivalry—to "keep up with the Joneses" or to get ahead of them. To this end people will endure much discomfort, including the consumption of costly goods for which they have a positive distaste. It must be understood that the economic interest, as such, is completely nonspecific; it is simply the desire for any end which requires the use of scarce means and so calls for "economy" of means. In one sense or another every interest has an economic aspect, and all human interests, including those of play and culture, find expression in economic activity. We can never say how far economic rivalry is really economic in motivation.

IV

We come finally to the major practical issue—the proposal to "change human nature" so as to reduce conflicts of interest, specifically between political groups, at least to the point where they will not break out in destructive violence. What is pertinent and can be said in brief compass will merely indicate the lines of intelligent discussion and point out the naivety of most of what is said and written about the problem.

Any judgment as to either the desirability or the possibility of such a change must rest on a clear notion of the respects in which the minds or "hearts" or habits of men would have to be different in order to eliminate war. Armed conflict would not occur if either (*a*) every existing state or other interest group would agree to accept the present situation (the "status quo") and would put into effect—enforce upon its citizens or subjects or members forever—all internal measures necessary to this end; or (*b*) all would agree in advance on all changes to be made and would enforce the requisite policies; at least enough would have to agree to enforce their will upon all.

The first alternative would mean the abolition of all progress or change in any direction; the second merely calls for general agreement on the issues or on some method for their adjudication. In terms of changing human nature, what would be required is elimination of all interests which give rise to group conflict or of their expression in action. There would be no war if every group would enter into a permanently binding agreement either not actively to resent anything which any other group might do or not to do anything which any other group might actively resent. And any single unit, individual, or group can always have peace through the same twofold policy. The democracies could, of course, have avoided war with the totalitarian states by joining in with the aims and projects of the latter for world reorganization. Even this would not necessarily banish war from the world unless some one totalitarian system succeeded in permanently establishing itself and imposing its will from pole to pole.

To universalize the policy of nonresistance—which seems to be seriously proposed by religious pacifists and by some who do not appeal to religious principles—would call for the abandonment by all, or at least the masses, of all rights, including life itself, except love and obedience, left, perhaps, to serve as "opium"; for any active effort to live and to perpetuate itself, on the part of any species, biological group, or individual, involves conflict with others, both of the same and of different species. If humanity were not to be reduced to the level of the nonsocial animals—with the "struggle for existence" in which they actually live—the only alternative way of preventing war is the organization of the whole race into a rigidly regimented society, with reproduction and all other interests and activities "frozen" along lines of custom and caste; it means a society of the nature of the beehive or some absolute authoritarian type. Of course, this might conceivably be universally accepted, passively or even joyfully, but a moral faith in human nature requires belief that men would prefer war.

It is, indeed, possible to imagine a universal "democracy," in which all issues arising out of conflicts of interests would be settled by a majority vote. Such a world government, representing any momentary nominal majority, would have to possess and employ force sufficient to prevent any minority, based on a regional or functional interest, from asserting its "rights" by force or to prevent such groups from coming into organized existence. Since such a system could not last a month if it existed, we need not speculate as to whether it would be better or worse than a despotism exercised by a limited self-elected and self-perpetuating "party," with an individual head, a "leader," chosen in some way. Such a group could not keep power and use it very far contrary to public opinion and will and "might be" about as democratic in reality as a representative government—with the vital exception that it would repress discussion and more or less make its "will of the people" to its own taste. But the limits of this procedure also are probably rather narrow.

Ultimately, the problem of peace is that of agreement, or agreement upon some method of arbitration, such as the majority vote. Agreement, direct or indirect, "may" be rational in any degree. In fact, emotion and tradition and force have always been the main factors controlling opinion. Only within fairly narrow limits is strictly rational agreement possible; for, even if men were so wise and good that each could be trusted to judge his own cause, there is no objective definition of justice. Rights as well as interests conflict and call for compromise, distant consequences are unknown, and ultimate principles do not answer concrete questions. There is not much sense in saying that men "ought" to agree, where no one knows what is right or best. It is surely the height of the immoral to contend that as a general principle men ought to yield right to wrong, or what they seriously believe to be such, either in the face of force or for love, i.e., for the sake of agreement and pleasant personal relations. How far they should yield for the sake of peace is a matter of balancing conflicting values, a matter of judgment. A minority is no more obligated to yield to a majority than the converse is true, except in so far as (*a*) an overwhelming majority opinion may carry a presumption of greater validity or (*b*) overwhelming force may make it foolish to fight. Intelligent people have never thought that democracy—and specifically federal democracy—is either a universally possible system or one that will solve all problems. Democratic federalism has never prevailed over component units of widely divergent culture except for very limited functions, chiefly war; and free government has never been able to keep the peace in the face of a serious disagreement between important sections of the population, requiring enforcement of any law against a large minority which did not believe in that law. On this point it is enough to mention slavery and prohibition in American history.

V

Omitting superfluous comment on the desirability of eventualities which would involve having peace through indifference to all questions of desirability—in effect, the peace of death—we next turn briefly to the scientific question of the possibility of changing human nature. On this point, one constantly meets with the supposed argument that human nature *has changed* in the course of evolution and of history and that "therefore" it *can be changed*. As to the major premise, no one can say whether or not "human nature" has actually changed, in any significant or relevant respect, within a time of which we have any knowledge. The capacity to learn new facts and relationships, to acquire new skills, and to modify emotions is undoubtedly an attribute of normal men. No one can say whether this general trait of human nature has or has not changed, qualitatively or quantitatively, since man crossed the line from the brute to the human.

Whether the vast concrete changes which have certainly occurred through learning in individuals and culture groups constitute change in human nature is a question which is meaningful for us in connection with the major differences and changes in attitudes and capacities in peoples of different cultures. The differences often appear very solid and real. But the inquiring student soon learns that the facts depend on "circumstances" so various and obscure that any general assertion merely shows ignorance or prejudice. We cannot go into the matter of the degree to which culture diversity corresponds with biological, i.e., racial, differences. Students find that the differences between major human groups are chiefly a matter of acquired culture rather than of different racial inheritance; but the facts are not fully known, and proof is impossible. *If* any proposed modification of human nature depends on biological change, the problem of action clearly falls in the field of eugenics or selective breeding; and it would be idle to comment on the possibility or the desirability of employing such measures, by political means, to any considerable extent.

Whatever the facts of change may be, the statement that human nature has changed, even if it is true, proves or implies nothing at all as to the possibility of changing it; this inference is merely absurd. However, human nature, viewed as a culture product, has in fact undoubtedly *been changed,* by deliberate action, in many cases. The scope of "teaching" is far more problematic than that of learning, but its reality will hardly be denied altogether. In this connection substantially every-thing depends on the personality (the specific human nature) of teacher and pupil and the social relations between them. It may be assumed, also, that some outstanding figures in history, such as authors and poets, religious prophets, and persons in a position of political authority, have at various times exerted some influence on the attitudes and interests of considerable population groups. How far the results were either permanent or intended or desirable is a question to be raised—but not one for us to attempt to answer here.

Our problem is that of the possibility that the persons interested in any particular change in political attitudes favorable to a peaceful world order "can" bring about changes that will lead to the result they wish to effect. About all that can be said about this question is that it is almost infinitely complex and difficult. At its simplest it has to do with the power of those in power—i.e., successful politicians—to mold the public opinion of the states or jurisdictions subject to their authority. Back of this is the question of the "right people" getting into power or "influencing" those who do, or affecting their selection—in competition with the efforts of multitudinous others to exercise influence in conflicting directions. In the immediate background of the present world situation we have seen a demonstration of the power of *dictators* to get into power and to effect substantial changes through education and propaganda, and especially the forcible suppression of similar activities opposed to their own. It will hardly be contended that the changes have been for the better, from the standpoint of international peace and amity. It seems probable, also, that, "human nature being what it is," it is easier for a dictator to effect changes which are bad from this point of view than to effect those which are good—easier, that is, to stimulate the growth of nationalism and group megalomania than to cause change in the opposite direction—and easier to get into power on the basis of the former platform.

However, "we," the parties to the present discussion, do not want a dictatorship on a world scale or for any power or group, including ourselves. We want a world order which is free as well as peaceful. Consequently, what may be thought as to the power of dictators or even of a technical majority, to "change human nature" is relevant only in a negative sense to our problem. In a democracy the possibility of progress by deliberate procedure in the direction of enlightenment rests on the hope that the more enlightened individuals finally have more influence, not merely in the pull-and-haul of concrete democratic politics, but back of that in molding public opinion, than have those who are less enlightened. Of course, we must make the prior assumption that individuals and voluntary groups have real power over the course of events in their own lives and that the choice of ends, as well as of means, can be more or less intelligent. If everything is determined by mechanical "forces" or some Cosmic Will, as pictured, respectively, by the scientific world view and by the religion or philosophy of theistic absolutism, there is no "sense" in conduct or in anything else. The possibility of freedom as an ideal depends on the reality of freedom as a metaphysical fact.

VI

The questions raised have the paradoxical character of being so "arguable" that they are rightly described as "unarguable." Further discussion would run into the ultimate issues of philosophy and ethics; and into that speculative region it cannot be carried here. It is not part of the aim of this article to give a solution of the problem of world organization, free from war but without sacrificing essential human values. The writer does not know the solution, if any exists. It is hoped that some contribution has been made to the comprehension of the problem and to its intelligent discussion, which is the first step toward solving it.

However, some constructive suggestions are implied in the argument. A more intelligent judgment of values, beginning with a more objective attitude toward culture differences, should be gradually achievable through education, if it is generally desired. This could reduce that form of patriotism and parochialism which assumes that particular institutions and ideas are ultimately valid and sacred because they are "ours"; that we should only teach other peoples, not learn from them; and that anything which will benefit an alien group or which it may wish to do in its relations with us must be bad for us and is probably motivated by a wish to injure us. If organized groups appealed to force only on issues rationally judged to be ethically real and important, the change would be a great improvement. Even though they would still occasionally fight, perhaps just as hard or harder, they would surely fight less often. The more accidental and immaterial differences, such as language and religion, should tend to disappear, as well as no longer to arouse antagonism. Groups might also be willing to stop fighting when they were clearly whipped and so avoid much useless destruction and post-war bitterness, which tends to a resumption of the struggle by the beaten side at the first favorable opportunity. When one party is clearly in a hopeless position before a war starts, the peace treaty might be written without the war; this would be a gain even if the treaty itself were no better, but the procedure also seems likely to result in better treaties.

XIII

Economics, Political Science, and Education

*O*ur topic covers three fields of knowledge and action, all vast and indefinite. The combination sets a rather bewildering task of saying anything reasonably true and relevant and not utterly trite; and one who says anything about it, needs to say a great deal. I shall not speak of methods of teaching (about which I know nothing), but shall restrict myself to content. And under that head I can only state a few results which must be achieved by social action in accord with sound principles of economics and political science if our society is to conserve and develop its recognized values of freedom and progress, along with the necessary minima of peace and order, and also of efficiency and justice. Nor can I more than mention immediate concrete issues. Of these the most important are doubtless monopoly and unemployment. They illustrate different types of problems, in that monopoly involves acute conflicts of individual and group interests,

Reprinted by permission from *American Economic Review Supplement*, vol. 34 (1944), pp. 68–76.

while unemployment is a matter of intellectual agreement upon effective measures.

My own approach is that of a "teacher" of fundamental economics, with the improvement of content in a secondary role. As I use the word teacher, it refers to an occupation, in which the craftsman presumably tries to earn his pay; it does not mean that learning, the logical correlate of teaching, actually follows as a result. My experience, of some three decades, has raised some other sober reflections in my mind. I fear that the urge to teach is largely a conceit and is a species of the lust for power and prominence, hence one of the immoral ingredients of human nature, a form of original sin. Also, I am more and more impressed with psychological and moral problems in education, and in thinking in general. In economics in particular, education seems to be largely a matter of unlearning and "disteaching" rather than constructive action. A once famous American humorist observed that "it's not ignorance does so much damage; it's knowin' so derned much that ain't so." But a purely negative conception would be an oversimplification. It seems that the hardest things to learn and to teach are things which everyone already knows, which are banal when explicitly stated. The main "principles" of economics are obvious, even insultingly obvious, to people at the intellectual level we should like to assume in the literate public, as well as university students. The problem here is to get generalities to "carry over" into political discussion and action, the field in which our two sciences are practically significant. In other connections, as will be shown, the problem may have the opposite form, of keeping professed principles from being taken literally or too seriously.

The situation is illustrated by the great American political issue of protectionism. No one denies the general advantage of specialization, or its enhanced advantage for parties living in different regions and differing in natural resources and culture. And no one holds that the facts are altered by political boundary lines. All that can really be said about the issue, in economic terms of the effective use of resources, is covered by Adam Smith's example of wine-growing in Scotland, or more pointedly by Bastiat's petition of the candle-makers for legal prohibition of windows in houses, to exclude the destructive competition of cheap light from the sun. But such witticisms would never have been thought of unless suggested by the stupidity of actual discussion and policy. The problem here is less intellectual than the moral one of getting people to use common knowledge and ordinary gumption. I think it is not primarily a moral problem in the more usual view, of getting men to prefer the social interest to private gain. The protectionist is honest enough, as honesty goes, though the capacity for honestly confusing the two aims is a leading trait of human nature. (It is needless to explain here that in this case the private interest itself is largely an illusion.)

However, the other side of the question is equally important. Realities, including some which are unchangeable or even ought not to be changed, afford sound reasons for political interference with the "natural" course of foreign trade, in response to the economic interests of individuals. But men do not advocate and vote for protection on these grounds, and they rarely justify the measures adopted. On the other hand, again, we never get tariff laws which would actually offset the difference in cost of production at home and abroad, to say nothing of the principle that what one party gains in an exchange the other must lose, both of which principles are also widely believed and professed. Moreover, yet again, the chief intellectual merit in much of our classical exposition of the advantages of trade is the ingenuity of its confusion and error. In short, as I see it, the main problem of political-economic education centers in the role of general principles, or theory. Such principles never solve any concrete problems, but they are indispensable for analysis. Valid principles can be cited on both sides of any question, and even the same principle, if it is sufficiently general and abstract. Witness the appeal to freedom in support of antithetical policies—indeed of nearly any policy which anyone cares to advocate.

A rational, common-sense approach to the subject matter of political economy begins with the fact that the economic problem for any individual or group is to make the best of what it has, through comparison, selection, and combination of competing alternative ends and procedures in the use of means. All practical problems arise out of conflicts of interest and differences of opinion. Economic problems arise out of conflicts due to limitation of resources in relation to total needs or wants, and these are social problems when the ends are those of different people. But human nature is clearly averse to such rational comparison. Men seize on particular aims or courses of action and treat them as absolute. Our whole moral tradition, sanctioned by our religious tradition, stresses disdain for the counting of costs. It is anti-intellectual; it teaches that if the heart is right, in relation to emotional or transcendental values, all concrete problems will be solved automatically. In this connection, it is the failure of men's professions to carry over into practical thinking and action which saves them from disaster instead of causing it. Even "scientific" economics has slowly and as yet imperfectly come around to the comparative point of view, to recognition that the only cost which makes sense is a sacrificed alternative. Economists "of the cloth" must concede that progress in this regard has met with ingenious obstruction from the profession itself, and the doctrine of "real" or absolute cost probably still predominates in elementary instruction.

Social action is a matter of achieving desirable social changes and avoiding changes which are undesirable. In our own culture, most of the immediate and acute issues arise in connection with the terms of economic association, co-operation, or organization, though essentially similar problems arise in play and other types of associative life. An intelligent approach to economic problems must obviously begin with understanding the situation which it is proposed to change, including the possibilities, methods, and probable costs of change. The objective is to show what changes are at all worth their cost, and which are best in relation to the cost. This means, first of all, understanding the "enterprise economy." But actual discussion has always been saturated with propaganda. In the early classical treatises, it was propaganda for the liberation from social control, while of late it has swung in the opposite direction. The first requirement is to get ethical and political, as well as merely sentimental and romantic, presuppositions out of social science. This task encounters a real and serious difficulty. In dealing with phenomena of life, even in biology, description must run largely in functional terms of how the organic process is kept going, and even of the adaptive modification of structure and function for better performance.

This applies, *a fortiori,* and in greatly enhanced degree, to the treatment of human phenomena, social and individual, where conscious purpose cannot be ignored. But functional explanation smacks of justification or apologetic. On the human scene, moreover, apologetic is justified up to a point. What is, must be considered good, until something attainable and enough better ideally to be worth the cost of change is in view. The abstractly ideal may be the worst enemy of attainable good; in a strictly practical sense, calling a situation hopeless amounts to calling it ideal. But human nature inclines to one of two equally pernicious extremes, either sanctifying what is, against all change, or abolishing without serious reflection about replacement, to say nothing of replacement by something better.

In practical thinking, principles are significant in two ways. First, as an instructional device, they shorten the process of "acculturation" of the young. And second, thinking in terms of principles is essential for rational change, though, to repeat, principles alone never solve real problems.

Analysis of any subject matter employs a hierarchical series of principles presenting a descending order of generality and scope of application. Compte's classification of the sciences gives the general picture, and the relation between physical mechanics and engineering is a sound analogy if not pushed too far. In the latter field, the first step is to formulate the universal conservation principles—mass, momentum, and energy, quantitatively defined in primary units of space, force, and time. (Relativity refinements are not in point here.) Such principles convey little concrete information to such a practitioner as a builder of automobiles, and that little is chiefly negative—things not to try to do. General physics has the same claim as economics to be called a "dismal science." Yet this negative information is vitally important. And further, general concepts are positively essential for stating problems in terms in which they can be solved. The principles of theoretical mechanics are directly contrary to the facts for most problems of action. They abstract from friction, while our human control of energy is finally directed to overcoming friction—including the activities of our own bodies. In practice, the theoretical relation between the general and the particular is reversed; the builder's main problem is to apply energy in driving a car against frictional resistance, with acceleration and deceleration against inertia as exceptional cases. Even in mechanics, human nature does not take naturally to sound analysis; perpetual motion is the problem which appeals to the tyro, and notably to the ingenious tyro; it is by no means the dolts who waste time and resources on such schemes.

Similarly, economics must begin with principles that are abstract and unrealistic, such as perfectly economic behavior of an individual and the perfect market, and stationary and moving equilibrium. Even the use of money is a consequence of imperfection, uncertainty, speculation, and must be excluded at the most general level of theory. But the ideal barter economy is no farther from reality than theoretical mechanics; in fact, as it would be easy to show, both involve logical contradictions. Yet abstract economic principles are universally valid, however society is organized, even without formal exchange and markets. The one necessary condition is conflicting ends, for individuals and between individuals, requiring a twofold allocation of means. Sound general theory excludes unemployment of resources, when both terms are correctly defined. As in engineering, only confusion will result from interchanging general and special cases to correspond with empirical facts and interests, as the "Keynesites" propose. The theory of equilibrium, unrealistic as it is, must precede the study of disequilibrium. And I must add that the treatment of disequilibrium and unemployment is merely confused by using such "gobs of language" as "liquidity preference" and "propensity to consume" in place of talking about what one is really talking about; namely, speculative hoarding and dishoarding and their causes and consequences. By the same token, perfect competition must be studied before monopoly of various degrees and kinds.

The relation between general or abstract and empirically more realistic theory runs into the problem of application. The latter is the political problem—the role of the state in economic life. All economic activity takes place in a framework of "institutions," partly of natural growth, partly formed by deliberate law making. These define the given conditions of market behavior, and also perform many essential functions, beginning but by no means ending with policing markets against force and fraud. These facts do not enter into sound general analysis; they merely set the main educational problem, since they are "caviar" both to the "million" and to many professional students.

The activity of the state takes two main forms. It provides an alternative mode of organization, partly independent of the market system, and it imposes various regulations upon individual market behavior. Both markets and the two forms of political action will always exist. Apart from the theoretical similarity of all mutual relations to formal exchange, there has been no society without markets, more or less free, at least since a low stage of savagery; no socialist has proposed their abolition, and no totalitarian regime has attempted it. Politico-economic problems relate to a mixed system of organization, comprising the three elements, free, regulated, and public enterprise, and their study is a joint task for the sciences of economics and government. Further, both of these sciences must use data from other branches of knowledge, from moral philosophy "downward" through the social disciplines, psychology and biology to technology and physical science. A main problem of education is to get the public and its politicians, administrators, and various experts, to look objectively at the nature and interrelation of the three factors in the economic organization as a whole, and to see what is patently there.

Market competition is the only form of organization which can afford a large measure of freedom to the individual, as consumer or as producer. Socialists have begun to recognize this fact, that state economy can preserve freedom only by operating through a system of markets. As to regulation, there is a strong presumption against much of it, beyond simple police measures and prevention of monopoly. But there is a large place for general activities, especially in such fields as money, and also for the conduct of enterprise by public bodies, where it is not feasible to make competition effective. Of course (though it may be improper to say it), individual freedom and prevention of monopoly exclude large-scale collective bargaining. This is merely a seductive name for bilateral monopoly (monopoly and monopsony, in current jargon) and means either adjudication of conflicts in terms of power, or deadlock and stoppage, usually injuring outside people more than the immediate parties to the dispute.

In a mixed economy, the difference between public and private enterprise is far less than is commonly assumed. On the one hand, the large productive units required by modern technology are (regardless of their detailed internal organization) much like the government; and on the other hand, public enterprises must compete with private in the purchase of productive services, and more or less in the sale of products, even as monopolies. (That they insist on monopoly status is highly significant, but the point cannot be developed here.) One main lesson of our war experience—specifically the rise in the production index (as far as it tells the truth)—is that the costs of freedom are high in terms of theoretically possible efficiency, and other theoretical losses are also involved. There is great danger that the public will misread this lesson, especially that it will greatly exaggerate the likelihood that both freedom and other values which conflict with freedom would in fact be realized under political planning and administration. One task of general education which tends to fall on economics is to make people realize that any one value must be had at some sacrifice of others; hence that we must be content—though not satisfied—with possibility and reasonable progress. The compromise is always a matter of judgment, not of fact or rule. The tendency to make impossible demands is of course largely due to the organization of special-interest groups, employing paid spokesmen, who inevitably become agitators and makers of promises impossible to fulfill.

Only a few remarks can be offered on the specific problem of cooperation between economics and politics or government as sciences, and between these and other disciplines involved in describing and explaining the structure and operation of the threefold politico-economic order. Neither of our two disciplines deals at all with either ultimate factual data or the ultimate ideals which must guide intelligent action. It is difficult, even analytically, to distinguish between the political and the economic and still other aspects of the mixed organization and its problems which must be understood merely to predict how any proposed measure will work. Discussion of the problems of monopoly and unemployment, already mentioned, would illustrate the difficulty of intellectual division of labor and cooperation, but that discussion cannot be undertaken here.

The public seems relatively willing to leave technical problems of legislation to specialists, holding them responsible for results; but in practice the specialists are chiefly lawyers, trained from a private professional point of view. Neither political scientists nor economists are highly esteemed as advisers by the public. In economics in particular, this is no doubt partly because what attracts general attention is not the scientific work, theoretical or empirical, but moral and political speculation and preaching. Where economists are agreed, as illustrated by protectionism—and I will add a national legislative minimum wage—the situation is summed up in the adage that free traders win the debates but protectionists win the elections. On the whole, the educational task in political science is more largely the training of experts; in economics, more largely raising the general level of public understanding. Both the economist and the political scientist must expect to work for, and take orders from, a third species, described by Adam Smith as "that insidious and crafty animal vulgarly called a statesman or politician." It would surely be helpful if the two groups could learn each to understand the language of the other, and the elements of the other discipline, so as to work together intelligently; but this consummation would presuppose more unity and objectivity than now exist within the disciplines themselves.

Another difference between the sciences of economics and government pertains to method. Political science proceeds chiefly by historical induction, making relatively little use of general axioms, while in economics the balance rightly inclines the other way. Neither type of knowledge gives very full or reliable answers to concrete questions of prediction or control. We have already commented, though very inadequately, on the practical limitations of abstract economic principles; statistics may carry us further, but still not very far. It should be emphasized that the concept of economic rationality, as efficiency in the use of given means to achieve given individual or group ends, excludes a large part of the purposive life of men as social beings—the ideal as well as the actual. My economist colleague on this program, Professor Clark, has somewhere pointedly commented on the craving for dispassionate rationality as itself an irrational passion. The real problems of social economy must in particular be understood in the light of the nature of man as a playing as well as a working animal and that of his workaday life as a competitive game or sport as well as cooperation for the sake of increased efficiency. And fellowship and other social interests demand consideration.

Limitations are fully as important in political science as in economics, particularly from the standpoint of education. Because reliable prediction, in terms of scientific laws, is impossible, because judgment is more important than rules, the way is open for the ignorant and romantic, the wish-thinkers, to picture political measures as working out in any way they feel to be desirable. One of the most vital needs in the education of the citizen is a fair knowledge of the possibilities and limitations of democratic political machinery—of government by law, based on discussion, and responsible administration. Electorates educated in and by democracy tend to combine lack of respect for "politicians" with the belief that elected officials will satisfy any craving by fiat, if only the right pressure is brought to bear. If we are to keep our liberties, preserve peace, and make orderly progress, political science must—I do not know whether it can or not—teach the people, as well as specialists, the major realities of human behavior in relations of power and obedience, and must give them realistic notions as to how many problems, and of what degree of difficulty, can be solved at the same time by group deliberation, and at what speed.

The most serious popular fallacies are due to a combination of economic and political ignorance and bias. "The government" is supposed not merely to miraculously multiply loaves and fishes and so distribute any amount more than is produced, but to defy the laws of arithmetic by making everybody better off in comparison with, and at the expense of, everybody else; it is asked to raise all selling prices while holding down if not reducing the same prices for the buyers. Many political scientists teach their students to view politics as a struggle for power rather than a mechanism of cooperation. In political economy, we are up against the problem of educating people to the right use of concepts and principles, in a field where the results of analysis can be applied to the problems to which they are relevant only if the bulk of the people either understand them or will recognize and follow specialists who do. The difficulty, to repeat, is not primarily intellectual; the failure to understand both principles and their limitations is due more to prejudice, either crude self-interest or naive reformist theories, the latter probably the worse corruption of the two.

In conclusion: The first step toward better cooperation

among the disciplines which deal with different aspects of social action must be their development separately, as sciences. Only on this foundation can their results be combined intelligently. In particular, the social sciences must be purified from presuppositions, especially from romantic ethics; and ethics must be developed as an independent critical discipline, not a science, in the accepted meaning of the English word. Of the role of the specialist or expert in ethics—specifically social ethics or political philosophy—we can only note that it is at best an especially difficult problem, and is made vastly more difficult through the traditional pre-emption of this role by spokesmen for organized religion, always a special-interest and pressure group. Currently, traditional religion is being replaced by ideology—also organized, and quite as dogmatic and intolerant and power seeking—and no improvement, if you ask me!

All the special disciplines must confront in various ways and degrees four tasks: to raise the general level of public intelligence; to raise their own level through research and critical thinking; to train specialists for active and cooperative participation in the political process; and to inculcate a right attitude of mutual understanding and respect in the public and in the functional specialists. Free society requires intellectual and moral leadership, but this merely defines the problem and locates the difficulty. Democratic leadership must keep the right distance in advance of the masses, and in the right direction—and not too many directions—and must lead by education, not dictation. The only guarantee of this relation is that leaders shall be constantly forced by an educated clientele to follow more than they lead.

XIV

The Planful Act:
The Possibilities
and Limitations of
Collective Rationality

*C*onscience compels me to begin this lecture with a disclaimer and a caveat, with respect to my role in starting off this series with such a discourse. Like the Lacedemonians at Thermopylae, I am here in obedience to orders, and would not have much ground for either surprise or complaint if I also were left dead upon the field. If my advice had been asked, I should have recommended against both the topic and the speaker. In my opinion, the series should have begun, if not exactly with a "pep talk," at least with something that would stimulate interest, and not with a heavy philosophical and critical discussion of presuppositions which must seem to throw cold water on the whole project. Such inquiries should not be pushed too far, even in one's private thinking, to say nothing of a public oral address, and one of a series, which to some extent the audience is bound to take whether they like it or not. I can only point out that

A public lecture given at the University of Chicago in 1944, the first of a series on planning.

the question of possibilities and limitations is logically fundamental and also practically important if discussion of planning is to look toward action and not merely intellectual entertainment, or propaganda. If those interested in planning mean business, they surely need to have reasonable expectations as well as romantic faith, or dreams. My assignment being what it is, and I being what I am—on which point my superiors should have sufficient knowledge to tell them about what to expect—I must use my allotted time to say what seems to me most needful to be said about collective rationality and its possibilities and limitations.

As I suppose we all recognize, men as individuals, and as groups, have to live largely by a mixture of two ultimately irrational faiths, the faith in reason, which we know is fallible, and the faith in inspiration, which we know is arbitrary. The modern student of history and social process soon learns that societies have lived in a state of relative peace and order by not raising problems they cannot solve and discussion of which would only stir up antagonism and probably lead to conflict, if not to a social nervous breakdown. Scientific sociology shows further that one primary function of social institutions has been to prevent the raising of such questions. This is done through "conditioning" the individual from infancy to acceptance of what is established. Social custom, tradition and authority are either not consciously questioned at all, or they are sacred. The burning problems of modern civilization, which are currently discussed with so much heat and an uncertain amount of light, particularly under the head of social planning, arise largely out of the partial replacement of this age-old type of institutional order and mental attitude by active critical inquiry and endeavor toward improvement and progress.

Freedom to criticize and to change things is the fundamental meaning of democracy. Its origin may be dated a couple of centuries ago, at the Age of Reason or the Enlightenment, which represented by far the greatest cultural revolution on record. In that historically short period, man's increasing knowledge of man has in some respects verified the ancient Scripture, "in much wisdom is much grief, and he that increaseth knowledge increaseth sorrow." It has become clear that people individually, and much more so in collectivities, are not very rational, they could not be if they would, they don't want to be, and the impartial spectator inclines to the view that they are largely right. On the other hand, we have democracy on our hands, as it were, and the situation forces us to solve our problems, for better or worse, through discussion or an attempt at "collective rationality." The fact that we here are discussing the problem publicly commits us to the assumption that it is to be solved by public discussion. And in any case, the members of such a group as this, as informed and intelligent people, must want the fullest knowledge of the process by which "climates of opinion" are formed and may be expressed in group action. The current vogue of social planning is an excellent illustration of the realities of collective rationality, namely one part of rationality to an indefinite number of parts of irrationality and romanticism. People of all sorts, but especially many of the most intelligent and best educated, clearly "believe in" the idea and project. The grounds seem to be similar to those which underlie the belief in heaven and hell, or the faith that prosperity is just around the corner, or the opposite conviction, that the world is going to the dogs. People believe because they want to believe; but this is no explanation, since it merely shifts the question to the reasons for the desire, which has no satisfactory answer.

The type of "reasoning" involved in this case, is illustrated by an address recently given at an academic conference at the great University of Chicago. The speaker referred to the strange way of thinking which leads nearly everyone to believe that individuals should plan their conduct and their lives, but at the same time to be horrified at the idea of governmental planning. Now the thinking which seems strange to me is that of the learned professor himself. His idea of logical consistency is that one who believes in individuals planning for themselves should at the same time believe that government, always meaning some group of politicians, should take the job out of their hands and do it for them. In fact, of course, both views are completely irrelevant to any real issue. Everyone actually believes in intelligent planning both by individuals and by governments; the real question is simply the perennial one as to what activities individuals and governments respectively should carry on and be responsible for. Or, more accurately, the question is the proper division of function in social life between individuals, voluntary groups of innumerable kinds, and political units almost equally various.

Noting that this apportionment of functions, freedoms and responsibilities, between itself and other agents is the primary function of law and the state as the supreme authority, the essence of keeping the peace, the statement suggests the fantastic scope of the topic assigned for this lecture. It calls for discussion of rationality and irrationality, in thinking and in action, with respect to means and to ends, and also to the large area in which the instrumental pattern of thinking itself has little application; and all of this must be considered in the individual life and in the two general types of groups, the voluntary and the legally compulsory. Obviously, all that one hopes to accomplish in a lecture is to show something of the complexity and difficulty of the problem and to emphasize the romanticism and the practical fatality of yielding to the craving for easy solutions through words or phrases like "reason" or "doing right," which mean whatever anyone wants them to mean and serve chiefly to intensify controversy.

The one general principle that can be stated—and which chiefly needs to be stressed—is that the solution of moral and social problems must be pluralistic. Most of the solutions advocated are sound in general terms, and "the" solution must take the form of compromise and balance among a vast number of conflicting principles, and must be a matter of judgment, not of formula or verbal rule. Perhaps the most serious practical difficulty is that thinking tends to over-simplification and that in general usage all the main terms are largely defined and employed for propaganda purposes, for begging some question in favor of some interest which it is a part of the propaganda technique to conceal. Thus our argument as a whole ought logically to consist largely of philosophical discussion of terminology, which would condemn it to futility at the outset.

The ideal meaning of "government by discussion"—Lord Bryce's neat definition of democracy—would be establishment of unanimous agreement through intellectual process or activity, without any employment of coercive power. That is, it would be anarchy. But we must assume as admitted that this ideal is impossible, hence not really an ideal, for groups of substantial size and with important problems to solve on which it is imperative to secure agreement. This observation suggests the limitations of collective rationality. In practice, group action virtually always takes the form of delegation of power to individuals or in fact to small groups within which there actually is a working unanimity of opinion. But this unanimity is always based in part on a common special interest, which conflicts in various ways and degrees with the interests of the governed group and its other members. In this special interest, ideals and theories may be as important as "crude self-interest" and even more dangerous. In any society, the ruling group or party must get and keep power, and this always involves "propaganda," which to be effective must diverge in varying degrees from "discussion" in the ideal meaning of objective treatment of facts and issues.

We may assume for the sake of the argument that the seeker of power is utterly sincere in wanting general agreement on what is really right and true. But this commonly means that other people should agree with him on what should be done, and should unanimously choose and follow him as their leader; those who disagree are irrational, incompetent, indifferent, or selfish and wicked and all such people it is his right and duty to coerce or destroy. This attitude prevails increasingly as any leadership succeeds in entrenching itself in power, and to the extent that it has ideals in which it sincerely believes. The alternative possibility is leadership which believes in compromise as the first principle of government and strives to preserve an atmosphere in which the best possible compromise will be achieved. This attitude is undoubtedly the main requisite for the preservation of freedom, but idealists tend to repudiate it as intrinsically immoral.

Human nature being as it is, there are fairly narrow limits to the achievement of collective rationality, i.e., rational agreement, even with respect to the means for realizing given ends. The procedure for maintaining physical health is a good example, and will later be considered. The limits become narrower as we think beyond such an objective end as health and consider the more remote, and higher, ends or ultimate purposes, the meaning of "the good life," to which all objective ends are admittedly means. Since it is inevitable that groups act through leaders or rulers who want power, while completely rational delegation of power is a self-contradiction, and that any group in power is in a favored position for keeping power and getting more, the problem is the perennial and familiar one of combining effective power to act with responsibility to society as a whole in its use. Excluding supernaturally inspired leadership and authority, the final decision must rest either with the governed, or with some individual or group ruling by force. Even this exception is logically unreal, since the governed must be the judge of the validity of the inspiration, or higher knowledge and wisdom claimed by its rulers, unless acceptance is forced, either overtly or through some form of "persuasion" which is really force or fraud. The ultimate question is the twofold one of freedom as a means to good government, and of the relative value of political freedom and efficiency, insofar as the two conflict.

The general thesis of this discourse is the old-fashioned liberal position that the main emphasis needs to be placed on freedom, on both counts. We shall argue that very "strong" government is more likely in the long run to be bad than good, and that freedom itself is of transcendent importance as a condition of the moral life. Accordingly, sound policy requires restricting the positive functions of government to things on which there is general agreement. Its main task is the negative one of preserving freedom by preventing coercive action by individuals and groups, through force or fraud. This view runs counter to present tendencies in the climate of opinion, even in our own society, which is still formally committed to the democratic ideal and is actually carrying on a terrible war for its preservation in the world. The present vogue of the "planning" idea is a natural social-psychological product of a condition of economic crisis; this situation makes men think in terms of security rather than freedom, and hence romantically exaggerate the need and possibility of action by governments, ignoring its evils and dangers. (It goes without saying that a considerable amount of "social planning" is inevitable, as well as that maximum freedom itself calls for sweeping restrictions upon the literal freedom of individuals and groups.)

A comprehensive and logically ordered survey must break

up our general topic into four or five heads. First, something must be said about the possibilities and limitations of rationality in the individual life, insofar as human life can be individual. Second, we must consider rationality in "casual" association, without formal organization. The third head is more or less enduring and stable organization on a "voluntary" basis. The final and main problem is rationality in the political unit or collectivity; and here we must distinguish between political organization under the dominance respectively of a majority and of some minority, specifically a minority "party," which always has an individual head, "leader," or "father," usually in a more or less religious, prophetic, or "charismatic," role. Even in the group of two individuals, doctor and patient, the position of the former is typically surrounded by something of an "aura" of inscrutable superiority in wisdom and power.

I. Individual Rationality

That "man is a rational animal" is one of those interesting statements which do not have to be proved, since the subject admits it. In fact he says so himself; and the objective value of the statement is to be appraised in the light of that fact. It must also be viewed in the light of other statements "man" makes about himself. By the same authority, he is also a groping ignoramus, a fool, and a miserable sinner, quite unworthy of redemption. The list of opposite characteristics could be indefinitely extended, and all the statements would be true, in varying degree and numerous interpretations. But by the same token each is false or, taken singly and alone, is an exaggeration and over-simplification. Man is certainly a romantic animal. For a general characterization, he is perhaps less distinctively *homo sapiens,* the knower, than he is *homo mendax,* the liar, deceiver, hypocrite, actor, pretender, practicer of make-believe. Other animals have effective if not

405

explicitly conscious knowledge, and an interest in truth; man alone prefers fiction to fact, with respect to the world and especially to himself. He covers his body with clothes and that is trivial compared to the concealment and misrepresentation of his intellectual, emotional and moral nature in language and expressive behavior. This is by no means all to the bad. Insofar as man is wise or good, his "character" is acquired chiefly by posing as better than he is, until a part of his pretense becomes a habit.

In no case are rationality and its opposite to be identified with what is respectively good or bad. A leading American economist has observed that "an irrational passion for dispassionate rationality" would take the joy out of life. It would also exclude most of the esthetic values, which depend upon taste (and about taste there is proverbially no argument) and also most of its real morality; hence it is not truly rational at all, nor moral. "Love is blind"; but this does not mean that devotion and loyalty ought to be abolished. Rationality is paradoxical in another sense. If it has a definite meaning, it is the interest in truth, as "naked" and "cold." But our real interest in truth is in the last analysis largely romantic. Truth is interesting chiefly because it is either "useful" or marvelous, or at least novel. "Mere" truth, completely established and beyond question, is a commonplace and a bore. Especially, truth is interesting because it is controversial, and in any case it is something to be pursued rather than to be possessed. And the ordinary meaning of rationality in action, its most objective meaning, is efficiency. But you may have heard the story of the football club that hired an efficiency expert as manager; his first step was to put all the men on the same side, because of the waste and absurdity of half of them pushing against the other half.

Individual rationality—or irrationality—may be illustrated by Plutarch's story of Pyrrhus and Kineas. Pyrrhus, you will recall, was that king of Epirus in Greece, who set out to conquer Rome about 200 B.C., and gave to language the expression, a Phyrric victory. Kineas was his favorite counsellor, and the story is of a conversation between the two on the eve of the great adventure. Briefly, Kineas pointed out the difficulties and hazards of the enterprise, and asked just what his master expected to gain by it in the not too probable event of success. He was told that the answer was obvious; victory over Rome would clear the path to Sicily. And when Kineas pursued the question into the gain to result from this further conquest, he was reminded in a similar tone that Sicily was on the way to Carthage and all of Africa. Led on as to what he would do when he had conquered the whole world, Pyrrhus laughingly observed that perhaps he would sit down and take his ease. Asked if he would really be in a better position to do this than he was in the beginning, again in the improbable event of ultimate success, Pyrrhus changed the subject; and Plutarch ends the account by observing that the conversation embarrassed the king considerably, but produced no change in his plans.

This story suggests another, which illustrates collective rationality. It was told at the University by Professor Radcliffe-Brown, and said to be authentic. After the first World War, some missionaries in South Africa got the bright idea of improving the life of the natives by beginning with its economic foundations. This meant teaching them more "rational" procedures in farming, such as they would be in a position to practice. But it was to be done with wisdom and subtlety, through example rather than precept. An intelligent young man was selected from each of a number of villages and taught the rudiments of "dry farming," in accord with the local requirements. These students were also instructed not to preach or exhort, but simply to practice what they had been taught, each in his own village and plot of ground, leaving others to imitate the obviously better practice. It happened to be an exceptionally dry season, and the particular young farmer of the story was achieving excellent results while on the other plots vegetation was drying up. The anthropologist told the story to illustrate ideas and practices of witchcraft, but remarked that it was not a very typical example, since the case was too obvious. With little of the ritual or formalities characteristic of more doubtful cases, the community simply took the young man in hand, cut his body into as many pieces as there were fields in the village, and buried one piece in each field. The next year, being a season of adequate rain, everybody had a good crop. And at the same time, the white inhabitants of the South African republic voted the government of General Smuts out of office, because of the hard times due to the same drought. As you all know, essentially similar things are done in our own contemporary culture, especially in the field of medical beliefs and practice, to say nothing of mob action and religious revivals in some parts of the country.

Returning to the notion of rationality in the individual life, a thorough-going analysis would require use of the Crusoe hypothesis, sometimes employed in economic theory. It was once more employed than it is now; it has been found that any rigorous conception of rational behavior seems too un-realistic to the public and to students to be useful for expository purposes. But if this is true in the discussion of the use of means for ends taken as given, it seems pointless to attempt a definition of completely rational thinking about ends, outside of the narrowest philosophical circles. Modern civilized man has in quite recent times become "reasonably rational" in his thinking and conduct in economic life, where the exigencies of the market force concrete choices into the form of quantitative comparison. But this is not the case with our thinking and discussion of more general interests. The best illustration is the case of health and disease, where both the end and the procedure for realizing it are in the highest degree subject to objective determination. While our own civilization has largely gotten away from the crudest techniques of primitive exorcism, magic and witchcraft, the treatment of illness is still saturated with superstition, occult practices and quackery of many sorts, which are based on reasoning of the same kind. Not long ago, I asked a well-informed medical friend at what date in history he would say that even professional medical practice began to cure more people than it killed, or help more than it injured. His answer was that scientific, professional and general education should probably be allowed another generation or so to reach this point. With respect to collective rationality in dealing with the problem of social health, we are still mostly in the "moralistic" or retributive stage of finding someone to blame for any supposed ailment and treating the case by punishment or "liquidation," which is strikingly similar to primitive witchcraft.

More remote and general ends, individual and social, are the province of esthetics and morals, which are admittedly in a sadly "unscientific" state. Of course it is an absurd and romantic idea that their treatment should or could be made scientific, or that the mental activity of thinking, deliberating and judging, could be planned in advance. Rational mental activity is problem-solving or question-answering, and cannot be thought of as either mechanical process or pursuit of a foreseen end. Moreover, each of these conceptions—mechanical process and the intelligent pursuit of given ends—excludes the other; and yet, to a very large extent the "best minds" in modern civilization contend that human conduct fits both descriptions. The thinking of the intellectual elite, and vulgar thinking, take us to the heart of the problem of collective rationality.

On the other hand, ultimate ends, and specifically moral ideals, make us think of religion, which is commonly held to be the only foundation for the validity of such values. Man seems to be a religious animal. But it is obvious that religious beliefs are for the most part inherited—in the cultural or social meaning, of course, not that of biological heredity. Frequently, to be sure, religion is based on conversion, but the least examination of this phenomenon reveals that it is rarely much more rational than cultural inheritance. The principle of social inheritance applies also to political allegiance and general moral convictions, such as the disapproval of head-hunting, cannibalism, and incest or non-monogamous marriage. It is true that men typically defend their political, moral and religious convictions with great intellectual ingenuity, but this fact does not reduce the irrationality of the grounds on which they actually rest. The logic of the polemic may be meticulously correct, but it is evident to critical examination that the premises are really inferred from the conclusions.

Moreover, scrutiny should make it clear that the connection between religion and morality in which men so commonly believe is unreal or rather, again, the causality is inverted; religion "sanctions" moral beliefs already established on different grounds. This is its general social function. An illustration is the attitude of the churches towards slavery, in our own country and only a short time ago, historically speaking. The position of religion, and of moral idealism, depended on the geographical location, north or south of the line dividing the territory in which the institution was or was not established. Religion has also sanctioned witchcraft wherever and whenever people generally believed in it (Cf. Exodus 22:18; "Thou shalt not suffer a witch to live") and "God" and even the same churches, as well as "right" are still on both sides in every major war. In religious ethics, the end justifies any means believed appropriate, and religion makes it wicked to inquire critically into either ends or means. The meaning of religious belief seems to be that it is sinful to question it; and again, apart from formal religion, it is immoral to inquire into the grounds of any moral conviction which is effectively established in any community. If we wanted to use language "rationally," in the sense of stating truth, we should undoubtedly say that men "cherish" or are "devoted to" or "love" their deeper convictions and not that they "believe" them, when the source is social conditioning in infancy, or mental processes for which "thinking" is hardly a correct name. Individuals who on their own initiative form or change their fundamental beliefs through genuine critical reflection are so rare that they may be classed as abnormal. Moreover, the "true" value of truth is so limited by conflicting moral and esthetic values that the communications of a human being of competence and good will are doubtless less than half motivated by the aim to tell the truth, the whole truth and nothing but the truth.

II. Rationality in Unorganized Social Relations

Our discussion of the first topic has unavoidably carried us well over the boundary into the second, since there really is no such thing as individual rationality. Rationality itself is social in nature and a product of stable group life. This would even be true of any Crusoe capable of self-maintenance, as to his fundamental beliefs and conduct. Certainly, any conscious idea of general truth and untruth is a late arrival in the growth of civilization.

Man is a social, or political, animal. This is another statement he makes about himself; and in this form, though literally true, it is essentially misleading. What is distinctive of human nature and society must be defined by contrast with animal life, particularly where it is highly organized, as among the social insects. The structure of human society rests to a negligible extent on biological instinct, correctly defined. It is in the first place a mixture of unconscious conditioning, imitation, and habit—which are as mechanical as instinct—with conscious processes; and the latter are a weird, unanalyzable mixture of various emotions with more or less rational types of thinking. The basic factor is always, even now, the mechanics of culture—custom and tradition. But undoubtedly also, man has "always" been an individualist—we should not call him human if he were not. He is more or less antagonistic to his fellows, incipiently rebellious against the socially established beliefs and patterns of behavior. But society means order and order means continuing conformity to some pattern, until it can be changed by general agreement or consent, achieved in some way. Throughout most of human history, there was little thought of change and then only to abhor it. The social problem was the enforcement of conformity; the "mores" defined what was right, and culture changed—shall we say progressed?—gradually, by unconscious drift (exemplified by language) or in some departments of social usage through the erratic intervention of prophets or lawgivers.

It seems to be a part of the social nature of man both to require rather definite and fixed forms of association and to feel consciously restrained by established usage, as "law"; it is always enforced both by human authority and by fear of the supernatural. A social order based solely on free casual association is a dream of the romantic imagination, more or less supported by argument. A greater amount of such free association actually comes as a more elaborate traditional and compulsive system develops. The outstanding fact is the paradoxical one that the freedom of association is "spoiled" by any serious purpose, on the part of the group or its individual members, in their relations to one another and to the group. In other words, it is play rather than work, and the absence of serious purpose is the essence of play, while the differentiation between play and work attitudes is a feature of the progress of civilization. The paradox lies especially in the fact that play has its serious purpose; for developed human beings it is undoubtedly essential to health, and even to sanity, as well as to enjoyment. But if it is directly motivated by these ends, both forms of functional significance are destroyed; it ceases to be recreative and also to make its contribution to healthy life. Nothing further need be said about rationality in this type of associative life, beyond the fact that it must be implicit rather than explicit.

We have referred to anarchy as the final meaning of the democratic ideal, government by discussion. Discussion itself may or may not be a conscious serious purpose in association, and in any society of considerable size and permanence, the discussion, or intercourse, which leads to the agreement necessary for group life presents a wide range of forms. It is probable that that which occurs spontaneously and without a conscious serious purpose is most important in the large. But the final stages which secure agreement, on the scale of political units, and which embody decisions in law and administration must obviously be organized. Further, there is practically no organization without authority. But it is ana-lytically useful to distinguish between voluntarily organized discussion and democratic political process. We here use organization with a formal reference which implies law, but no provision for coercive enforcement. Such voluntary orga-nization is anarchy, but is to be distinguished sharply from the "antinomian" meaning of the term. Whether a society entirely without law (or custom regarded as sacred) is con-ceivable, depends on the definition of law and is a disputed point; but it is at least commonly asserted that universal good-will or "love" (or perhaps "reason") would make law superfluous, as well as the state which enforces (and makes) law.

The present treatment must be restricted to social processes which go on within the type of social order represented by modern states, whether or not the processes are directly a part of political life. Here the essential fact is the inevitable mixture and combination of practically all conceivable varieties of social relationships. The fundamental features of social order, and the great bulk of what is involved in it, are, and always must be, traditional. The basic fact is of course a common language, but this is hardly separable in thought from the more fundamental beliefs and attitudes which prevail in any culture and are taken for granted in practically any communication or private thinking for which its language is instrumental. This is true practically regardless of the form of government, from the freest democracy to a dictatorship. And it is also universally true that the great bulk of social change, beyond unconscious "drift," must be in harmony with public opinion and a common will formed in casual social intercourse, in small-scale face-to-face association, with little or no formally organized discussion. A dictatorship secures most of its real power through manipulating public opinion and emotional attitudes rather than direct coercion of overt behavior. Apart from such manipulation (based on force) the process of change in the public mind is for the most part unplanned and is not true discussion, since it is not consciously oriented to the solution of problems, intellectual or practical, and its character is not primarily intellectual. It obviously presupposes a large amount of tolerance and good will. Moreover, it may be more educative and "rational" in its results because of the absence of consciously rational motivation. A "principle of indirection" seems to be inherent in the social nature of man.

Genuine, purely intellectual discussion is rare in modern society, even in intellectual and academic circles, and is approximated only in very small and essentially casual groups. On the larger scale, what passes for discussion is mostly argumentation or debate. The intellectual interest is largely subordinate to entertainment, i.e., entertaining and being entertained, or the immediate interest of the active parties centers chiefly in dominance, victory, instructing others, or persuading rather than convincing, and not in the impartial quest of truth. In practice, discussion of substantial scope, with respect to the number of persons involved, centers in and arises out of difference of opinion—with a complex relationship to conflict of interests—associated with a recognized need for securing agreement and preserving the group— or conceivably of forming a new group. In fact, such discussion must take place under both law and authority, and must be to some extent planned and managed; and the parties must exercise moral restraint and a will to compromise, if it is to progress to agreement rather than to intensify disagreement, all of which again requires good-will. However, genuine discussion is the quest of the solution of some problem, and in the nature of the case can only be planned in broad general terms; it cannot be directed to a preconceived end, since it contradicts the notion of a problem for the solution to be given or known in advance.

III. Collective Rationality in Voluntary Organizations

The treatment of voluntary organization, from the point of view of collective rationality, will best be oriented to the organization of discussion itself, which is in fact the main substance of all group life, as rational. A realistic discussion of this topic, with reference to modern conditions, would deal with two main topics. These are the proceedings of deliberative bodies, using the spoken word, and various types of publication, now including the radio as well as writing and printing. The complexity under both heads would be vast. The chief observation allowable here, and which may be assumed to be obvious, has already been suggested. It is the necessity for law and for authority in the making and enforcing of law, beginning with constitutional law. In an assembly, only one person can be allowed to speak at a time, since only one can be heard at a time, though with mechanical aids one speaker can make himself heard unilaterally by practically any number who are disposed to listen to him. The limitation upon general discussion increases rapidly with the size of the group. Further, utterance must be restricted to what is relevant to the business of the meeting, and preference given to what is more relevant and more important, and this "business" must be defined and agreed upon. Under the principle of freedom, or the nearest approach to freedom which can be achieved, enforcement is finally through exclusion from the group, by some mixture of direct group action and constituted or accepted personal authority. This fact especially needs emphasis because it means that effective freedom depends upon an alternative open to the non-conforming individual of leaving the group without suffering loss or damage. In fact, freedom is chiefly a matter of "competition" between groups for members, and if it is not to mean indefinite social subdivision, the problem is transferred to the field of relations between groups. Inter-group relations are of course the main actual problem of modern free society, both within states and in the world as a whole. It is a matter of common knowledge that in any assembly of substantial size, a constitution and rules of procedure have to be made and administered and that this is largely done by individual leaders accepted and acting as agents of the group as a whole. Also, that the really funda-mental rules which govern discussion, beginning usually with the language to be employed, have just grown up, while the detailed superstructure has been built through a previous process of the same kind as the current deliberation.

In line with what has been said, a deliberative body is usually concerned with action as a group either with or upon outsiders, individually or organized, and upon the material environment, and its own constitution and procedure are instrumental to action. It must be kept in mind that a scientific or philosophical convention rarely tries to settle any question, or to commit itself as a body to a conclusion on any issue. It is primarily a medium of publication, but typically with some provision for discussion at various levels. What is most important is usually the printed publication of "proceedings." We can only record our amazement at Professor John Dewey's contention that economic and political organization should be or could be patterned on "science," which he takes as the embodiment of "organized intelligence." As a matter of fact, these gatherings are not taken very seriously, as more than social occasions. With reference to the subject matter, what importance they have is chiefly that of giving rise to subsequent informal, casual discussion, and independent publication.

Turning briefly to publication as a form of discussion, two facts are obvious. First, someone in command of substantial resources has to decide what is to be published, and must expect either to donate the cost or to recover it in some way, including in the cost the rate of return on the investment which might be had through its use in other fields. Second, every potential reader must decide for himself between any particular book or article and other opportunities, and also as to whether he will purchase the work or be content with temporary access to it through other channels. The amount of effective freedom involved in these choices is a question too large to discuss—like freedom to listen or not listen to a paper publicly read, and any person's effective voice in determining what will be so presented. The individual cannot possibly have very much rational freedom, since the only way to form an intelligent opinion as to whether any paper is worth reading or hearing would be to read or hear both that paper and all other reading or listening one might have done, and to consider other possible uses of time and energy. Of course there are various ways of forming an opinion more or less rationally, by sampling, inquiry from others whose judgment one respects, reading reviews and comments, etc.

Everybody, every competent adult, knows how these problems are met and solved in nominally free groups, i.e., how the necessary minimum of agreement is first of all itself determined, and (second) achieved, and (third) acted upon. Some pronouncement on a general objective and line of action is first arrived at on the basis of a majority vote. This is called "policy determination." Second, action itself is delegated by a majority to agents or representatives, who must by similar methods be selected and given authority, and power, or means of enforcing their detailed decisions as to methods and results. Any dissident minority has the choice between acquiescing, organizing a revolution, and getting out—if it actually "can" secede without starting a war or incurring serious loss. In reality, the procedure has to be still more indirect, in large groups, especially political bodies. The constitutional and other legislative functions are themselves delegated to "representatives," on the basis of still more vague formulation of instructions or their promises as to what they will do if given power—their campaign pledges or party platforms.

The theory of representation is a large and vague subject. The theoretical function of an "agent" varies from doing exactly what his principal would do, to act for him purely as a matter of convenience, to acting as a custodian and judge of his principal's interests, or the means of achieving interests of any degree of remoteness and generality up to selecting his wife, or saving his life, or even his soul. In a democracy, officials are theoretically the agents of the group as a unit, which they represent. Analysis of their sphere and mode of action, in relation to the problem of group rationality, would carry us into the problem of ends and means in various kinds of group life, since rational discussion inevitably runs in these terms. The most important concrete function of most groups is education. This is often a hard problem even in connection with means, though when the ends are given the means are objective, and may be determined by logic and experimentation, as to the results of which ordinary men will agree. Vastly more difficult and serious is the educational problem with respect to ends, or esthetic and especially moral education. The latter is tied up with religion and innumerable forms of partisanship, loyalty, and absolutism.

The problem of rational group action through agents is best discussed with reference to the state and the relations of the political sovereign to other groups within its jurisdiction. In this connection we must keep in mind that in social life rational freedom takes one of two forms, freedom to influence the action of the group, and freedom to get out of it. To the extent that the constitution and laws of any group effectively preserve equal freedom, they exclude exercise of power by the individual over the group or its members, since we must distinguish power from rational argument leading to intelligent conviction. But the effective voice of an individual in free and rational group discussion necessarily decreases rapidly as the size of the group increases, and soon becomes infinitesimal or a matter of accident.

IV. *Collective Rationality in Politics*

Everyone must be presumed to know the general relation, similarities and differences, between the state and other organizations characterized by contrast as voluntary. However, a few reminders may be worth stating, and the first is that "voluntariness" is a matter of degree in groups of both classes. The modern state is based on "sovereignty" over a definitely bounded geographical area. Subordinate political divisions, colonies, etc., have various degrees and kinds of sovereignty within particular areas, under the ultimate sovereign—whose sovereignty is in fact limited in various ways, including international law, if there is such a thing. The practical peculiarity of the state or other political unit is that submission to its laws (as far as they are actually enforced) is a condition of living within its territory, and that a typical resident cannot "get out" without inconvenience of all degrees, up to impossibility. (Technicalities regarding citizenship must be passed over.) The difference to the individual may not be very real, since under not unusual conditions membership in other groups may be a condition of securing a livelihood, or even of not being murdered. When states do not coercively prevent the egress of persons, or their property, they at least coercively limit ingress, and in the actual world, one cannot get out of one state without getting into another. Further, states correspond largely with language and culture areas, and these differences constitute a very serious obstacle to transfer, not to mention the physical transportation costs. The result is that the typical individual is under strong compulsion, apart from legal coercion, to belong to the state in which he is born, and to obey its laws and authorities. And his freedom to change these, while a precious moral possession, is of negligible practical significance unless he strives successively to get power which restricts the rational freedom of others.

Although the distinction between political and voluntary organization is largely one of degree, it is supremely important, because of the vast size of states and other political units, and of the practical limitations of choice of one's place of residence. Both considerations apply even to the city, which is primarily in question in this series of lectures. Both elements of compulsion are in fact present in connection with organizations classed as voluntary, particularly those of an economic sort. Some American labor unions and farmers' organizations have more members than some states, and some business corporations are comparable in size. Apart from legal control, such bodies also have far less effective safeguards of individual freedom or provision for discussion of policies. They practically cannot have the three main recognized safeguards, an opposition party, a free press, or an independent judiciary, and many do not actually afford the poor recourse of regular and free general elections. Such bodies have an important bearing on the collective rationality of the larger community in which they operate. We shall presently give some attention to the particular case of professional organizations in the field of medicine.

As to the national state, we can only note that all known democracies operate through party organizations of some sort—which we call "machines." They first make platforms and nominate candidates—or select candidates subject to endorsement at a popular primary, which is different in form rather than in substance and is not generally believed by students to be an improvement over the party convention. At the second stage, the voters, meaning those who take sufficient interest in the outcome, choose between the offerings, and the majority prevails, assuming the election to be honestly conducted. What happens subsequently may be lumped together as the third stage in the whole process, and the literate adult must be left to judge how far all this constitutes "collective rationality." The party system usually carries over into the state and municipality; and if anyone is interested in forming a rational judgment on the "collective rationality" of the process at this level, a familiar and excellent case study is at hand in the great city of Chicago, where these lectures are given.

Of course, the "planner" will answer that everything "might be" altogether different, "if only . . ." Different objectors will finish out the sentence in the most divergent ways, each according to his individual preferences, predilections and prejudices; and that is the most important fact for the whole argument. It is also pertinent for the subject of rationality, individual and collective, to note that the "scientificists" in the study of society, including a large proportion of the very best minds, insist that it is all a matter of cause and effect. This dogma would make the notion of rational action completely illusory, and if carried out consistently would mean that there is no difference between making a statement and making (more accurately, occasioning) a noise. A great French philosopher said that we are able to say grammatically that anything "might be different" only because language itself was made by ignorant barbarians.

In practice (to repeat) the problem of collective rationality in action, for any group of appreciable size or permanence, is that of rationally delegating power. It involves rational choice of the agent, giving him rational instruction on the end to be achieved and the procedure to be followed, and holding him "responsible" for acting in general accord with the instructions. Actually, the group chooses among competitive seekers of the position or job of representing it, on the basis of some platform or promises, and general personal impression. To the extent that effective power to act is delegated, effective responsibility is attenuated, and working democracies have to rely upon the moral force of public opinion aided by some system of "checks and balances" between a plurality of power organizations, or branches of government. In place of further analysis in general terms, it seems best at this point to consider briefly a real case. And the best case for illustration seems to be the social problem presented by medical service, already mentioned several times. It is an especially favorable case, from the standpoint of rational collective action, since the end, the preservation of health through the prevention and cure of disease, is accepted by everyone and its meaning is quite accurately agreed upon.

V. *The Organization of Medical Service*

To begin with, medical service is an economic good, and its provision might be organized in any way from pure individualism to pure collectivism. The former method would leave it entirely to the individuals concerned; the person needing or for any reason desiring the service might practice upon himself (or his family) or hire as doctor anyone he pleased, among those offering it, on various terms. All regulation would then be left to market competition, with political authority in its minimum preventive role of assuring freedom of exchange by prohibiting force and fraud and monopoly. Or, as an alternative, the state, acting through its officials, might go to any length. It might even adopt the Platonic system of selecting its future doctors in childhood and compulsorily giving them the training deemed appropriate, fixing the terms on which the service would be rendered, including the assignment of individual doctor to the individual patient in every case, and enforcing its orders through criminal procedure. The illustration is favorable to the system of collective planning and control to a considerable extent at least, on the further ground that a close approximation to "free competition" is universally admitted to be intolerable. Health is for special reasons a social as well as an individual concern; and in spite of the comparative objectivity of health and the means of preventing or curing disease, medical service itself cannot be standardized and labelled as to kind and grade and so brought under effective market competition. Further, the organization of medical service is typical of the whole range of social-economic problems in that modern scientific technology can yield its enormous benefits only through a high degree of specialization or division of labor. On the other hand, the problem is comparatively simple in one respect, if we confine our attention to the general practitioner, the "country doctor," isolated from specialists and elaborate facilities representing a large capital investment and minute specialization, within an elaborate unit. At this level, it is a "handicraft" industry; and while the tendency is for medicine to go over to the "factory system" and even the corporate form, we may fix attention here on the more primitive case.

No doubt all specialization is theoretically bad, since it is opposed to the complete and well-rounded development of individual personality; and it also gives rise to serious problems through interdependence and the need for coordinating specialized activities. The separation of direction from concrete behavior is especially bad, in terms of modern ideals which give rational active freedom rather than unquestioning obedience the primary position in the scale of ultimate values. (This of course is the major ultimate ethical issue on which modern liberalism has reversed the Greek and medieval-Christian ideal; the earlier ethics also exalted freedom, but defined it in "spiritual" terms as submission to a higher will, assumed to be expressed in the established social order and hierarchy of authority.) A society which accepts the ideal of active freedom in the choice of ends and means, rather than submissiveness—"not my will, but thine, O universe"—as an ultimate principle, must face the fact of an intricate conflict between freedom and the conditions necessary to order, efficiency and progress that arise out of modern science and technology. In this respect, medicine is like every other branch of economic provision.

A problem of action in relation to health arises when an individual himself, or someone else on his behalf, is disturbed about his present or prospective state and disposed to do something about it. The question whether this disturbance is justified is the first one that must be answered by special competence. In the simplest case, where it is an adult as potential patient who raises the question, he must first of all decide whether to consult his physician or to doctor himself, which he may do within limits and in various ways. If he decides to seek outside help, he ordinarily has, even in our society, at least in a modern city, a very wide range of choice. For simplicity, we will assume that he rejects the whole group of alternatives presented by "occult" practitioners and other "quackery," and that he knows the difference, and decides upon orthodox scientific medicine. Under individualistic procedure, he must still select some particular doctor. Of course he is free to "inquire around," to seek advice from any source he may respect, before making a final commitment. Theoretically, he may also "shop around" among doctors themselves, but for practical reasons (rational or irrational) not much of this is generally done.

The essential point is that, for individual choice, rationality is extremely limited, if not theoretically almost excluded. To choose a doctor rationally, the individual would have to know all medical science, and in addition know how much of this is available through each of the possible selections, their respective competence, and also their trustworthiness. He is comparatively helpless, even assuming that his freedom is not restricted by power considerations either in the way of monopoly or limitation of means in relation to the price of different services.

Some escape from those limitations may be offered by organization in either of the two forms, voluntary or political-coercive. The individual may join—or in anticipation of such contingencies may already belong to—some medical panel, or insurance group, or the like. Without detailed discussion, it is obvious that similar limitations affect the rationality of this individual decision, and also affect the choices to be made by the organization, which involves all the problems of collective rationality. Finally (as already suggested), the "state" of which the individual is a citizen or subject may take action in a wide variety of ways. It may define standards and either publish information or prohibit practice without conformity to some minimum standard of training and demonstration of competence, to the satisfaction of some political authority, or it may directly appoint and assign doctors. Regulation of this general sort is in fact universal. It varies infinitely in objective reliability, depending on the competence and trustworthiness of politically chosen authorities and the enforcement of their pronouncements. In any case, regulation limits the freedom of the individual, even if it is for his own good and that of others. Regulation is both narrower and far better enforced in primitive society, where by civilized standards it has little reliability.

With respect to political control, the nature of the case requires that in practice action must be largely committed to the hands of the medical profession itself, since it alone has the necessary special competence. The medical profession must then be formally organized, under some mixture of the voluntary principle and political compulsion. In a modern nation, or even a typical city, the doctors are a large, heterogeneous, and widely scattered group, and must act through general rules and delegated power. As already observed, such an organization allows few safeguards of the freedom of its own members. Its officials cannot be disinterested in their relations to the profession at large, and they have much arbitrary power. The public is largely at the mercy of the "professional ethics" of the profession, the officials of its organization and the individual doctor, and none of these are disinterested in relation to the society they serve.

This is true of all expert service, and the main facts and problems are evident enough without detailed treatment here, particularly of the "politics" of the relation between an organized profession and the state.

When relations have been established in any way, between a particular doctor and a particular patient (passing over the equally interesting problems of public health) we confront an interesting situation as to individual rationality on both sides. The problems are of general importance, because even two people, acting together in any relation, constitute a group. In the doctor-patient relation, an infinite variety of emotional factors are not only present, but must be operative in the interest of effective functioning. Medical practitioners both admit and vehemently insist on the importance of the personal relationship, and the "bedside manner." The ideal situation includes a mixture of friendliness, respect and deference, a degree of the parent-and-child or priest-and-parishioner relation.

The doctor-and-patient relation is an excellent case for bringing out the meaning of authority in relation to rational freedom. Ideally, the authority of the doctor is not his own, is not personal, but is that of medical science; but he necessarily has wide arbitrary power. The immediate relation is one of command and obedience; the patient is "under the doctor's orders," though he has selected the doctor, ordered him to give the orders, and may do as he pleases about obeying any order, or—under individualism—may dismiss the doctor at will, i.e., withdraw from the two-party group. But at best this freedom, or power, is theoretical rather than real. The connection once established, change is difficult and may be a matter of life or death to the patient; and the doctor has every incentive to make him believe that it would be serious, and is in a position to do so—only more or less limited by ethics and various social forces. Limitation of the doctor's power is largely in the hands of his profession, which is naturally inclined to give him the benefit of the doubt, or it depends on competition, to the degree to which actual conditions give rise to an effective market.

As the earlier argument should make clear, the difficulties in the way of rational action are indefinitely multiplied when it is a group of substantial size, and not an individual, that requires service of specialized competence, which is to be had only through the delegation of power. This is typically the case in economic production; technical efficiency requires that men work in groups, including those who furnish property and those who furnish labor, both of various kinds and grades. Such a group requires administrative as well as technical direction, and the question of its selection and control, its responsibility to the group itself, and the responsibility of the group to society at large are the main problems of economic organization, or specifically of "social planning." As already observed, medical service tends to pass out of the hands of the individual practitioner and into those of public or private corporations.

VI. Market Competition: The Alternative to Planning

Individual freedom of patients to select their doctors, and of men generally to be doctors, is exactly the meaning of what is called free competition, or more accurately, the open-market organization. Social planners usually misconceive these facts. There is no implication of competition in the psychological sense of a feeling of rivalry, or action motivated by this feeling; on the contrary, such feeling and action are definitely irrational, in the instrumental or means-and-end definition. Economic competition is one of the unfortunate accidents of terminology; what it means is simply the freedom of individuals to cooperate through exchange with the others who offer (or accept) the best terms. The idea of "bargaining" is likewise misleading. In an effective market there is no bargaining in the sense of higgling or discussion or influence, and in most real markets there is very little.

To discuss market competition as a method of organized action would mean summarizing the science of economics. It may be viewed either as an alternative to collective rationality or as an alternative form of the latter or method of achieving the same general result. We can only assert "dogmatically" that the theoretically perfect, or "perfectly competitive" market has certain consequences for the given individuals involved. It leads to the "maximum" of efficiency consistent with individual freedom, in the only sense in which association can be free, i.e., based on rational mutual consent, and also results in "justice" in the sense of exchange of equal values. That is, the return to each participant is equal to his contribution to the total result of the joint activity; each takes out the equivalent of what he puts in, in the only possible meaning of quantitative equivalence.

This of course is "theory." On the other side we note two general facts, also without explanation or argument. The first is that real markets are more or less imperfect; the second, the far more important fact that the ethical quality of the result is limited by the consideration that the individuals are taken as given, specifically with respect to their desires and their possession and control of productive capacity in all forms. The main mechanical limitations are monopoly and the business cycle. Popular ideas about monopoly fantastically exaggerate both its amount and the evil of that which exists, particularly when society is not already demoralized by crisis conditions. A considerable amount of monopoly is inevitable and more is natural and useful in a free and progressive economy. In extreme cases, where conditions make reasonably effective competition impossible or grossly wasteful (such as public utilities, railways, etc.) public authority always steps in to "regulate" the industry or to operate it directly. As to cycle phenomena, the main fact is that depressions benefit virtually no one and accordingly do not arise out of conflicts of interest. Consequently, the remedy does not present an ethical problem but is purely a matter of science and political competence.

The major ethical problem of economic organization arises out of the grossly unequal distribution of economic capacity, and consequently of the product, among individuals, and the fact that distribution is determined for the most part by forces beyond the control of the disadvantaged individuals and classes, while the working of the free exchange system naturally tends toward increasing inequality. The simple and obvious remedy for inequality, insofar as it is unjust and is practically remediable, is not planning by a central authority, but progressive taxation, particularly of inheritances, with use of the proceeds to provide services for the poorer people. Particularly in point are relief of destitution, health measures, and educational opportunities for the young. This remedy has long been widely applied. The ethical and administrative problems of its further development must be passed over here, except for the observation that popular and reformist ideas as to the causality of the evils and modes of treatment are largely palpable fallacies. For example, the sharp distinction usually made between property rights and personal or human rights will not stand critical examination from any point of view. All forms of productive capacity arise out of a similar complex of social forces and acts of individuals. The property system is a detail in the structure of economic power. It is to be kept in mind that in the liberal economic order based on the free market, any pair or group of individuals are free to exchange on any terms other than the established market price and to organize cooperation in any other way upon which they can agree as ethically better, or preferable for any reason.

The free market, with purchase and sale under competitive conditions, by free individuals or groups freely formed, can be described, as we have seen, in terms which make it appear to embody the ultimate ideal of collective rationality. It combines efficiency and freedom with justice in the most commonly accepted meaning of this term—"commutative" justice, or equivalence between what each person gives and what he receives. We have also briefly suggested the main limitations of all these pronouncements, and indicated the main type of remedial action, which is reduction of inequality in the distribution of burdens and benefits through a suitable program of taxation. This points in a very different direction from central planning, which obviously means curing the root evil of excessively unequal distribution of economic power through an enormously greater concentration—in economic terms, a universal monopoly. And if any prediction is possible, this would not tend either to equalize the distribution of income itself, or to increase efficiency, while freedom, the greatest of the fundamental human values, would be largely sacrificed. Within wide limits, free government is to be preferred to good government (in any other meaning) or freer to better; and the reasonable inference from history, current experience, and reasoning in general terms is that planning by any central authority would sacrifice the one and mean a loss rather than a gain in terms of the other. Any government which had the task of managing the economic life of a modern nation, to say nothing of the world, would have to be a dictatorship and to repress the primary freedoms of thought, communication and association. This would be true even if it were staffed with people who personally abhorred power— and the contention that power would fall into the hands of such people will appeal only to the most romantic credulity.

However, the problem is complex, and certainly calls for a combination of practically all conceivable forms of solution. The positive values in what we call economic life itself are more aesthetic, social and cultural than really individual; and even where they seem to be individualistic, there are limits to the possibility of allowing each individual to be his own judge of what is good for him, or the means of achieving it. The real defects of the "competitive" economic order as revealed by objective analysis are largely due to limitations of the rationality of individuals and free groups, and a general replacement of free action and voluntary association with political compulsion would certainly mean a decrease and not an increase in rationality. Centralization of authority within any political unit would be achieved through the domination, by force, emotional appeal, or outright trickery, of some particular interest group, and under conditions which probably mean mobilization for war against opposed internal interests or externally against other units. The unification of the world could result only from world conquest, as proposed by German National Socialism, and seems to be impossible as well as intolerable to contemplate, though it might theoretically achieve peace and a kind of order.

Yet there is a place for centralized planning under authority, with some use of force, of innumerable activities and with an infinite variety in the scope of the units. All government is by nature central planning. But there is a vast difference in principle between general laws, of the nature of traffic regulations or rules of the game, and concrete prescription of where, when, and how to travel or what game to play. The main difficulty is that planning always means replanning, and the imposition of some particular plan out of an infinite number of possibilities, and under some particular authority, among innumerable claimants. Most of the possibilities under both heads have both merits and limitations, and the real question is how far to go at the same time in most of the possible directions.

With reference to "the city," it goes without saying that practically all cities in modern civilization are constantly being more or less replanned as to their social and economic map, through action of their governments. The nucleus of most of them was doubtless to some extent planned in the beginning, at some date in history, and this is obviously the case in America. Ancient and medieval cities largely "grew up" through the uncoordinated action of individuals, under a minimum of political control, except for a political and religious center where the authorities acted as individuals rather than as agents of the community in any real sense. In the light of modern notions of esthetics, sanitation and health, and general conditions of life, the result is hardly one to be yearned for, even by the most romantic admirer of nearly anything long ago and far away, in contrast with the alleged sordid materialism of modern civilization. It seems almost superfluous to observe that what ought to be done in any particular case depends largely on the case, on the conditions "here and now" from which any change must start and proceed continuously. Discussion of details must be left to persons of special competence, general judgment and with knowledge of concrete facts, possibilities and costs.

Relatively recent history affords a striking example of what may be expected to happen in connection with a tolerably extensive replanning of a city. We refer to the transformation of Paris under the directions of Baron Hausmann and the authority of the Emperor Napoleon III. The story is too intricate to go into, but should be known to anyone actively interested in such projects. It is a sad one, or disgusting, or amusing, depending on taste and temperament. The primary motive, of course, was neither aesthetics nor convenience for the ordinary business of life, but a street plan which would

433

make it easy to suppress revolution by a suitable placement of a limited amount of artillery. Yet we do not say that the result was not worth the cost, in terms of the larger values of civilization.

VII. Collective Action Under Non-Democrative Forms

So far we have discussed collective rationality under what is called free government, meaning the freest possible political system, democracy, or government under law by legally elected representatives of a majority of the normal-adult population of a given area. This has been briefly contrasted with the alternative of voluntary as opposed to political association, with government restricted in the main to the negative function of preserving freedom, together with whatever positive functions may be so generally agreed upon that their performance by government will not involve an "undue" amount of coercion. This is the theory of traditional "19th century" liberalism. For two reasons, it is commonly referred to as "*laisser-faire,*" with specific reference to economic life. The first reason is the historical fact that the far more basic issues of intellectual (religious) cultural and social freedom had been tolerably well disposed of by the end of the 18th century; this left chiefly the state control of economic life which had become the main focus of governmental activity in the age of "mercantilism"—for which "economic nationalism" is a more descriptive designation. The second reason is that it was chiefly in the field of economic relations that conflict developed and became more and more acute during the history of the democratic states.

As a result partly of the effort to deal with economic problems, partly of other and deeper social forces, the later 19th century brought a resurgence of nationalism, and with it

a tendency to repudiate the democratic political form, culminating in the establishment of dictatorships in many countries
of European civilization. Interestingly enough, the first dictatorship, in Russia, was established under the theory of
Marxism, which is nominally cosmopolitan, like early liberalism. But Russia rapidly reverted to nationalism, as the
liberal democracies had previously done. Later dictatorships—
Italy, Germany, Japan—were established by "parties" ostensibly representing a reaction against communistic tendencies,
but explicitly based on nationalism as a quasi-religious creed.
Important differences and problems must be passed over here,
but something must be said about the "holistic" conception
of society and the state, with its logical implication of the
"leadership" form of political and economic organization,
and about the relation between freedom and power and
collective rationality under outright authoritarian organization
or dictatorship.

We have emphasized the limitations of collective rationality
under democratic forms, due to the fact that universal free
discussion does not seem to lead to general agreement, or
perhaps more accurately, that it raises new problems faster
than it solves those already recognized. Representative government depends on moral forces to set limits to the power
("tyranny") of a majority and to prevent political manipulation
leading to the seizure of power by an effectively organized
minority, with more or less recourse to literal force. On the
other hand, we have pointed out that no government can rule
predominantly through overt force, in opposition to a reasonably unanimous public opinion and will. The outright use of
force by a dictator must be largely indirect, acting upon and
through the opinions and sentiments of the people, not directly
against these. That is, it will "educate" public opinion,
through some romantic emotional appeal, using power to
control the channels of information and discussion. In a

stabilized dictatorship, the main reliance will be control of elementary education, under religious or quasi-religious auspices. Under such a system, most of the people may have far more of the feeling of freedom than they do in a democratic order with its inevitable differences, confusion, struggle and frustration. The pretense of a ruling minority party, that it offers the people real, positive freedom, as well as "freedom from" particular evils and problems, tasks and responsibilities to which they are unequal, may both be entirely sincere and have a substantial basis in fact.

Essentially authoritarian propaganda is put out in the contemporary world in three main forms, Marxism, religious Catholicism, and patriotic nationalism, with differences in detail under each head. The main real difference is the matter of "who is to be boss," in the familiar expression of Lewis Carroll. All three are ostensibly cosmopolitan, and more or less explicitly advocate world unity through conquest by force. Everybody is finally to be converted, through some mixture of education, propaganda and coercion, and incorporated into the party or church, as the case may be. Marxism most explicitly emphasizes the temporary and educational character of the dictatorship; after an interval, the state would "wither away," leading to a classless and therefore (in Marxian theory) stateless society, administered scientifically, with impersonal objectivity. The assumption seems to be universal intellectual agreement, the final ideal of collective rationality, and of anarchism. According to Catholicism, ultimate power should be in the hands of the Church, which gets both supreme wisdom and supreme power direct from God, and the righteous and enlightened (or properly conditioned) individual would find ideal freedom in obedience. Nationalism receives its light from the mind of the master race or folk. Each of the systems presupposes a special kind of "charismatic" leadership. The right of the ruling group, under its individual "leader," to rule, is always based on a combination of superior wisdom, from a super-intellectual source, matched with an absolute duty of emotional loyalty on the part of the ruled.

The merits of this type of political philosophy cannot be critically discussed and appraised in the compass of this lecture. We must be content with the observation, as an assertion, that it has merits. Within limits, a case can be made for freedom as well as order through a natural harmony of interest between a ruling class in some form and the general public, in contrast with an extreme democratic emphasis on freedom under equality of status and continuous responsibility of rulers to the wishes of the mass. Complete equality is anyhow unattainable, and orderly society is impossible without both authority and super-rational loyalty. The problem, as we have said before, is to secure the best compromise and balance between conflicting principles, each valid in its measure and place.

VIII. Conclusion

This address is not to be taken as an argument for aimless drifting, but for the intelligent use of intelligence, individual and social, beginning with an objective appraisal of its limitations and its real possibilities. The demand for centralized social planning rests on romantic claims on behalf of intelligence, especially that of the planners. Such claims mean the opposite of rationality for others, since the first presupposition of rationality is a free mind and freedom to act in obedience to its dictates. In the face of this romanticism, one is forced to recall that the human race and its pre-human ancestors both lived a long time and made considerable progress—from the first primitive slime up to a high state of civilization—before social and political theorists, and poets and prophets, came along to announce that everything is wrong and the way to fix it is through a revolution putting the right people in charge of social life. What this means, whether it is denied or more or less explicitly recognized, is setting the historical clock back a few centuries or a few millennia, to the state of affairs that prevailed before the common man became infected with the virus of aspiration for freedom. And one is also reminded that as much intellectual and humanitarian as well as material progress was achieved in the short epoch of liberalism as in all previous history, as such things are measured.

This argument leaves out of account the question of whether active freedom founded on freedom of thought and expression is intrinsically a higher ideal or ultimate moral value than either voluntary or unconscious submission to tradition and authority. The latter question we have not attempted to discuss, and it could hardly be argued, beyond pointing out (as we have already done) that public discussion presupposes acceptance of the principle of freedom on some mixture of utilitarian and absolute grounds. This conclusion would seem to be escapable only by holding that the idea of discussion itself is an illusion, that what purports to be discussion is really preaching and propaganda, on behalf of some interest, or that it is merely mechanical process. The former accusation will undoubtedly be brought against the present lecture by some at least in the audience who have embraced the doctrine of social planning.

We have assumed that our culture is committed to the ideal of freedom, which indeed the "planners" in our own society ostensibly accept for the most part, and have attempted to bring out some of the conditions requisite to preserving and progressively realizing this ideal. These conditions include, as we have attempted to show, a fairly narrow limitation of the functions of government, in accord with the doctrine of old-fashioned liberalism. This means in particular a limitation of the positive functions of the state, and a further development of the negative function of preserving freedom by limiting the powers of individuals and organized groups. Extensive positive action as a unit by any large group, defined by residence in a contiguous area, means delegation of power to a limited number of officials, politicians and bureaucrats. If this is done on an extensive scale, as advocated by planners and "neo-liberals," the agent cannot be held responsible for the use of power, even to a technical majority of those for whom he acts. Such grants of power tend to become irrevocable and the power itself tends to grow beyond assignable bounds. All this means that rationally free social change must be subject to the principle of gradualness.

XV

The Sickness of
Liberal Society

*T*he sickness of modern civilization is a familiar theme
and a fact which is obvious and not in dispute. The
occurrence of two world wars within less than a generation
is proof enough; and quite as sinister is the strong probability
that, in the second case at least, international conflict came
as the alternative to internal class war, or to chaos, in some
of the major countries involved. Antagonism, war, and
preparation for war between nations and allied groups can be
viewed as the one psychological force capable of overcoming
tendencies to conflict between interest groups within nations,
groups formed chiefly along economic lines.

Agreement on the fact of social unhealth does not carry us
far toward common acceptance of a program of action and
may, indeed, work in the opposite direction, aggravating the
malady. Awareness of social disorder makes imperative a
reasonable unity of opinion as to what is the matter and what

Reprinted by permission from *Ethics*, vol. 56 (1946), pp. 79–96, with substantial
additions.

to do about it, or—in medical terms—on diagnosis and treatment. In the current scene we find the most acute disagreement on these crucial points. There is intense controversy especially between two opposed schools of social-medical thought, as to the very meaning of social health. The one school views our social malady as a too-exclusive reliance upon science, upon knowledge as power, and the accumulation of means for making knowledge effective in terms of "material comfort," to the neglect of the "spiritual" values, intellectual, esthetic, and moral. The opposed diagnosis finds a failure to "follow through" with the scientific development, especially to apply scientific method to the solution of the social problem, and more specifically the economic organization. The methods of treatment advocated follow obviously from the diagnoses. The first position is typically advocated by our humanists and literary intelligentsia, as well as by the "preachers" in the narrow religious sense, but perhaps derives its most serious support from organized religion. The countermovement is represented by a substantial proportion of contemporary scientists, including the human and social as well as the natural sciences, and philosophers of the "pragmatic" school.

In this essay criticism of these social philosophies will be incidental to a more constructive task. This is the ambitious one of surveying the twofold problem, of indicating the nature of the trouble and the method or methods of treatment most likely to be effective. Our main concern is with the meaning of social health, especially the facts as to what are the ideals or spiritual foundations of modern civilization. These ideals will be referred to as liberalism or individualism. The former term directly suggests the ethical ideal of freedom, and freedom is the fundamental moral value exalted in the modern view of life, individual and social, in thinking and in practice.

Freedom, the ethical meaning of liberalism. The first major difficulty, both for analysis and in the practical application of freedom as the ideal, is, of course, the ambiguity of the concept. The word has been claimed as a designation, and used as a slogan, by the most diverse ethical and social philosophies and programs, ancient and modern; in our day, this applies also to "democracy," its synonym in political discussion. Both the older and the newer antiliberal ideals of social order, the ecclesiastical authoritarianism surviving from the Middle Ages and the contemporary totalitarianisms—communism, fascism, and "naziism"—claim to be or to embody the "real freedom," or democracy, in opposition to liberalism. Further, the new use of the word "liberalism" to refer to supposedly democratic stateism—socialism or economic planning—now compels us to restrict the term explicitly to the conception which went by that name in the nineteenth century social-philosophic theory and was the norm of social policy in countries where it was accepted. Our task is to show, in relatively concrete terms, the meaning of freedom, the autonomy of the active personal self, in its relation to the social problem. (A philosophical discussion of freedom would merely lead into endless metaphysical speculation.) The main point for emphasis is that freedom is an ethical principle. Its acceptance does not involve a repudiation of morality or idealism, but rather does involve an inversion of the ethical principle which has ruled in all civilizations prior to liberalism. All these earlier systems of social order have been rooted in tradition and authority, and it is by opposition to these that liberal freedom is to be defined.

The important fact is that liberalism asserts a new ethical ideal, thereby rejecting or modifying ideals which had previously been accepted; this rejection of old ideals has frequently been misinterpreted as an abandonment of all morality and ideals. Our first task is to make clear the content of the liberal ideal. Two points need emphasis at the outset. The first is that freedom is an intrinsic value, as well as instrumental to other goods. It is assumed that greater "well-being" will result if, in general, each person is the final judge of his own and of the means of achieving it. But historical liberalism has probably overemphasized this utilitarian argument. It is also a part of the liberal faith in human nature to believe that normal men prefer freedom to objective well-being, within limits, when the two conflict. Freedom always includes the right to consult others, provided one may choose his own counselors and follow or reject their advice. But the liberal doctrine goes further, holding that men "ought" to prefer freedom; and the institutions and laws of liberal states do not allow anyone to contract away his freedom, to sell himself into servitude for any price, however attractive. Thus freedom is paradoxically limited in the interest of its own preservation. An agreement binding the individual for the future will be invalidated if it is shown that he has entered into it under duress or deception or even gross incompetence to manage his own affairs.

The second point is that freedom does not mean unregulated impulse, or "license," but action directed by rational ideals and conforming to rational laws. The ideals and laws are to be discovered in individual and social life and recognized and imposed upon themselves by individuals and groups. Somewhat paradoxically, again, conformity to law is combined with spontaneity in choice. The fundamental notion of obligation is found in problem-solving activity, the raising of questions and quest of the "right" answers. But, at the same time, liberalism exalts a more literal spontaneity, a limitation of the whole "serious" side of life; it has meant an ethical rehabilitation of the play interest, along with a new conception of work. Thus it has brought about an enormous extension of the field of value and of the human interests and activities accepted as ethically worthy. Freedom must mean the freedom to change; hence, a central feature of liberalism is the ideal of progress, viewed as the goal of rationally directed action, in addition to its recognition as an evolutionary and historical fact. Earlier thought, particularly in our own religious-ethical tradition, inclined to view history in terms of degeneration from an original perfect state, recovery of which would be the supreme ideal. Modern ideas place the "golden age" in the future, not in the past, and regard betterment as to be achieved gradually by human action, not through a supernatural cataclysm.

Liberalism conceives of progress in terms of cultural values, intellectual and esthetic as well as moral, all based on material advance. It is a cumulative achievement in the individual life, and in various societies and the world as a whole, through the ages. The maintenance of a civilized standard of living, defined in cultural terms, and its progressive advance or elevation, has come to be the serious business of life. This involves the gradual transformation of the world, of society, and of the individual human being, including his appreciations and his creative powers. This is the meaning of "work," defined as purposive activity, in which the real motive is some desired result. But the good life includes play as well as work. In play, also, activity is usually directed toward some end, but the relation is reversed; the end is not "real" but symbolic and instrumental; it is set up for the purpose of making the activity interesting. The value lies as much in the activity of pursuit as in the enjoyment of the result. The work and play interests are actually so mixed on both sides that concrete activities can hardly be classified between the two heads. The ambiguity is particularly evident in the direct pursuit of cultural values, the professional intellectual, and esthetic life. But all work is ideally, and to some extent actually, affected by the play interest.

On its serious side, liberalism might be called "secular rationalism," in contrast with naïve theism, ethical and

444

metaphysical idealism, and also with that philosophical rationalism which finds the solution of all problems of life in immutable principles, supposed to be known, or somehow accessible, to all men.

Liberal thinking about conduct tends to proceed in two steps—the critical evaluation of ends and the selection of appropriate means or modes of using means. The main subject of discussion in these pages will be "economic liberalism," or individualism, since it is chiefly in the domain of economic life, the organization of the use of means, that the reaction against liberalism centers and radical reform or revolution is advocated. However, it is to be emphasized that economic liberalism is merely a part, an aspect, of a system of values centering in individual liberty and applicable to all departments of human interest and activity and all social relationships. Economic freedom and other freedoms are inseparable, and authoritarianism must likewise be all-inclusive. The term *"laisser-faire"* actually means simply freedom; and it is for historical and rather accidental reasons that the phrase has come to refer to the economic life, or what is usually thought of under that designation. A thorough examination of the relation between ends and means, or between duty and pleasure, will make it clear that more is finally to be learned about life and morality, even in the economic field, from the study of play and of cultural pursuits than from the direct study of economics as ordinarily conceived and in terms of the assumptions usually made in economic discussion.

Economic individualism. Discussion of economic problems has been prominent in liberal theory for two main reasons. Achievement of most ends, higher as well as lower, depends on the use of means and is limited by an actual scarcity of means. The world is poor; and so are the wealthiest countries, compared to the resources, material and human, that would be required to give everyone a "decent"—morally and esthetically satisfactory—life or standard of living, to say nothing of what men would like to have. The basic ethical principle, the meaning of freedom and democracy, is the equal right of everyone to the good life, or a fair opportunity to get the means necessary for it. It is wrong for one to have these at the expense of another or by using another as a means. It follows that social betterment requires an increase in total means available—resources or capital—along with an equitable distribution, and also the most effective use of means, and improvement in "technology." Liberalism finds hypocrisy as well as falsehood in the older ethical attitude of exalting poverty—which always tended to mean that poverty was an ideal for others, the masses, not for the "elite" who preached the doctrine. The contempt for means, and for the common forms of work, which persists among the élite today is a survival of the attitude of a slaveholding aristocracy, always supported by religion. (In our own country and within the lifetime of people still living, slavery was defended on scriptural grounds, where it was established; in Europe, official Christianity never condemned it until it was undermined by other forces.) Means are emphasized, then, because progress depends on increase in means and their better distribution.

The second reason for emphasis on means is that according to liberal theory each individual ought to be and in the main can be free to choose his own ends, while access to means is more directly dependent on the social situation. Consequently, means present a social problem, a problem for unitary social action, while ends, in the main, do not. These statements are, indeed, subject to limitations, which liberal political thought has doubtless tended to underestimate. The subject of qualifications will come up at a later point. Liberal society first came under severe criticism in terms of its own fundamental values, and specifically with respect to the economic organization. Opposition developed, not on grounds of a repudiation of the liberal ideals of freedom and equality (or "just" inequality) and progress, but rather the failure of the liberal order to realize these ideals, in a way reasonably satisfactory to a major section of society, which has felt itself unfree and unjustly treated. (We refer here to the countries which have remained democratic, primarily the English-speaking world; we shall not go into the explicitly anti-liberal, totalitarian social philosophies and movements, now painfully familiar.)

The course of events under liberalism, beginning even in its formative period in the eighteenth and nineteenth centuries, led to increasing discontent and to an attempt to organize the "disadvantaged" classes. Later, other functional interests have been organized. They try to secure economic advantage for themselves, partly through unitary economic action—essentially monopolistic—under existing law, and in part through legal change or government action, by acting as political pressure groups. We must also remember that all through the liberal period there were movements advocating revolution to replace the "capitalist" system with some form of politically organized collectivism. Originally, the collectivist order was to be thoroughly democratic. But after the middle of the nineteenth century, socialism in the "scientific" version, under the lead of Marx and Engels, lost faith in democracy as a method of change. It was felt that the "vested interests" were too strong, and the movement looked to forcible seizure of power by a small "party," claiming to represent an advanced section of the working class; hence the "dictatorship of the proletariat"—meaning a dictatorship of the propagandists. This would theoretically be a transitory measure, to reorganize society and re-educate the people toward the ultimate classless—and hence stateless—society. The ultimate ideal was an anarchist utopia, administered "scientifically," without any exercise of power by men over men. The scientific social order advocated by Professor Dewey, referred to earlier, is essentially identical except for omission of the transitional dictatorship—without replacing it by anything else; and the professed ideals of the moralistic school, and indeed of utopians or reformers of all ages, are strikingly similar.

The basic ideals of liberalism have been indicated briefly but, in order to deal with contemporary problems, it is necessary also to sketch briefly the main facts and principles involved in the application of liberal ideals to the political and economic order. For the economic system envisaged and partially constructed by liberalism, "free enterprise" is perhaps the most descriptive designation—certainly less misleading than "capitalism." An adequate treatment of this topic would obviously extend first to a treatise on economics and then to a similar treatment of politics and the more basic social sciences, including psychology. We can point out only a few of the main general principles and conclusions; these will be contrasted with popular misconceptions, and attention centered on the merits and defects of the system.

From the standpoint of social and political ethics, free enterprise *in its theoretically ideal form* is an embodiment and application of the fundamental principle of liberalism, i.e., individual liberty, including free association. In economic discussion liberty means the right of the individual to choose his own ends and the means or procedure most effective for realizing them. And association, in economic terms, means cooperation, for the purpose of greater "efficiency," more effective individual action in realizing individual ends—always including community ends freely chosen by all members of any group.

It is easy to show that, wherever goods and services are roughly standardized, free cooperation must take the form of regular exchange and will result in the establishment of "markets." The theoretically ideal market is described in terms of "perfect competition." This is a most unfortunate term since psychological competition or emulation is not involved and is in fact inconsistent with economic motives. A free market means simply provision for effective intercommunication, so that every man as buyer or seller (or potentially one or the other) is in a position to offer terms of exchange to every other, and any pair are free to agree on the most favorable terms acceptable to both parties. A free market will establish a price, uniform for all, on every good or service, with the general result that all parties will specialize in production in the manner and degree which secures for each the greatest advantage compatible with the free consent of all. The market rests on the ethical principle of mutuality with each party respecting the equal freedom and rights of others. The mutual advantage of free exchange is the meaning of the "invisible hand" directing each to serve the interests of others in pursuing his own. It replaces the idea that what one gains the other must lose. Any two parties are always free to exchange on terms other than those fixed by the market, upon which they can agree as better, or preferable for any reason.

Free association also allows for the organization of groups to act as units in production or trade, in the interest of still greater efficiency. These, again, may have any form of internal constitution on which the parties can agree. As things have worked out historically, such groups have been widely set up, chiefly under the "entrepreneurial" form. Either an individual or a more or less numerous body takes the initiative in production—decides all detailed questions, and assumes financial responsibility for the economic result by buying labor and property services at definite prices fixed in the open market. Typical today is a group of comparatively large size, organized in the legal form of a "corporation," with a representative system of control similar to that of political democracy, except for the different basis of voting power.

Effective competition between industries will tend to direct production into the lines most in demand by consumers; and competition within any industry tends to compel every productive unit to adopt the most efficient methods—as a condition of remaining solvent and staying in the business. The price of any product will be equal to the money costs of the productive services required to produce it, i.e., to the prices that must be paid for these to meet the competition of producers of other products, fixed by the demand for the latter. Thus the entrepreneur will have neither a profit nor a loss. Product prices will be as low, and prices for productive services as high, as is compatible with freedom of choice of consumers and producers. Any profit will reflect superior achievement by the enterprise-unit receiving it, either in gauging consumers' demand or in technical efficiency, and any loss a similar inferiority. Profit or loss can only occur temporarily; a profit to one unit means a loss by others, and vice versa, and the inferior unit or units must either do better or be eliminated.

This form of organization is widely condemned on various moral and economic grounds. Criticisms usually center in the idea that ''profit'' is unnecessary and reflects ''monopolistic exploitation,'' of consumers or those who supply productive services (labor and property), or of both groups. Critics ignore the facts about profits that have just been pointed out and are obvious or easily verified. (Theoretical reasons which we cannot go into here lead to the expectation that losses will actually exceed profits, and this conclusion is on the whole confirmed by the best statistical evidence available.) Those who oppose the entrepreneurial or ''profit'' system have frequently experimented with organization under other forms. These are commonly distinguished as ''cooperative,'' reflecting failure to understand that exchange itself is a method of free cooperation. The results of these experiments have usually been failure (with some exception for the special and limited field of "consumers' " cooperation). The facts are a matter of common knowledge; the reasons are not hard to find and need not be given here.

The theoretical merits of free enterprise. The brief description just given should suffice to show that the free enterprise system of organization, *in its theoretically ideal form,* combines maximum efficiency with freedom for all. It produces for every individual the largest yield from his "resources" (person and property) that is compatible with the free consent of others. Further, it embodies "justice" between individuals, in the "commutative" sense that what is given up in exchange is equal to what is received; hence the individual share in the total product is equal to his contribution to it, including personal services and use of property. This is "natural" justice; each receives the consequences of his own conduct. The conclusion is commonly drawn, both by those who condemn the system and those who defend it, that these three features constitute an ethical vindication of it as socially ideal. This conclusion is wholly unjustified, and its rejection in no way discredits the theory itself, as is commonly assumed. Its validity clearly depends upon two sets of facts or conditions and may be destroyed by facts contrary to either set. On the one hand, the system as it actually exists may have "mechanical" imperfections; it may fail to work in accord with the theory. And, on the other hand, the principle of reward on the basis of productive contribution may be rejected on ethical grounds. The facts under the two heads must be briefly summarized.

Two major mechanical weaknesses. The mechanical imperfections of the system as it actually works are only too familiar. Two ways in which reality deviates from the theoretical ideal are especially important. Monopoly, and other tendencies, partly inherent in the "given conditions," physical and human, partly contrived by individuals and groups for their own advantage, make competition more or less imperfect. Popular criticism with respect to monopoly is, indeed, much exaggerated and misconceived. Every monopoly obviously has competition, and the notion that monopoly is always bad may be met by the two reminders: monopoly is often deliberately created by social action, as in the case of patents on inventions; and other monopolies commonly function in the same way, to stimulate and reward useful innovation and compensate for the risk and the losses that they involve. Most monopolies are in fact relatively temporary. Yet monopoly is certainly a real evil in many cases and presents a very difficult problem. No simple legal procedure can preserve freedom and the incentive of profit and at the same time prevent individuals from seeking economic power and organizing for this end or from seeking gain through monopoly and restriction.

Far more important in practice is a second mechanical weakness. This is the familiar tendency for economic activity to expand and contract in more or less regular "cycles" of prosperity and depression, both in particular fields and in society as a whole. Depressions involve widespread suffering and the equal or greater evil of insecurity and fear. The worst feature of the situation, from the political point of view, is the "panic" type of thinking which seems to be natural to human beings in a crisis. The drowning man not merely grasps at straws but is likely to seize hold of one who attempts to rescue him in a way which results in the death of both. It would take us too far afield to show in detail the falsity, or very limited truth, of the two common assumptions that depressions are inherent in the nature of capitalism and that the problem would be avoided under any other system of organization, or at least any which allowed individual freedom of purchase and sale. (Most theories of collectivism, and the practice of both communist and fascist states, do embody these activities as basic to the social-economic structure.) It should, however, be evident that the cycle problem is purely one of scientific knowledge and political competence. It is not one of conflicting interests, since all classes suffer in varying degree from a depression and practically no one is profited.[1]

Ethical limitations of individualism. This brings us to consideration of the ethical postulates of economic individualism, specifically the principle of reward according to contribution, or "reaping what one sows." If men's behavior is "economically intelligent," competition will mean sharing in the social dividend in proportion to "productive capacity." We then face the question whether this "commutative justice" is defensible as an ideal of human rights, or how far it is even compatible with social necessity. The ethical limitations of this principle are far more serious than the mechanical imperfections of the market in invalidating an apologetic interpretation of economic theory. The social result of the principle will clearly be any degree of inequality—opulence at one end of the scale and poverty at the other—in accord with inequality in ownership of productive capacity, in its two forms. In an exchange economy, the principle directly implies destitution for any who have nothing to sell in the way of services, of person or property, for which—or for their products—other persons are both willing and able to pay. The principle can be defended only to the extent either that the distribution of productive capacity itself is ideally just or that nothing can be done about it, and both these assumptions are patently contrary to fact.

It is a fallacy, rooted in prejudice and superficiality, but

---

[1] These mechanical imperfections do not (as the uninformed public tends to assume) invalidate the economic theory which at the most general stage of analysis pictures them absent. Theoretical mechanics similarly has to assume the absence of "friction," and deal with idealized conditions in other respects, which diverge quite as far from literal realism. Analysis must begin with general principles which must be properly qualified in application to practical problems.

nearly universal in popular and reformist thinking, that economic inequality is, or is mainly, associated with the ownership of "wealth" or property. To begin with, many of the largest incomes are actually derived from personal services; for example, "prominent" lawyers, doctors, and artists, including prize fighters and movie stars. Moreover, the difference is largely unreal, since property and personal earning capacity come into the possession of individuals through practically the same channels—inheritance, effort, and thrift, all largely affected by "luck." It follows that the familiar sharp distinction between the ethical claims of the two sources of income to their economic earnings is indefensible. All forms of capacity for rendering useful service are largely artificial, but chiefly in the social and historical sense, not that of individual creation. They are components of "civilization," and so, in fact, is appreciative capacity, or economic wants. The whole problem of inequality and injustice is rooted in the two factors of natural endowment and the participation of individuals in a total accumulated social inheritance, and this is mental or spiritual or "cultural," as well as "material." And to all these sources of inequality must be added the large factor of accident.

Individualistic theory versus facts. What has just been said does not mean that the moral qualities of the individual are economically unimportant. It does not even logically imply that superior inherited capacity ought not to have a superior reward. These propositions set problems that are to be discussed on their merits and in the light of facts and social ideals. But it does follow that the whole social philosophy of individualism is subject to sweeping limitations. Freedom is a sound ethical ideal, but "effective" freedom depends on the possession of power as well as mere absence of interference, at the hands of other individuals or of "society." And it is also relative to tastes or wants. The assumption underlying the individualistic economic ethic is that the individual is either unalterably "given" as he stands, or is morally "self-made" and that in either case he is the real social unit. The element of profound truth in this view is basic to the moral life and to all serious discussion of human and social problems. But it is only part of the truth, and liberal thought, particularly in its formative stage, tended to neglect other factors fully as important. Freedom and power are like the factors in an arithmetical product; the result varies in proportion to each separately and disappears entirely if either factor is zero. Both wants and "capacity" (in both forms) result from a complex mixture of individual effort reflecting moral qualities, with various forces and conditions that are beyond individual control. As is usually the case in human problems, no clear or accurate analysis is possible; "judgment" must be used in comparing and combining factors which seem important but are never measurable.

The limitations of individualism are particularly obvious from the standpoint of economic analysis. The theory of market competition takes individuals as given, with respect to their three economic attributes, i.e., their tastes or wants and their productive capacity, the latter in turn consisting of personal qualities, and external agents and materials owned, and recognized and protected by the existing legal order. In sociological terms it may almost be said that the individual is unreal; any nation or other society which acts as a unit in external or internal policy is a complex of "institutions"— traditions, knowledge or belief, and common-interest groupings, rather than an organization of independent individuals. Our "individualistic" society would be more descriptively called "familistic" and—as it has worked out in the past century—nationalistic and "classistic." The individual is not a datum, and social policy cannot treat him as such.

Again, it is useful to think of social life as a game, and

consider its particular features. It is played by groups, or teams—in this case an indefinite number. In fact, inequality and injustice exist far more in the relations between groups than between literal individuals. The family, in some form, is the minimum real unit, and many other communities, up to states and even larger units, are only less important, both as interest groups and in making the individual what he is on entering social life as a functioning unit. The fact that inequality applies "fundamentally" to families and communities, regions and states, rather than to literal individuals, is the basis for the rivalry and conflict which result both in international war and in the "class struggle." The tendency to conflict is greatly aggravated by differences in "culture," as well as wealth, and by cultural, group, and national loyalties; such groups always feel an urge to perpetuate themselves and their way of life, and to expand at the expense of others. Secondly, the social game is played for stakes which involve the major values of life. And, finally, it goes on continuously, generation after generation, with "players" constantly dropping out and being replaced. Hence, in addition to the procedure of play itself, the rules must cover the terms of admission of new players. Any new entrant must be trained to play, and dealt a "hand," and must also be given some share in the "chips"— the stakes which the activity must not only distribute but maintain and increase by using it.

In free society the preservation and increase of wealth and culture are largely left to individual, family, and voluntary-group initiative. The inevitable result is a tendency toward increasing inequality, between self-perpetuating groups of all sorts, as well as (or rather than) between individuals. This is most conspicuous with respect to productive capacity (internal and external) though just as true of all elements of culture. It is a case of "to him that hath shall be given." Any individual or other unit which at any time has more is in a better position to acquire still more. Capacity and taste develop together and inseparably, though wants typically grow more rapidly than the means of satisfying them—human nature being as it is (and probably ought to be). The tendency goes beyond the individual life, through various forms of inheritance, appearing in each new generation as the injustice of an unequal start in life.

Liberal societies have as a matter of course, if gropingly, recognized these problems in practice and have tried to meet them through such measures as progressive income and inheritance taxation. This is designed to reduce inequality, at both ends of the scale. It sets some limit to accumulation, and the proceeds are used to provide a decent minimum for all and especially to provide education and other requirements for the young. The liberal ethic goes beyond law, in many directions. Modern civilization has been as much distinguished from others by humanitarianism and "charity," voluntary and politically organized, as it has by the unprecedented development of science and technology. The attitude toward rights of convicted criminals and toward animals is in point here.

Complexity of the problem of free society. The facts briefly pointed out make the social-ethical problem of liberal society one of tremendous complexity, scope, and difficulty. Liberal society may be defined by the fact of consciously facing its own future as a social problem. It is a human or world problem, not merely a local or national one, and is spiritual as well as economic or "material," even in those aspects which can at all properly be even roughly distinguished as economic. It is rather an accident that the conflicts which threaten peace and order arise in the economic field, even when this is properly defined to cover the use of means for all ends, higher as well as lower, and the distribution of means. A little reflection, along the lines of the foregoing argument, should make it clear that harmony and conflict of interest, giving rise to problems of lawmaking and enforcement, are characteristic of informal association, play, and cultural activities, as well as of ''business'' life, and that the problems have essentially the same form in all fields. Without law and obedience to law, and moral ideals and self-restraint going far beyond law, even a casual conversation may degenerate into a quarrel and then a fight. It is increasingly recognized that conflicting economic interest is relatively unimportant as a cause of war. The parties could almost always gain more through peaceful exchange and cooperation, and they really know that this is true. All this is true also of ''class struggle,'' and all clashes of economic interests. Careful calculation shows that even colonial exploitation is not usually profitable economically. In European history religious differences loom large as a cause of war—supplemented by cultural competition and by sheer partisanship. Economic interests, real or supposed, are also involved, but an ''economic interpretation'' is largely rationalization. In war, as in general, the real motives are unanalyzable and often seem paradoxical and inscrutable and in any case irrational.

The deeper meaning of liberalism. One who approaches the social problem from the economic side, and who at the same time tries to be objective and face obvious facts, must be struck by the limitations of the economic view of conduct. Economic analysis treats production as a ''means'' to consumption, or at least to some ultimate use of some result. But reflection will show that in ''economic'' life itself the motives are highly mixed and in large part not distinctively ''economic.'' That is, the ''value'' to individuals and groups of the goods and services they want and strive to get is not mainly intrinsic; they are symbols of success. Economic activity has at least as much the character of a competitive game or sport as that of providing the means for satisfying substantive wants or needs. This applies both to consumption and to production; people are largely motivated by "keeping up with the Joneses"—and/or getting ahead of them. Economic "success" is largely competitive; and the symbols are in large part culturally determined, and their concrete form more or less a historical accident.

In so far as the ends of action are real, i.e., valued for any intrinsic quality, the content is primarily esthetic, as indicated by the expression, a "decent" standard of living. But esthetic values also are distinctive of particular cultures and are much affected by the motives of emulation and prestige considerations. Real beauty cannot be separated at all sharply from rarity and costliness, and these clearly reflect the craving for conformity and distinction. But it is "beauty" in a broad interpretation, which makes up the bulk of the cost—beyond purely competitive standards—of a scale of living, even at a "decent minimum" in modern society. Physical comfort, in anything like a literal interpretation, is hardly at issue in civilized life under ordinary conditions. It is a right, both recognized and provided for through charity, public and private, and even for incarcerated criminals. If anyone is physically destitute, it is because of the repugnant social terms on which "relief" is offered. Nothing is more familiar than the voluntary sacrifice of comfort and security for "appearances," or even the mere love of adventure. Esthetic creation, in contrast with the reduplication of existing works, is so much more than a matter of economy in the use of limited means that it seems trivial, absurd, if not repulsive, to think of it from the latter standpoint at all, though it always has this aspect also.

Beyond obvious and fairly narrow limits, it becomes entirely unrealistic to look at the good life in economic terms, or under the form of means and ends, even with the choice of ends not treated as given but also included in the problem; indeed, there are limits to viewing it as a problem in any sense. As an American economist has observed, "an irrational passion for dispassionate rationality" would take all the joy out of life. And it is just as true that an irrational passion for duty can destroy goodness. The castigation and lampooning of Puritanism (or of its caricature) is a familiar theme. That social life is much more than cooperation for increased efficiency has been illustrated by the story of a football club which hired an efficiency expert as a manager; his first innovation was to have all the men play on the same side, it being obviously wasteful to have half of them pushing against the other half. Our ethical thinking runs into similar paradoxes, if pushed too far along any line. J. S. Mill, perhaps the leading representative of liberal social philosophy and ethics as well as economics in the nineteenth century, held that pleasure is the ultimate end but had to admit that, to get maximum pleasure, we must to a large extent forget it and pursue other explicit ends. The observation can be generalized for all ethical theory; all thinking about conduct seems to run into a principle of indirection. Friendliness and generosity toward others lose much of their ethical quality if the motive is merely a sense of duty—and even more obviously if it is personal salvation, in terms of eternal heaven and hell.

To get at the real meaning of liberalism, we need to consider more fully the observation made earlier, that the ideal of freedom involves both a rehabilitation of play and a changed conception of work. Liberal thought recognizes that man is a social being—though in the light of many radical differences between human society and that of nonhuman species, it may be misleading to call him a "social animal." The liberal ideal of society in accord with the principle of freedom is free association. It is useful to distinguish at least four forms or aspects of a good social life. Arranged in a descending order with respect to the degree of reflective seriousness involved, they are work, cultural activity, formal or organized play, and pure or spontaneous, even frivolous, "sociability," typified by casual conversation. The different types overlap and fuse, beyond the possibility of clear distinction, and all have both individual and social aspects. The point here is to emphasize that "the good life" involves all of them inseparably, particularly the last—and that more is to be learned about liberalism by considering the roles of the other three factors than that of work. This last term may be used to include all "economic" activity, everything that is undertaken primarily for the sake of some end felt to be intrinsically or "finally" desirable, or necessary. A vague and largely arbitrary distinction must be made between work in which the value of the end is individual and that in which it is social or involves the "good" of others. The latter seems to be the meaning of ethical value, or "duty," though personal enjoyment or avoidance of pain, beauty, and moral obligation all enter into all four forms of activity, in varying ways and degrees.

The permeation of all conduct by the different factors or aspects may be brought out by noting the paradox in the meaning of play and work, as the main contrast in the rationale of conduct. The difference is largely a matter of the more or less arbitrary attitude of the participant. It depends on whether the end is "real" and the activity instrumental to it, or the reverse is the case. No empirical classification of activity into play and work is possible; it would be hard to find any concrete activity which may not be one or the other, depending on "circumstances." On the one hand, play has its serious purpose; as exercise, it is developmental, and undoubtedly necessary, to man, for health, physical and mental. But if the player thinks about the activity in terms of its purpose, it becomes work and not only loses its distinctive value as enjoyment, but may also fail to accomplish the serious purpose. On the other hand, work ideally has the play aspect of being interesting, and doubtless always does have more or less of it, at least if it is above the lowest drudgery. Perhaps the most serious human activity or work is the task of democracy, the discussion of ethical and social problems. But discussion itself is largely mixed with the play interest—and also with esthetic motives. These tend to outweigh the reaching of sound conclusions, and we cannot say that discussion is in general more fruitful in its primary function if attention is seriously fixed upon the serious end, excluding the other interests.

The paradox perhaps comes to a head in the attempt to discuss conduct itself, in the abstract, to give a truthful description of it, hence in the "methodology" of the moral and social disciplines. The urge for scientific objectivity calls for ignoring motives and reducing behavior to purely physical process—the "behavioristic" point of view. But in such a treatment, in a rigorous sense, conduct ceases to be conduct and becomes mechanical reaction—and it is a manifest absurdity to take this view of the discussion itself, which is also a form of conduct. A similar paradox applies to all mutuality in social relations; we cannot verbally define free association, or state the distinction between exchange and "robbery" through either fraud or force. All human relationships involve an unanalyzable mixture of mechanical interaction, free exchange of things or services, and also both giving and taking, by coercion or deception, on both sides. We cannot realistically ignore motives—especially because we are usually more interested in these than in the physical facts—though we can never say at all accurately what the motives are. It is a scientific truism that an individual's motives are known only to himself; they cannot be observed by anyone else. But the facts are often to the contrary; the motives professed, and even actually felt, depend largely upon the norms which are currently "fashionable" in the cultural setup. Men give, even honestly give, moral or sentimental reasons for their acts—

affection, patriotism, or religion—when an observer cannot help seeing that the "real" reasons are largely of the opposite sort and the converse situation is perhaps equally typical. In the Middle Ages thought and expression were dominated by an ascetic-religious ideology; the counsel of perfection was the monastic ideal of poverty, chastity, and obedience. But, as everyone knows, the monks assumed that the world owed them a living, and they expected and normally secured a degree of comfort and security as high as contemporary civilization afforded and far above what was possible for the mass of the population which supported them. Further, the means considered legitimate for securing this support often amounted to pious fraud and violated modern standards of common honesty. In our own day the opposite situation commonly prevails. The modern spirit abhors sentimentality and pretense. This results in the familiar "hard-boiled" pose, where the real motives are often clearly sentimental.

The modern devotion to critical objectivity—as soon as we reflect about that—"brings the eternal note of sadness in." While our better instincts run in the direction of making work into play, our inclination toward "too much thinking" has the opposite effect, converting our play into work. Philosophy as well as science tends to destroy romance and only partly to replace it with another "beauty" of a colder intellectual kind. But all the distinctively human values are romantic; love must proverbially be blind. And beauty also, to a degree; it is hard for the scientific botanist not to lose the beauty of the flower, which, of course, he cannot find with his micro-scope or by any use of the scientific method; and the argument applies as well to the economic botanist.

The ethical significance of play. We have suggested that for an understanding of the social ethic of liberalism, its general principles and their application to political and economic life, it is highly important to consider carefully the phenomena of play and the cultural pursuits. Both will be discussed without reference to any economic aspect, though this is always present in one form or another and cannot finally be ignored. We have also pointed out that economic life, in the meaning ordinarily understood, really has much of the character of play. It is a mixture of solitaire and competition and also "ritual"; but attention may here be confined to competitive play. The ethics of play or sport is a topic strangely neglected by moral philosophers, even in modern free society, and is virtually ignored in all discussion under religious auspices. (In the Bible one finds no explicit reference to having "fun," or to rivalry or emulation, as a part of the good life.)

The first characteristic of play, as of all social activity, and indeed of that which is called individual or private, is that freedom is conditioned and limited by "law," in several meanings of the word. Even in the most informal sociability, such as casual conversation, not usually thought of as play, there must be a common language and this in itself implies a vast stock of common ideas, meanings, and values and of accepted formalities. These are necessary to mutual understanding and anticipation by each of the way in which the other will "react." However, this foresight is and must be limited. An element of curiosity and surprise is equally essential to interest in any activity. There is always an element of luck; there are games of pure chance, but a game of pure skill is a self-contradictory idea. The basis of mutual understanding is a common cultural background. This is never perfectly uniform, and cultural as well as individual differences are a source of misunderstanding and strife; the former are the main factors in international relations.

In the pure ideal form of play all the "laws" are taken for granted; the moment they give rise to any problem, the nature of the activity and of the association is fundamentally changed.

Law, in the inclusive sense, is the essence of any social group, and the acceptance of the laws is a condition of membership. In free and progressive society, every social problem centers in differences as to what the law either is or ought to be and takes the form of interpreting, enforcing, and eventually changing the constitution and laws. In free association, this is done by ''discussion,'' ideally leading to unanimous agreement. ''Government by discussion'' is Lord Bryce's well-known definition of democracy. Discussion is an activity not directed to any concrete end but to the solution of the problem, necessarily unknown in advance. A social problem always combines conflict of interest with difference of opinion about what is right. Further, the differences must be associated with a common interest, the interest in perpetuating the group—in play, ''the game''—while improving its character. It follows that freedom in social relations has three forms or components. First, every system of law allows some latitude for literal freedom of action by individuals and free groups. Second, social freedom requires equal participation in the activities of lawmaking—or this is a condition of full membership in a group. Finally, since complete unanimity is not usually to be had, complete freedom implies the right and the power to leave the group, hence to join other groups, and eventually to form groupings at will. In principle, any group is ''political'' to the extent that its members do not have this third form of freedom. In common usage political groups are defined by territorial sovereignty; leaving one group means physical removal to another and is limited by material cost, by cultural differences, and by the laws governing departure and especially entry into other political units, which practically cover the earth. The first task of law is to define its own scope, i.e., the scope of individual freedom within the law, or tolerance of differences.

In play, not much literal enforcement is possible, without

destroying the play spirit. It takes the form of excluding the recalcitrant individual—which is also the ultimate sanction of political law. Breaking the rules, or "cheating," is the primary meaning of crime, and of "sin" as well. But it is human nature to feel a temptation to cheat, in spite of its irrationality (scoring or winning by this means is not really doing so at all). The satisfaction of the individual interest in winning and of the group interest in having a good game are completely interdependent.

All problems of social ethics are like those of play in that they have the two components of obeying the rules and improving the rules, in the interest of a better "game"—or other associative activity. We cannot here develop in detail the extensive parallelism between play and political and economic life. Both present problems of distribution of the "reward" in some relation to capacity, effort, and luck; and the fundamental values to be achieved—morality, intelligence, good taste, and enjoyment—define the philosophical problem. Intelligence is always both a form of capacity to act and a requisite for the use of capacity in other forms—a means and a mode of use of other means and an end. It is a vitally important fact that capacity to play intelligently, from the standpoint of winning, is much more highly and more commonly developed among human beings than is the capacity to improve the rules or invent better games. The difference between sport and action in the larger social arena is partly bridged over when a game is played for "stakes," in contrast with mere points—i.e., for values felt to be substantial as well as symbolic of success.

Perhaps the most important ethical principle of secular liberalism—in contrast with our traditional religious ethic—that is to be learned from the consideration of play has to do with competitive self-assertion. As a matter of course, every party in a game must "play his own hand" to the best of his

466

ability; otherwise, there is no game. The ideals of charity or service simply have no place. Further, rigorous equality in the distribution of the results is self-contradictory (as is the complete elimination of luck, as already pointed out). The ethical ideal is a "fair" and an interesting game. Sportmanship is a large part of liberal ethics. The conception of fairness calls for a certain minimum of inequality in capacity among the players. This need is often met by classification of players, choice of the game, handicaps, etc. Such devices are obviously needful in connection with the larger social, economic and political game, and the difficulty of working out and applying them is a major aspect of the whole problem. The moral attitude of liberalism, being defined by the notion of law, is primarily impersonal. It is a matter of respect for the rules, and of ideals for their improvement, rather than a feeling toward persons, and the two things are as often conflicting as harmonious. The law is, of course, supposed to express the rights of men, which are in question only where these differ, or seem to differ, from their felt interests. The principle is not "love," which covers a group of special feelings, all restricted in scope, and hardly a matter of duty or obligation. Friendliness and courtesy are, of course, good, and there is always a margin for generosity in interpreting and applying rules in doubtful cases. A game is more or less spoiled if the players are "too much" interested in winning, even in strict accord with the rules.

Cultural values; development and progress. In contrast with casual association and play, the cultural values are the content of liberalism on the "serious" side. The primary values are intellectual and esthetic; morality or "goodness" is chiefly a matter of distribution rather than a distinct value; personal relations, as obligatory, are largely comprehended in good manners or courtesy, which is more an esthetic than a moral category, and in "giving" in special cases of distress. In the liberal view the serious values of life are intellectual and esthetic enjoyment and creativeness. From the standpoint of discussion or of reflective thinking, as we have seen, all values are serious. They are included in "truth," since all questions relate to the truth "about" whatever subject matter is in question. Truth is assumed to be ultimately the same for all, but it is neither necessary nor desirable to have universal agreement. Genuine belief cannot be coerced, and freedom of belief is the ultimate concept in terms of which all freedom is defined. The overt expression of belief can, of course, be controlled through reward and punishment, and even the feeling of believing freely can be established by social conditioning in infancy or by playing upon the emotions. But these procedures are abhorrent to liberal ethics, which calls for a sharp distinction, as a matter of personal integrity, between true intellectual conviction and any so-called belief which is at bottom an emotional loyalty or an esthetic appreciation or which rests on any ground other than the truth. To draw these distinctions clearly is one of the tasks of a liberal education.

The core of liberalism—what most distinguishes it from other views of life—is a manifold revolution in the conception of truth. We need not attempt to answer Pilate's famous question, "What is truth," as we need not give a formal definition of freedom in any metaphysical sense. We assume that there is an intelligible difference between believing, on the basis of facts, reasoning and the critical evaluation of evidence, and "prejudice," or believing by choosing to have faith in some traditional dogma or myth or authoritative pronouncement. These usually have no concrete meaning until interpreted with explicit reference to a particular issue, by an authority, itself based on traditional faith or some form of force.

To say the belief is free is to say that truth is inherently "dynamic," subject to change and actually growing and changing. The liberal interest in truth is one of curiosity and quest, not of mystical contemplation or adoration. Truth is the right—or the best—answer to some intelligent question, and when a question is definitively answered it is no longer a question. Hence, any truth that is really "established" is no longer interesting, but a commonplace, even a bore. Truth is the supreme example of the principle that liberal idealism looks at the values of life in terms of pursuit as well as possession; they belong to the activity as much as to the result, to means as well as to ends. Truth is an end when it is unknown or uncertain, and especially if controversial; hence the truth interest is finally a romantic one. Established truth is valued instrumentally, as a means to the acquisition of further truth, or of other values, to be had through thinking and acting. Truth is the solution of a problem, and its pursuit is partly explorative, the goal more or less an unknown. This is clearly the case in mathematics, where we make the nearest approach to "absolute" truth; the answer to a problem is that unknown result which satisfies certain prescribed conditions.

The second feature of the liberal conception of truth is that it is a social category; its only test is unanimous acceptance in some community of discussion. Further, truth as social is ultimately democratic. As in most cases, democracy is indirect, and implies some kind of aristocracy, and some form of leadership. The consensus which defines truth is that of the competent and unbiased, even in factual observation. For most people, and in most of the field of knowledge and opinion, what to believe is necessarily a matter of accepting tradition or selecting the authority to be followed. Thus a truth judgment is moral as well as intellectual. But competence and freedom from bias are to be judged by the whole community of interested persons, and finally by each individual for himself. No sanctity attaches to tradition or to any authority; intellectual leaders secure their position exclusively through appeal to the free judgment of their followers. It follows that telling the truth in social relations is a primary ethical value. However, literal truthfulness in discourse is seriously limited by conflicting goods, and every person is both free and morally obliged to make the best compromise he can between literal veracity and other values. Among the latter, the moral value of courtesy and kindliness is conspicuous, and the conflict is a familiar problem. Fully as important are esthetic values of many kinds. Far more statements are interesting because they are not true, but imaginative and fictional, than are significant because of objective accuracy.

On the vital subject of esthetic value, and its relation to truth and to utility, only a few words are in order here. The concept covers a very wide range of experience, suggested by such words as "amusing," "exciting," "chastening," "cathartic," "edifying," and "thrilling"—"comic" and "tragic," "realistic," "romantic," and "classical." Undoubtedly, beauty is connected with and overlaps both truth and utility, yet some contrast is of the essence of the meaning of the word. The poetic statement that "beauty is truth, truth beauty," etc., is beautiful but not true. And so of beauty and utility—with due respect in this case to Ruskin instead of Keats. Recognition of beauty, natural as well as artistic, its enjoyment and creation, on their own account, as a part of the good life for everybody, is a distinctive feature of liberalism, almost on a par with the free and critical-skeptical pursuit of truth and its appreciation. Other systems of values have used art for didactic purposes and as a part of the "pomp and circumstance" making religious and political authority impressive to the masses. From the liberal point of view, all this represents special privilege and emolument, and prestige, for the elite. (In the Semitic religious tradition, a part of the original Christian inheritance, representative art is explicitly prohibited.)

Liberalism and religion; absolutism; pragmatism. At this point, some negative observations are called for. The social and ethical philosophy of liberalism involves no repudiation of religion, specifically the more basic tenets of Judaism and Christianity, such as the belief in God, moral freedom and responsibility, personal immortality, churches, and even "faith." It does involve a radical re-interpretation of these fundamental doctrines, but it is one which large numbers have been able to accept while retaining allegiance to either of the two great religions of European civilization. The idea of God does not necessarily mean more than some kind of "ground" in the cosmos for the validity of spiritual values. Modern physics recognizes that matter itself is finally metaphysical in nature, not physical in the naive meaning. The church is for the liberal a free association of individuals for the pursuit of the religious life, not a supernatural entity with special authority to tell people what to believe or to do, or to dispense "salvation" on arbitrary terms. The belief in immortality will function as extending and enlarging the moral life and providing additional meaning and motivation. Otherwise, it is not practically significant, since the liberal will hold that the problems of the other world can be dealt with only by working as intelligently and conscientiously as possible at those presented by the present life. As to faith, all reasoning finally goes back to premises which cannot be demonstrated, or rationally argued, and usually to following authority with special competence.

Liberalism is also a "faith," a faith in the world and in man. It views the world as an environment in which it is possible progressively to achieve a better life, in terms of the values of truth, beauty, goodness, and enjoyment; and it imputes to men at large the intelligence and the will to work for these values. It is a qualified optimism, in contrast with the doctrines of the vale-of-tears and original sin, which make men helpless, morally and materially, and dependent on miraculous intervention and aid. In practice, the latter doctrines have meant a duty of submission to the authority of some human group claiming to speak for God, and also claiming the right to enforce, by torture and execution, both belief and conduct. The liberal ethic is democratic; it exalts freedom against obedience and power. Either will be "abused"; but it is held both that the abuse of power generally leads to worse objective evils, and that even doing what is actually good, under authoritative command, is contrary to the ideal of the moral life. Within limits, self-government, by the individual and society, is to be preferred to good government, where a choice must be made. But only within limits; the liberal ideal is always one of balance and compromise, on the basis of "judgment," between conflicting principles and values, as well as interests. The best balance cannot be described in formal rules concrete enough to answer real questions, or not subject to criticism and revision.

In short, as we have stressed, liberalism is a faith in the capacity, and the courage, of man to find and follow truth and right. This implies a faith in the nature of the world as "such that" truth, carried as far as facts and evidence allow, will be finally in harmony with other values, including utility. Truth is to be believed because it is true, and for no other reason, though in particular cases objective accuracy may be subordinate to other considerations, as we have seen. For liberalism, no form of value is "absolute"; but this does not mean that one opinion is as good as another, or that error, moral choice, or good taste, is unreal. These things are rather "relatively absolute"; they are valid in the same sense that the objective world is real; i.e., we think in terms of a substance or sub-stratum which may be "eternal and immutable," but its nature is to be progressively discovered, and never fully or finally known. The liberal faith begins with skepticism, and repudiates dogma and wish-thinking on absolutistic grounds or "rationalistic" in the idealistic meaning; but it equally repudiates the reduction of intelligence to will in the rational-utilitarian or "pragmatic" manner. It is assumed that men should know and face the truth, and will wish to, even when it is unpleasant; and also that the world is "such that" truth will be useful, in leading to the enlargement of personality and to cultural progress, and ultimately to "happiness." This does not exclude humor, frivolity, play, and esthetic escape, setting more or less arbitrary bounds to serious thinking and acting. The scientist must both believe that truth will be useful, while pursuing it as truth and not as utility, and at the same time accept it as a moral, and even a religious, value. There can be no science either if scientific workers are dogmatic absolutists or if their motive is utilitarian, not to mention the self-seeking interest of the charlatan.

Freedom of thought implies freedom of action as a corollary, as well as freedom of verbal expression, which is obviously necessary to freedom of thought itself. The ultimate contrast is between intellectual freedom and various forms of obscurantism. Freedom of association, or mutuality, in action, may be viewed as a form of freedom of expression. If the historical change to liberalism from "religious," i.e., ultimately theistic, idealism, with its logical implication in social practice of ecclesiastical authoritarianism, and a static social order based on caste, constitutes moral degeneracy, the liberal can only say, "Make the most of it." The only "proof" that can be offered for the validity of the liberal position is that we are discussing it and its acceptance is a presupposition of discussion, since discussion is the essence of the position itself. From this point of view, the core of liberalism is a faith in ultimate potential equality of men as the basis of democracy. There are two possible alternatives. One is a conspiracy to seize power by force. The other is "preaching," which itself is really a form of force and can finally be successful only through "preaching down" or overt repression of other preachers of competing programs or gospels.

The liberal will admit that much is to be said for an aristocratic constitution of society, including slavery, in an idealized form—if it could be assumed that there is any practicable way of having it in an ideal form. This "if" is enough by itself to give away the whole case. An idealized "caste" relation between leaders and followers, in accord with the romantic picture of parents and children in the family, can be defended in terms both of "happiness" and of the possibility of a higher absolute level of cultural achievement. Such a system might endure indefinitely, preserved by conditioning each new generation to accept it, and in obeying to feel free. But there does not seem to be any way for a society once liberalized deliberately to "go back." It would have to give to some particular selected individual or group a perpetual blank check on power; and this is hardly thinkable as a rational performance—apart from actual belief in some special channel of access to a superhuman source of knowledge and taste open only to the ruling caste. If the change comes about, it must apparently be through some self-appointed leader and party seizing power by some combination of force and deception.

The place of economic conflict in the social problem. Enough was said earlier of the ultimate unreality of the economic basis of conflict, or the more or less accidental reasons for conflict appearing in this form. All conduct has the economic aspect, as far as purposive action involves the use of scarce means; and all associative life involves power relations. And on the other hand, the ends are never economic,

474

but are a mixture of esthetic and symbolic values. It is a serious question whether, if all economic limitations and conflicts were removed say, by the discovery of some effective magic for producing all material goods and services without effort or the use of scarce means, social antagonism and conflict would be removed, or even reduced, or essentially changed in form. It appears probable that conflict would be more intense, unless other interests and other traits of "human nature" were at the same time miraculously transformed, removing all desire to "get ahead" and all occasion for organized action of any kind.

However, there are obvious reasons why conflict, within and between societies, arises in the economic field. These begin with the two facts, that means are necessary for the good life, and that in any community they are "scarce" in comparison with what is required for a satisfactory standard of living for all. Thus arises the problem of distribution, since men have individual interests (in contrast with bees), and there is no generally accepted or acceptable norm for a "just" distribution, especially because the problem is tied up with family interests and the institution, and with the motivation of production. Finally, a tolerably effective use of means requires organization. And moreover, the progress of civilization and the accumulation of means require organization on a larger and larger scale. It is now on a scale where cooperative relations are largely "impersonal," and the moral forces that operate more or less effectively in the small face-to-face groups (and might operate even in a small democratic group) practically lose all their force. To utilize modern technology, economic organization has in many respects to be world-wide.

When we look at the problem of any society, or of the world, in economic terms, and from the standpoint of the disadvantaged individual and group, the major "real" evils are on one side the esthetic sordidness of life for the poor, and on the other the dreary monotony and lack of effective freedom which affects highly specialized work under the direction of technical and administrative specialists. For completeness, we should add the overwork of those individuals who incur and accept responsibility, and the "boredom" of those who are independent and do not.

For the liberal moral sense, the major evils may be actually worse if they are not felt by those directly affected. A bad condition presents a social problem only if it is socially recognized. The diseases of liberalism may be viewed as results of the general inculcation of ideals of equal rights, combined with failure to impart an understanding of the limits of equality and of the methods and costs of securing that which is possible. This fact raises the difficult moral problem of the role of the "agitator" on the one hand, and the dispenser of philosophic or religious "opiate" on the other. The critical spectator finds discrepancy both ways between discontent actually felt and that which "ought" to prevail. People are satisfied with conditions they ought to rebel against, and dissatisfied with conditions better than they deserve or can reasonably expect—or they are justifiably discontented, but for wrong reasons. According to liberal theory, they ought to be discontented only with what is both bad or unfair, and remediable; it is irrational to object to what cannot be changed. But there is little agreement on these points, or upon rational procedure.

Moralistic and scientistic romanticism. Since the essence of liberalism is the reliance on rational agreement or mutual consent for the determination of policy, and since the amount of agreement attainable seems very meager in relation to the needs for action felt in a large-scale, rapidly changing society, it is easy to understand psychologically, though not to approve, the tendency to fly to one or the other of the two positions mentioned early in the essay under the names of moralism and scientism. There is much truth in both these positions; the error is in accepting either as true to the exclusion of the other (and still others), i.e., in the romantic disposition to oversimplify the problem. On the one hand, human nature is undoubtedly "sinful," and, on the other, the mind makes mistakes in the choice of means to achieve given ends. It is easy and attractive to generalize from either fact, and make it explain everything, and particularly attractive to account for the ills of society in terms of either the sins or the errors of other people. And as to the content of sin and error, there is much real virtue and wisdom in respecting tradition and established authority. There is also much truth in the idea that the desire to "get ahead," and especially to get ahead of other people, is the primary sin to be avoided. We can only mention the questions obviously raised—whether the play interest, including the emulative aspect, can be rationally condemned, whether civilization and progress are good, and whether it is possible to have them without the motives which religious idealism views as sinful. These views are as old as history.

The advent of modern science, with the power it has conferred on man to change the world and the conditions of life, has just as naturally produced the opposite romanticism, the "scientistic" oversimplification. It is perhaps true that, especially under the influence of frontier conditions, liberalism had tended to stress activity as such and the cruder levels of achievement, to some neglect of the higher appreciations, the intellectual and esthetic life, and the moral value of fellow-feeling and "aimless" sociability. In any case, the problem of life cannot be reduced to one of means for achieving given ends. And this is particularly true of the social problem. Here, the end is right terms of association, and the essence of it is the definition of the result to be achieved rather than any concrete achievement.

The "sickness of liberal society" is not to be diagnosed

either as moral degeneracy or as arrested intellectual development, specifically in the scientific sense. Both moralism
and scientism formally accept freedom as an ultimate value;
in form, both are anarchistic, though in contrasting senses;
but both eventuate in an authoritarian social order. Both
theories aim at unity through free agreement, to cure the
malady of social discord and strife. But such agreement is
not to be reached either through preaching abstract ideals or
through adopting the experimental method. The social-ethical
problem is an indivisible whole; means and ends must be
determined together, and by the same agent—either by society
as a whole, implying equal participation in its decision, or by
some prescriptive authority. Both the moralists and the "scientificists" really assume that other people "ought" to agree
with them and freely accept their leadership in dealing with
both ends and means. An anarchistic theory, in any form, is
essentially an invitation to all to "leave it to me" (and "my
gang"—those who already agree with me) to deal with the
problem as a whole. It is, finally, immaterial whether "utopia"
is pictured in moral or scientific-administrative terms. The
Marxists are merely frank in cutting the knot by proposing a
dictatorship—of themselves—for an indefinite period, to work
out the solution and "educate" society to accept it.

The alternative to dictatorship is simply democracy in
general as we have known it, struggling to solve its problems,
along lines already familiar. It means cooperation in thinking
and acting to promote progress, moral, intellectual, and
esthetic, with material and technical progress as the basis of
all, and all under the limitation of gradualism and "seasoned"
with humor and play. The combination is the meaning of
liberalism.

Index

This book was set in the Times Roman series of type. The face was designed to be used in the news column of the *London Times*. The *Times* was seeking a typeface that would be condensed enough to accommodate a substantial number of words per column without sacrificing readability and still have an attractive, contemporary appearance. This design was an immediate success. It is used in many periodicals throughout the world and is one of the most popular text faces presently in use for book work.

Book design by JMH Corporation, Indianapolis, Indiana
Typography by Monotype Composition Co., Inc., Baltimore, Maryland
Printed and bound by Worzalla Publishing Co., Stevens Point, Wisconsin